Shojo Beat

Fushigi Yûgi
Genbu Kaiden™

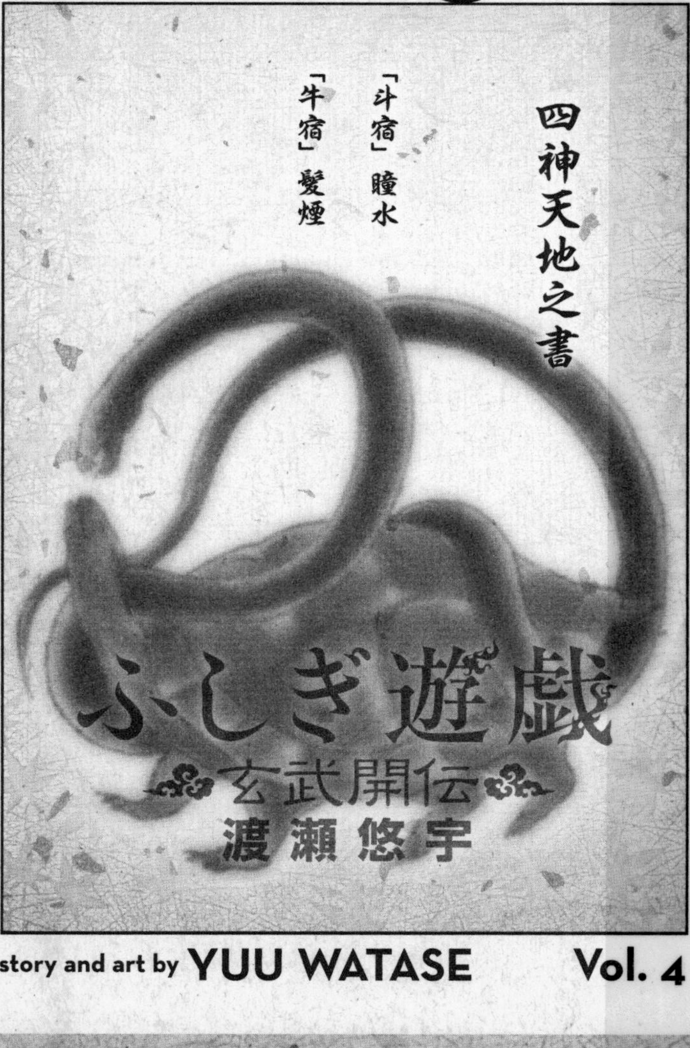
四神天地之書
「斗宿」瞳水
「牛宿」髮煙
ふしぎ遊戯
玄武開伝
渡瀬悠宇

story and art by **YUU WATASE**

Vol. 4

CONTENTS

TRANSLATION OF "THE UNIVERSE OF
THE FOUR GODS"

Hikitsu: Water Eye
Inami: Hair of Smoke

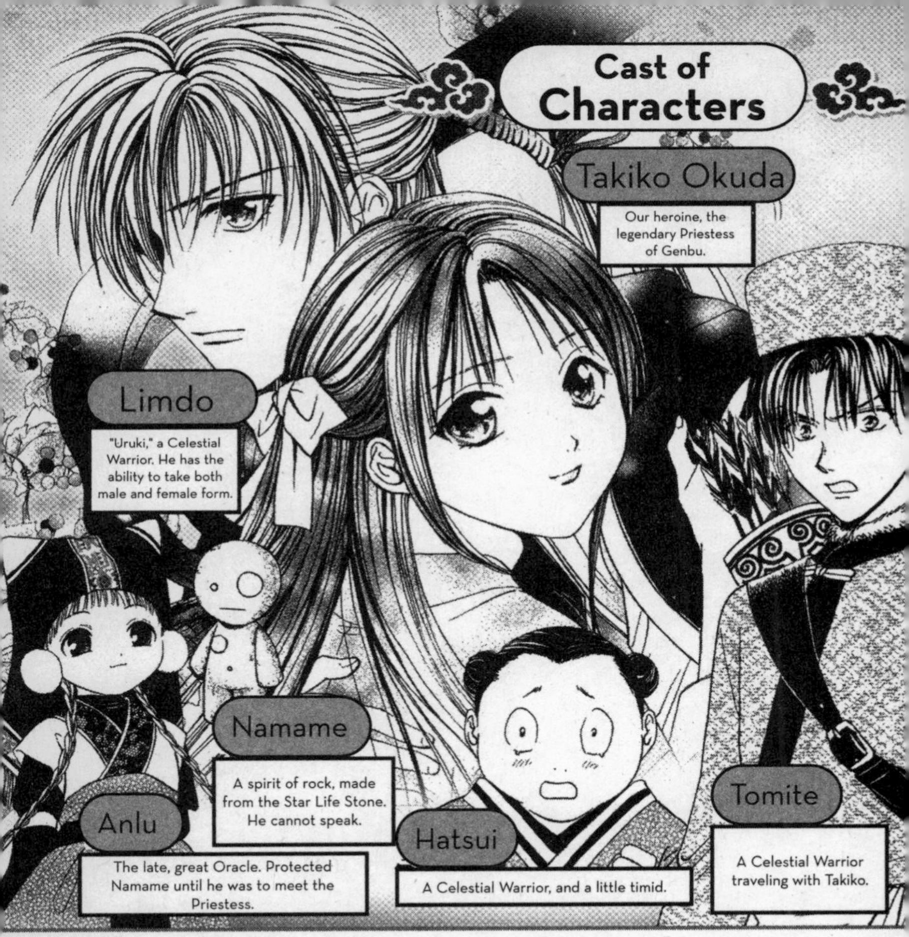
Cast of Characters
Takiko Okuda
Our heroine, the legendary Priestess of Genbu.
Limdo
"Uruki," a Celestial Warrior. He has the ability to take both male and female form.
Namame
A spirit of rock, made from the Star Life Stone. He cannot speak.
Tomite
A Celestial Warrior traveling with Takiko.
Hatsui
A Celestial Warrior, and a little timid.
Anlu
The late, great Oracle. Protected Namame until he was to meet the Priestess.

The Story Thus Far

The year is 1923. Takiko is drawn into the pages of *The Universe of the Four Gods*, a book her father has translated from Chinese. There, she is told that she is the legendary Priestess of Genbu, destined to save the country of Bêi-jîa. She must find the seven Celestial Warriors who will help her on her quest. In Bêi-jîa, however, the Priestess and the Celestial Warriors are seen as ill omens.

With Tomite and Hatsui, Takiko meets the Oracle Anlu, and Namame, one of the Celestial Warriors, at Turning Point Rockfield. Namame joins their group, but at the cost of Anlu's life. Now, with Anlu's necklace in their hands and her blessing in their hearts, their journey continues...

FUSHIGI YÛGI:
GENBU KAIDEN

KISSED BY THE WIND

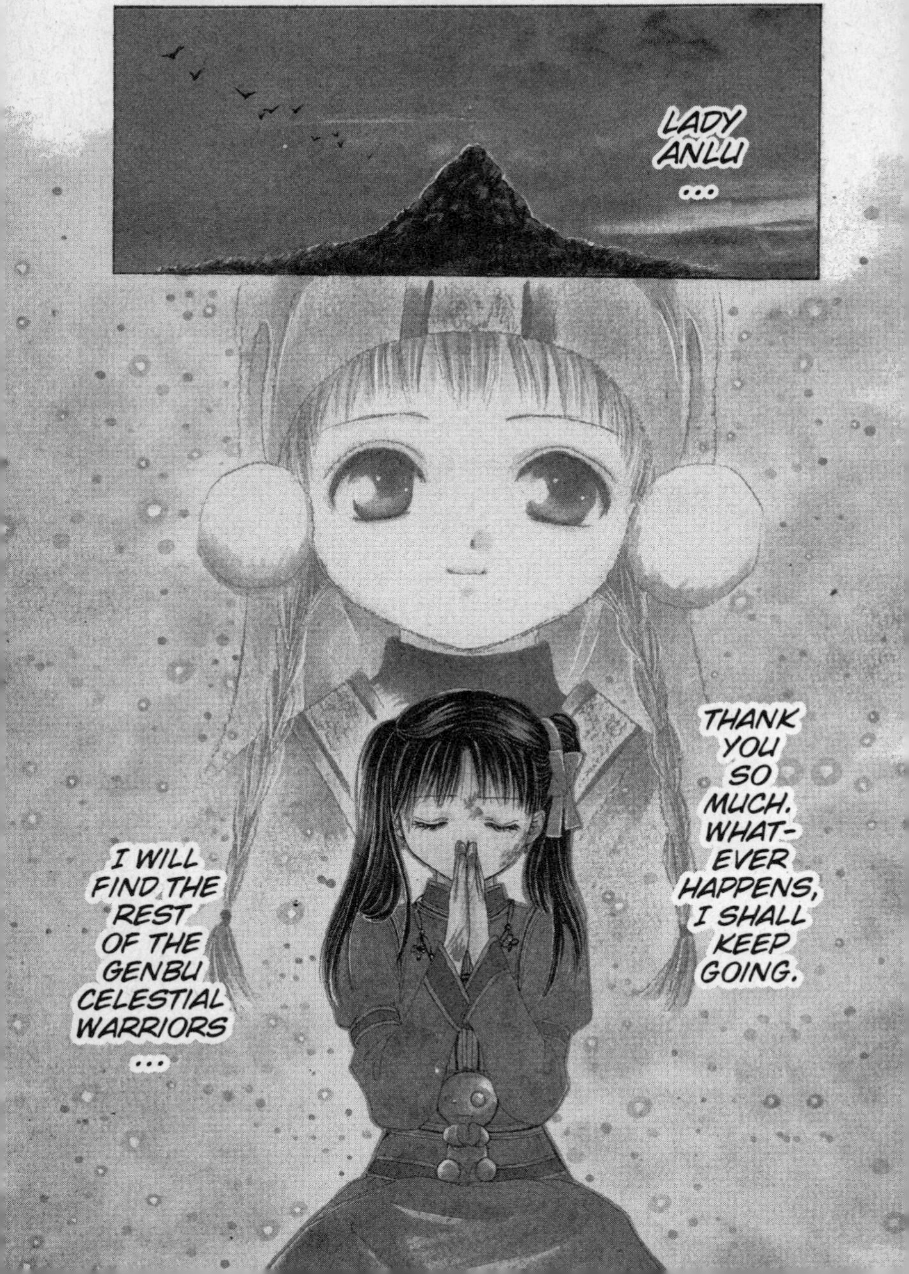
LADY ANLU ...
THANK YOU SO MUCH. WHAT-EVER HAPPENS, I SHALL KEEP GOING.
I WILL FIND THE REST OF THE GENBU CELESTIAL WARRIORS ...

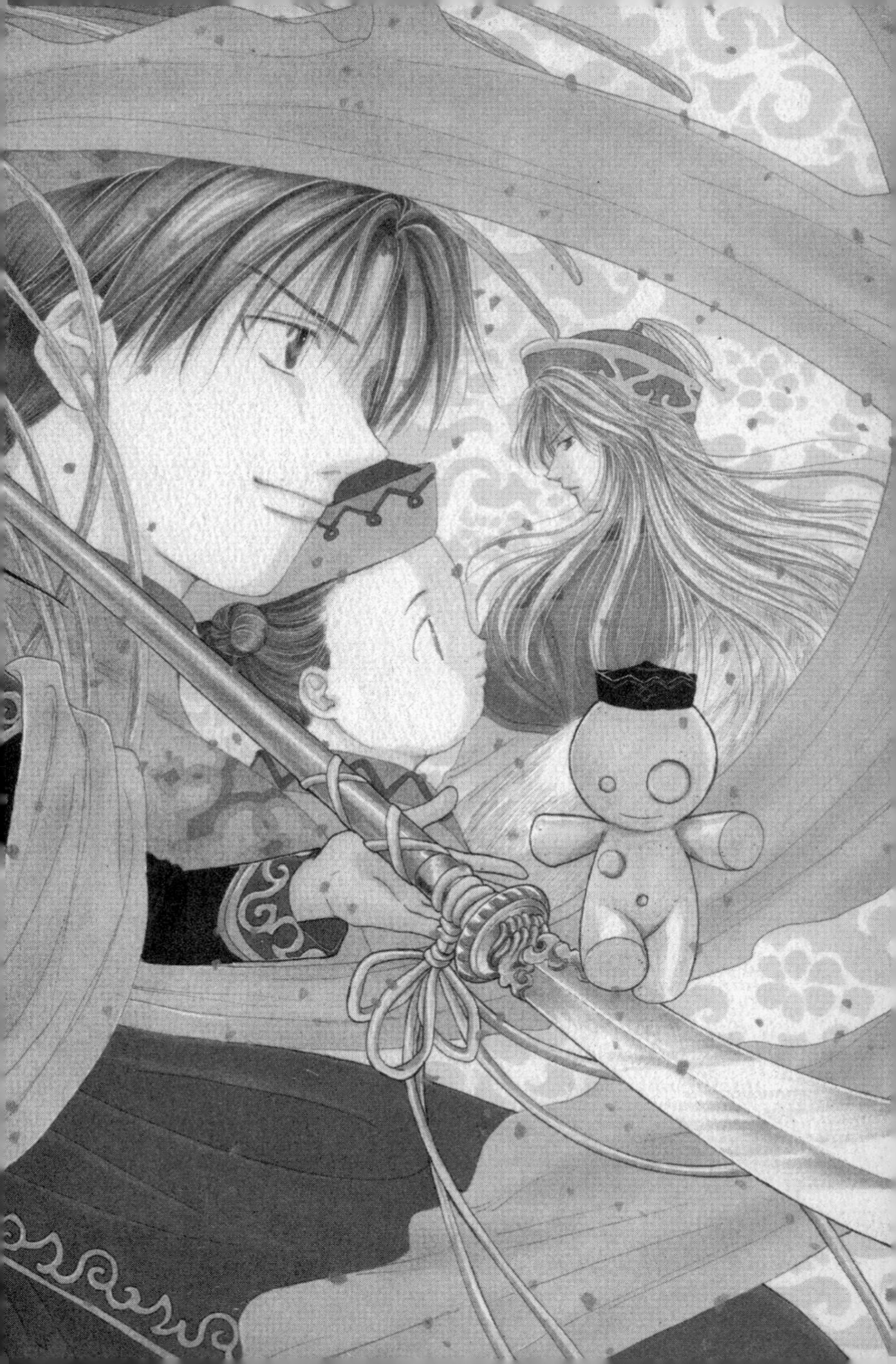

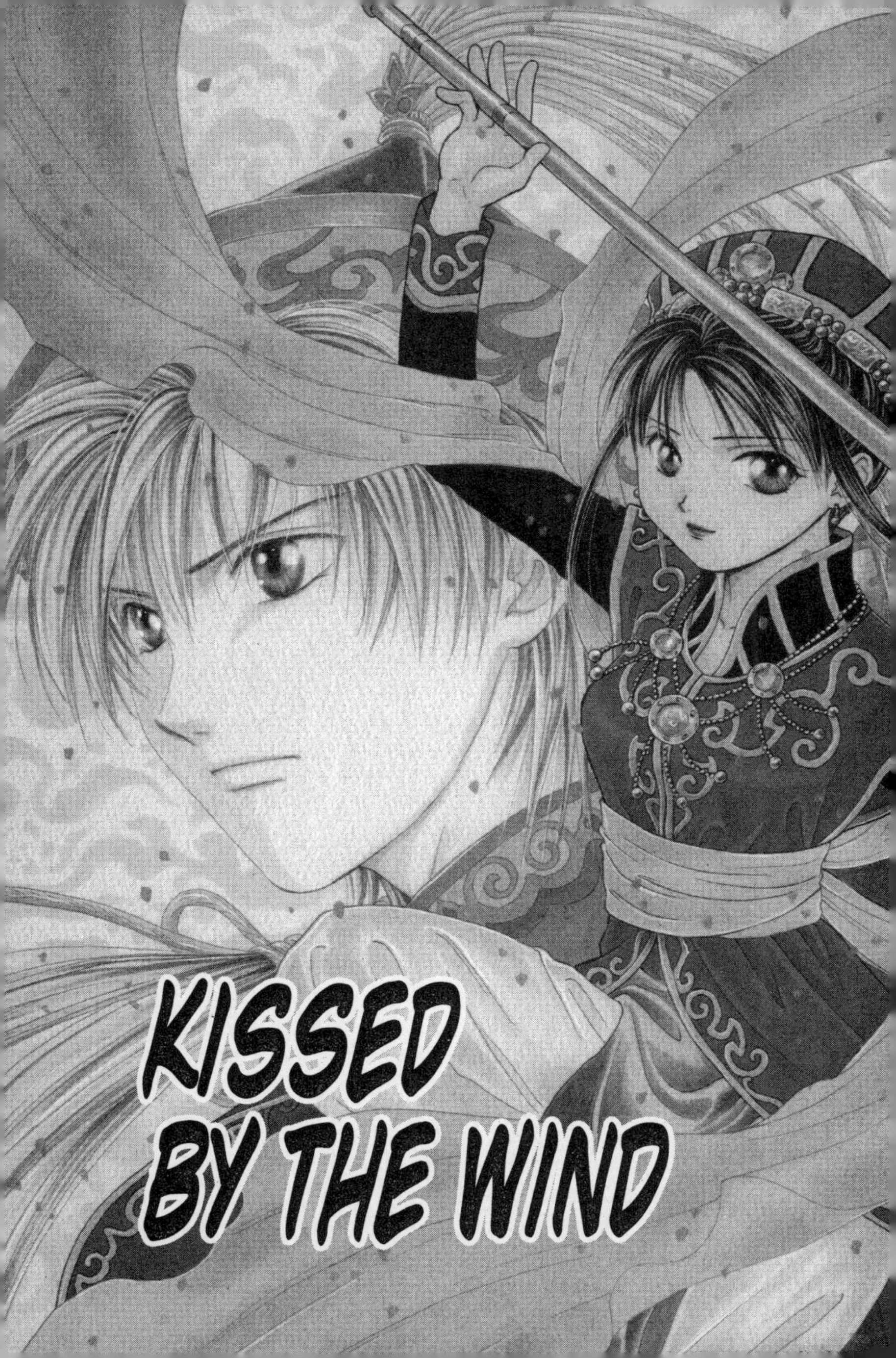
KISSED
BY THE WIND

FUSHIGI YÛGI:
GENBU KAIDEN

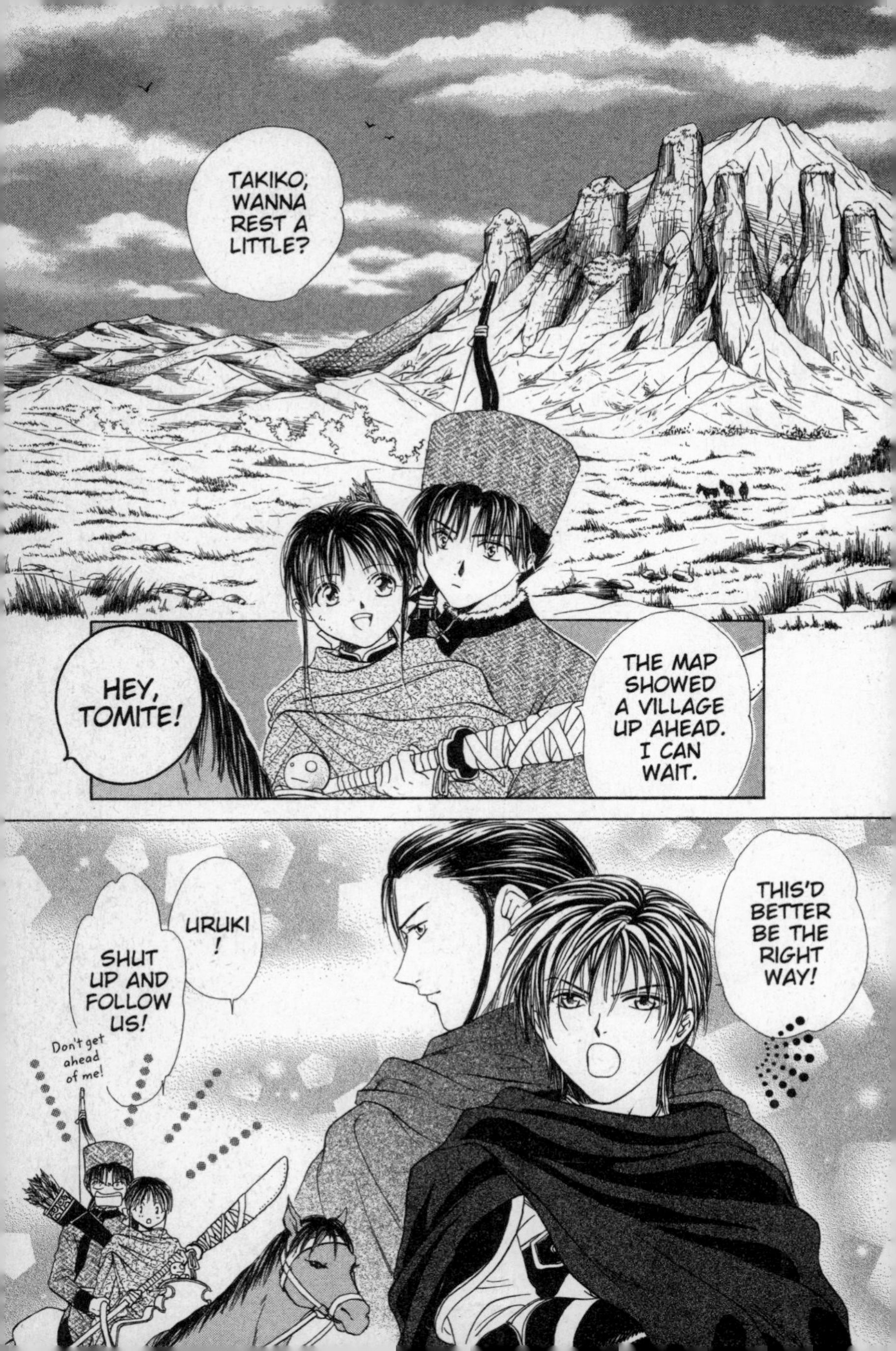
TAKIKO, WANNA REST A LITTLE?
THE MAP SHOWED A VILLAGE UP AHEAD. I CAN WAIT.
HEY, TOMITE!
THIS'D BETTER BE THE RIGHT WAY!
URUKI!
SHUT UP AND FOLLOW US!
Don't get ahead of me!

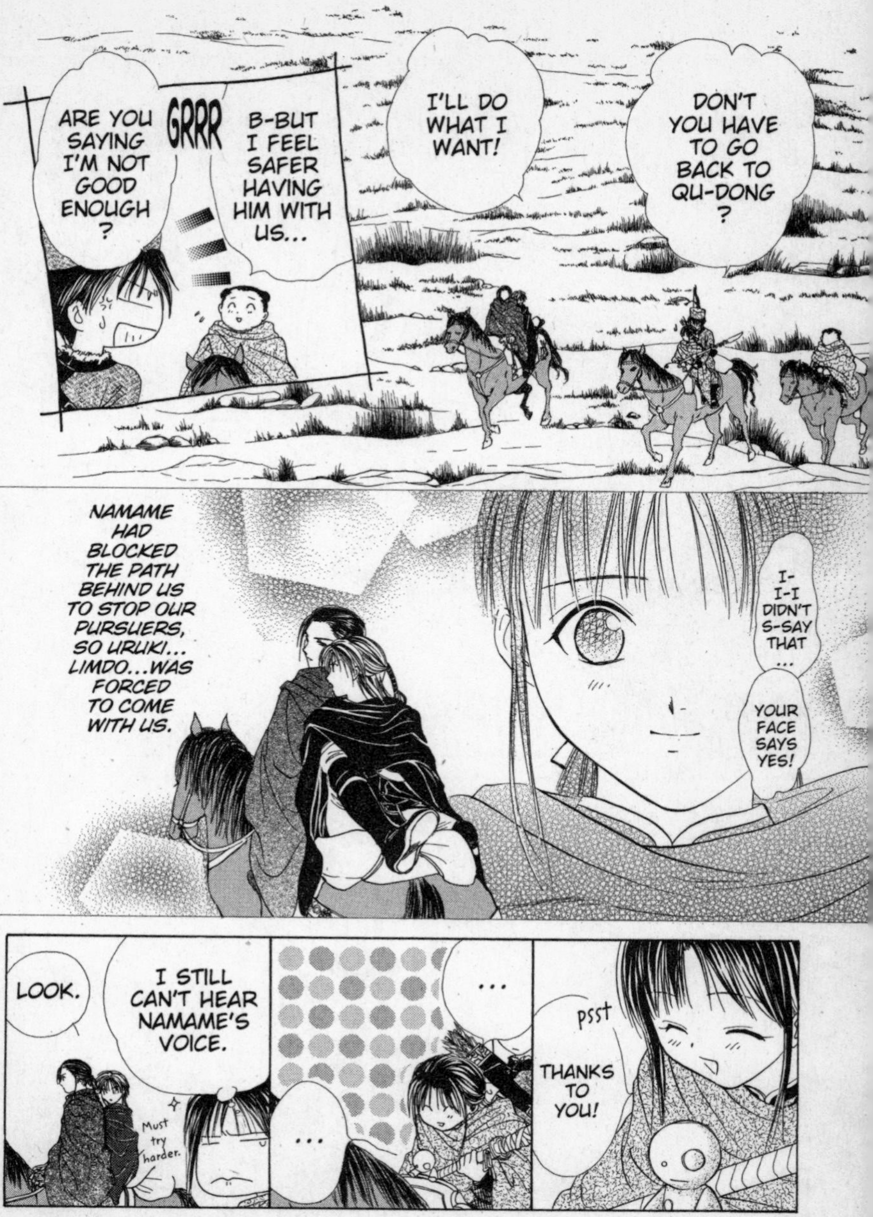
DON'T YOU HAVE TO GO BACK TO QU-DONG?
I'LL DO WHAT I WANT!
B-BUT I FEEL SAFER HAVING HIM WITH US...
GRRR
ARE YOU SAYING I'M NOT GOOD ENOUGH?
I- I-I DIDN'T S-SAY THAT...
YOUR FACE SAYS YES!
NAMAME HAD BLOCKED THE PATH BEHIND US TO STOP OUR PURSUERS, SO URUKI... LIMDO...WAS FORCED TO COME WITH US.
psst
THANKS TO YOU!
...
...
I STILL CAN'T HEAR NAMAME'S VOICE.
LOOK.
Must try harder.

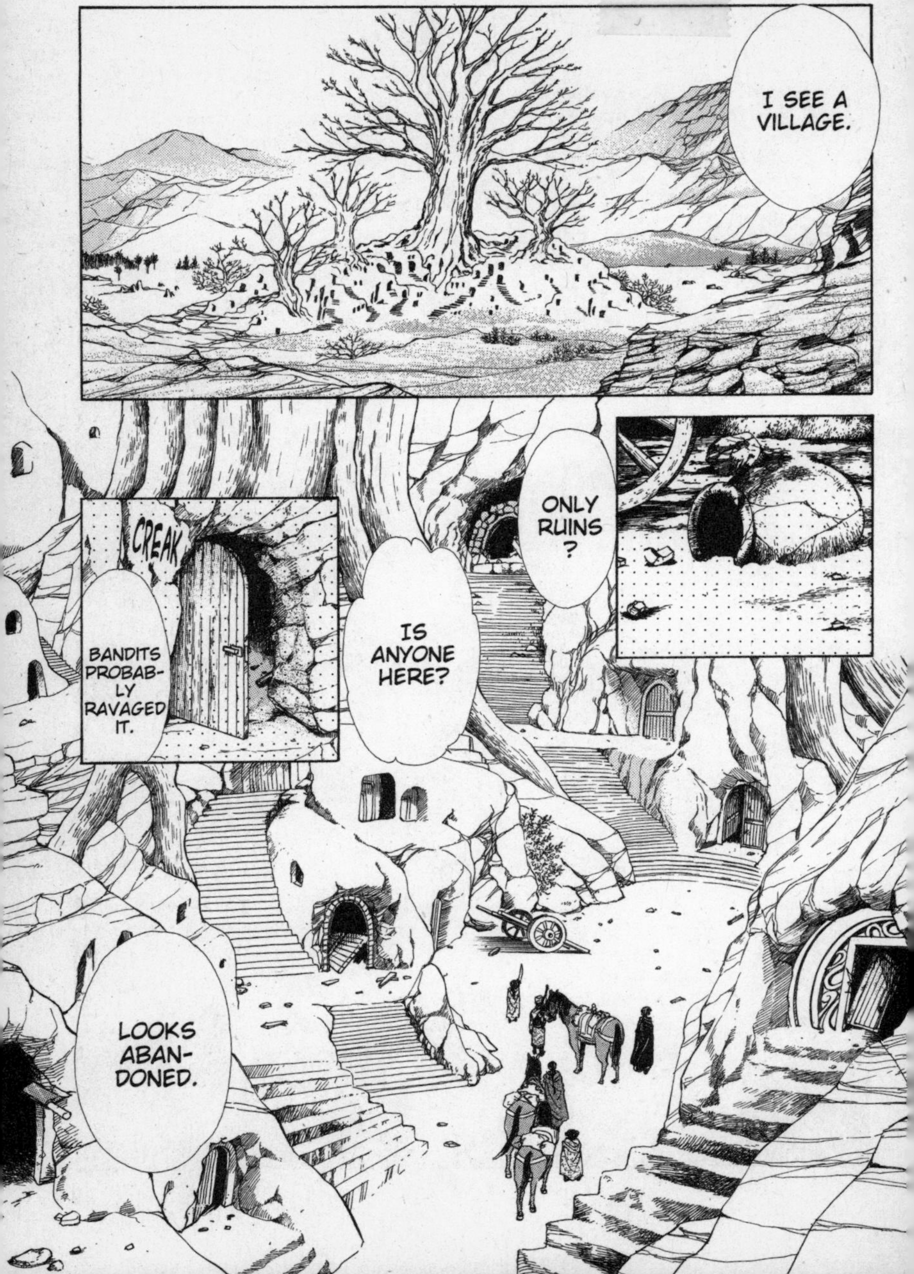
I SEE A VILLAGE.
ONLY RUINS?
IS ANYONE HERE?
CREAK
BANDITS PROBAB-LY RAVAGED IT.
LOOKS ABAN-DONED.

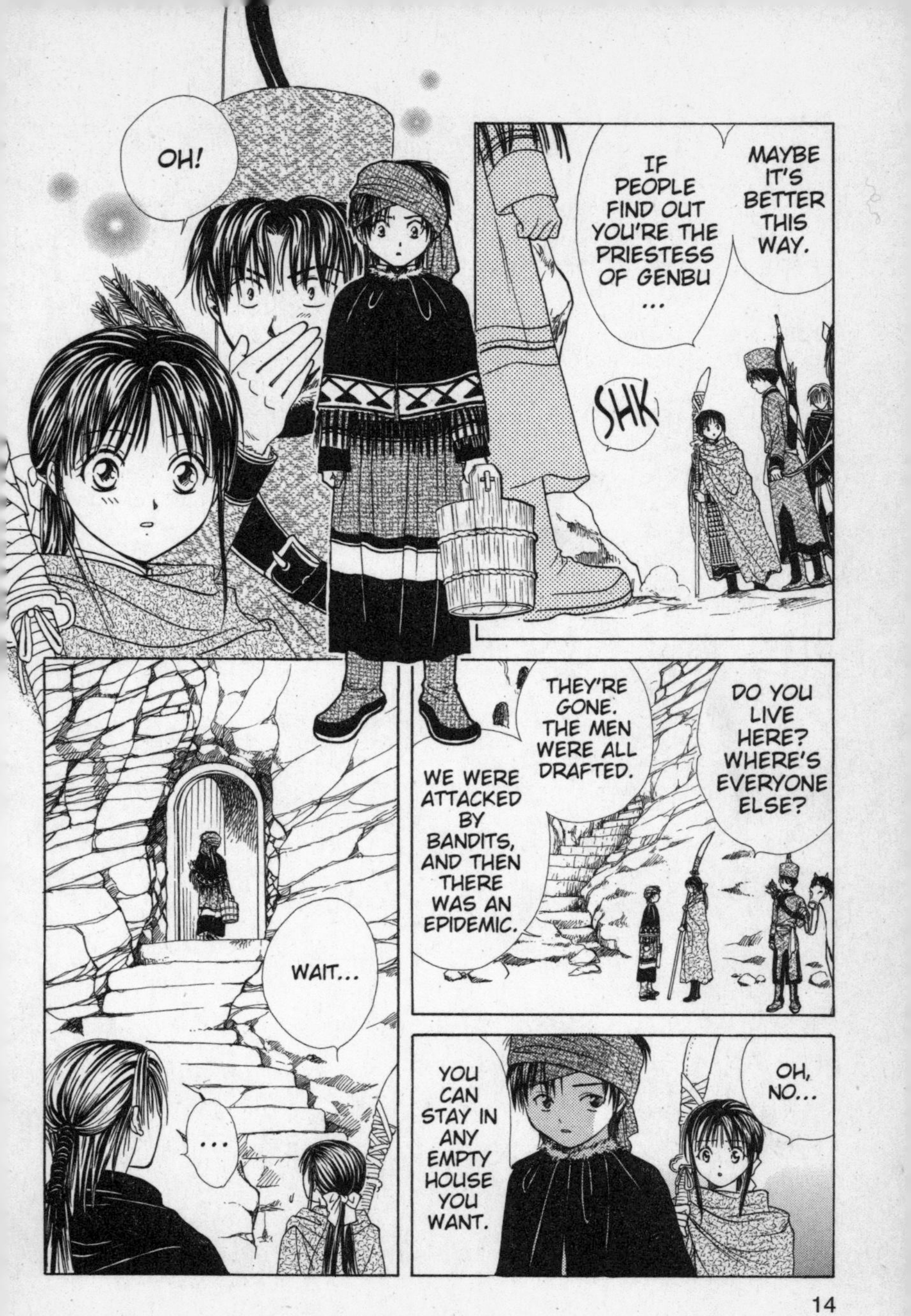
MAYBE IT'S BETTER THIS WAY.
IF PEOPLE FIND OUT YOU'RE THE PRIESTESS OF GENBU ...
SHK
OH!
DO YOU LIVE HERE? WHERE'S EVERYONE ELSE?
THEY'RE GONE. THE MEN WERE ALL DRAFTED.
WE WERE ATTACKED BY BANDITS, AND THEN THERE WAS AN EPIDEMIC.
OH, NO...
YOU CAN STAY IN ANY EMPTY HOUSE YOU WANT.
WAIT...
...

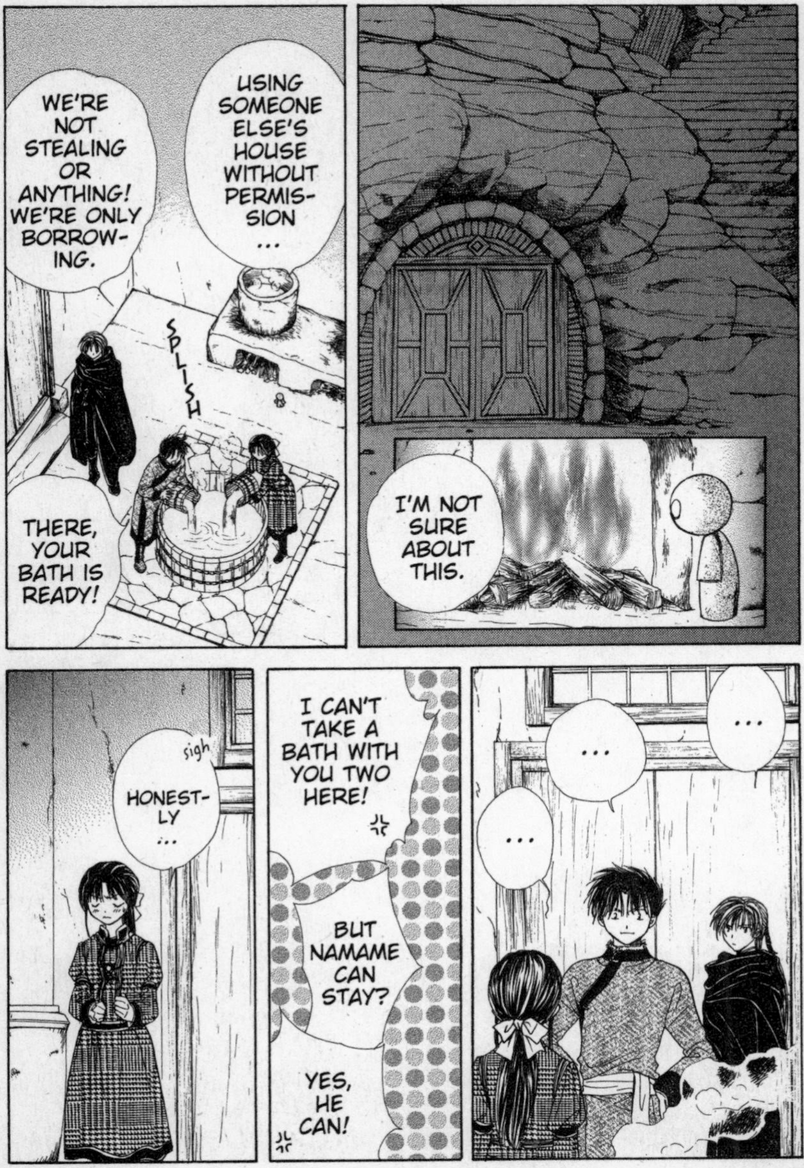
I'M NOT SURE ABOUT THIS.
USING SOMEONE ELSE'S HOUSE WITHOUT PERMISSION ...
WE'RE NOT STEALING OR ANYTHING! WE'RE ONLY BORROWING.
SPLISH
THERE, YOUR BATH IS READY!
...
...
...
I CAN'T TAKE A BATH WITH YOU TWO HERE!
BUT NAMAME CAN STAY?
YES, HE CAN!
sigh
HONESTLY ...

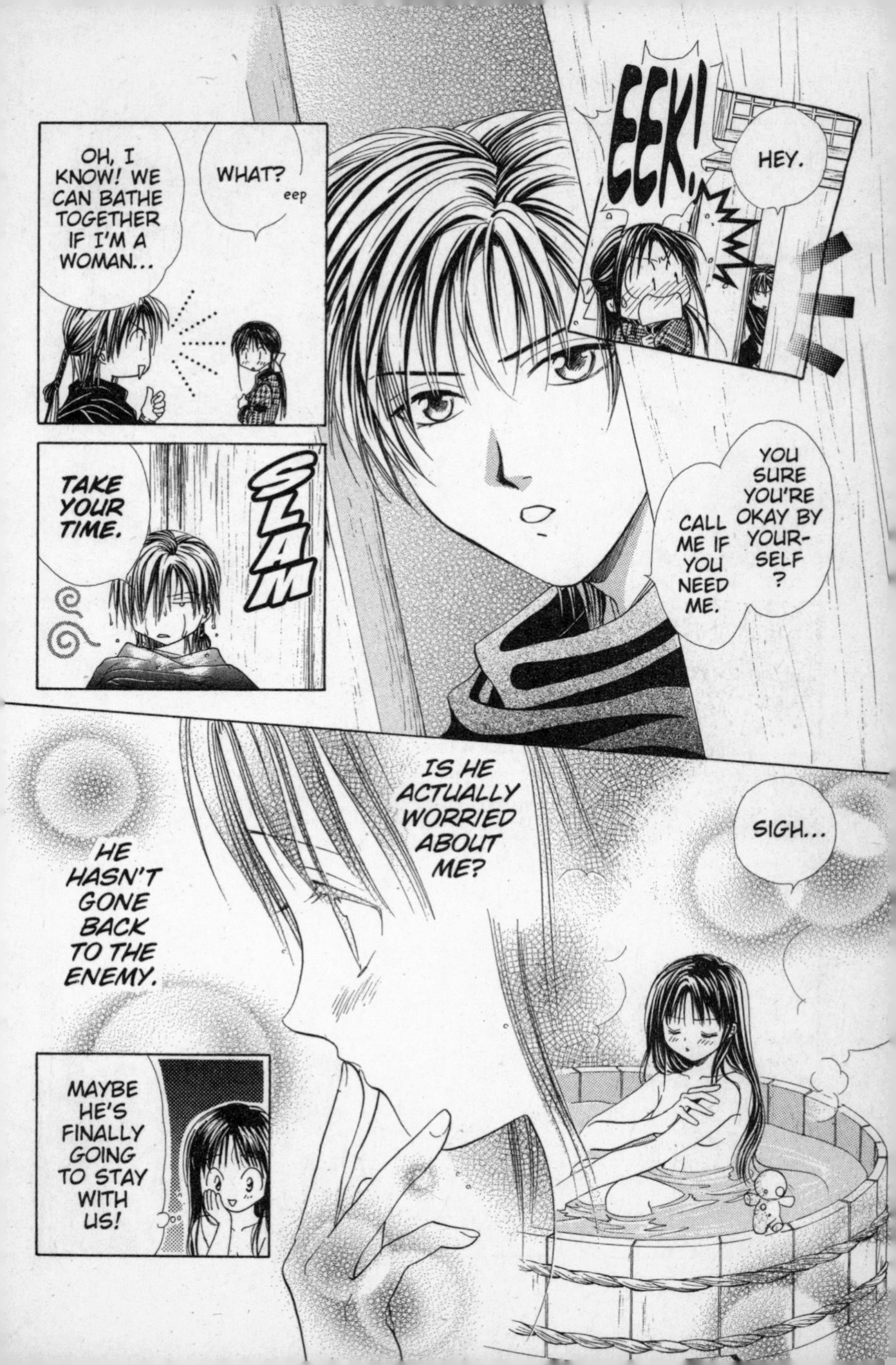
EEK!
HEY.
YOU SURE YOU'RE OKAY BY YOUR-SELF?
CALL ME IF YOU NEED ME.
OH, I KNOW! WE CAN BATHE TOGETHER IF I'M A WOMAN...
WHAT?
eep
SLAM
TAKE YOUR TIME.
SIGH...
IS HE ACTUALLY WORRIED ABOUT ME?
HE HASN'T GONE BACK TO THE ENEMY.
MAYBE HE'S FINALLY GOING TO STAY WITH US!

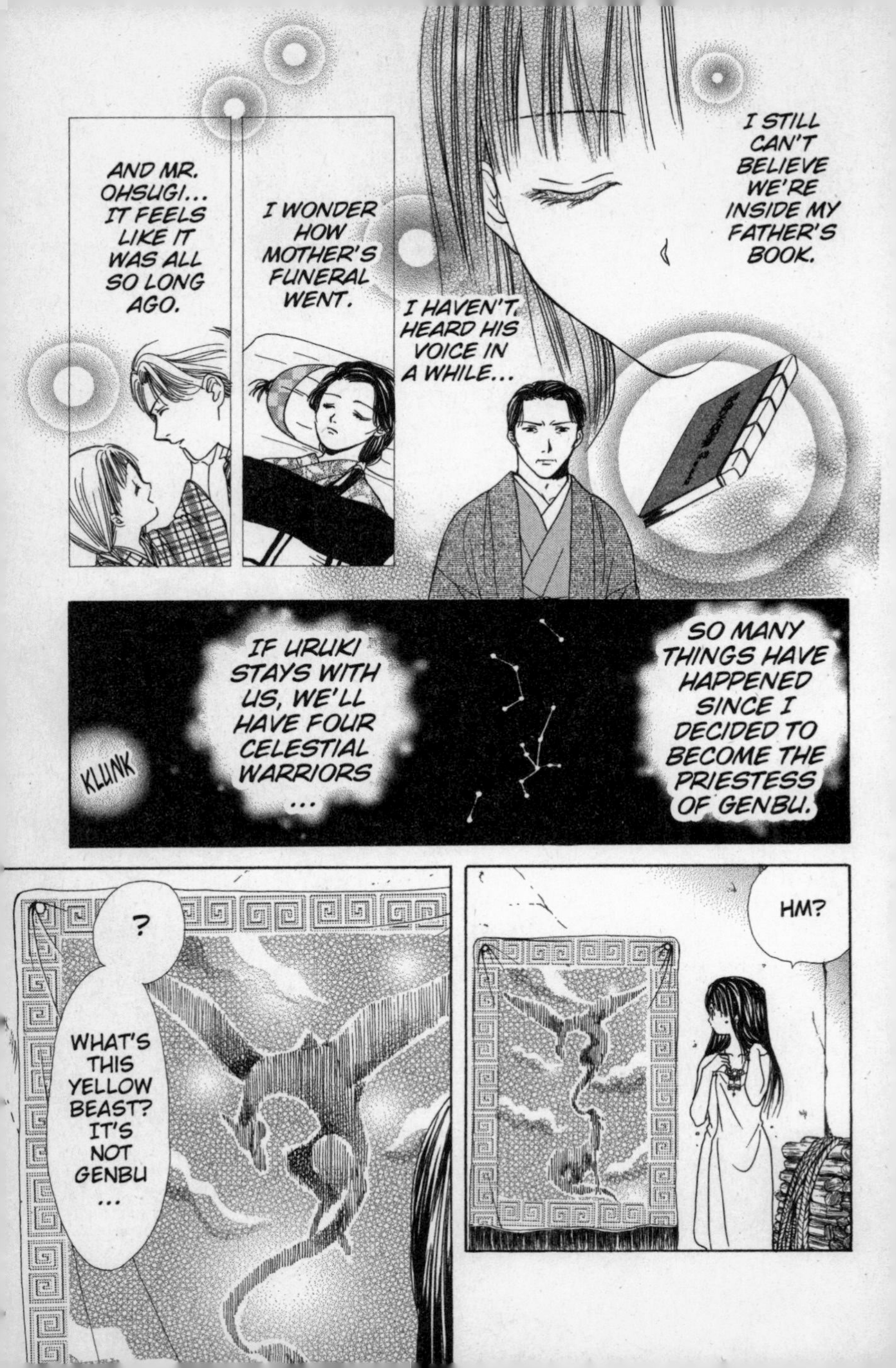
I STILL CAN'T BELIEVE WE'RE INSIDE MY FATHER'S BOOK.
I HAVEN'T HEARD HIS VOICE IN A WHILE...
I WONDER HOW MOTHER'S FUNERAL WENT.
AND MR. OHSUGI... IT FEELS LIKE IT WAS ALL SO LONG AGO.
SO MANY THINGS HAVE HAPPENED SINCE I DECIDED TO BECOME THE PRIESTESS OF GENBU.
IF URUKI STAYS WITH US, WE'LL HAVE FOUR CELESTIAL WARRIORS ...
KLUNK
HM?
?
WHAT'S THIS YELLOW BEAST? IT'S NOT GENBU ...

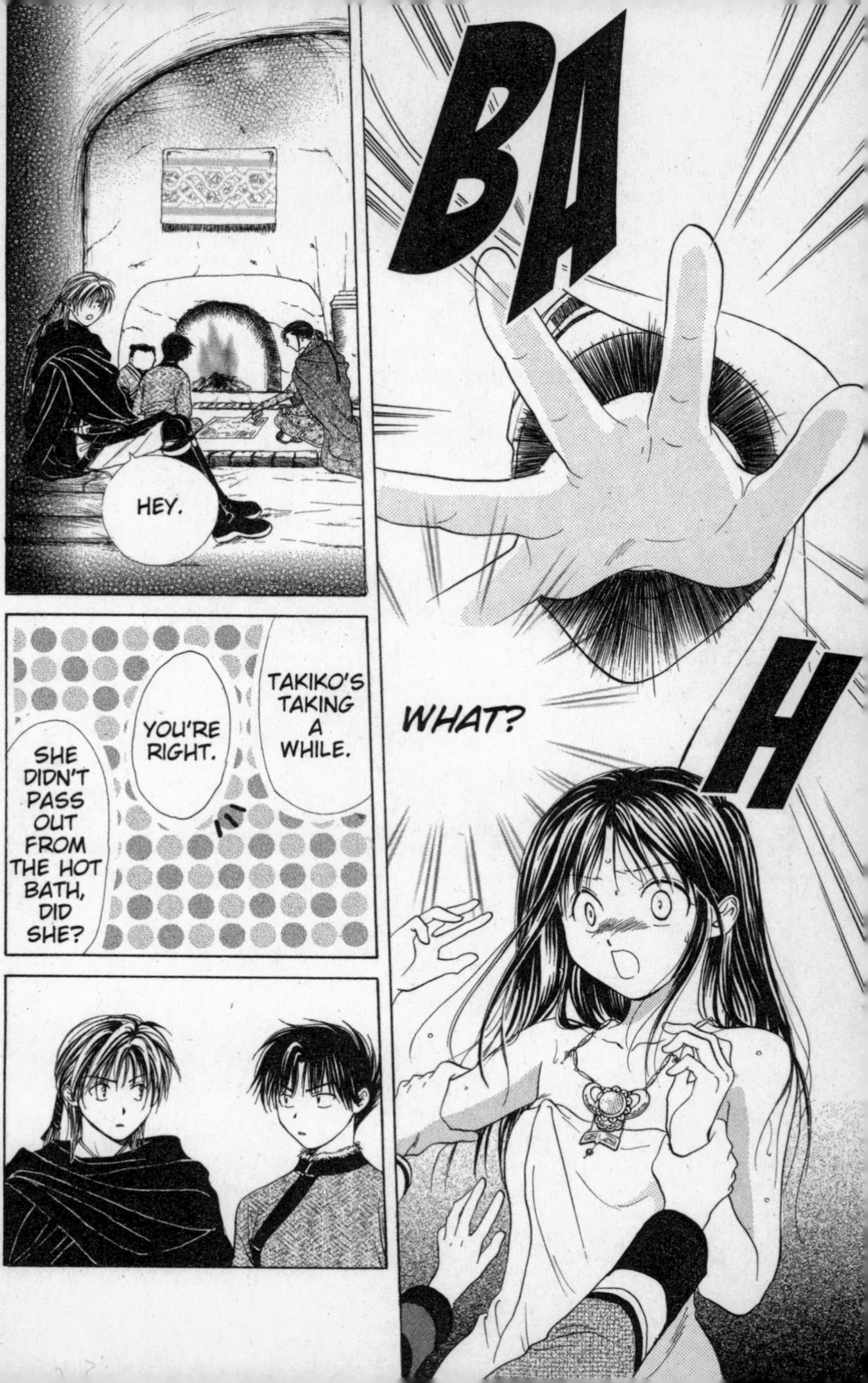
BA
H
WHAT?
HEY.
TAKIKO'S TAKING A WHILE.
YOU'RE RIGHT.
SHE DIDN'T PASS OUT FROM THE HOT BATH, DID SHE?

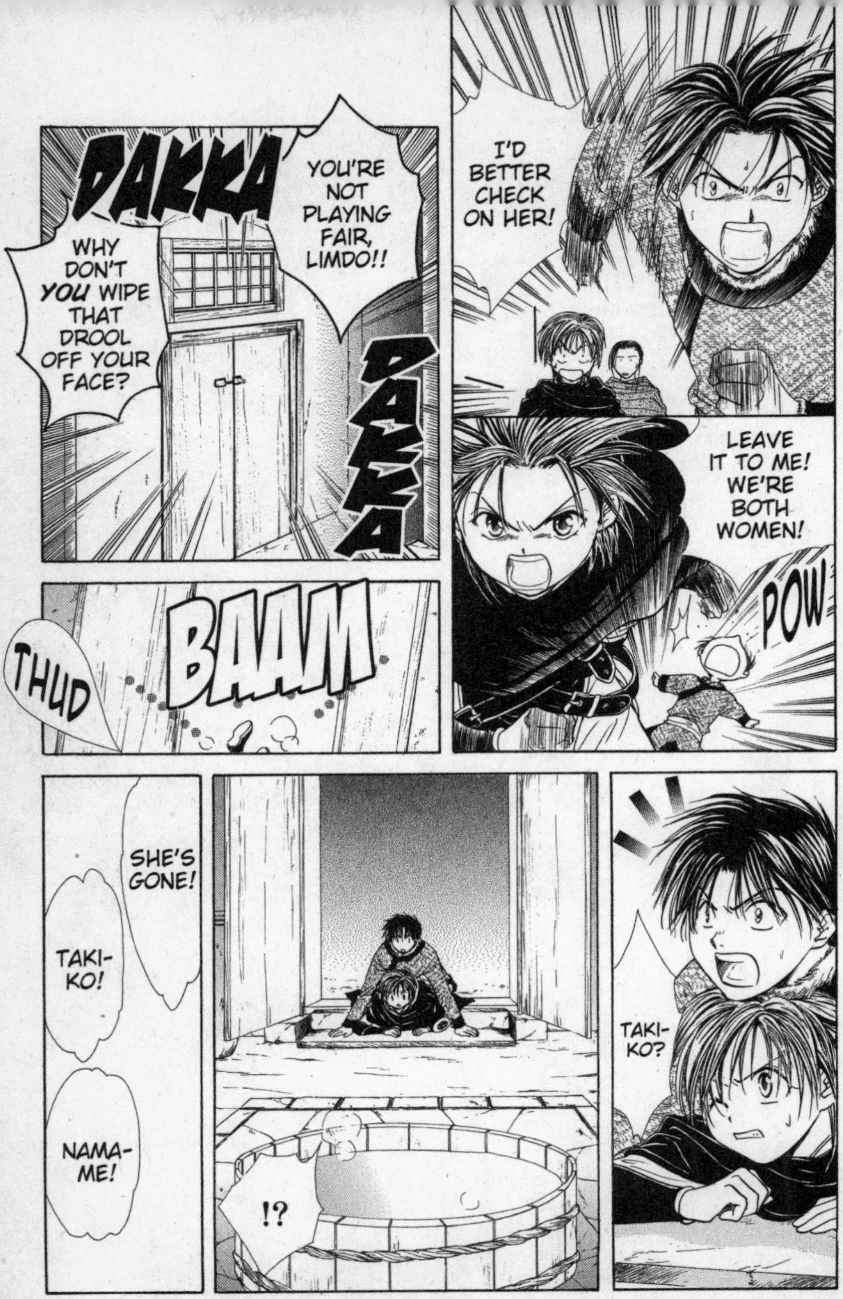
I'D BETTER CHECK ON HER!
LEAVE IT TO ME! WE'RE BOTH WOMEN!
POW
DAKKA
YOU'RE NOT PLAYING FAIR, LIMDO!!
WHY DON'T YOU WIPE THAT DROOL OFF YOUR FACE?
DAKKA
BAAM
THUD
TAKI-KO?
!?
SHE'S GONE!
TAKI-KO!
NAMA-ME!

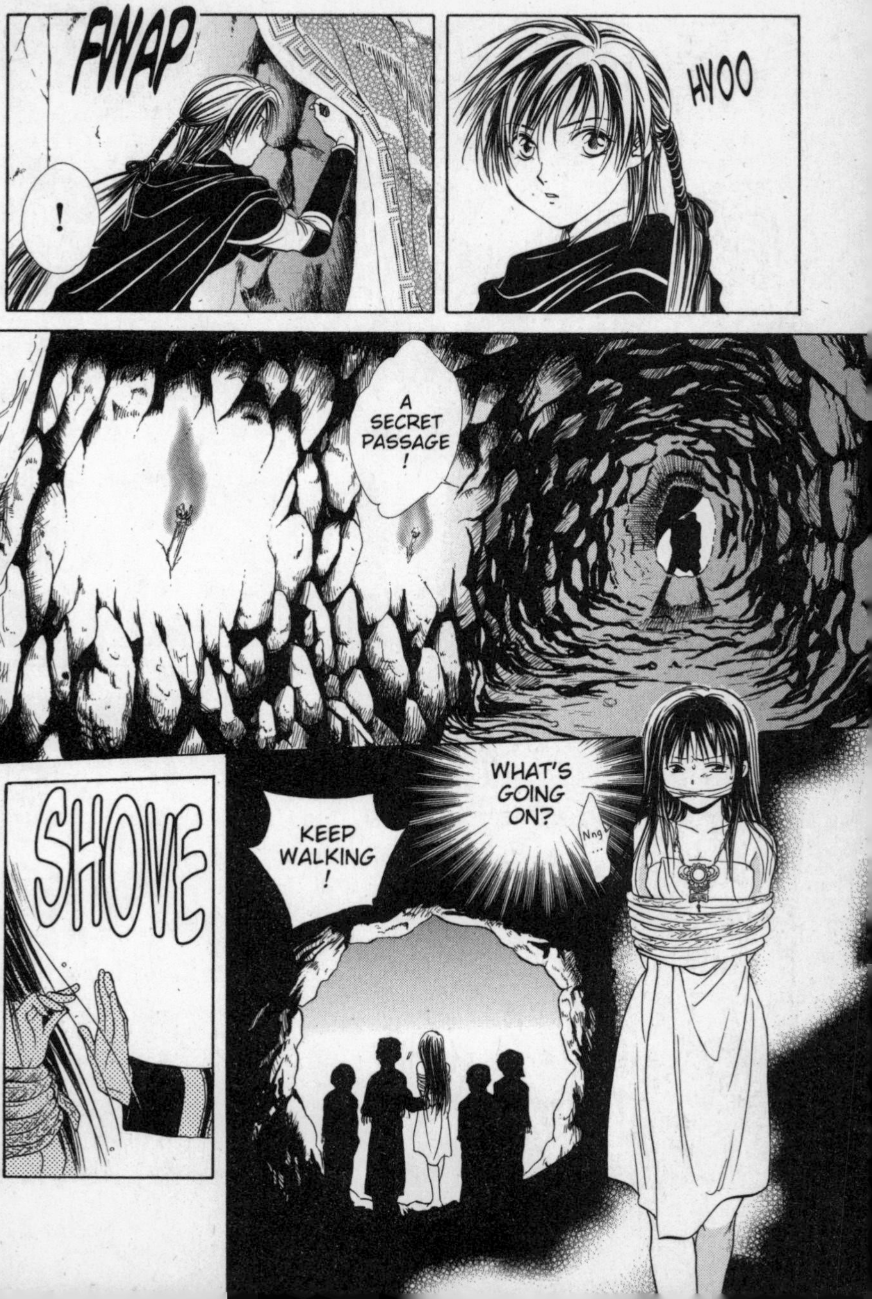
HYOO
FWAP
!
A SECRET PASSAGE!
WHAT'S GOING ON?
Nng...
KEEP WALKING!
SHOVE

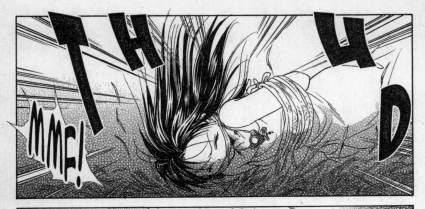

THUD
MMF!
UNH...
YOU'RE THE PRIESTESS OF GENBU!
WHAT'S HAPPENING? ARE THEY FROM QU-DONG?
THIS IS DIVINE PUNISHMENT!
WHAT?
IT'S ALL YOUR FAULT!
THOOM...

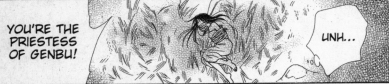

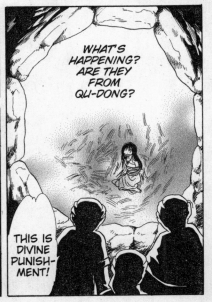

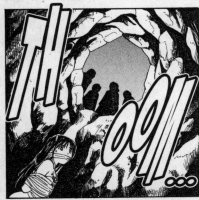

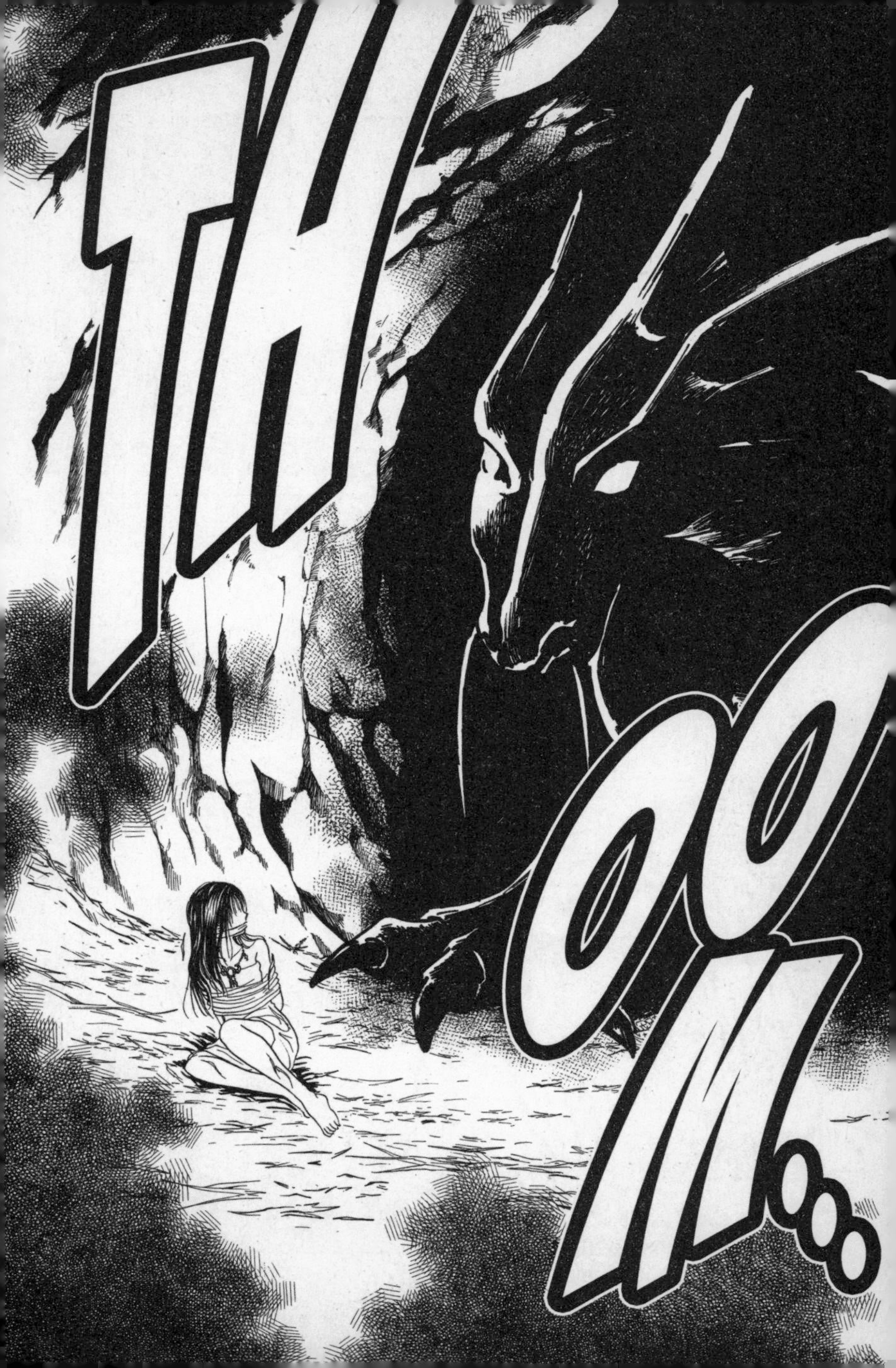
THOOM...

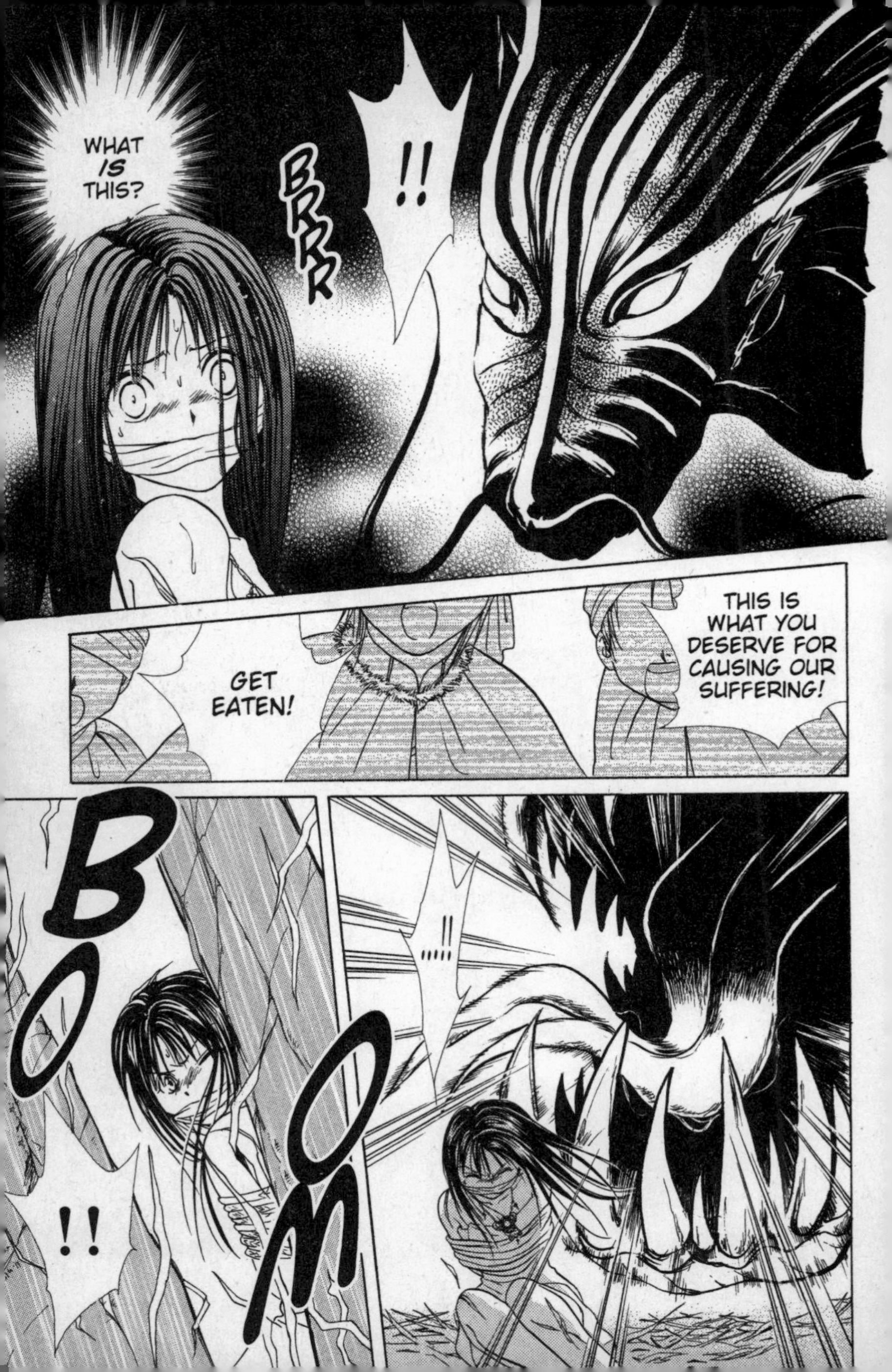
!!
BRRR
WHAT IS THIS?
THIS IS WHAT YOU DESERVE FOR CAUSING OUR SUFFERING!
GET EATEN!
...!!
BOOM
!!

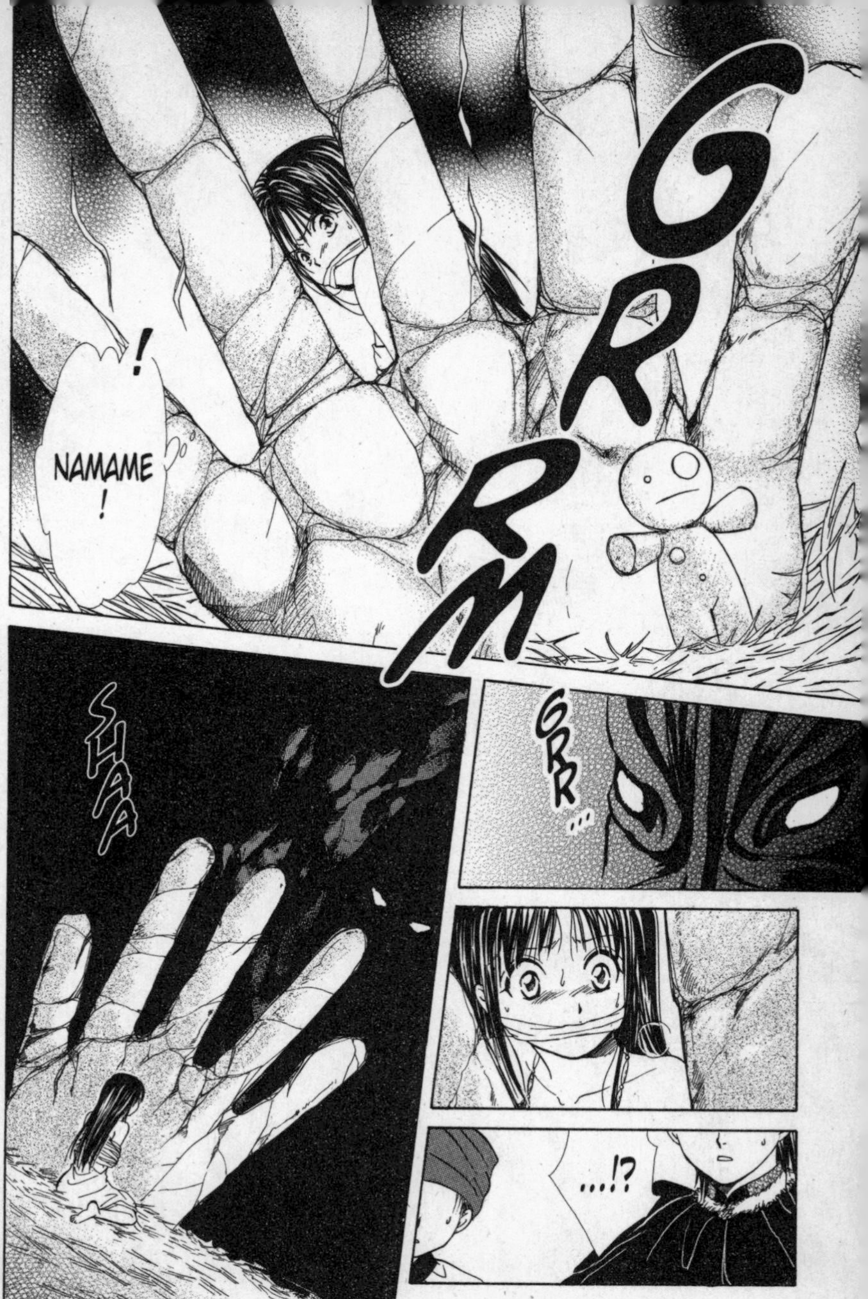
GRRRM
!
NAMAME!
GRR...
...!?
SHAAA

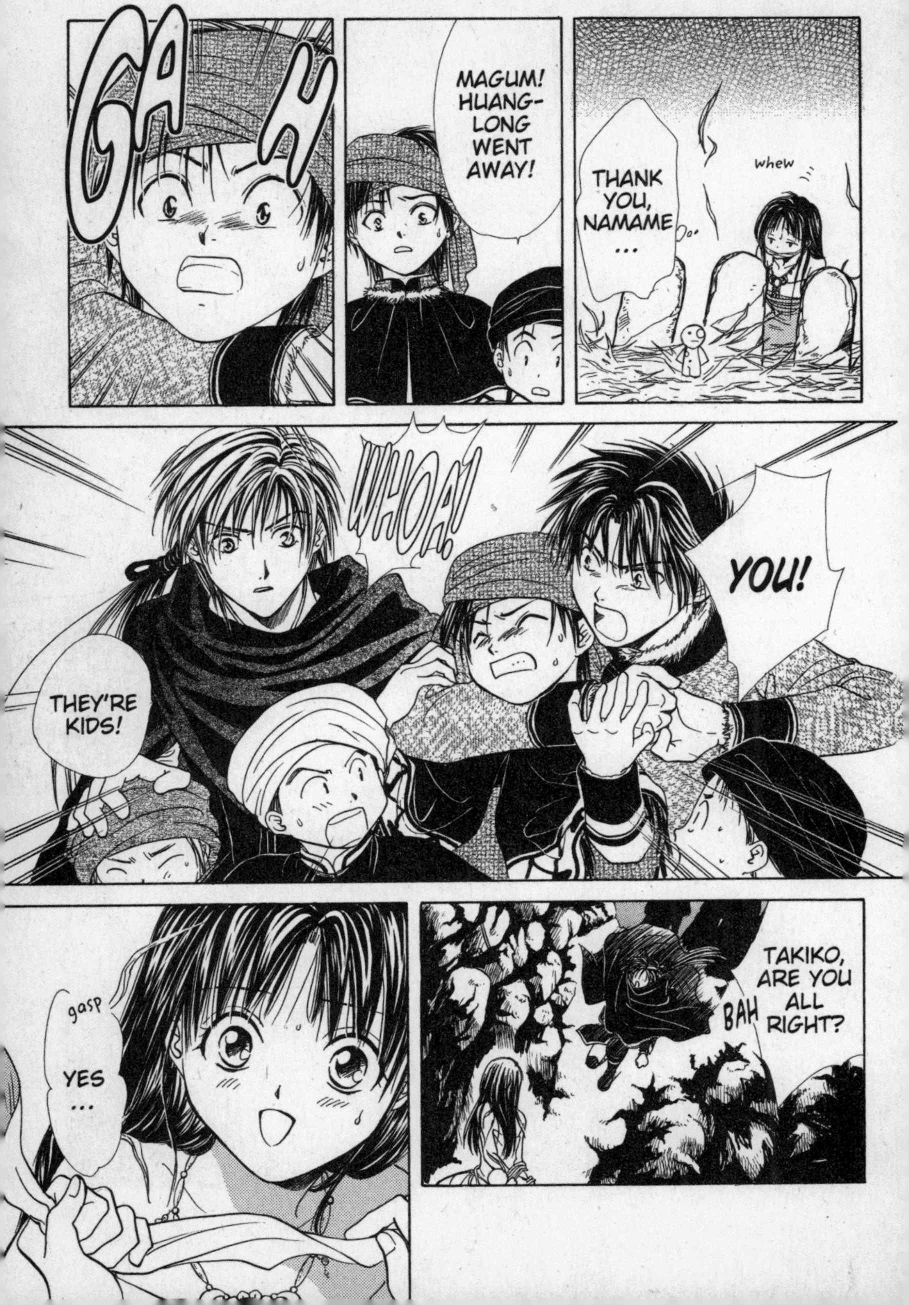
whew
THANK YOU, NAMAME ...
MAGUM! HUANG-LONG WENT AWAY!
GAH
YOU!
WHOA!
THEY'RE KIDS!
TAKIKO, ARE YOU ALL RIGHT?
BAH
gasp
YES ...

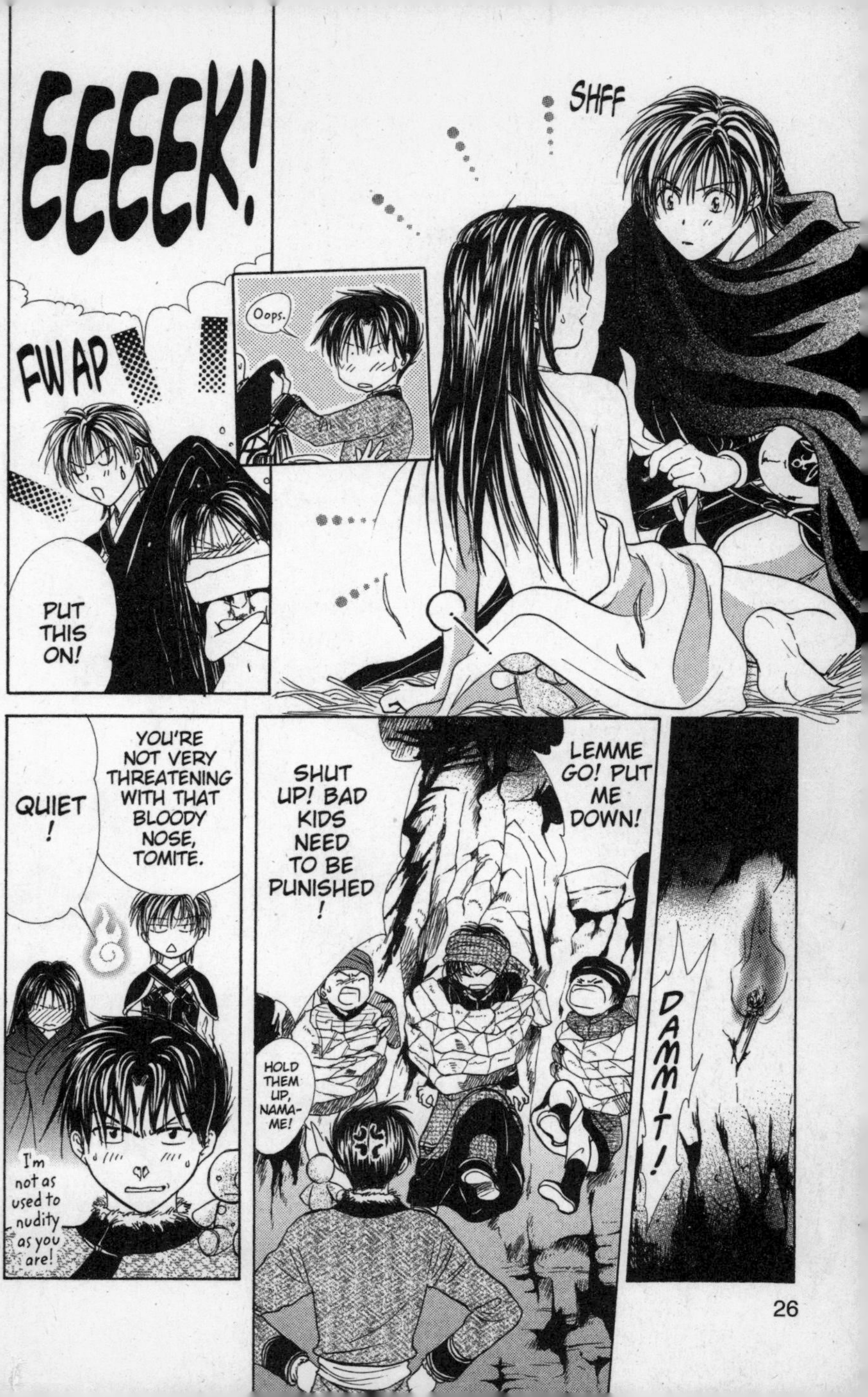
SHFF
Oops.
EEEEK!
FWAP
PUT THIS ON!
DAMMIT!
LEMME GO! PUT ME DOWN!
SHUT UP! BAD KIDS NEED TO BE PUNISHED!
HOLD THEM UP, NAMAME!
YOU'RE NOT VERY THREATENING WITH THAT BLOODY NOSE, TOMITE.
QUIET!
I'm not as used to nudity as you are!

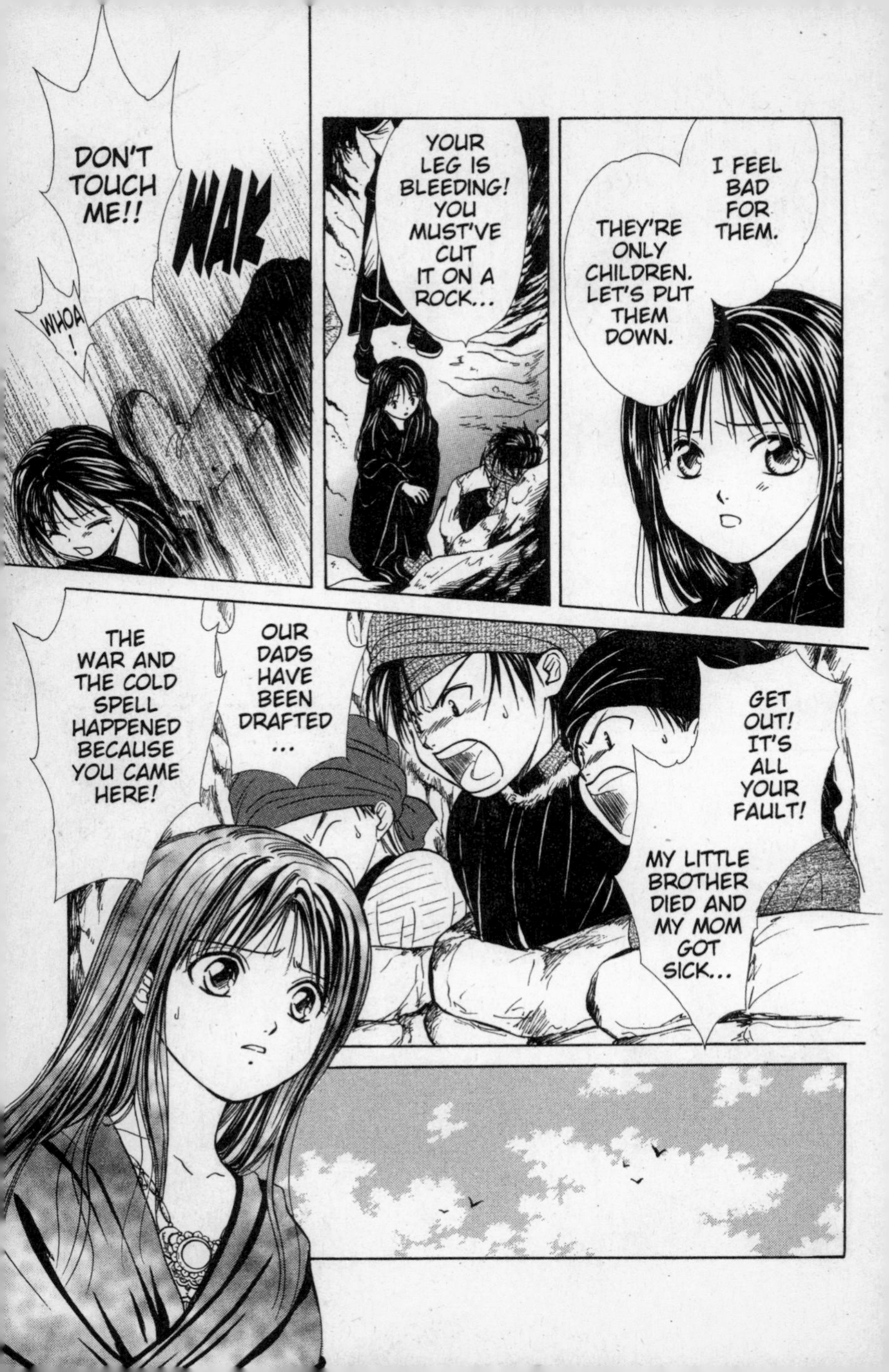
I FEEL BAD FOR THEM.
THEY'RE ONLY CHILDREN. LET'S PUT THEM DOWN.
YOUR LEG IS BLEEDING! YOU MUST'VE CUT IT ON A ROCK...
DON'T TOUCH ME!!
WAK
WHOA!
GET OUT! IT'S ALL YOUR FAULT!
MY LITTLE BROTHER DIED AND MY MOM GOT SICK...
OUR DADS HAVE BEEN DRAFTED...
THE WAR AND THE COLD SPELL HAPPENED BECAUSE YOU CAME HERE!

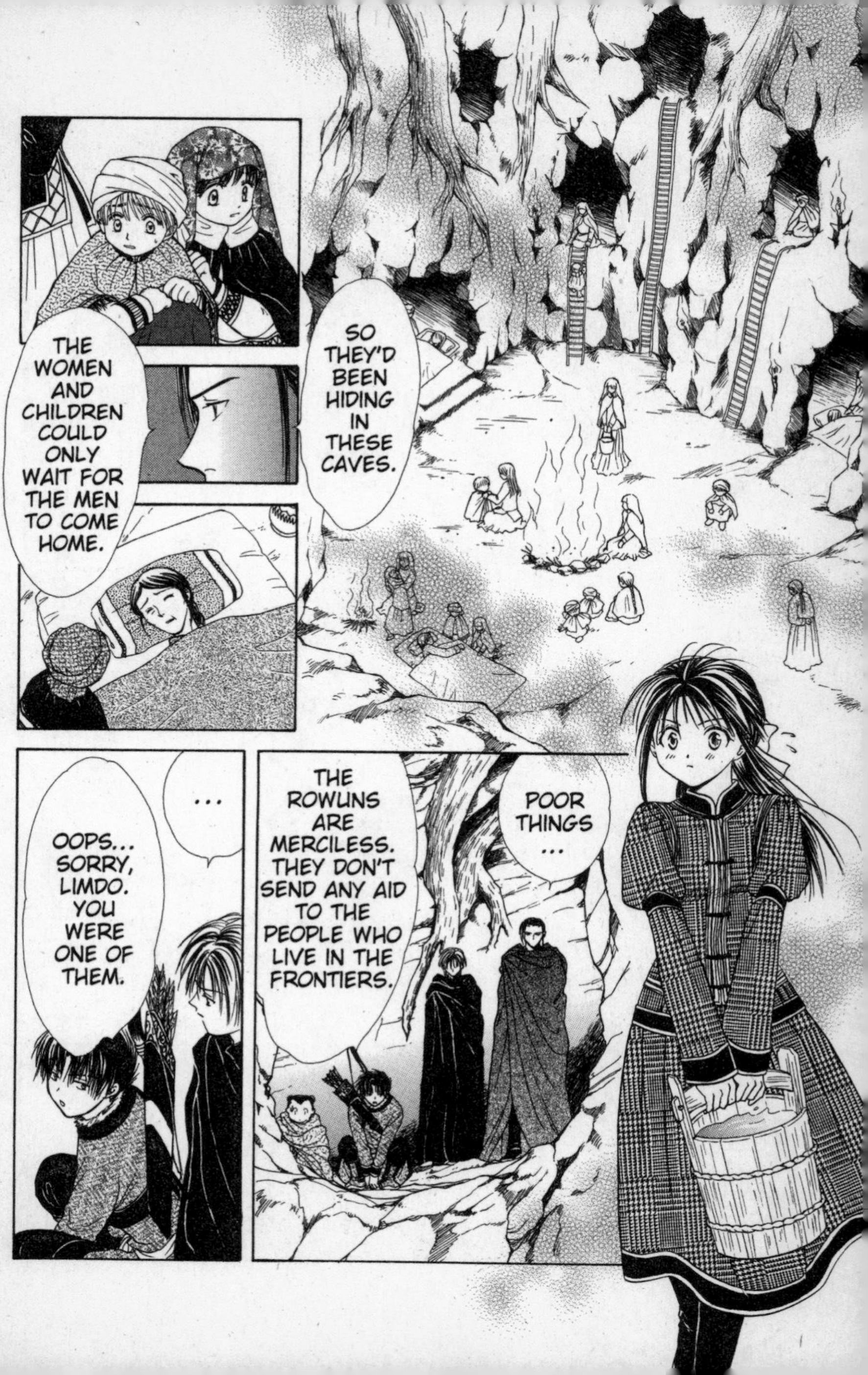
SO THEY'D BEEN HIDING IN THESE CAVES.
THE WOMEN AND CHILDREN COULD ONLY WAIT FOR THE MEN TO COME HOME.
POOR THINGS ...
THE ROWUNS ARE MERCILESS. THEY DON'T SEND ANY AID TO THE PEOPLE WHO LIVE IN THE FRONTIERS.
...
OOPS... SORRY, LIMDO. YOU WERE ONE OF THEM.

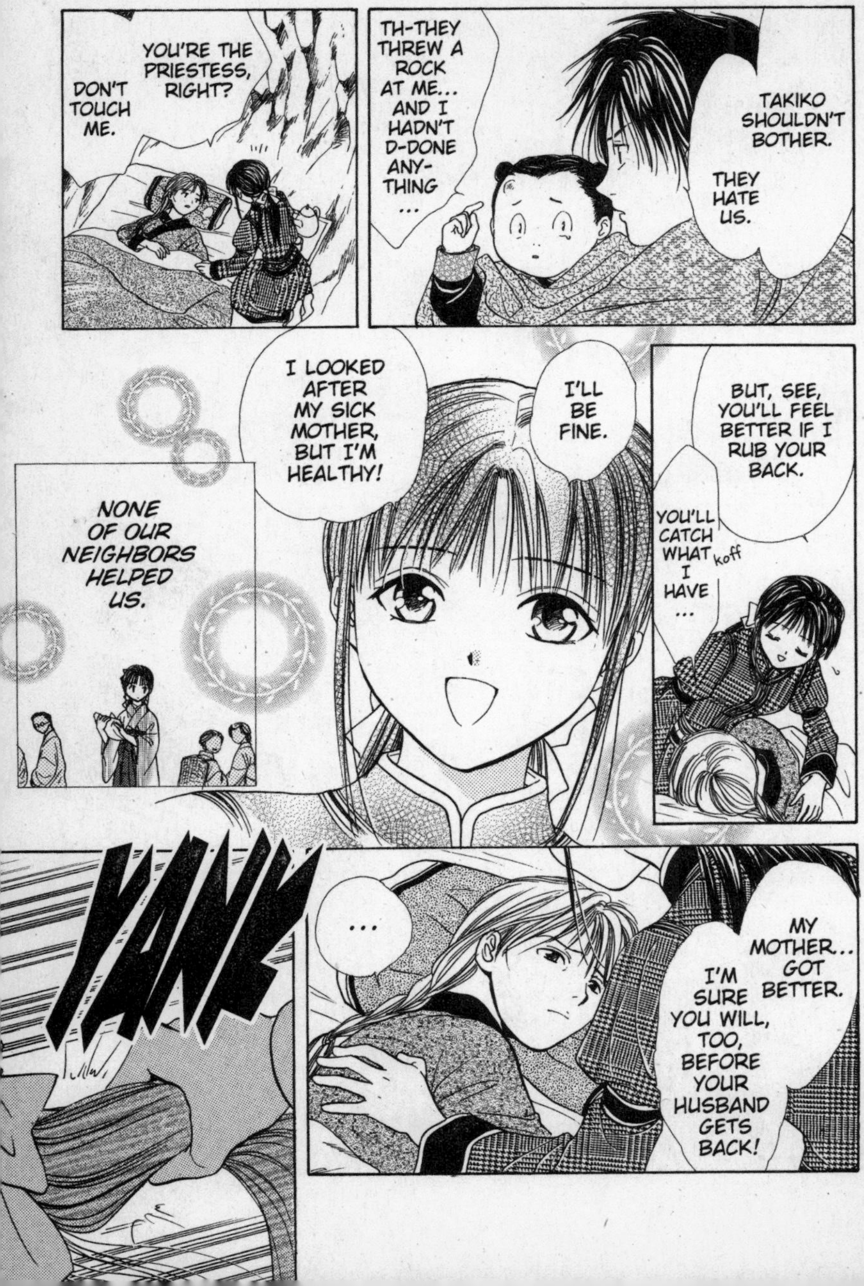
TAKIKO SHOULDN'T BOTHER.
THEY HATE US.
TH-THEY THREW A ROCK AT ME... AND I HADN'T D-DONE ANYTHING...
YOU'RE THE PRIESTESS, RIGHT?
DON'T TOUCH ME.
BUT, SEE, YOU'LL FEEL BETTER IF I RUB YOUR BACK.
YOU'LL CATCH WHAT I HAVE...
koff
I'LL BE FINE.
I LOOKED AFTER MY SICK MOTHER, BUT I'M HEALTHY!
NONE OF OUR NEIGHBORS HELPED US.
MY MOTHER... GOT BETTER.
I'M SURE YOU WILL, TOO, BEFORE YOUR HUSBAND GETS BACK!
...
YANK

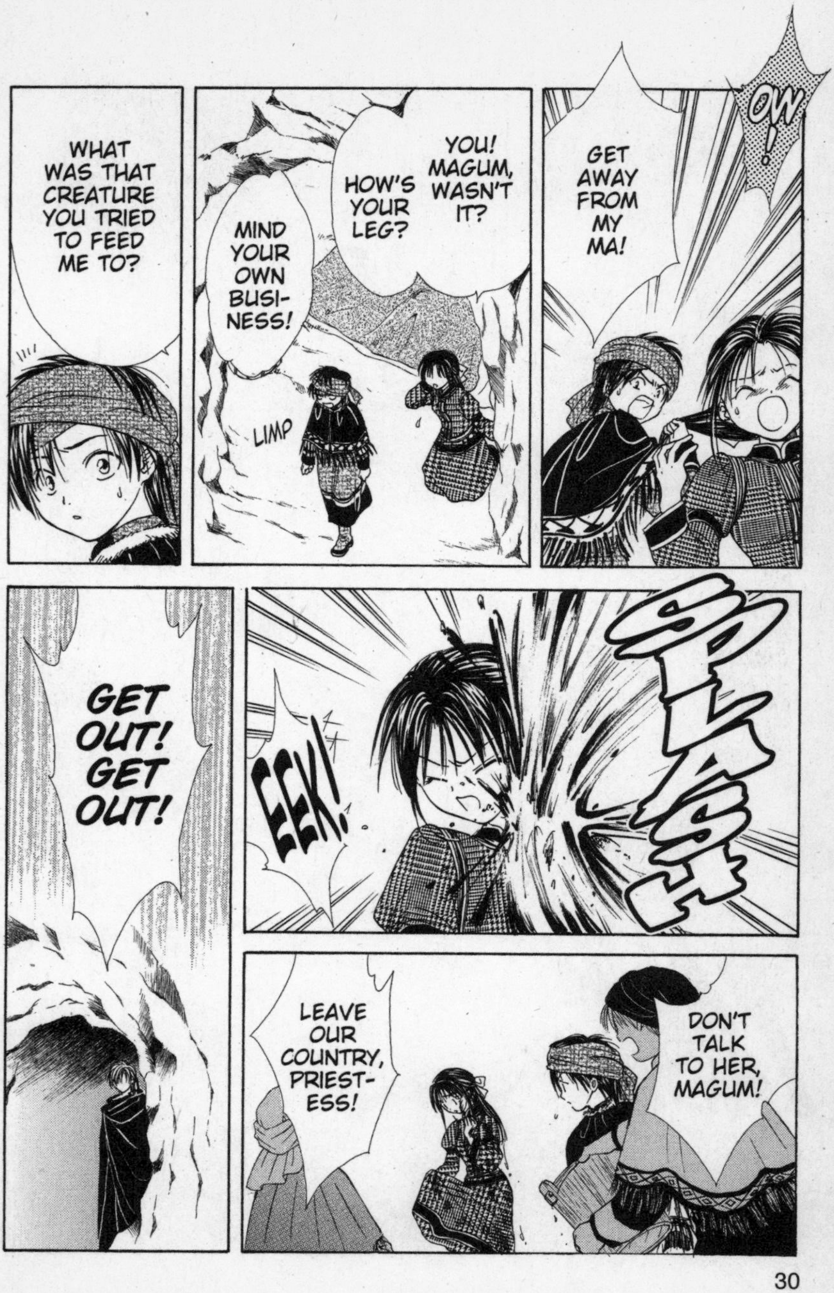
OW!
GET AWAY FROM MY MA!
YOU! MAGUM, WASN'T IT?
HOW'S YOUR LEG?
MIND YOUR OWN BUSI-NESS!
LIMP
WHAT WAS THAT CREATURE YOU TRIED TO FEED ME TO?
SPLASH
EEK!
DON'T TALK TO HER, MAGUM!
LEAVE OUR COUNTRY, PRIEST-ESS!
GET OUT! GET OUT!

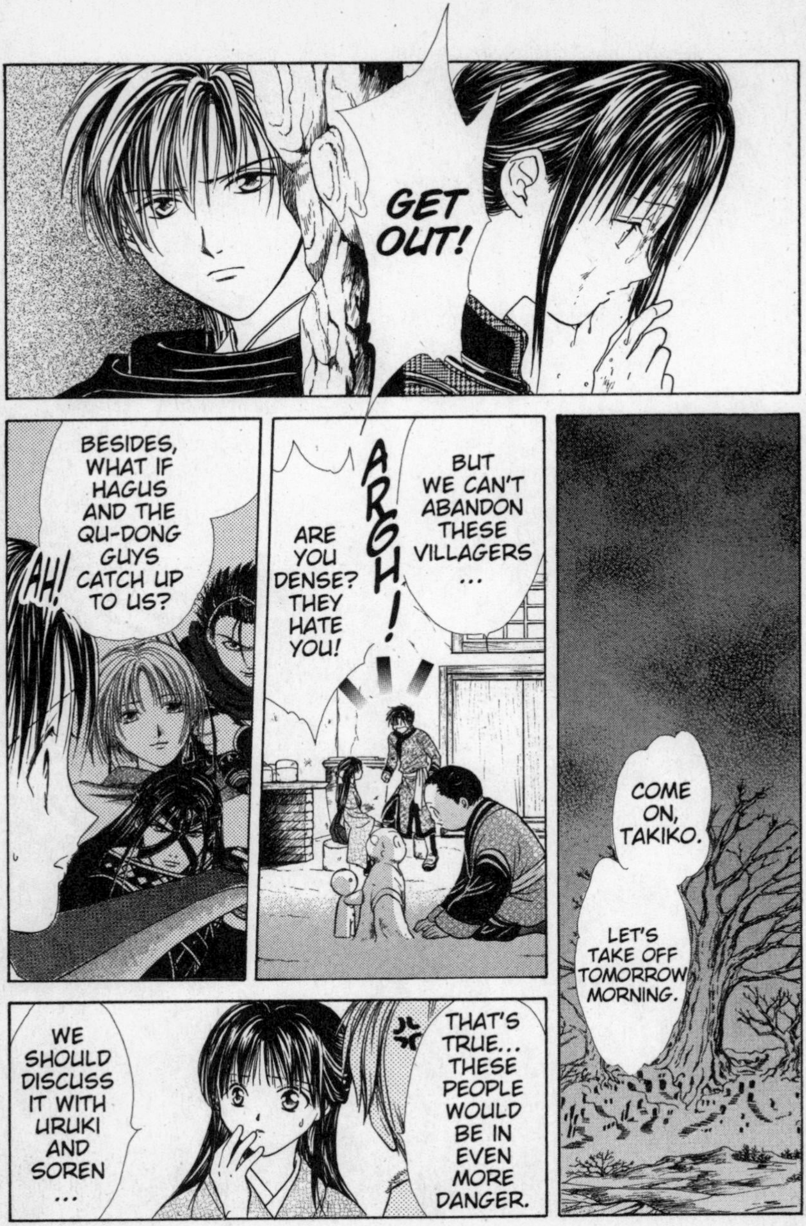
GET OUT!
COME ON, TAKIKO.
LET'S TAKE OFF TOMORROW MORNING.
BUT WE CAN'T ABANDON THESE VILLAGERS...
ARGH!
ARE YOU DENSE? THEY HATE YOU!
BESIDES, WHAT IF HAGUS AND THE QU-DONG GUYS CATCH UP TO US?
AH!
THAT'S TRUE... THESE PEOPLE WOULD BE IN EVEN MORE DANGER.
WE SHOULD DISCUSS IT WITH URUKI AND SOREN...

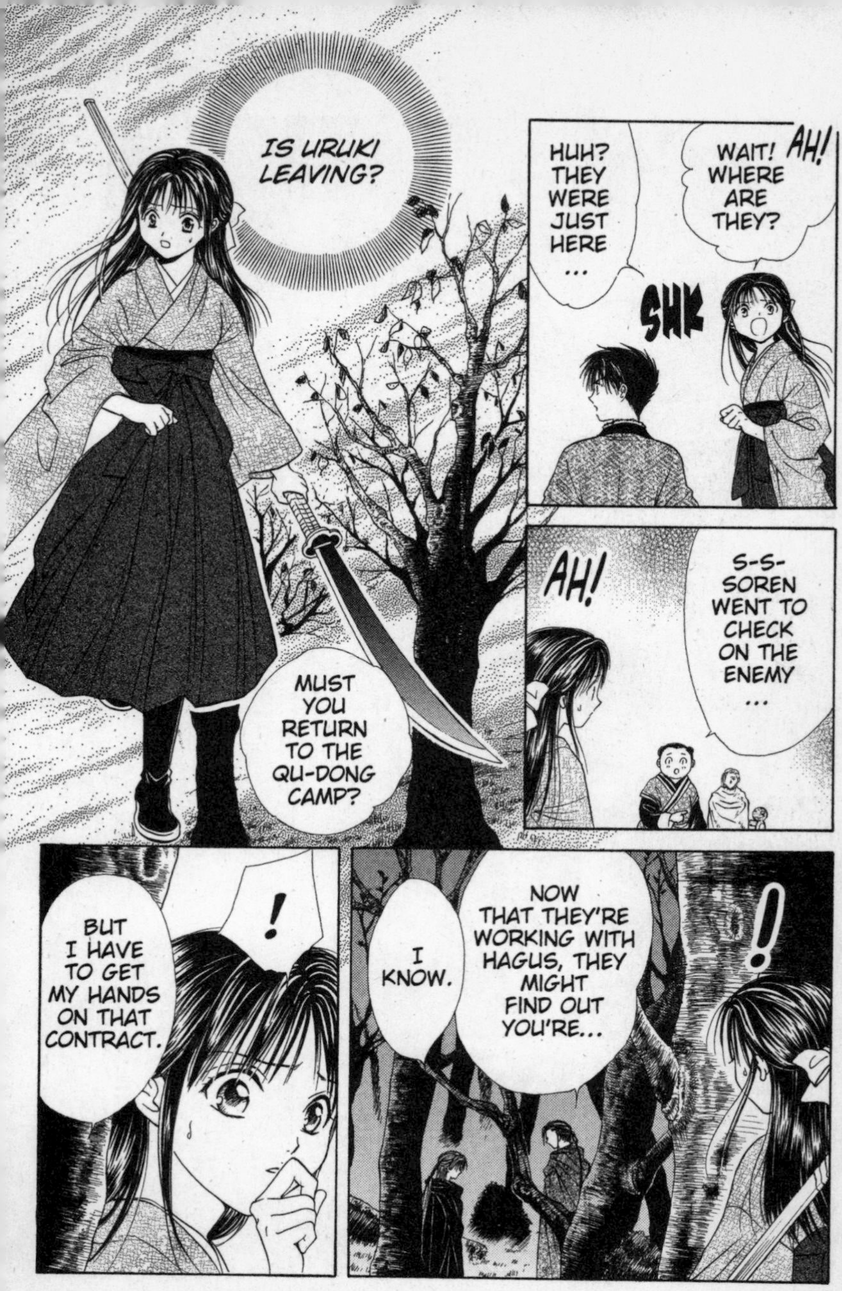
AH!
WAIT! WHERE ARE THEY?
SHK
HUH? THEY WERE JUST HERE ...
S-S-SOREN WENT TO CHECK ON THE ENEMY ...
AH!
IS URUKI LEAVING?
MUST YOU RETURN TO THE QU-DONG CAMP?
!
NOW THAT THEY'RE WORKING WITH HAGUS, THEY MIGHT FIND OUT YOU'RE...
I KNOW.
!
BUT I HAVE TO GET MY HANDS ON THAT CONTRACT.

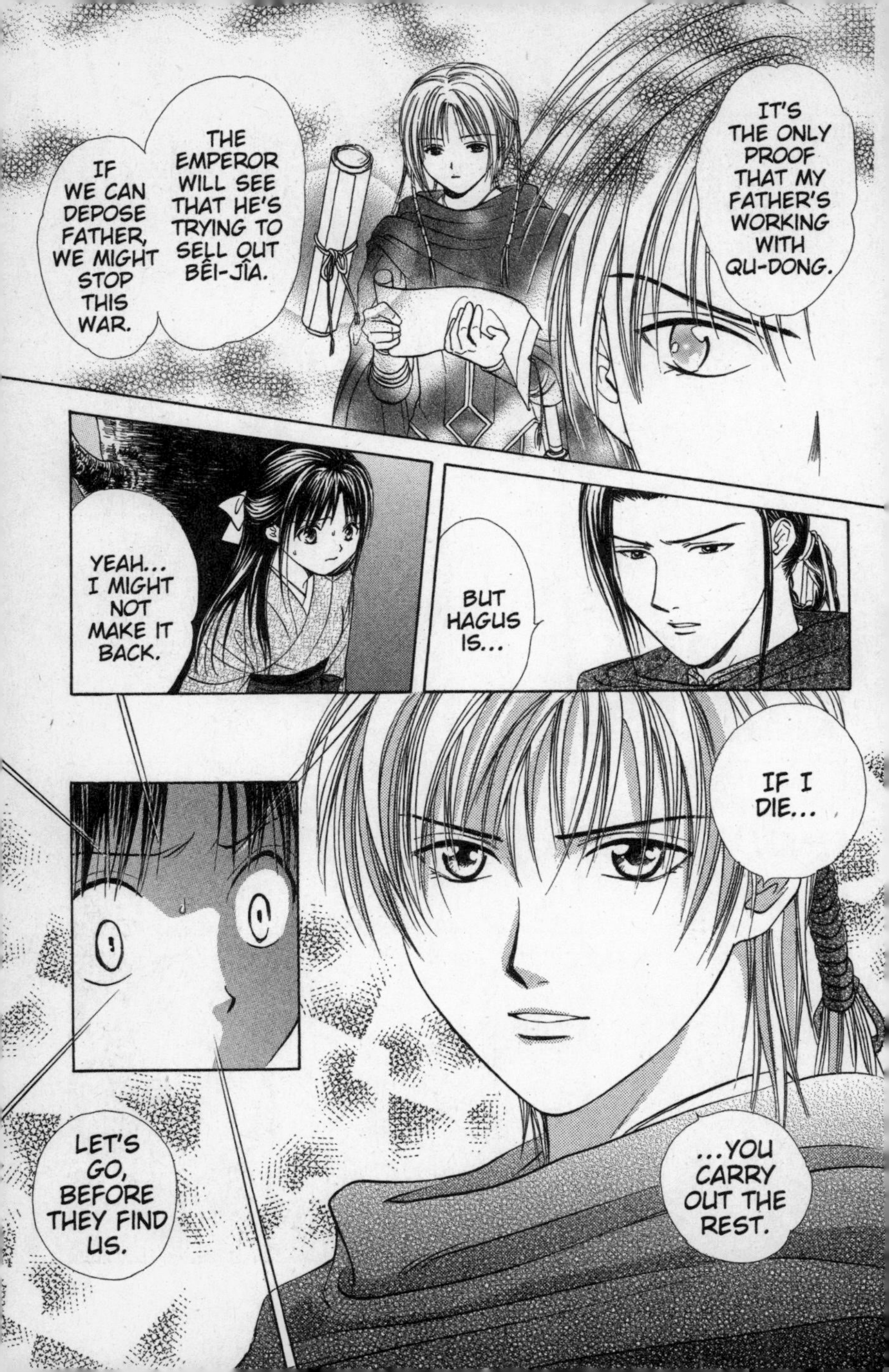
IT'S THE ONLY PROOF THAT MY FATHER'S WORKING WITH QU-DONG.
THE EMPEROR WILL SEE THAT HE'S TRYING TO SELL OUT BÊI-JÎA.
IF WE CAN DEPOSE FATHER, WE MIGHT STOP THIS WAR.
BUT HAGUS IS...
YEAH... I MIGHT NOT MAKE IT BACK.
IF I DIE...
...YOU CARRY OUT THE REST.
LET'S GO, BEFORE THEY FIND US.

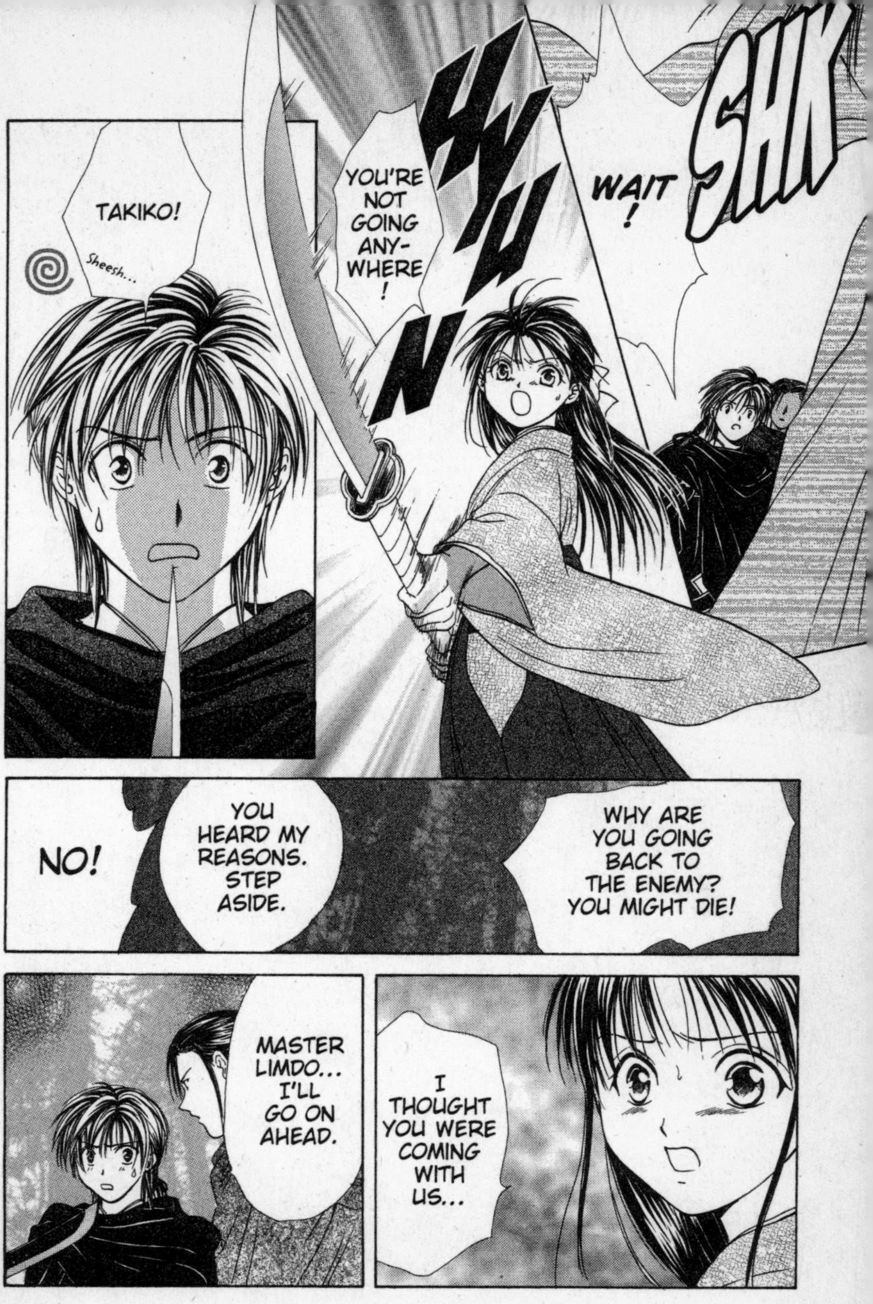
SHIN
WAIT!
SHUN
YOU'RE NOT GOING ANYWHERE!
TAKIKO!
Sheesh...
WHY ARE YOU GOING BACK TO THE ENEMY? YOU MIGHT DIE!
YOU HEARD MY REASONS. STEP ASIDE.
NO!
I THOUGHT YOU WERE COMING WITH US...
MASTER LIMDO... I'LL GO ON AHEAD.

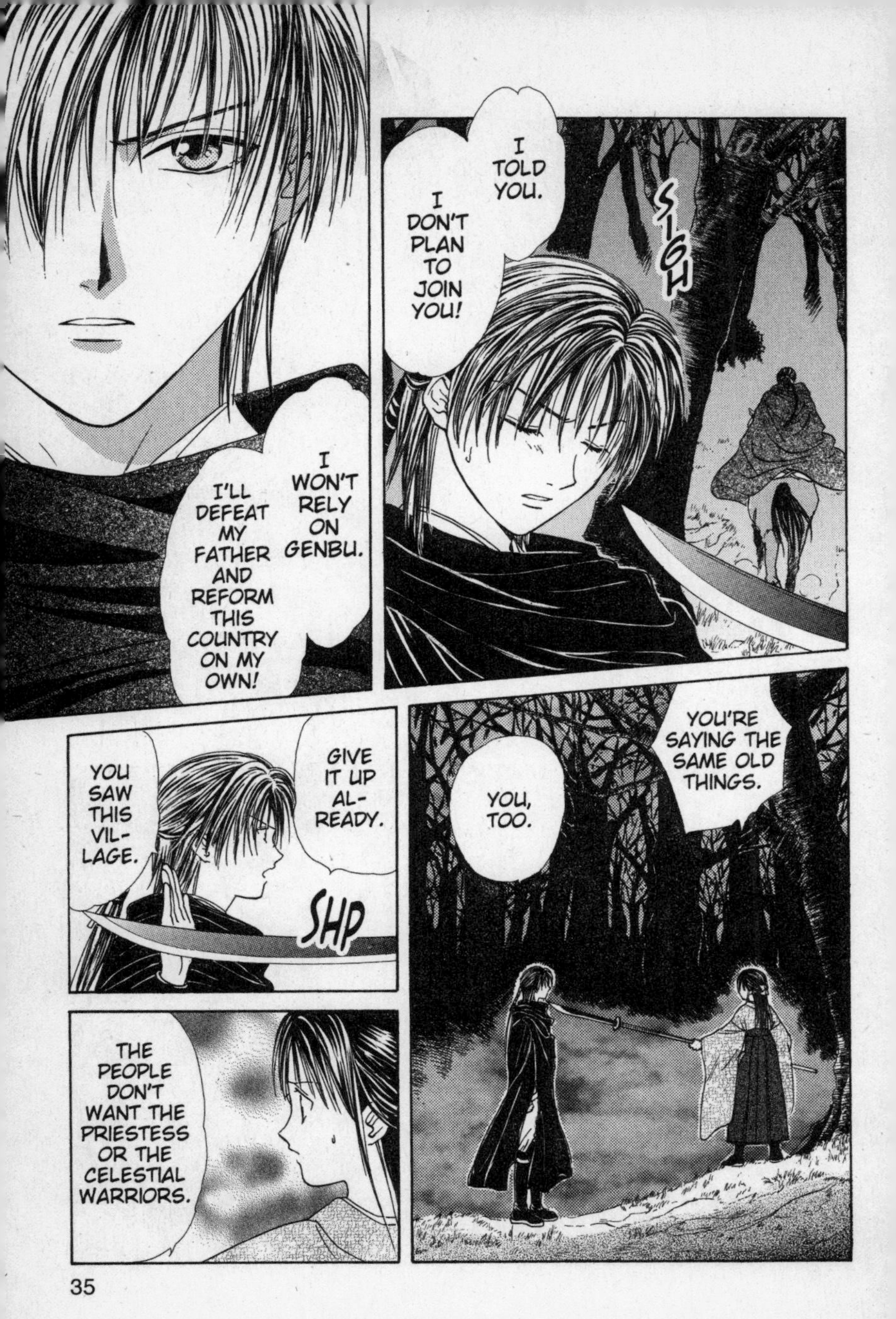
I TOLD YOU.
I DON'T PLAN TO JOIN YOU!
SIGH
I WON'T RELY ON GENBU.
I'LL DEFEAT MY FATHER AND REFORM THIS COUNTRY ON MY OWN!
YOU'RE SAYING THE SAME OLD THINGS.
YOU, TOO.
GIVE IT UP AL-READY.
YOU SAW THIS VIL-LAGE.
SHP
THE PEOPLE DON'T WANT THE PRIESTESS OR THE CELESTIAL WARRIORS.

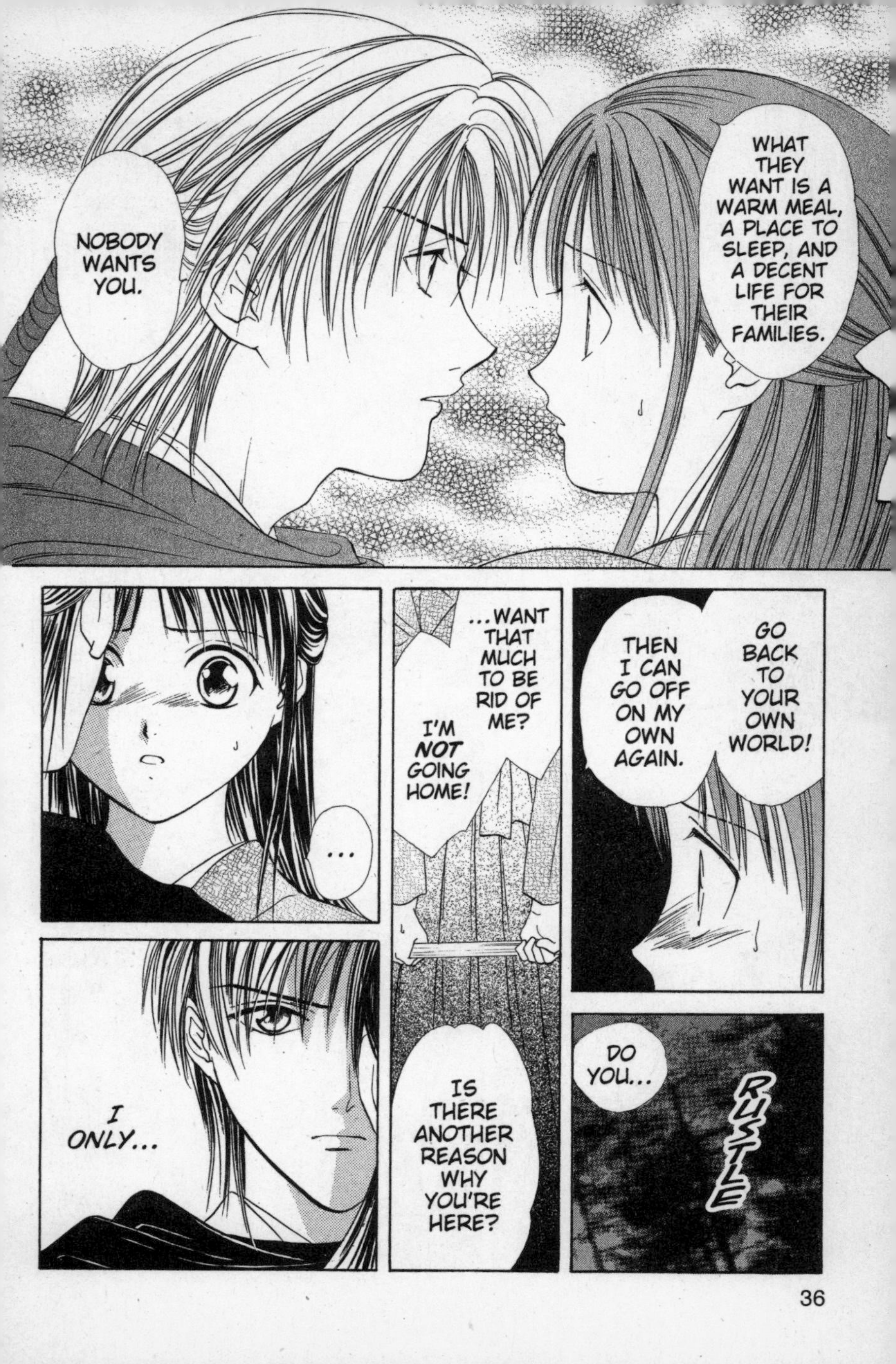

WHAT THEY WANT IS A WARM MEAL, A PLACE TO SLEEP, AND A DECENT LIFE FOR THEIR FAMILIES.
NOBODY WANTS YOU.
GO BACK TO YOUR OWN WORLD!
THEN I CAN GO OFF ON MY OWN AGAIN.
DO YOU...
RUSTLE
...WANT THAT MUCH TO BE RID OF ME?
I'M ***NOT*** GOING HOME!
IS THERE ANOTHER REASON WHY YOU'RE HERE?
...
I ONLY...

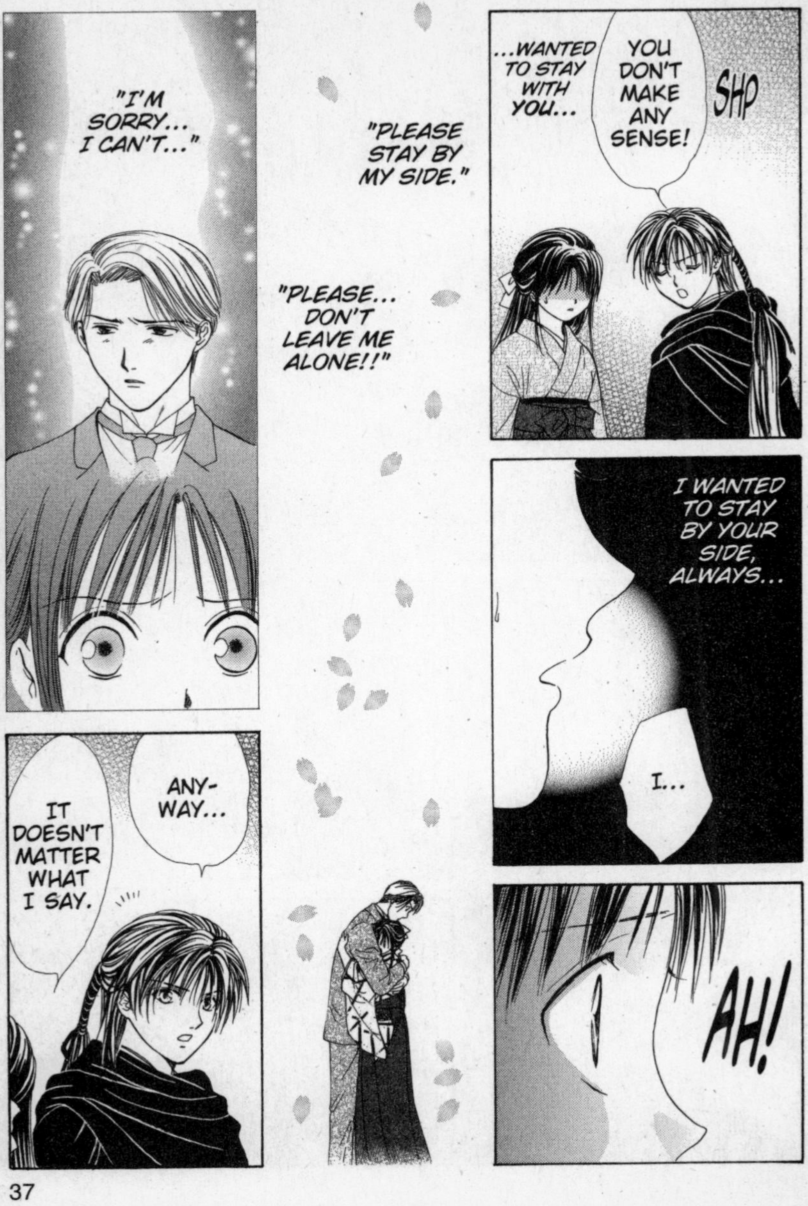
SHP
YOU DON'T MAKE ANY SENSE!
...WANTED TO STAY WITH YOU...
I WANTED TO STAY BY YOUR SIDE, ALWAYS...
I...
AH!
"PLEASE STAY BY MY SIDE."
"PLEASE... DON'T LEAVE ME ALONE!!"
"I'M SORRY... I CAN'T..."
ANY-WAY...
IT DOESN'T MATTER WHAT I SAY.

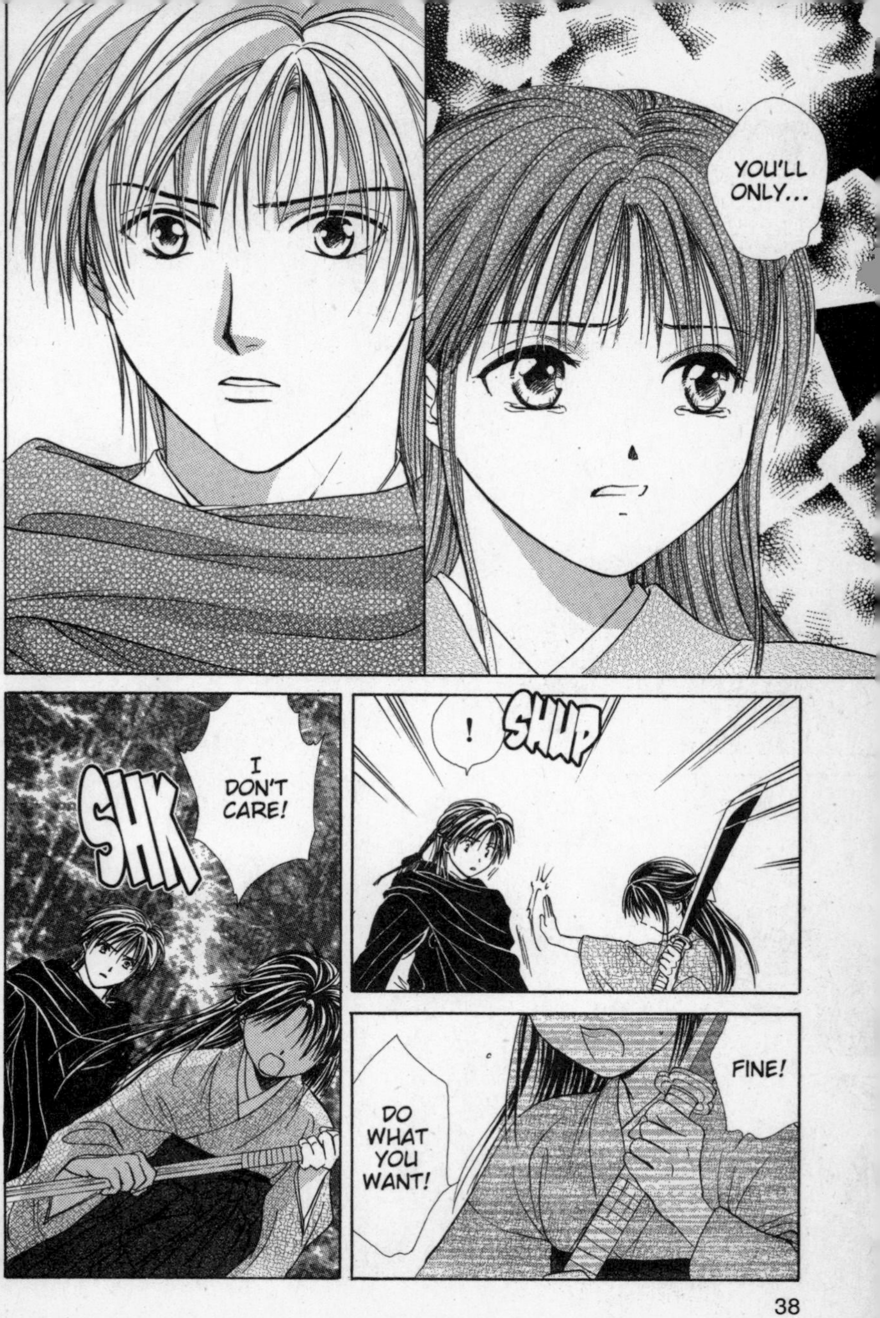
YOU'LL ONLY...
!
SHUP
FINE!
DO WHAT YOU WANT!
I DON'T CARE!
SHK

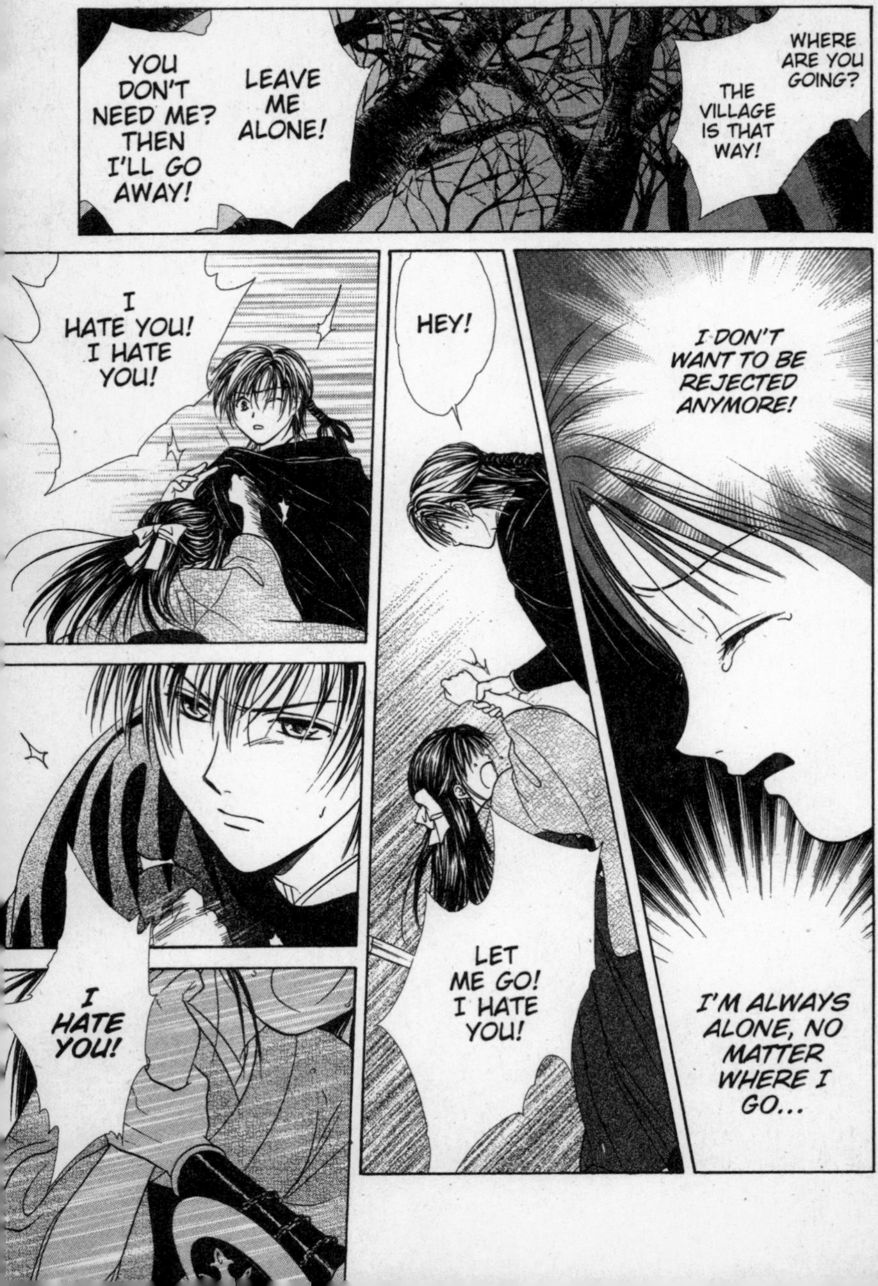
WHERE ARE YOU GOING?
THE VILLAGE IS THAT WAY!
LEAVE ME ALONE!
YOU DON'T NEED ME? THEN I'LL GO AWAY!
I DON'T WANT TO BE REJECTED ANYMORE!
I'M ALWAYS ALONE, NO MATTER WHERE I GO...
HEY!
LET ME GO! I HATE YOU!
I HATE YOU! I HATE YOU!
I HATE YOU!

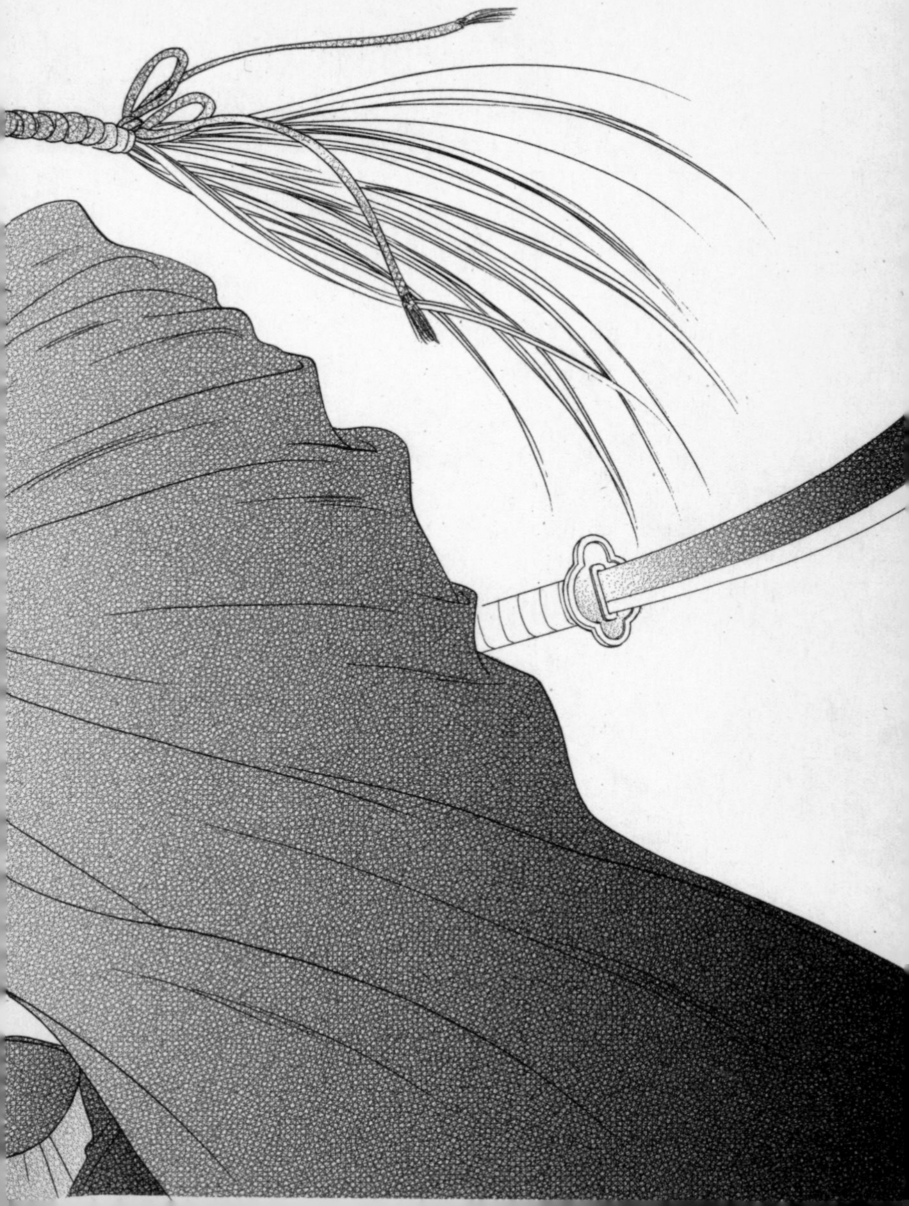

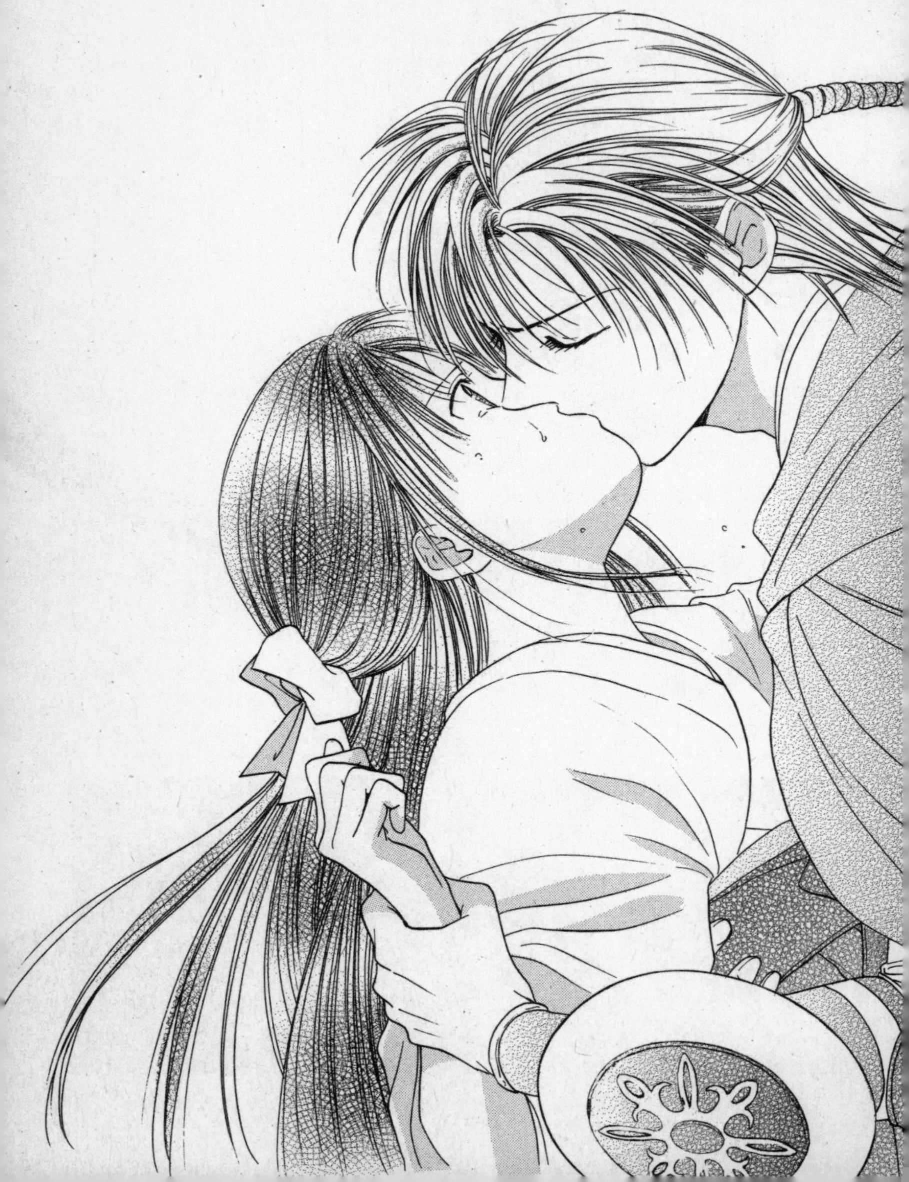

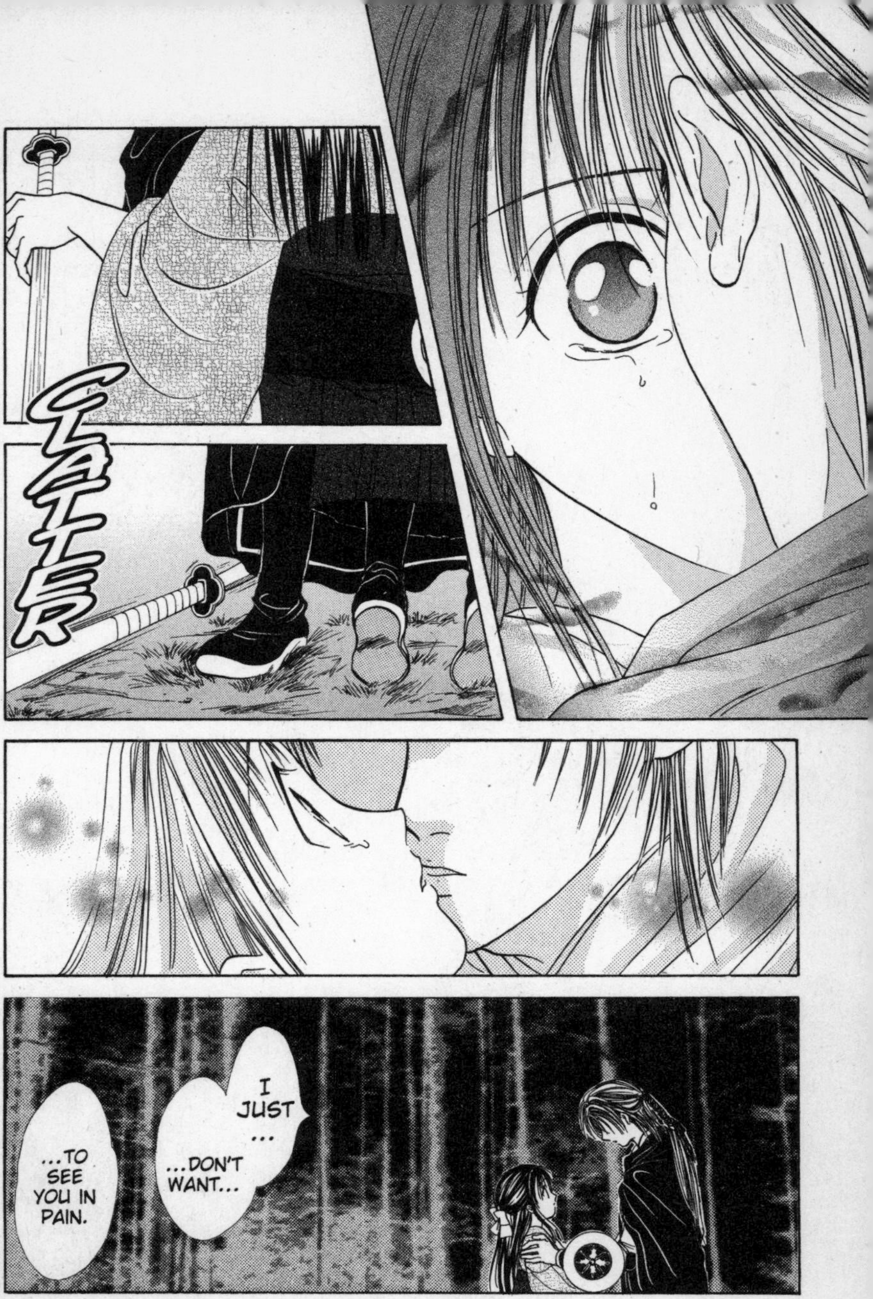
CLATTER
I JUST ...
...DON'T WANT...
...TO SEE YOU IN PAIN.

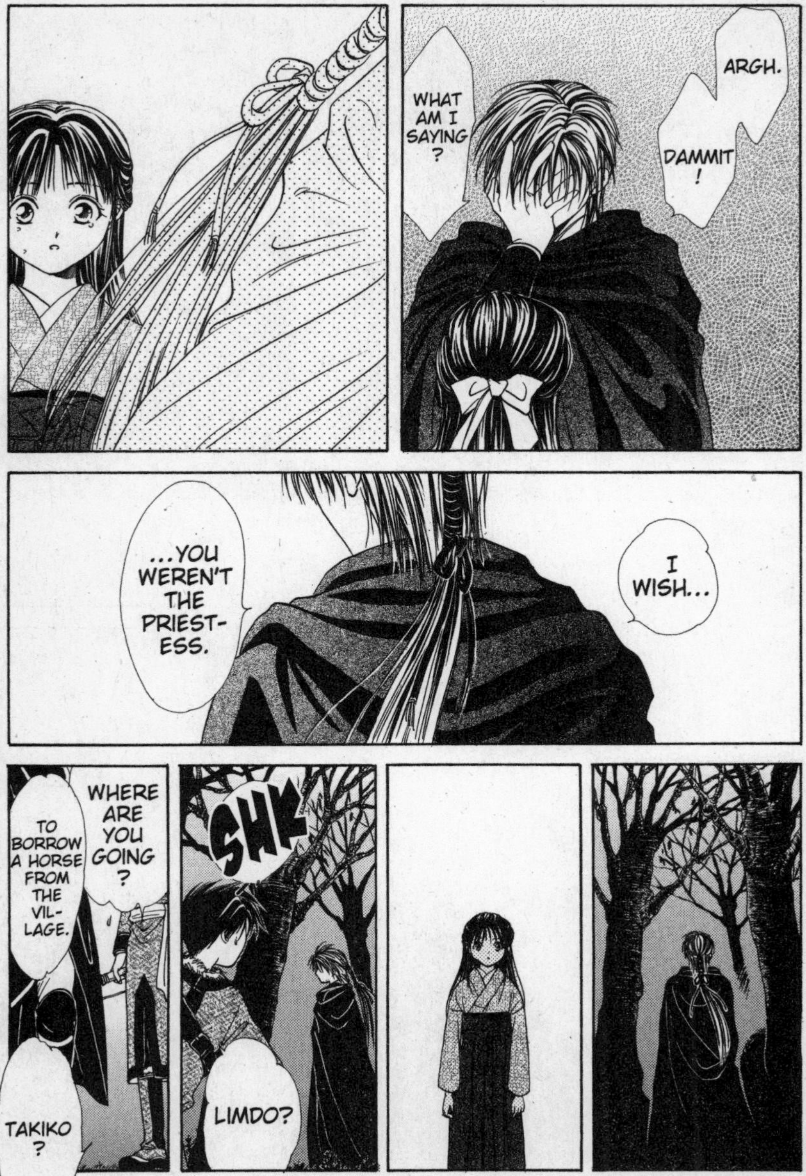
ARGH.
DAMMIT!
WHAT AM I SAYING?
I WISH...
...YOU WEREN'T THE PRIEST-ESS.
SHK
LIMDO?
WHERE ARE YOU GOING?
TO BORROW A HORSE FROM THE VIL-LAGE.
TAKIKO?

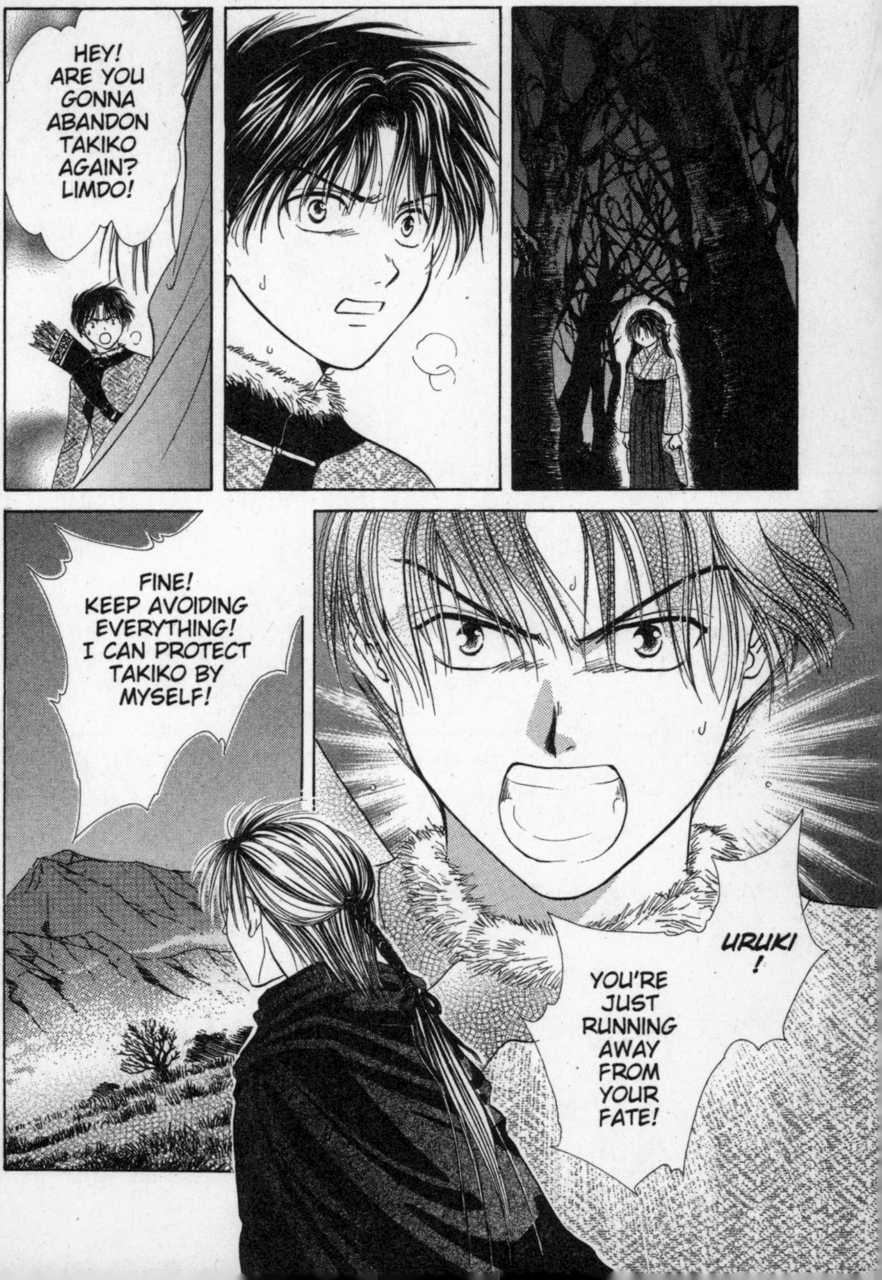
HEY! ARE YOU GONNA ABANDON TAKIKO AGAIN? LIMDO!
URUKI!
YOU'RE JUST RUNNING AWAY FROM YOUR FATE!
FINE! KEEP AVOIDING EVERYTHING! I CAN PROTECT TAKIKO BY MYSELF!

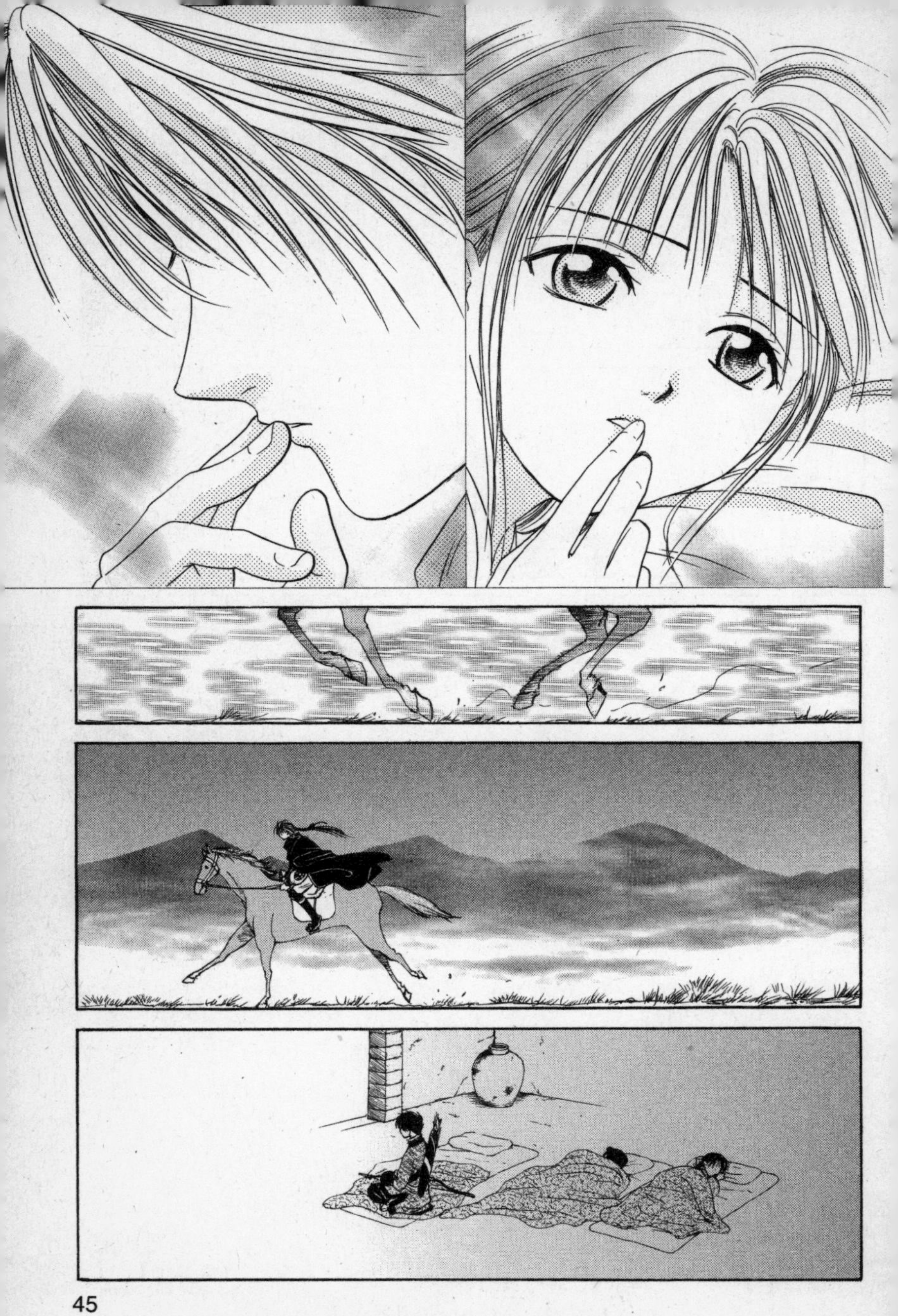

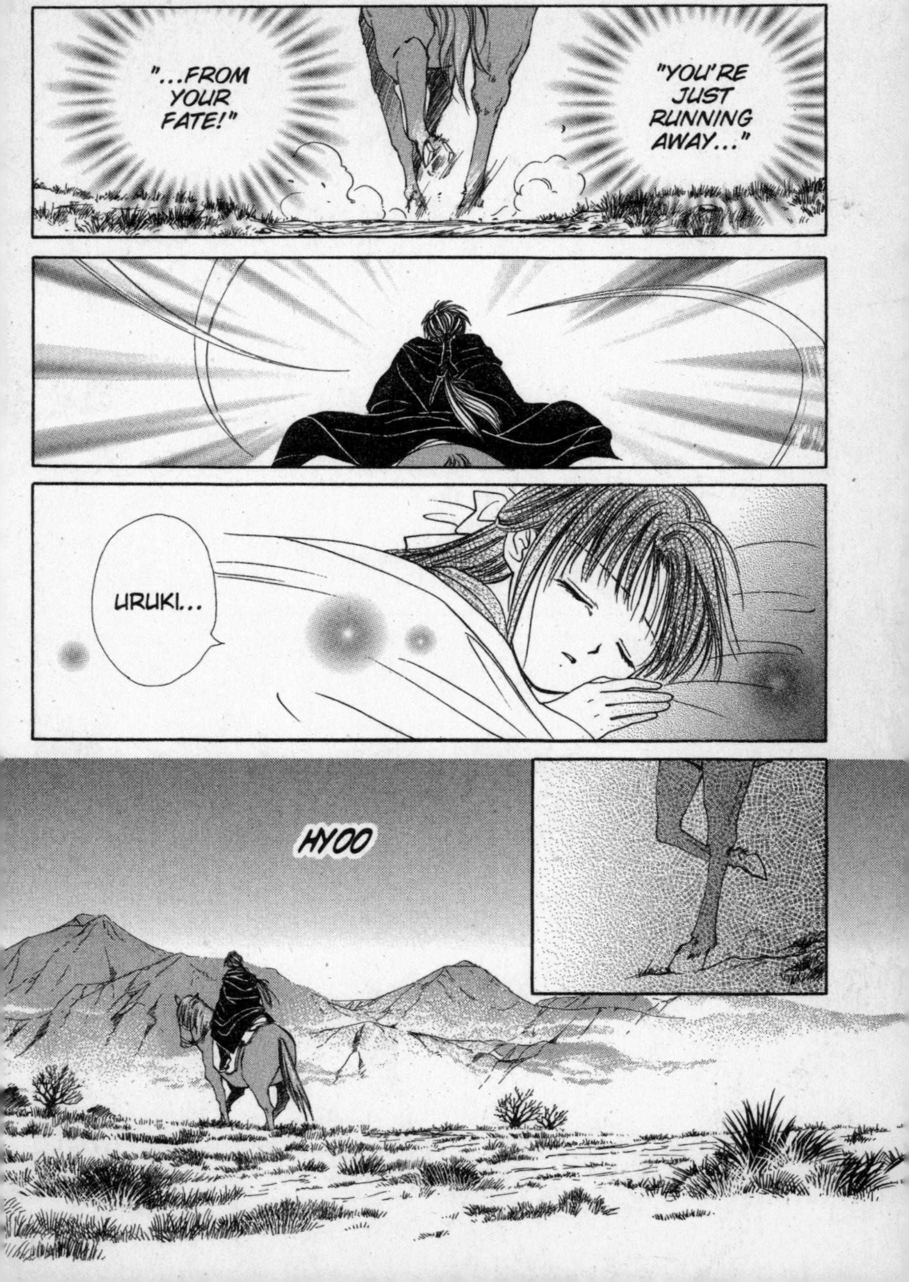
"YOU'RE JUST RUNNING AWAY..."
"...FROM YOUR FATE!"
URUKI...
HYOO

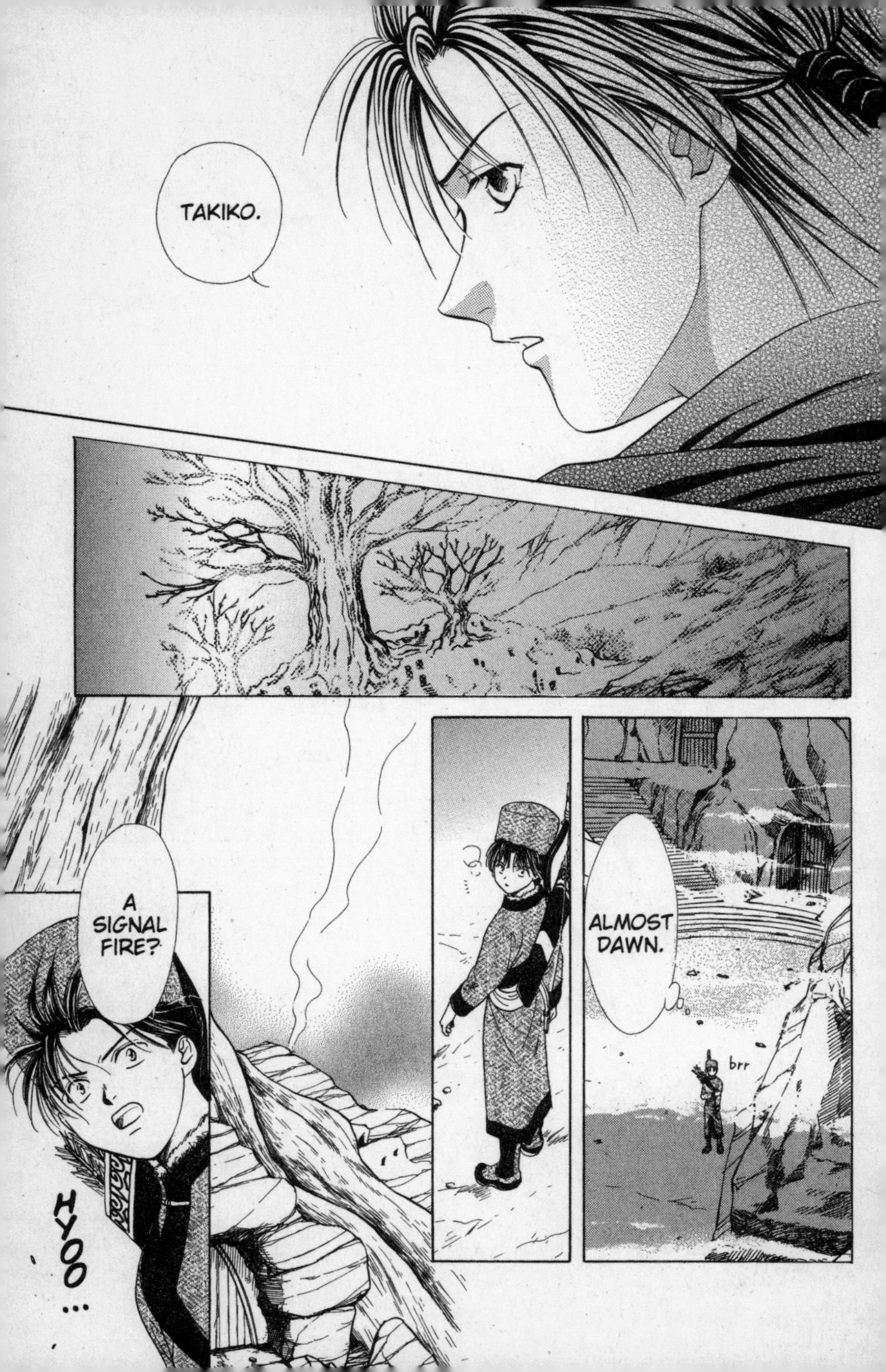
TAKIKO.
ALMOST DAWN.
brr
A SIGNAL FIRE?
HYOO...

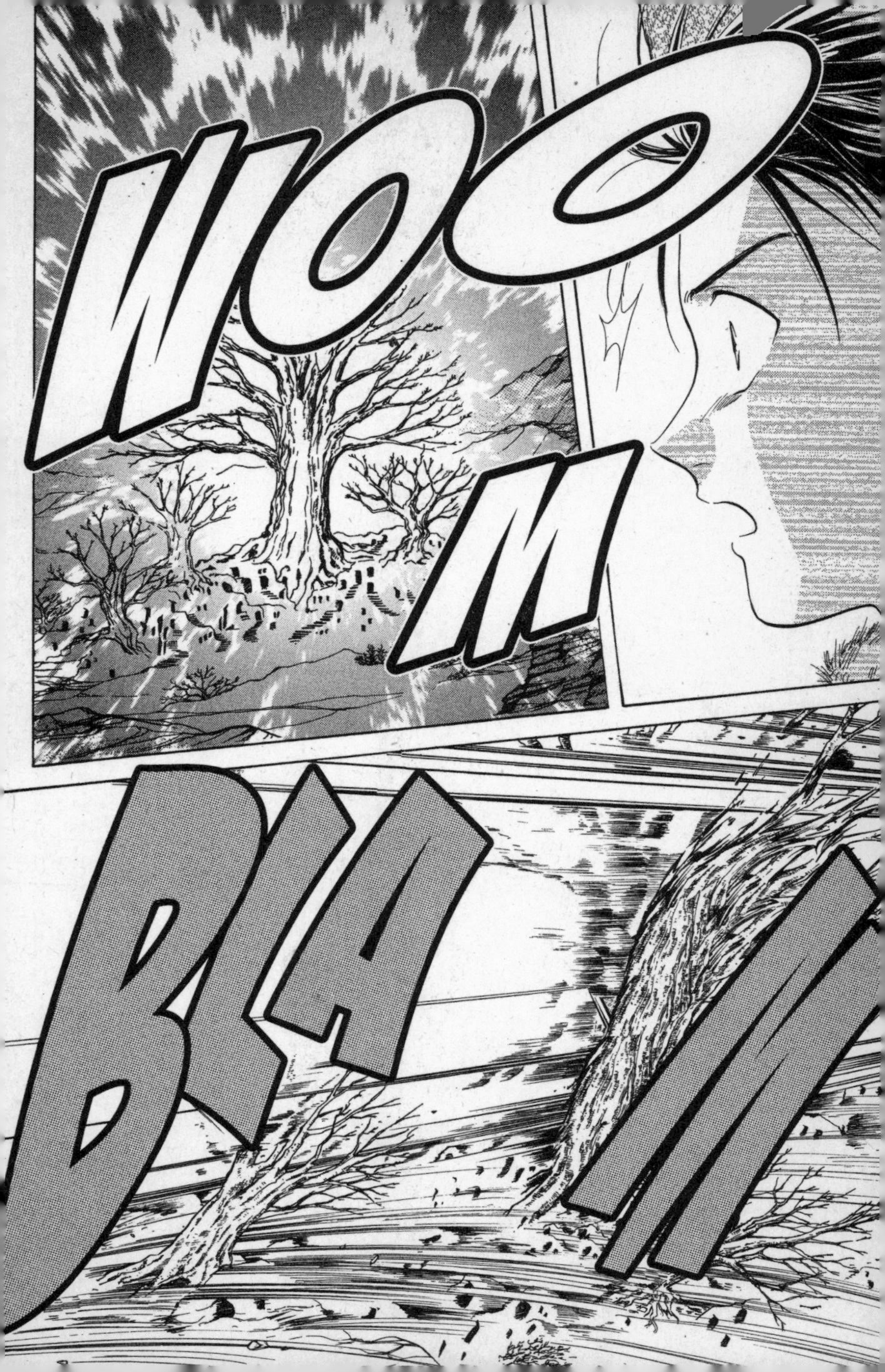
WOOM
BLAM

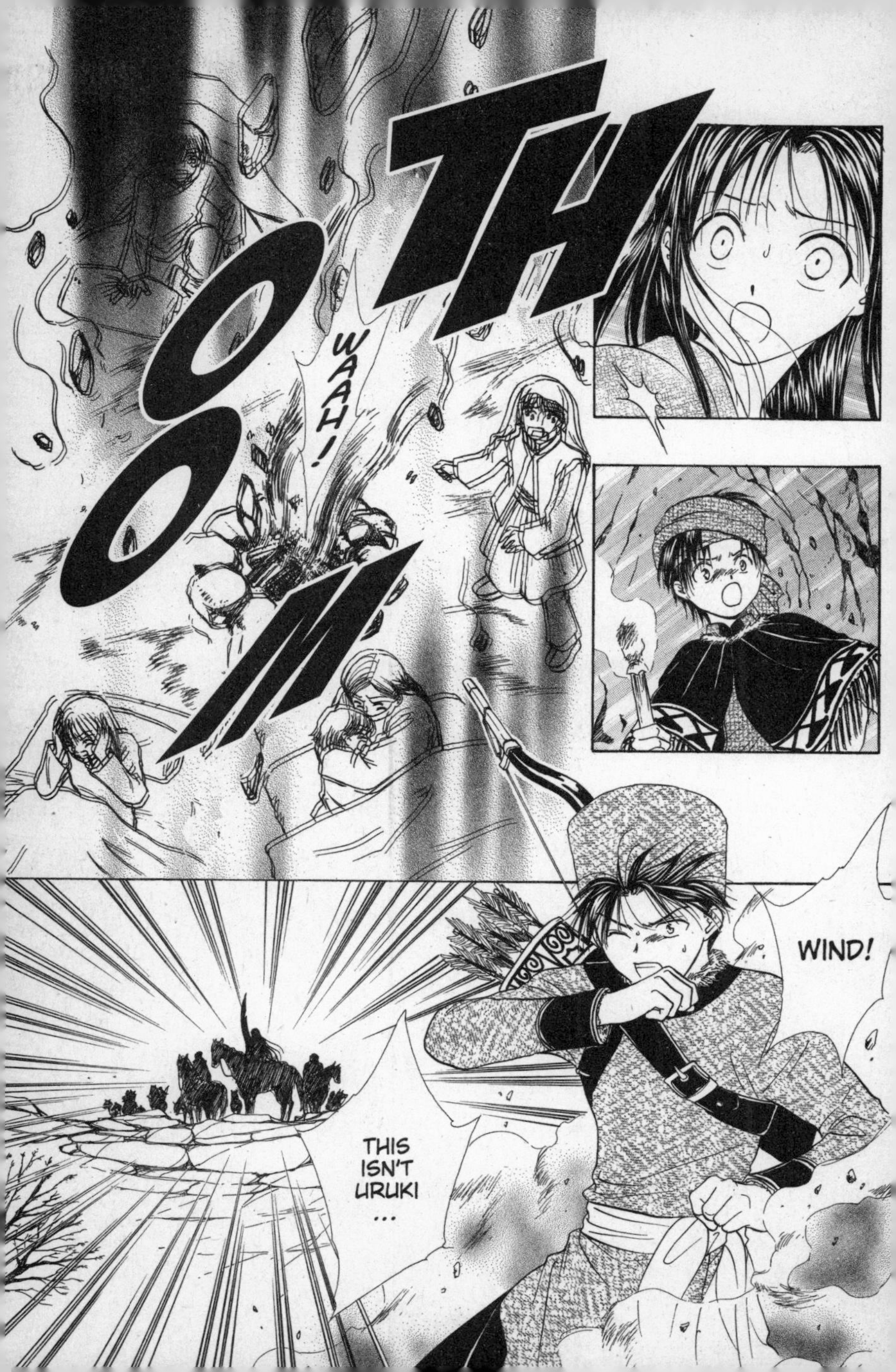
THOOM
WAAH!
WIND!
THIS ISN'T URUKI ...

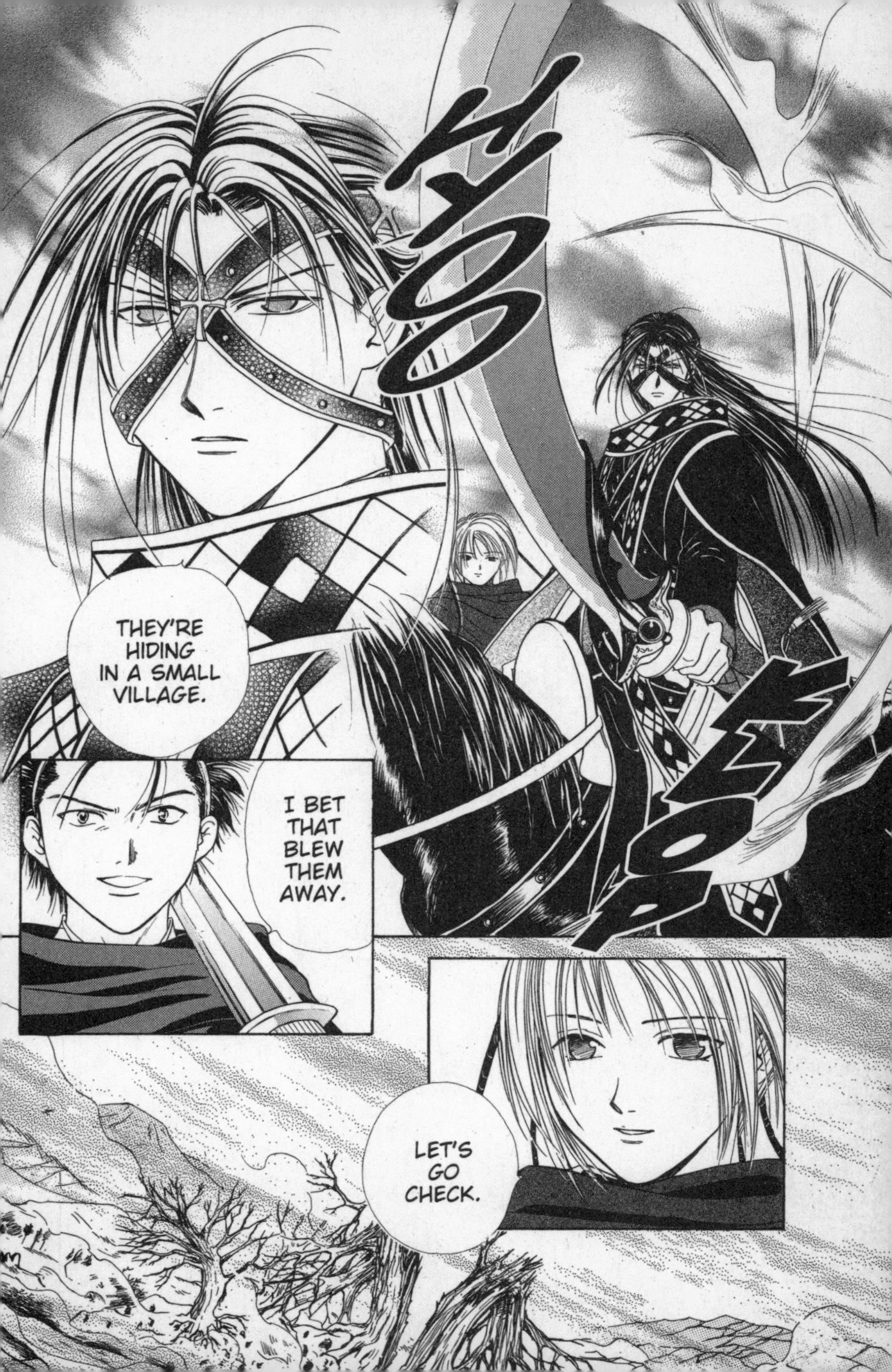
THEY'RE HIDING IN A SMALL VILLAGE.
I BET THAT BLEW THEM AWAY.
LET'S GO CHECK.

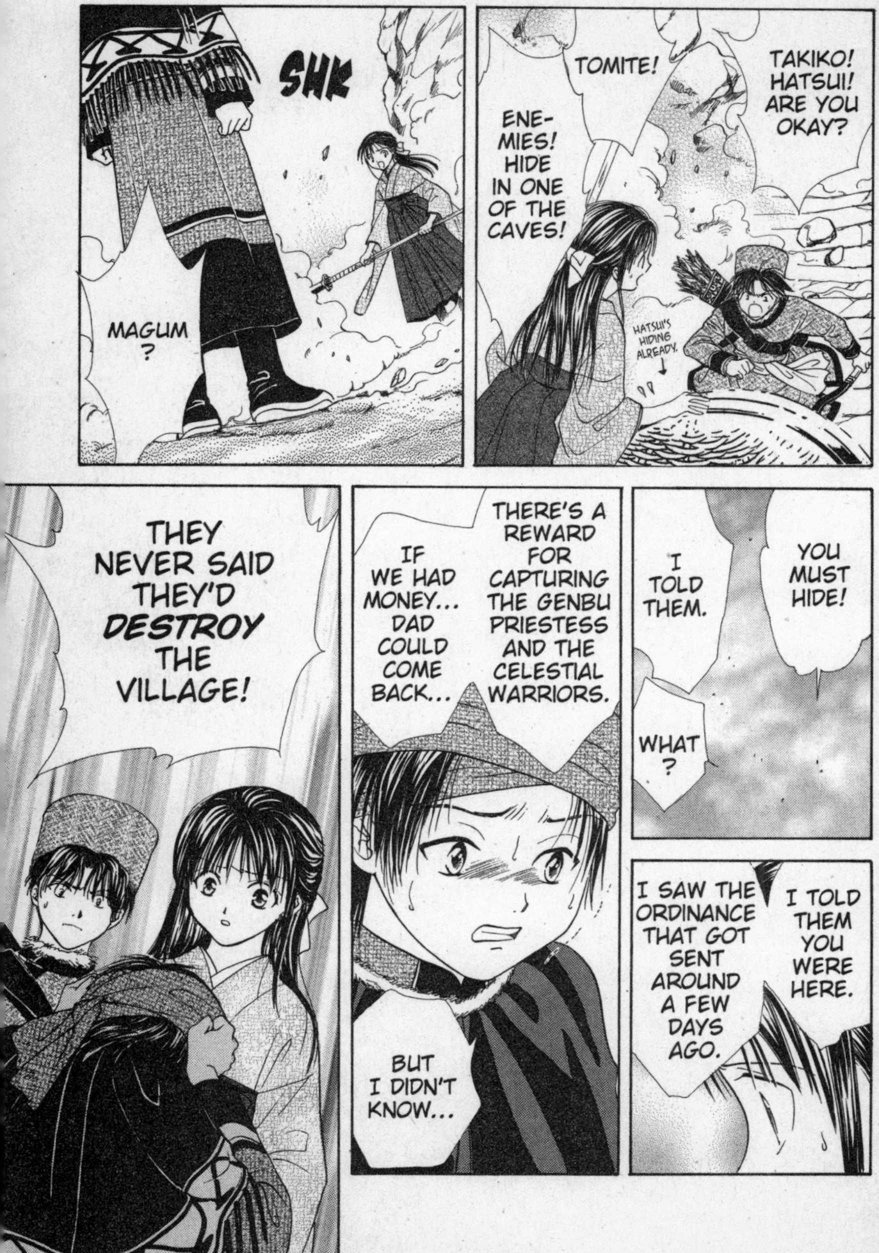
TAKIKO! HATSUI! ARE YOU OKAY?
TOMITE!
ENE-MIES! HIDE IN ONE OF THE CAVES!
HATSUI'S HIDING ALREADY.
SHK
MAGUM?
YOU MUST HIDE!
I TOLD THEM.
WHAT?
I TOLD THEM YOU WERE HERE.
I SAW THE ORDINANCE THAT GOT SENT AROUND A FEW DAYS AGO.
THERE'S A REWARD FOR CAPTURING THE GENBU PRIESTESS AND THE CELESTIAL WARRIORS.
IF WE HAD MONEY... DAD COULD COME BACK...
BUT I DIDN'T KNOW...
THEY NEVER SAID THEY'D DESTROY THE VILLAGE!

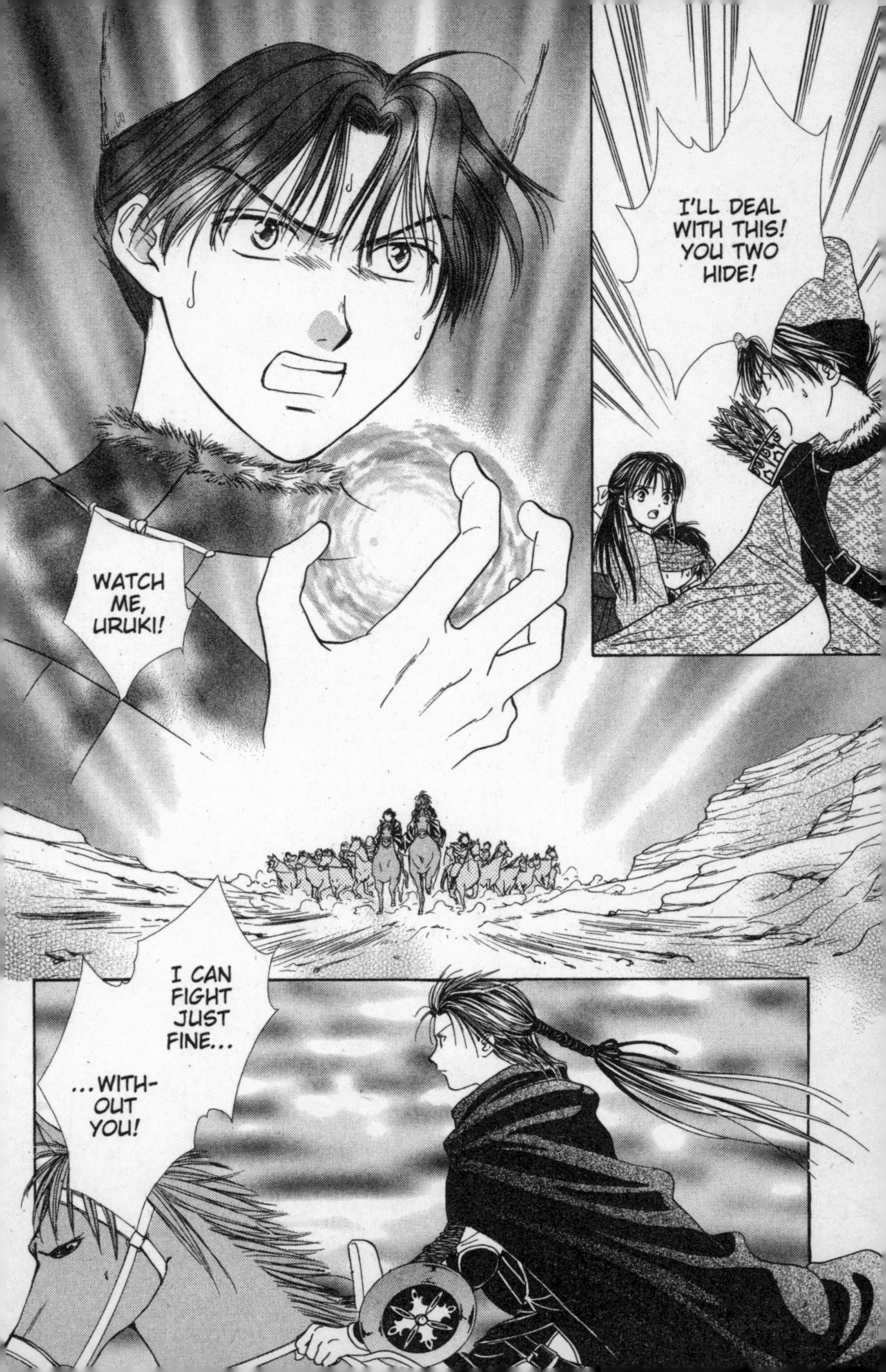
I'LL DEAL WITH THIS! YOU TWO HIDE!
WATCH ME, URUKI!
I CAN FIGHT JUST FINE...
...WITH-OUT YOU!

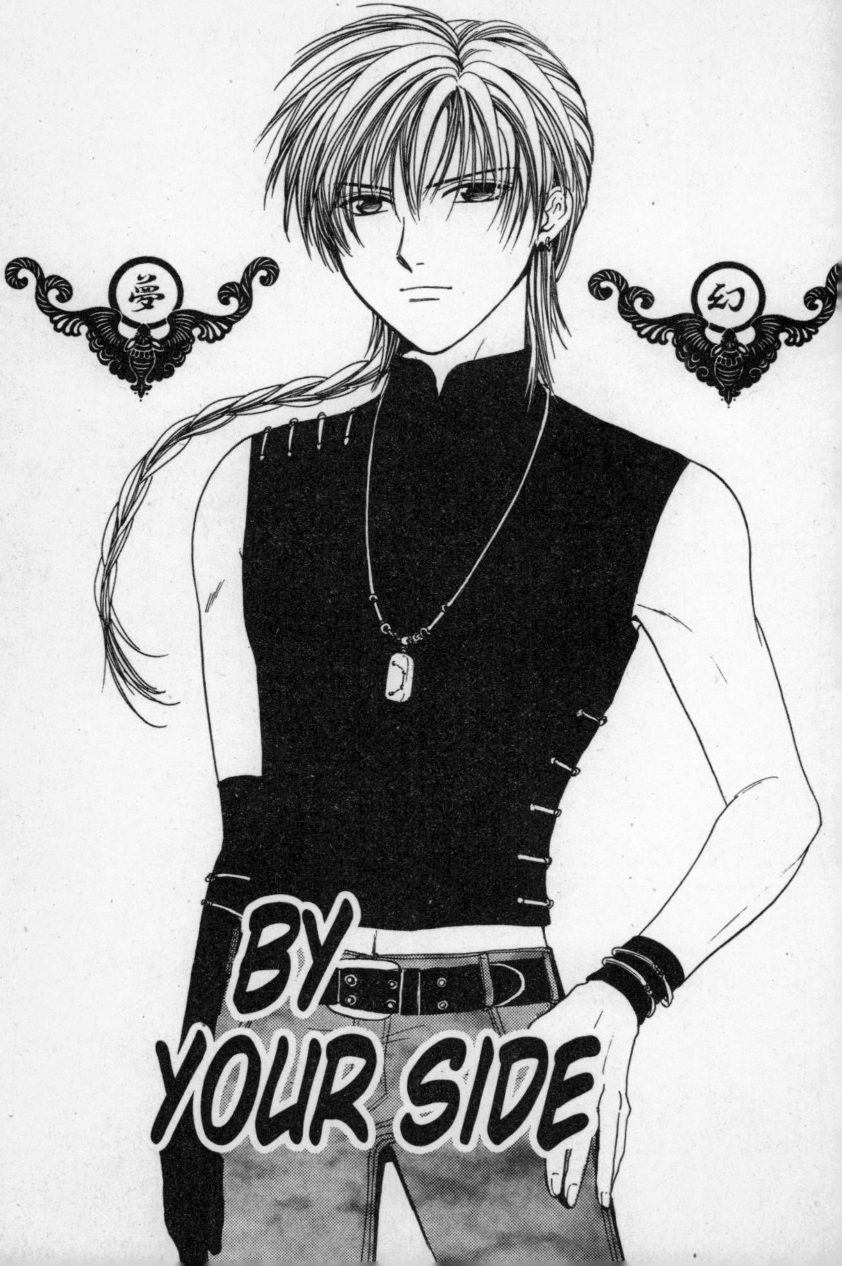
夢
幻
BY
YOUR SIDE

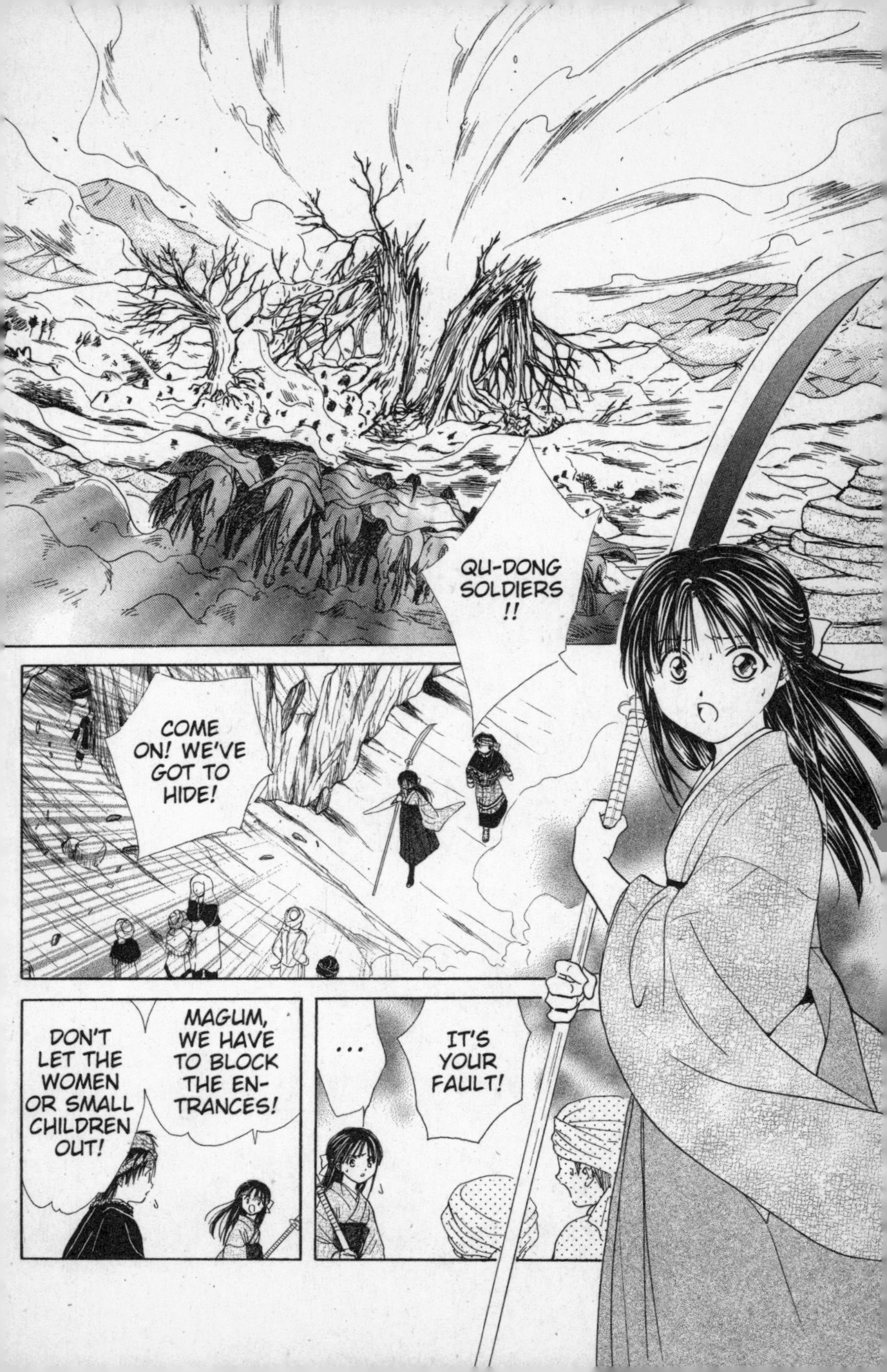
QU-DONG SOLDIERS !!
COME ON! WE'VE GOT TO HIDE!
IT'S YOUR FAULT!
...
MAGUM, WE HAVE TO BLOCK THE EN-TRANCES!
DON'T LET THE WOMEN OR SMALL CHILDREN OUT!

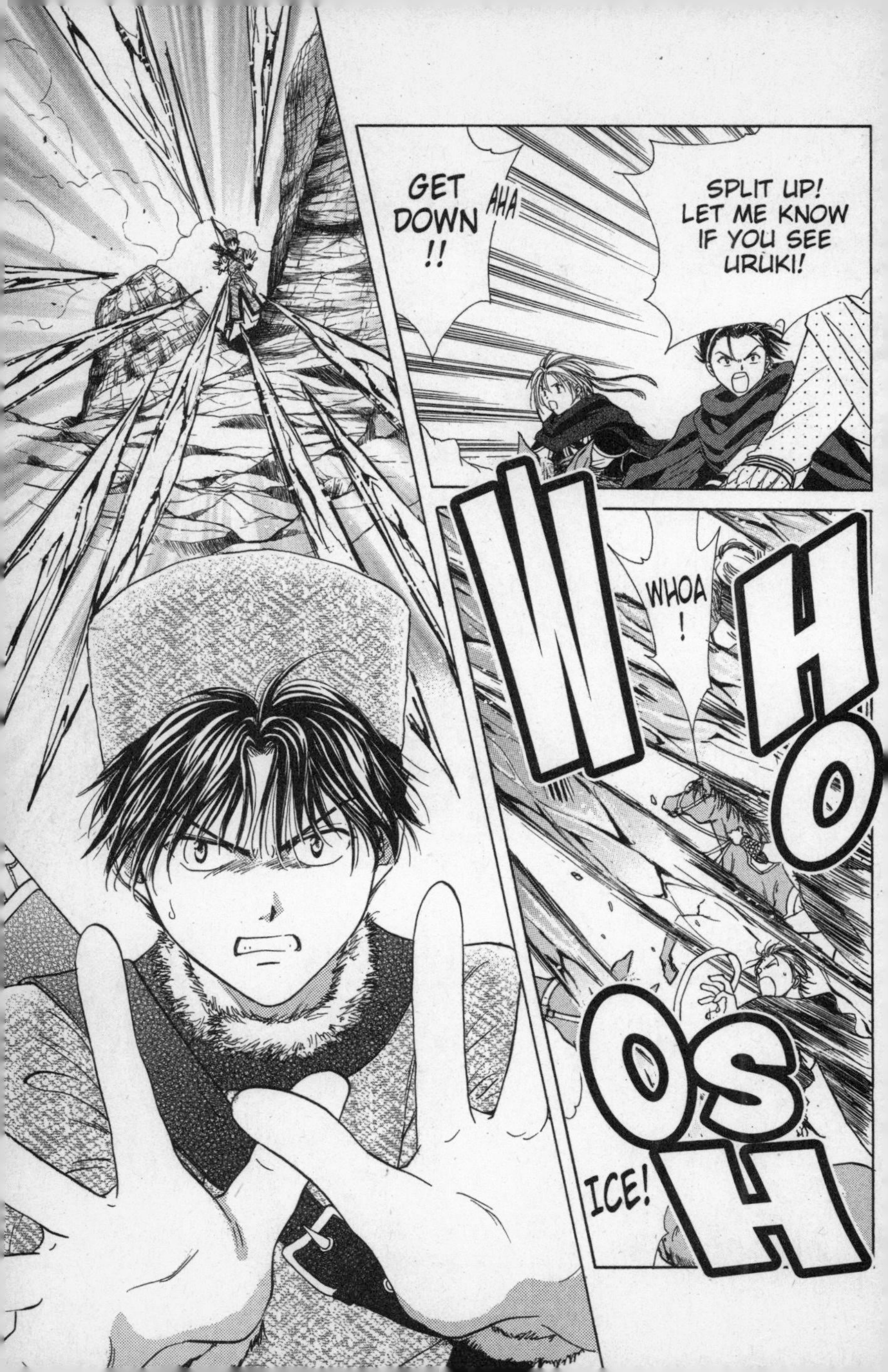
SPLIT UP! LET ME KNOW IF YOU SEE URUKI!
GET DOWN !!
AHA
WHOA !
WHOOSH
ICE!

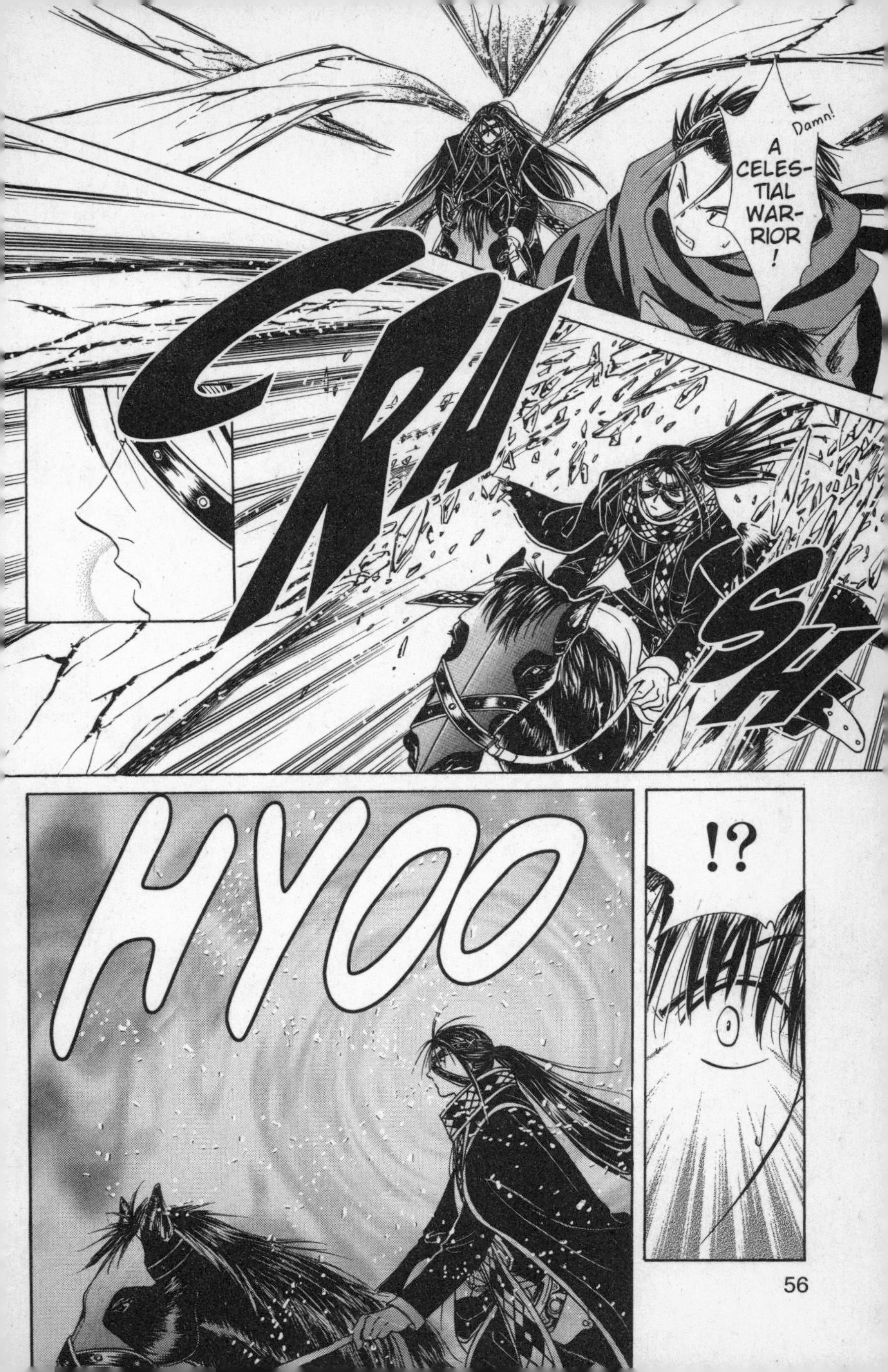
Damn!
A CELES-TIAL WAR-RIOR!
CRA
SH
!?
HYOO

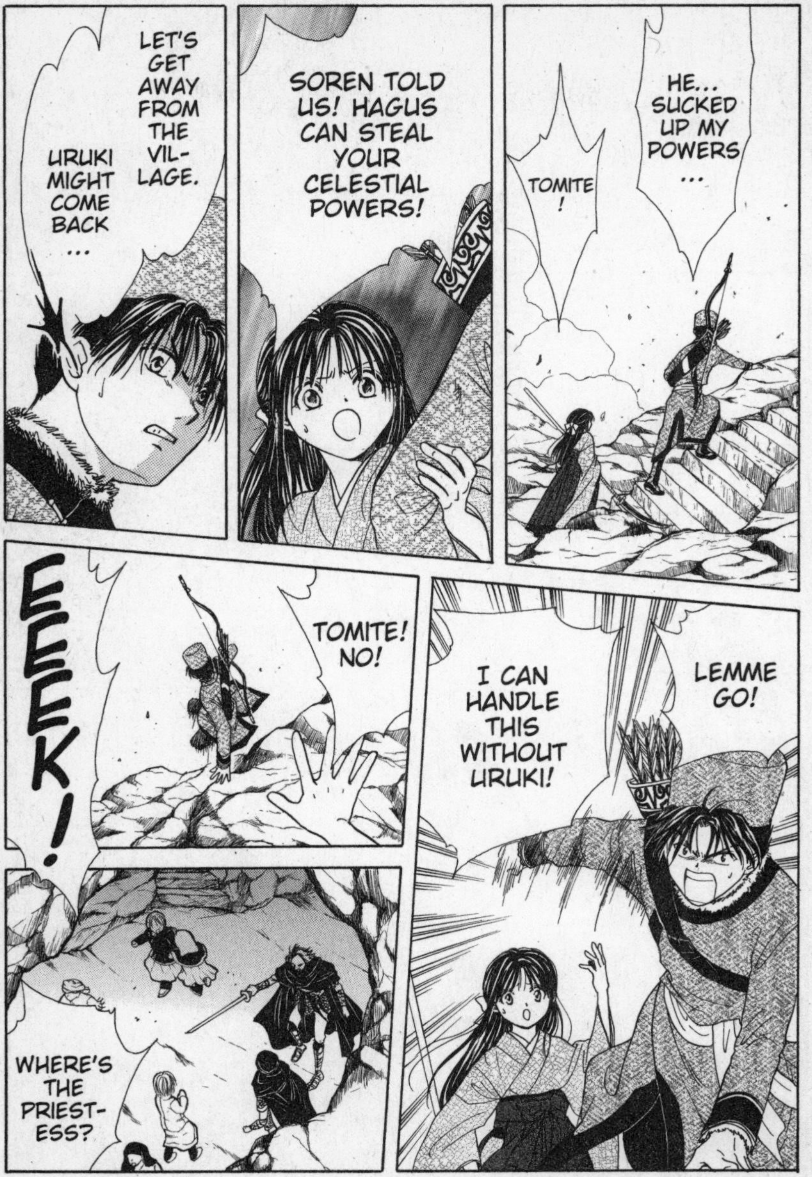
HE... SUCKED UP MY POWERS...
TOMITE!
SOREN TOLD US! HAGUS CAN STEAL YOUR CELESTIAL POWERS!
LET'S GET AWAY FROM THE VIL- LAGE.
URUKI MIGHT COME BACK...
LEMME GO!
I CAN HANDLE THIS WITHOUT URUKI!
TOMITE! NO!
EEEK!
WHERE'S THE PRIEST- ESS?

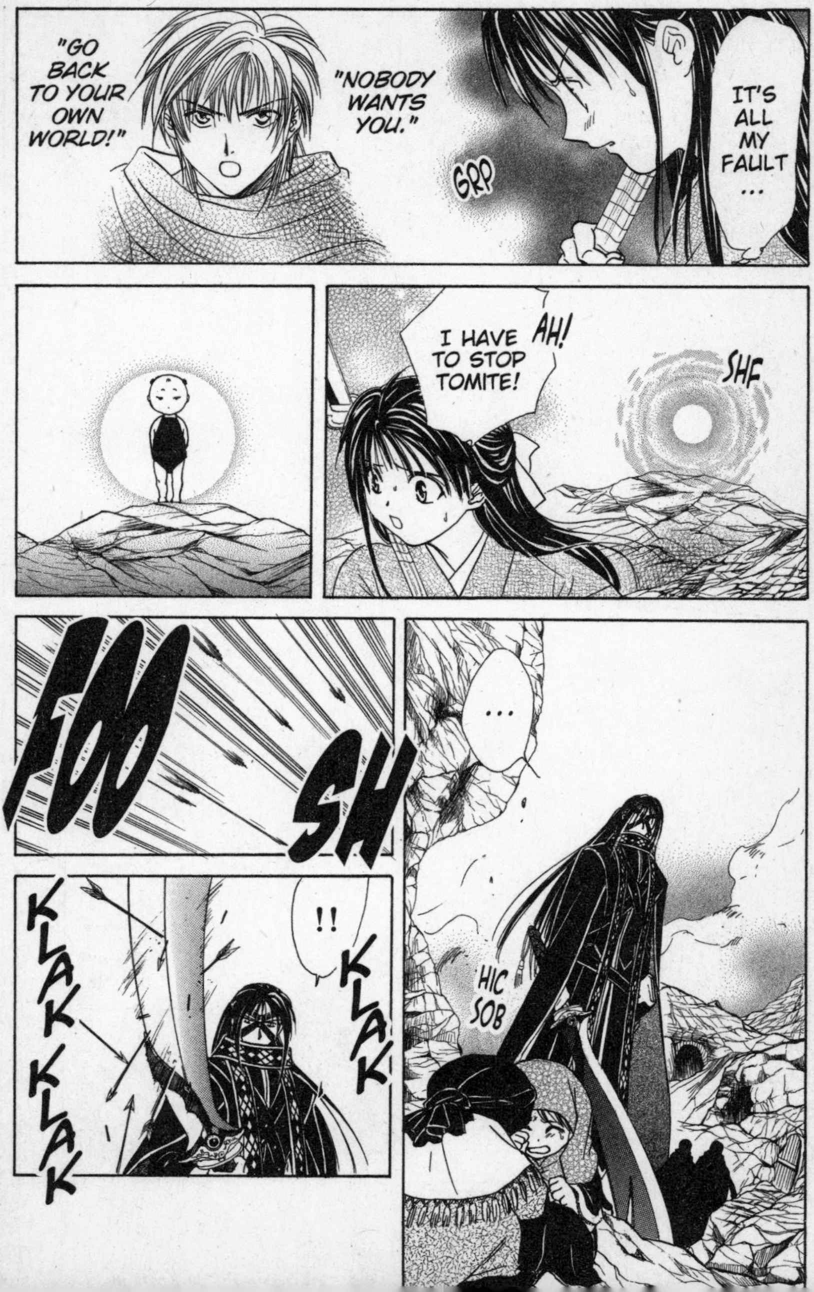
IT'S ALL MY FAULT...
GRP
"NOBODY WANTS YOU."
"GO BACK TO YOUR OWN WORLD!"
AH!
I HAVE TO STOP TOMITE!
SHF
...
HIC SOB
FOOSH
!!
KLAK
KLAK KLAK KLAK

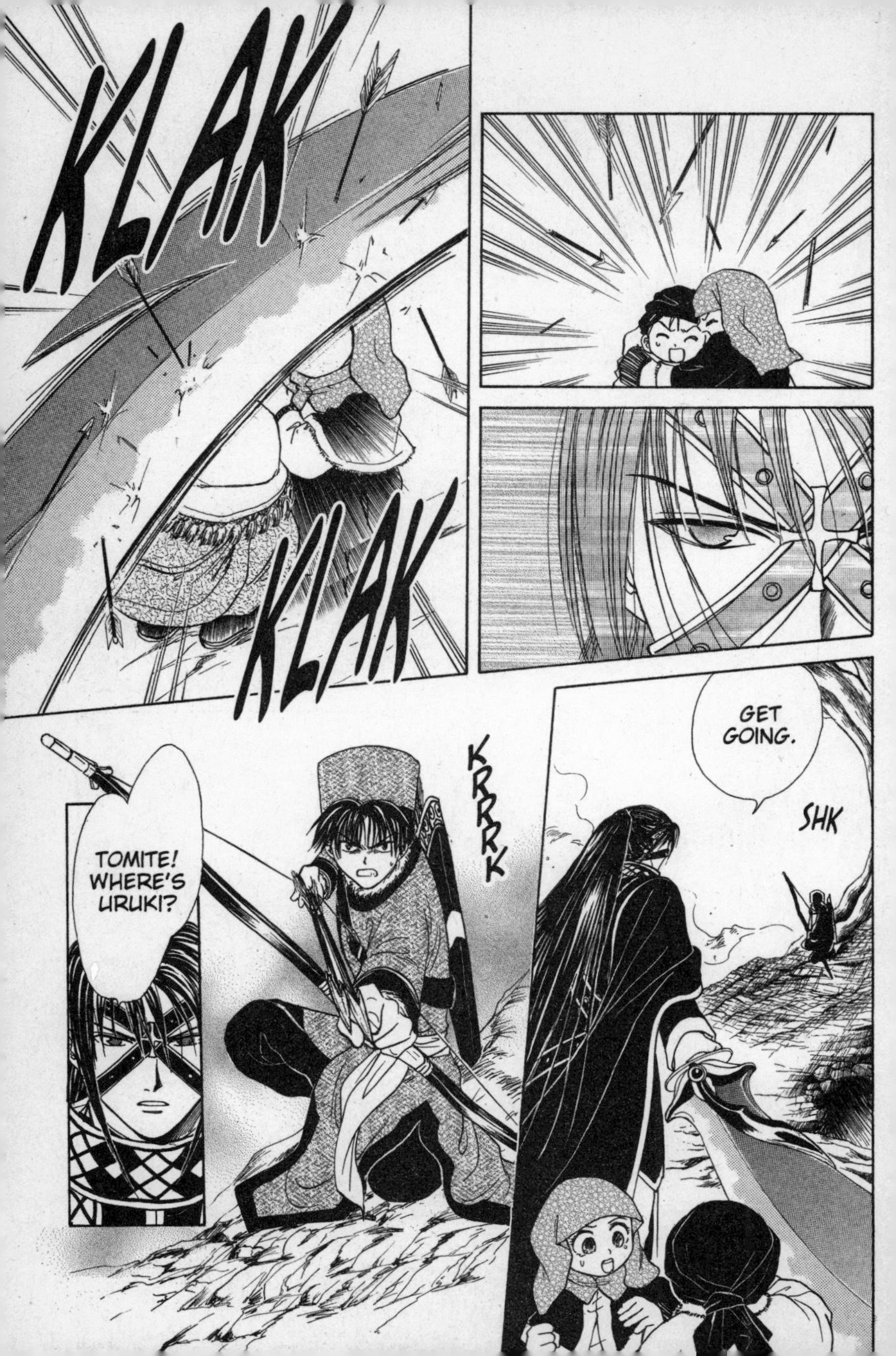
KLAK
KLAK
GET GOING.
SHK
KRRRRK
TOMITE! WHERE'S URUKI?

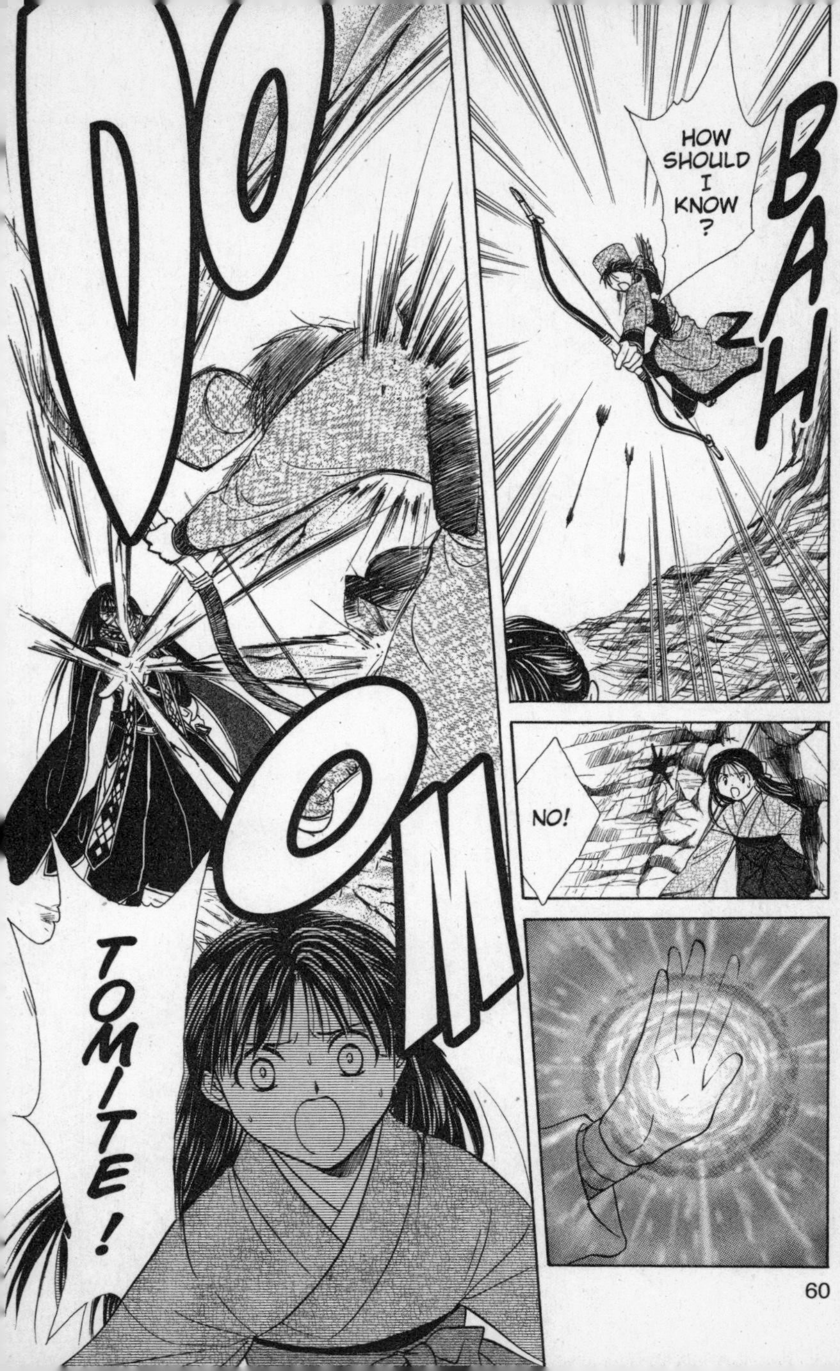
HOW SHOULD I KNOW?
BAH
NO!
DOOOM
TOMITE!

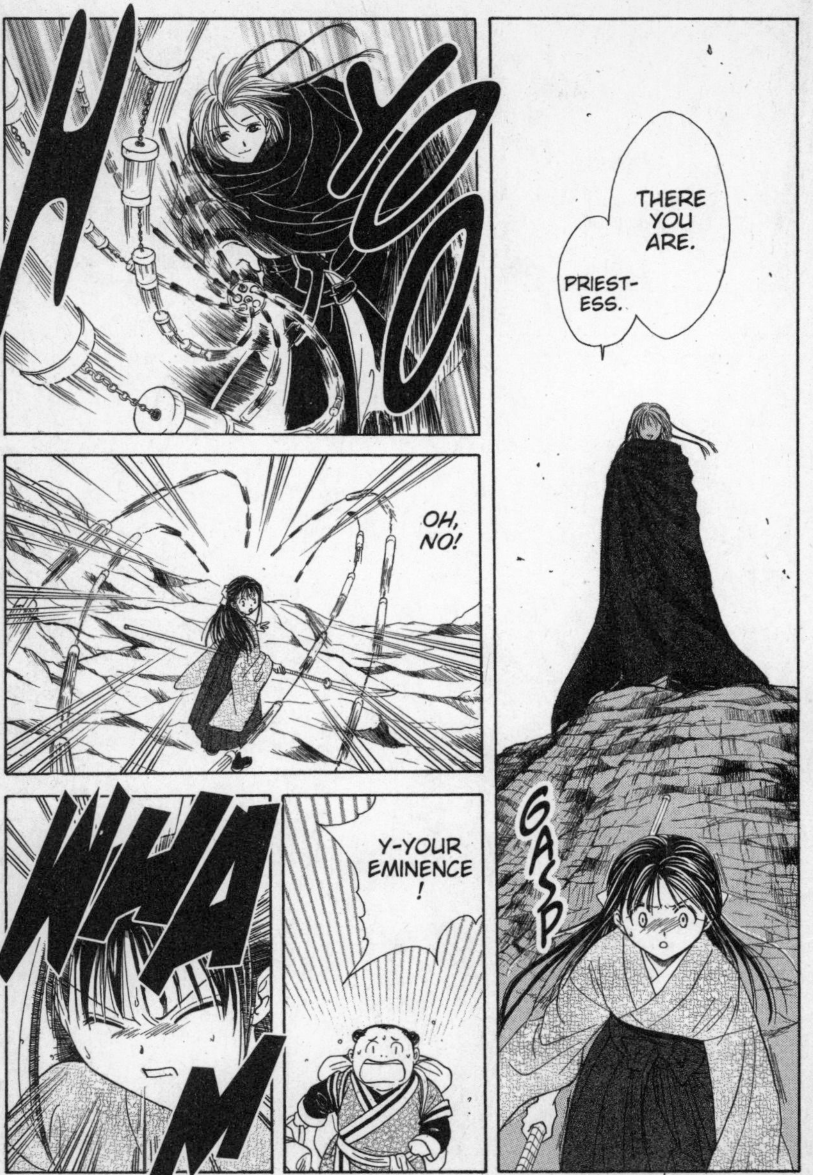
THERE YOU ARE. PRIEST-ESS.
GASP
HYOO
OH, NO!
Y-YOUR EMINENCE!
WHAM

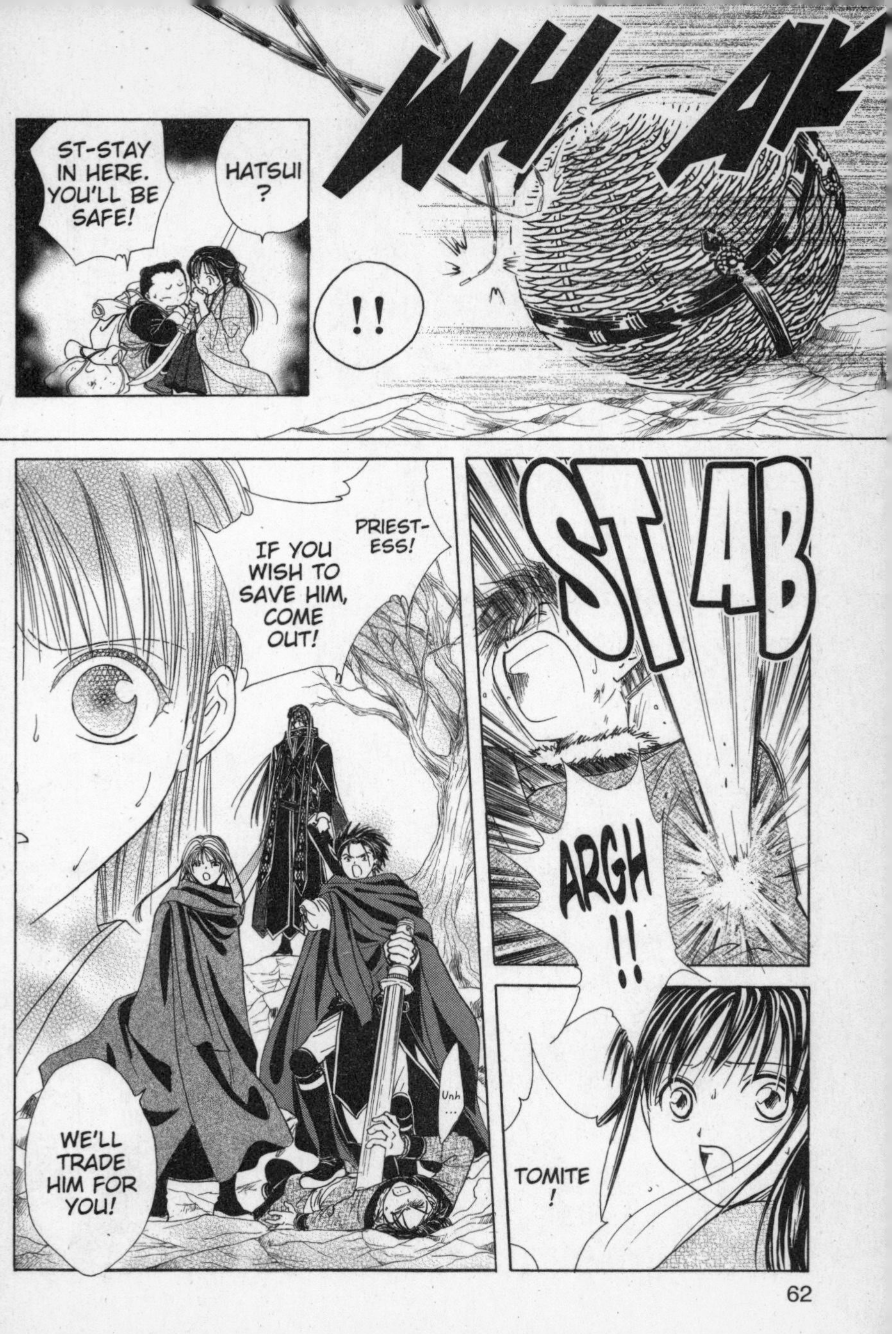
WHAK
!!
HATSUI ?
ST-STAY IN HERE. YOU'LL BE SAFE!
STAB
ARGH !!
TOMITE !
PRIEST-ESS!
IF YOU WISH TO SAVE HIM, COME OUT!
Unh ...
WE'LL TRADE HIM FOR YOU!

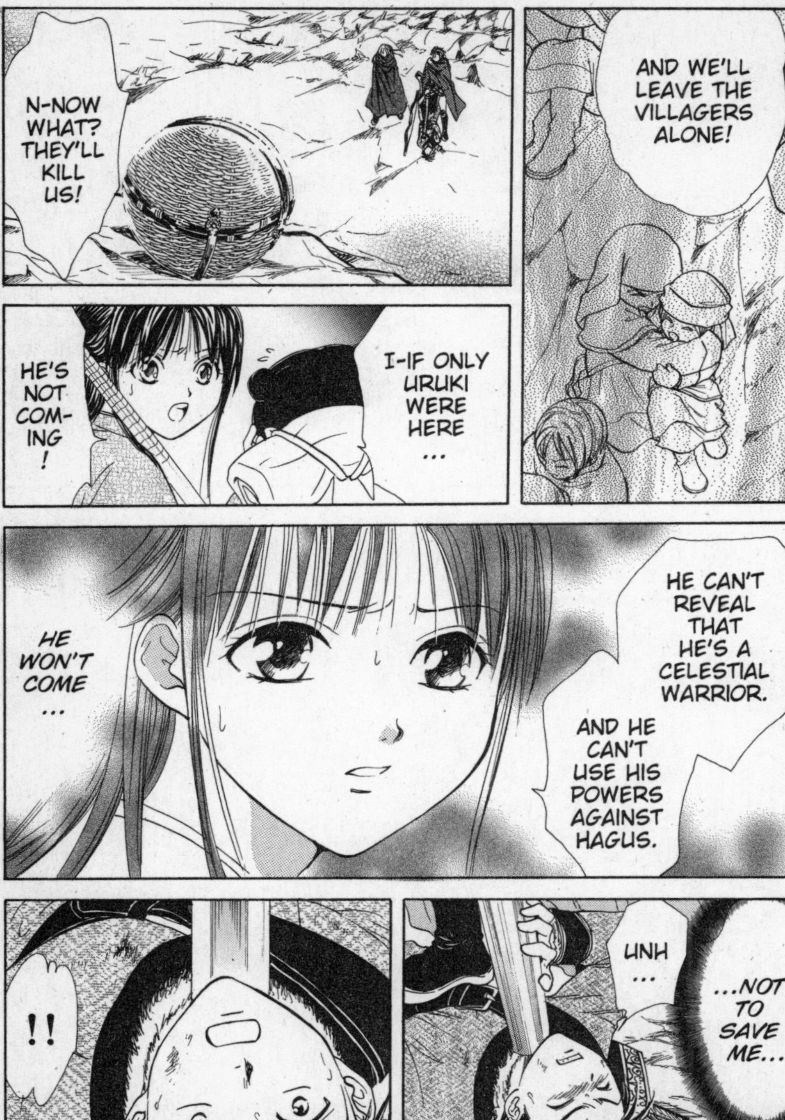
AND WE'LL LEAVE THE VILLAGERS ALONE!
N-NOW WHAT? THEY'LL KILL US!
I-IF ONLY URUKI WERE HERE...
HE'S NOT COMING!
HE CAN'T REVEAL THAT HE'S A CELESTIAL WARRIOR.
AND HE CAN'T USE HIS POWERS AGAINST HAGUS.
HE WON'T COME...
...NOT TO SAVE ME...
UNH...
!!

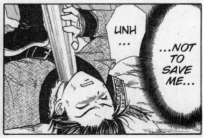

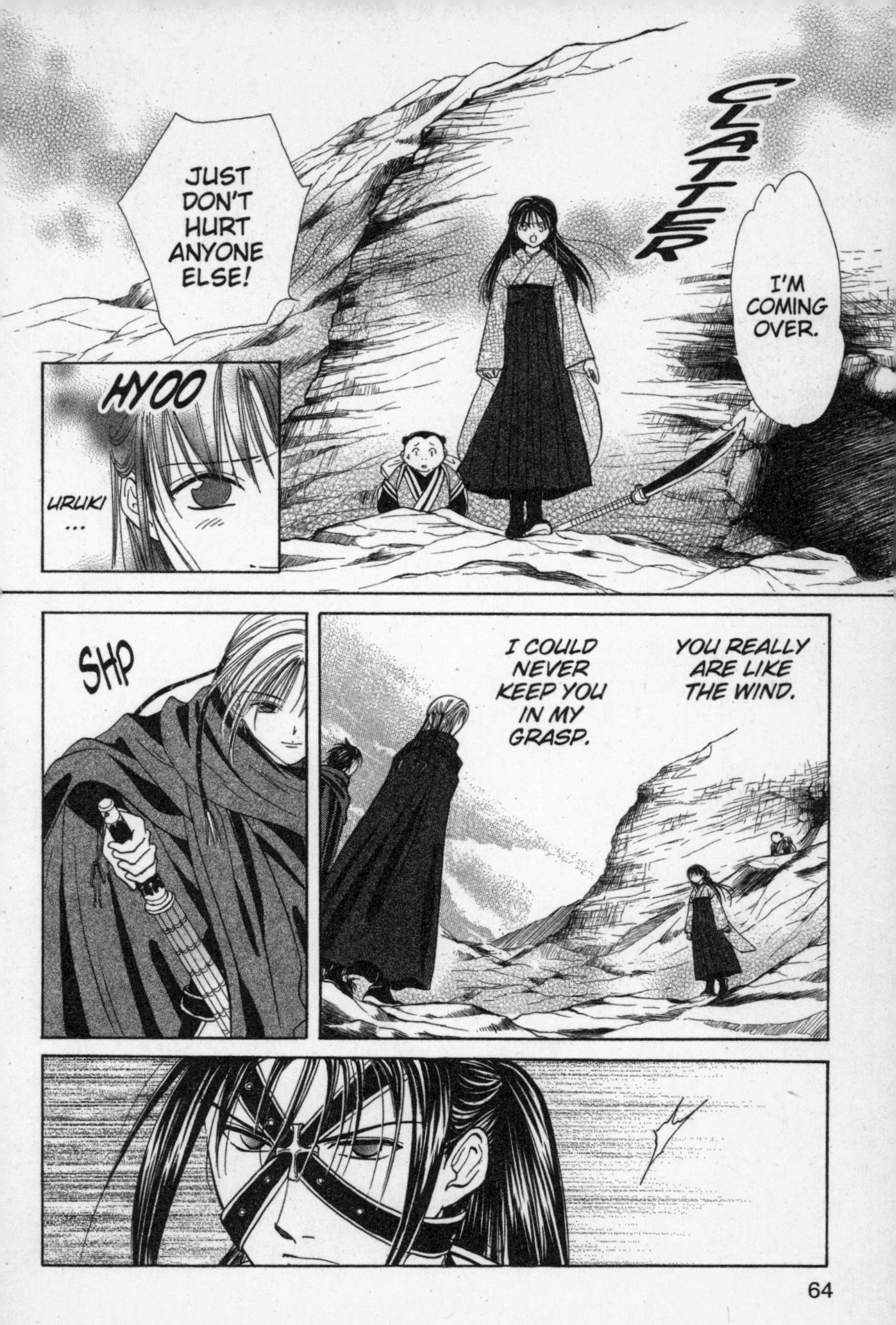
CLATTER
I'M COMING OVER.
JUST DON'T HURT ANYONE ELSE!
HYOO
URUKI ...
YOU REALLY ARE LIKE THE WIND.
I COULD NEVER KEEP YOU IN MY GRASP.
SHP

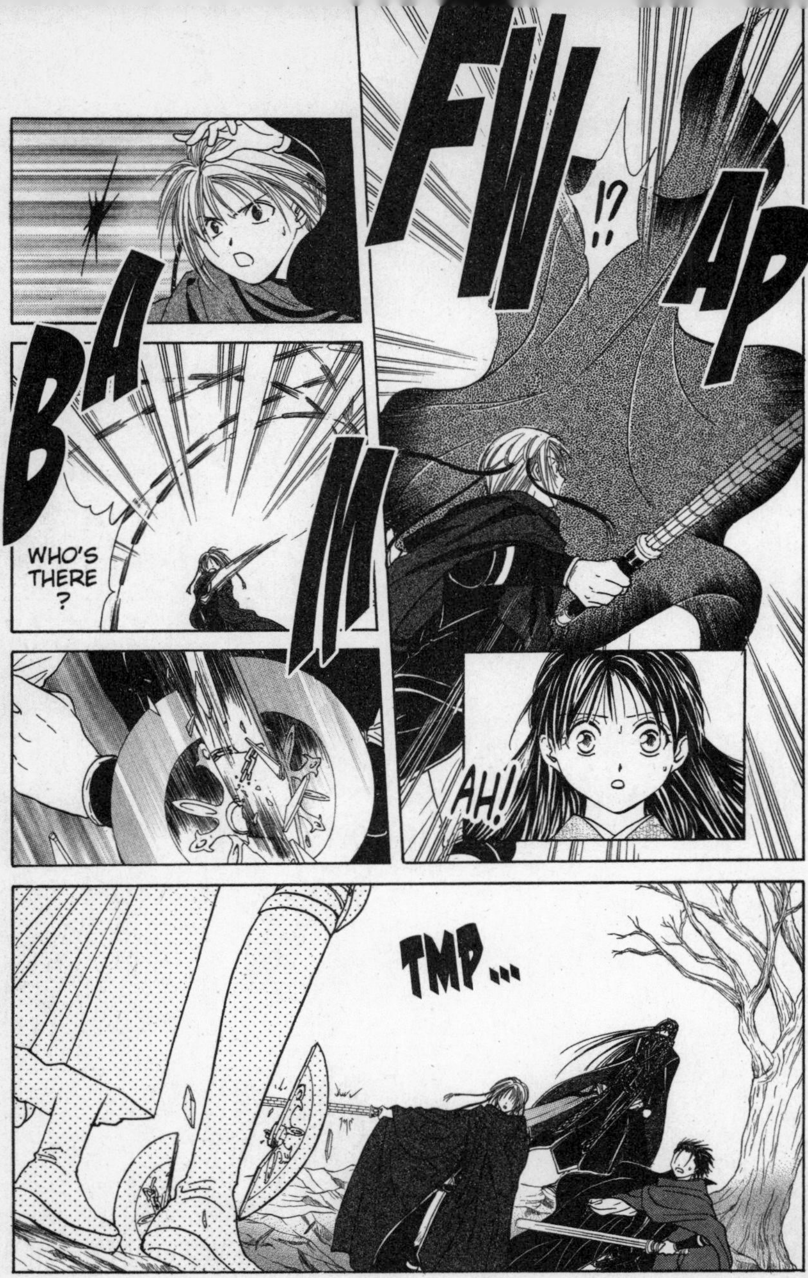
FW-AP
!?!!
BA-M
WHO'S THERE?
AH!
TMP...

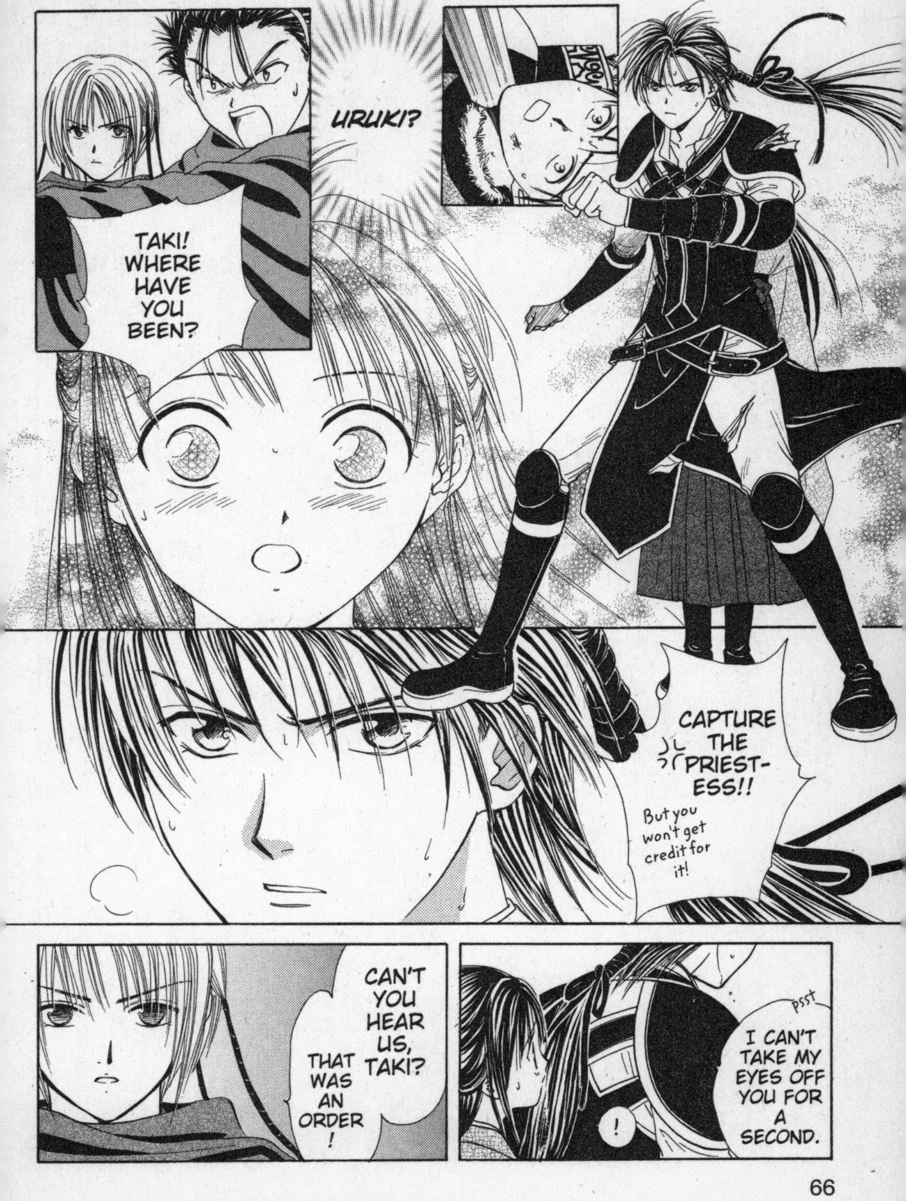
URUKI?
TAKI! WHERE HAVE YOU BEEN?
CAPTURE THE PRIESTESS!!
But you won't get credit for it!
psst
I CAN'T TAKE MY EYES OFF YOU FOR A SECOND.
!
CAN'T YOU HEAR US, TAKI?
THAT WAS AN ORDER!

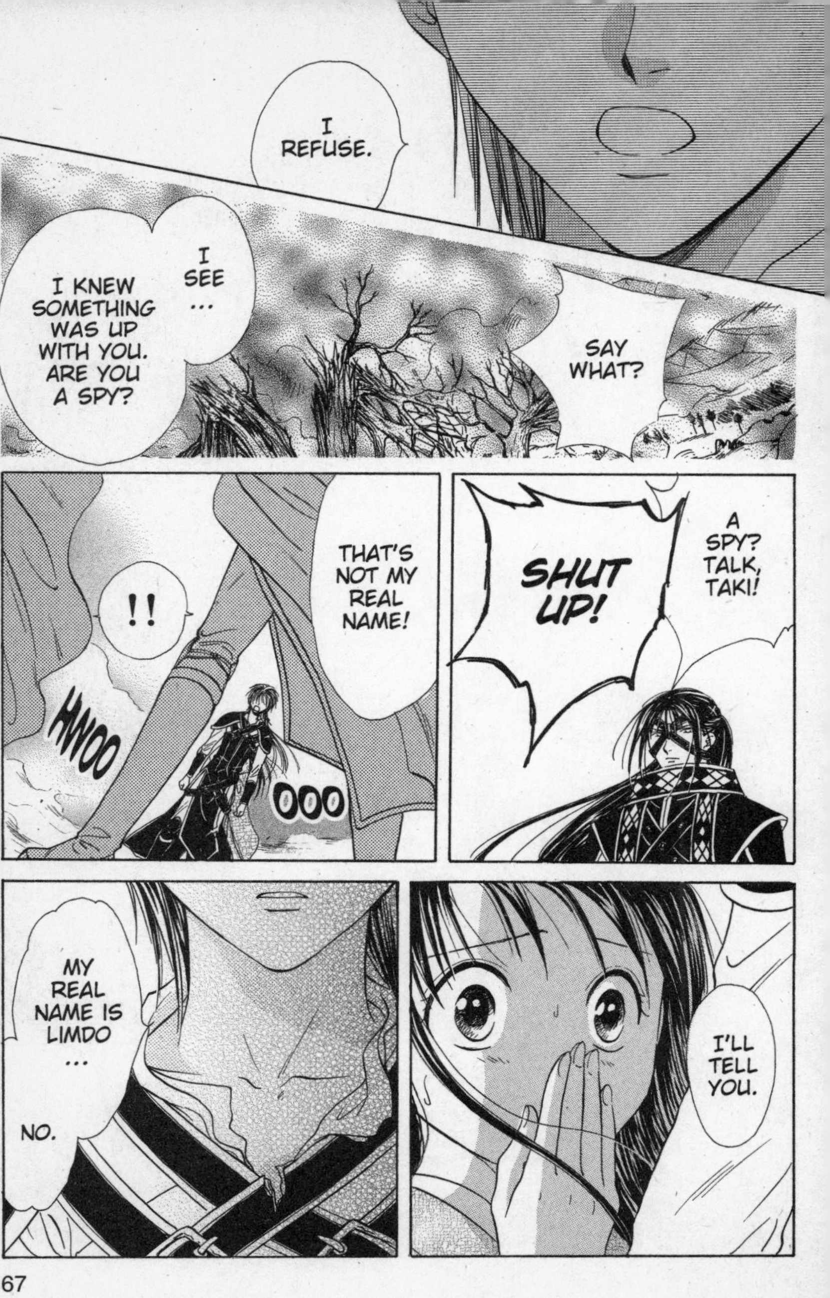
I REFUSE.
SAY WHAT?
I SEE ...
I KNEW SOMETHING WAS UP WITH YOU. ARE YOU A SPY?
A SPY? TALK, TAKI!
SHUT UP!
THAT'S NOT MY REAL NAME!
!!
HWOO
I'LL TELL YOU.
MY REAL NAME IS LIMDO ...
NO.

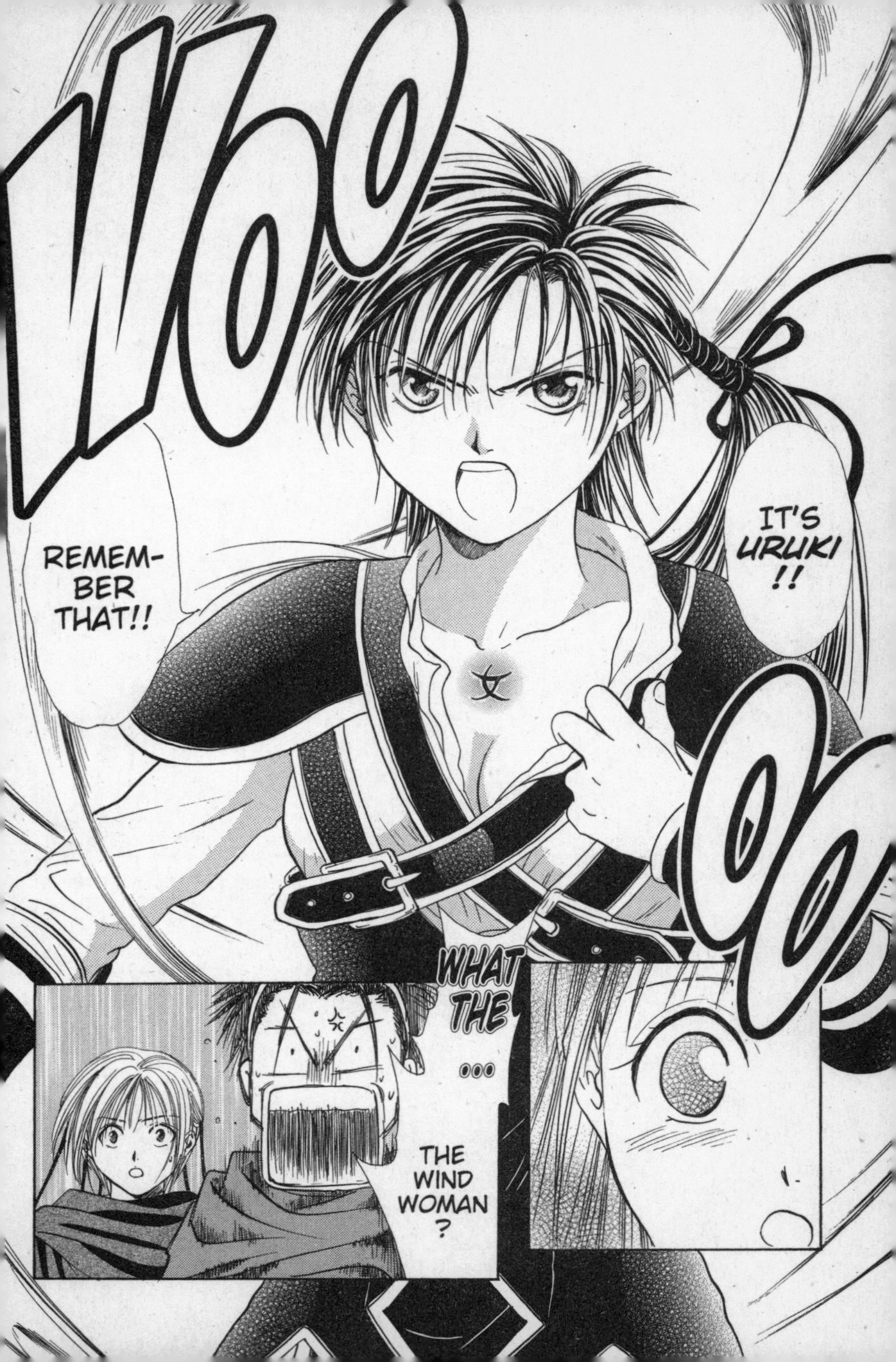
IT'S URUKI!!
REMEMBER THAT!!
WHAT THE ...
THE WIND WOMAN?

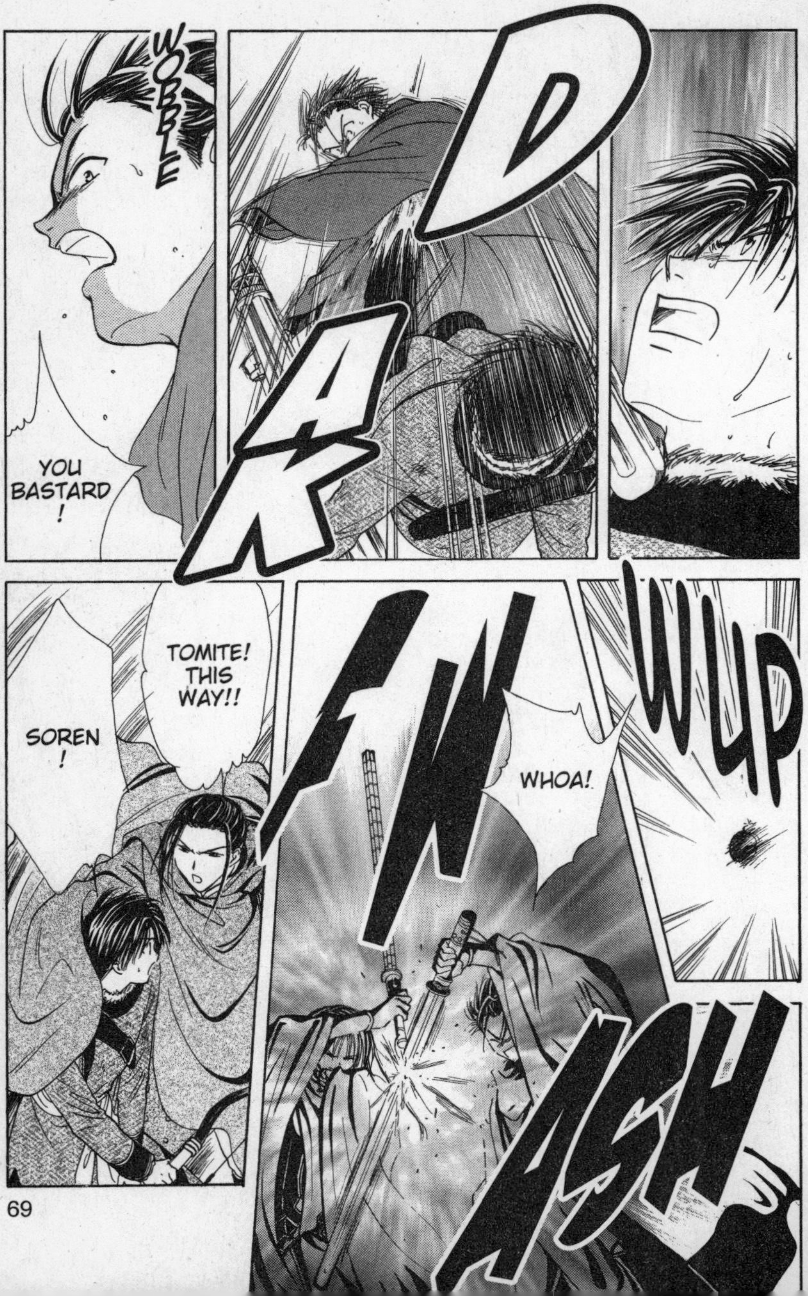
DAK
WOBBLE
YOU BASTARD!
WUP
WHOA!
FW
ASH
TOMITE! THIS WAY!!
SOREN!

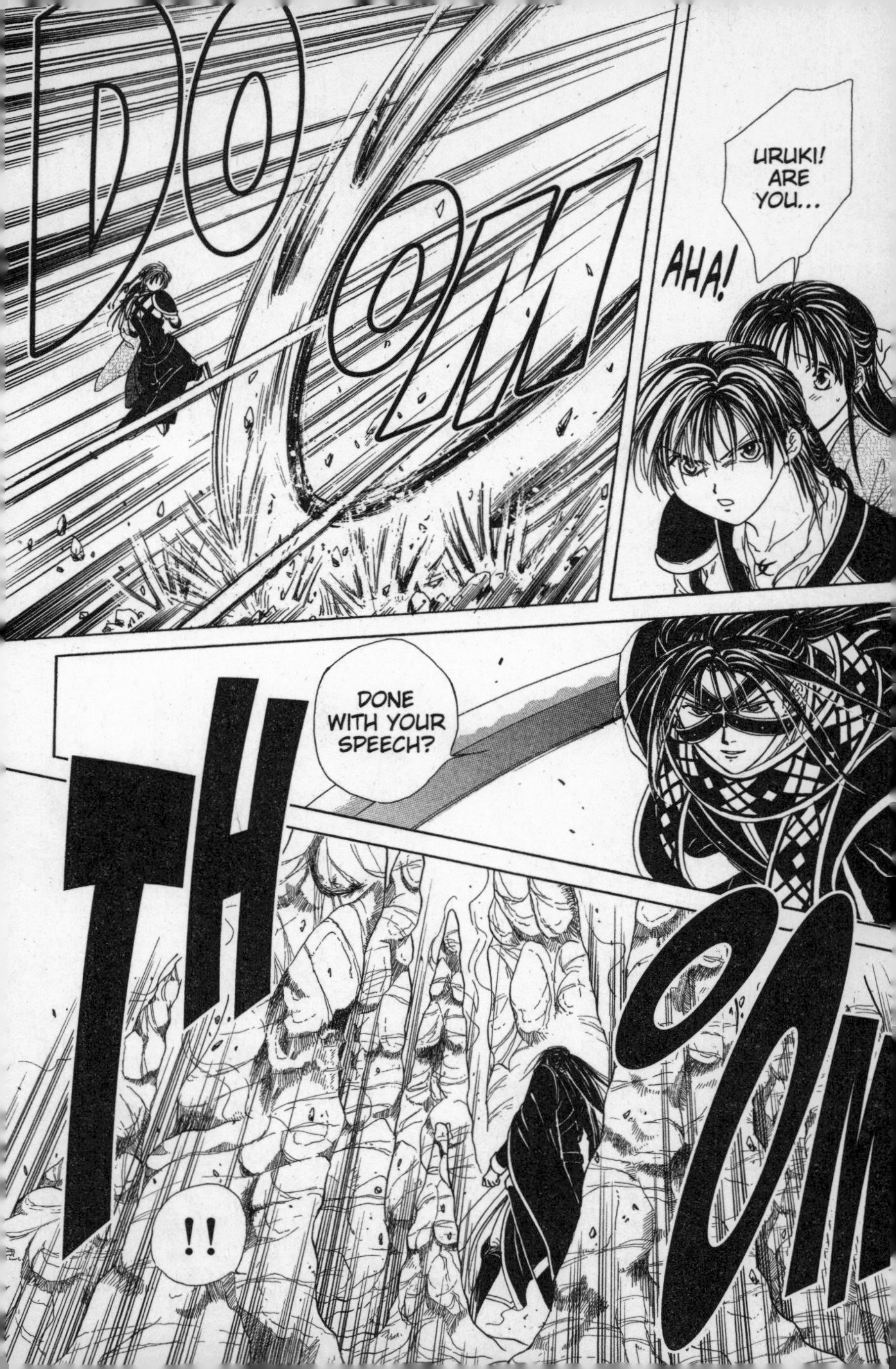
URUKI! ARE YOU...
AHA!
DOOM
DONE WITH YOUR SPEECH?
!!

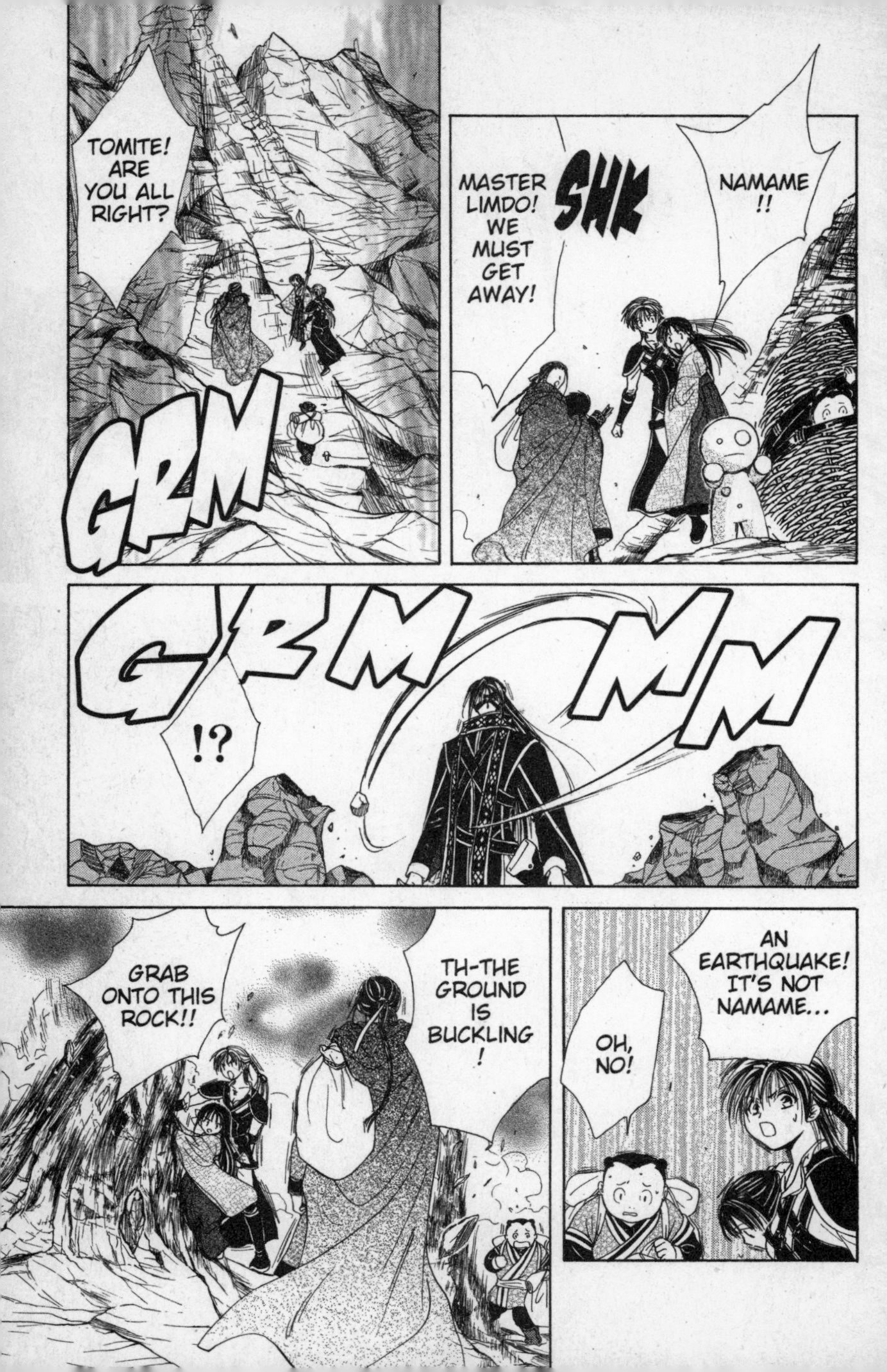
NAMAME !!
SHK
MASTER LIMDO! WE MUST GET AWAY!
TOMITE! ARE YOU ALL RIGHT?
GRM
GRM MM
!?
AN EARTHQUAKE! IT'S NOT NAMAME...
OH, NO!
TH-THE GROUND IS BUCKLING!
GRAB ONTO THIS ROCK!!

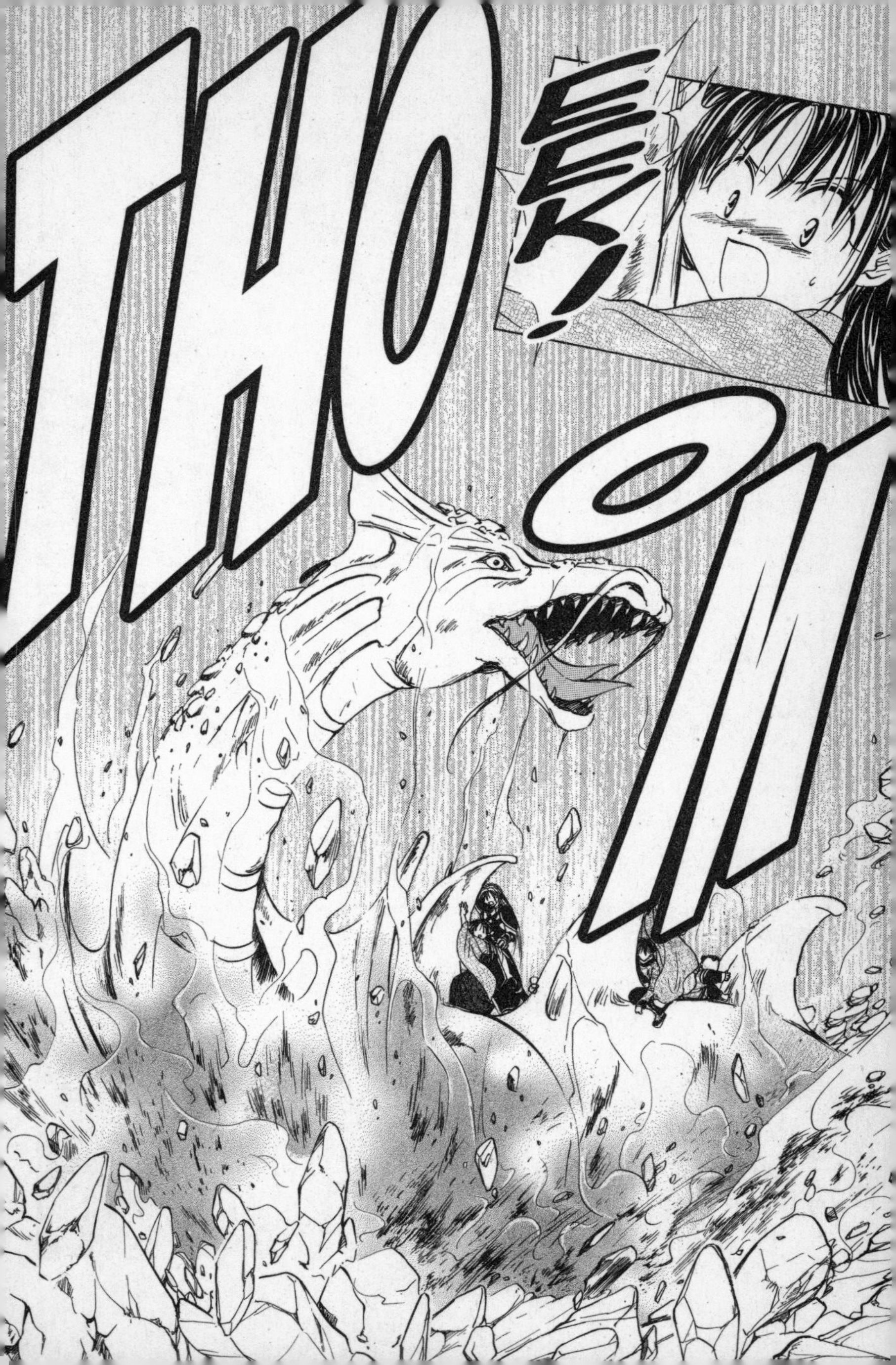
EEK!
THOOM!!

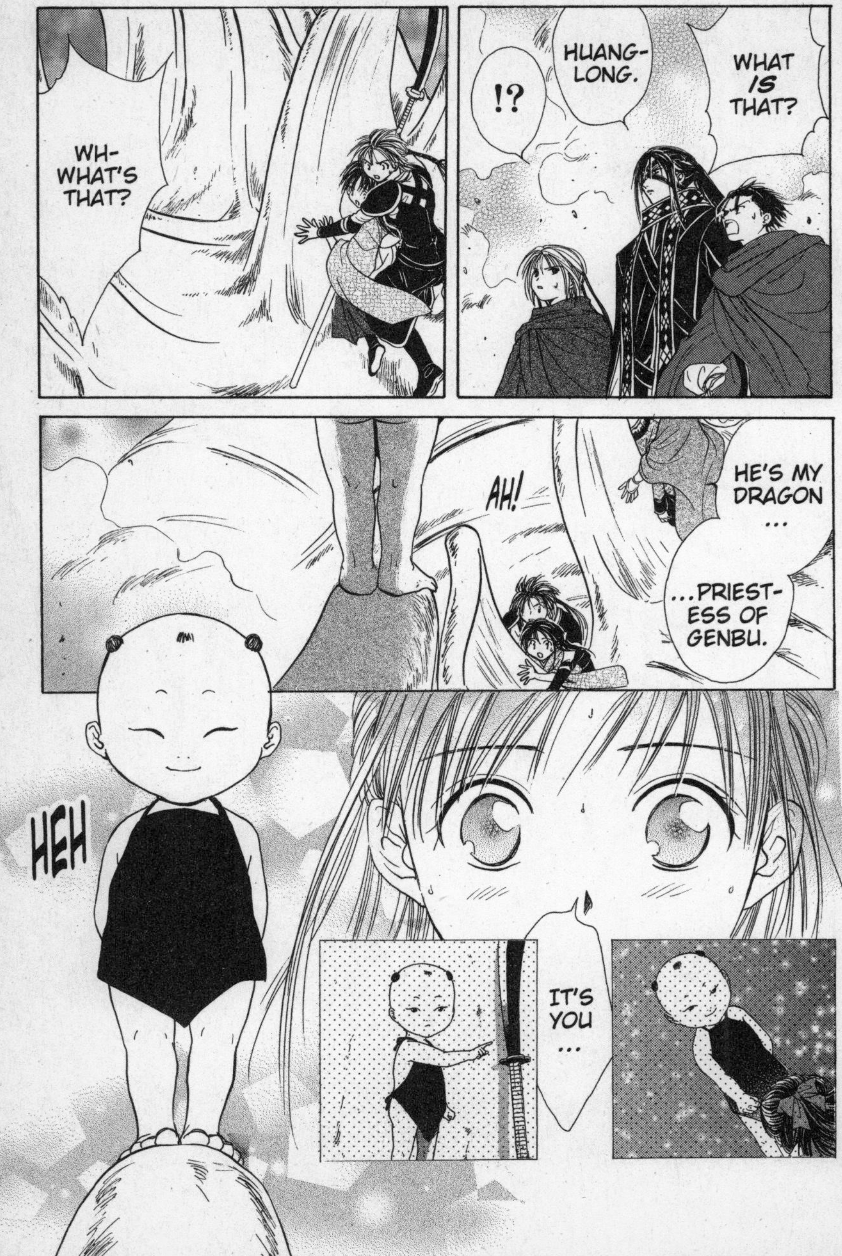
WHAT *IS* THAT?
HUANG-LONG.
!?
WH-WHAT'S THAT?
HE'S MY DRAGON ...
AH!
...PRIEST-ESS OF GENBU.
IT'S YOU ...
HEH

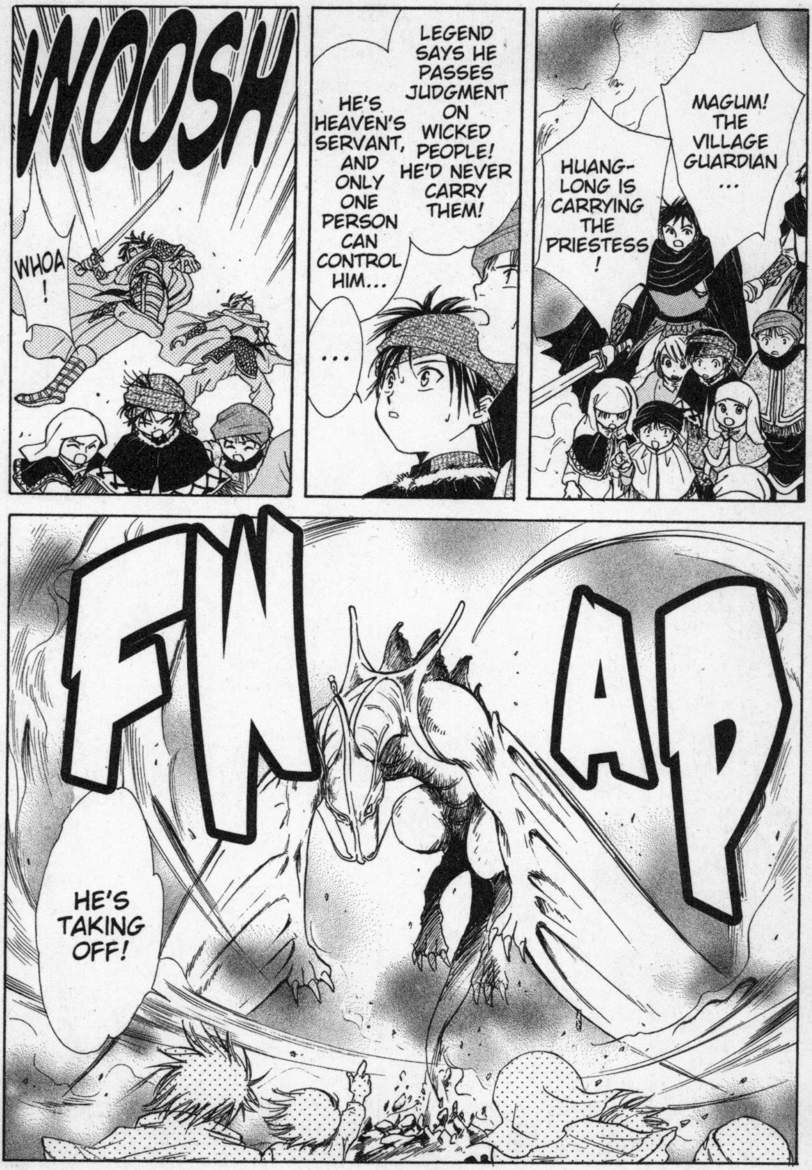
MAGUM! THE VILLAGE GUARDIAN...
HUANG-LONG IS CARRYING THE PRIESTESS!
LEGEND SAYS HE PASSES JUDGMENT ON WICKED PEOPLE! HE'D NEVER CARRY THEM!
HE'S HEAVEN'S SERVANT, AND ONLY ONE PERSON CAN CONTROL HIM...
...
WOOSH
WHOA!
FWAP
HE'S TAKING OFF!

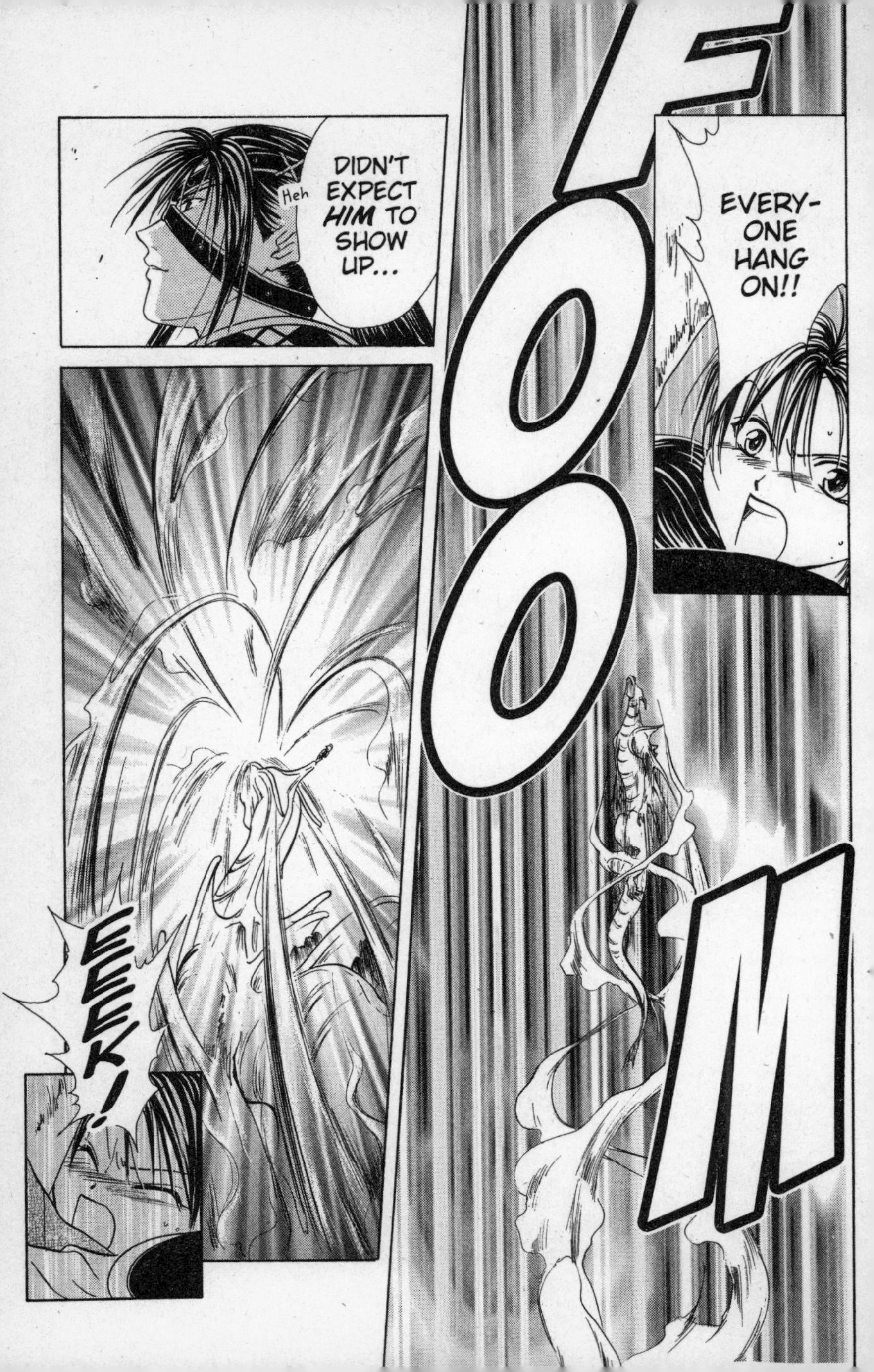
EVERY-ONE HANG ON!!
Heh
DIDN'T EXPECT HIM TO SHOW UP...
FOOM
EEEK!!

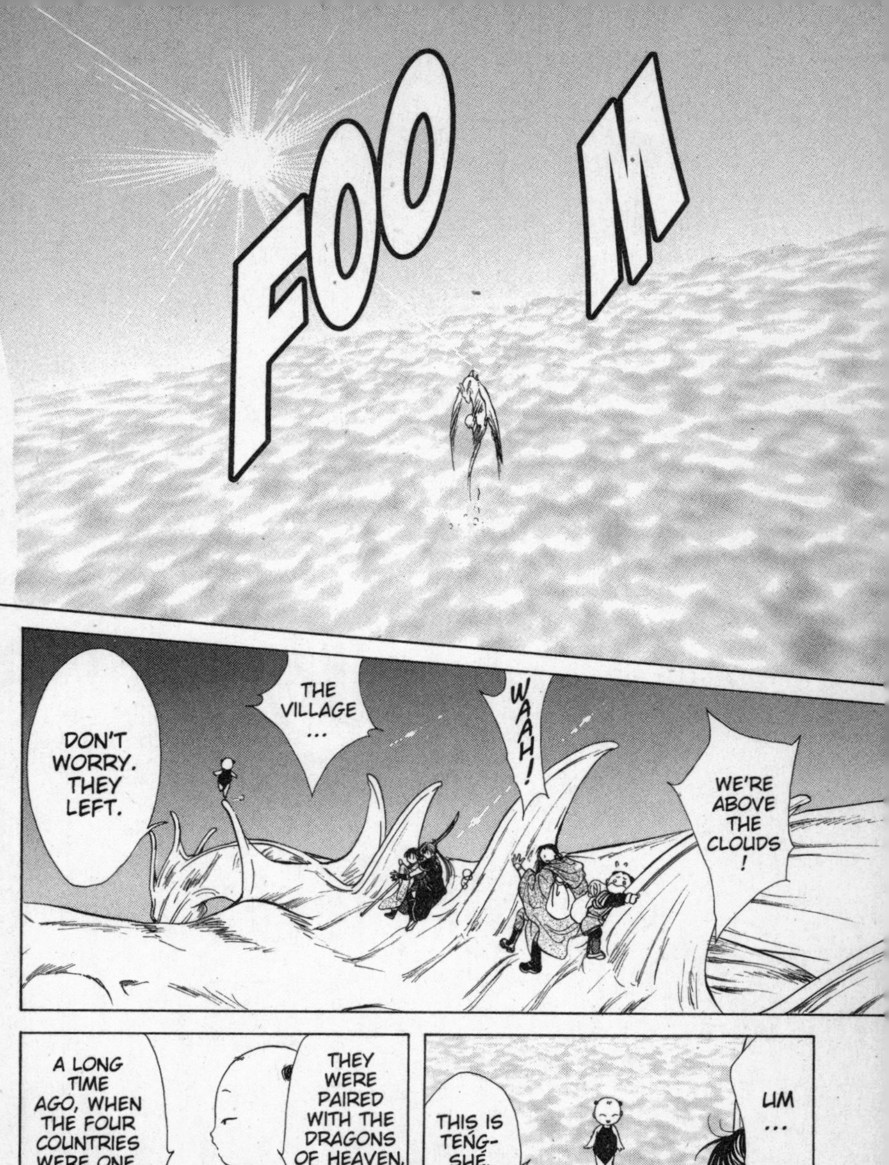
FOOM
WE'RE ABOVE THE CLOUDS!
WAAH!
THE VILLAGE...
DON'T WORRY. THEY LEFT.
UM...
THIS IS TEŃG-SHÉ, A DRAGON OF EARTH.
THEY WERE PAIRED WITH THE DRAGONS OF HEAVEN, BUT HE'S THE ONLY ONE LEFT.
A LONG TIME AGO, WHEN THE FOUR COUNTRIES WERE ONE, THERE WERE MANY DRAGONS OF EARTH.

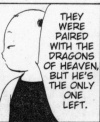

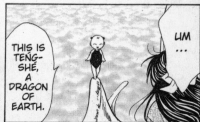

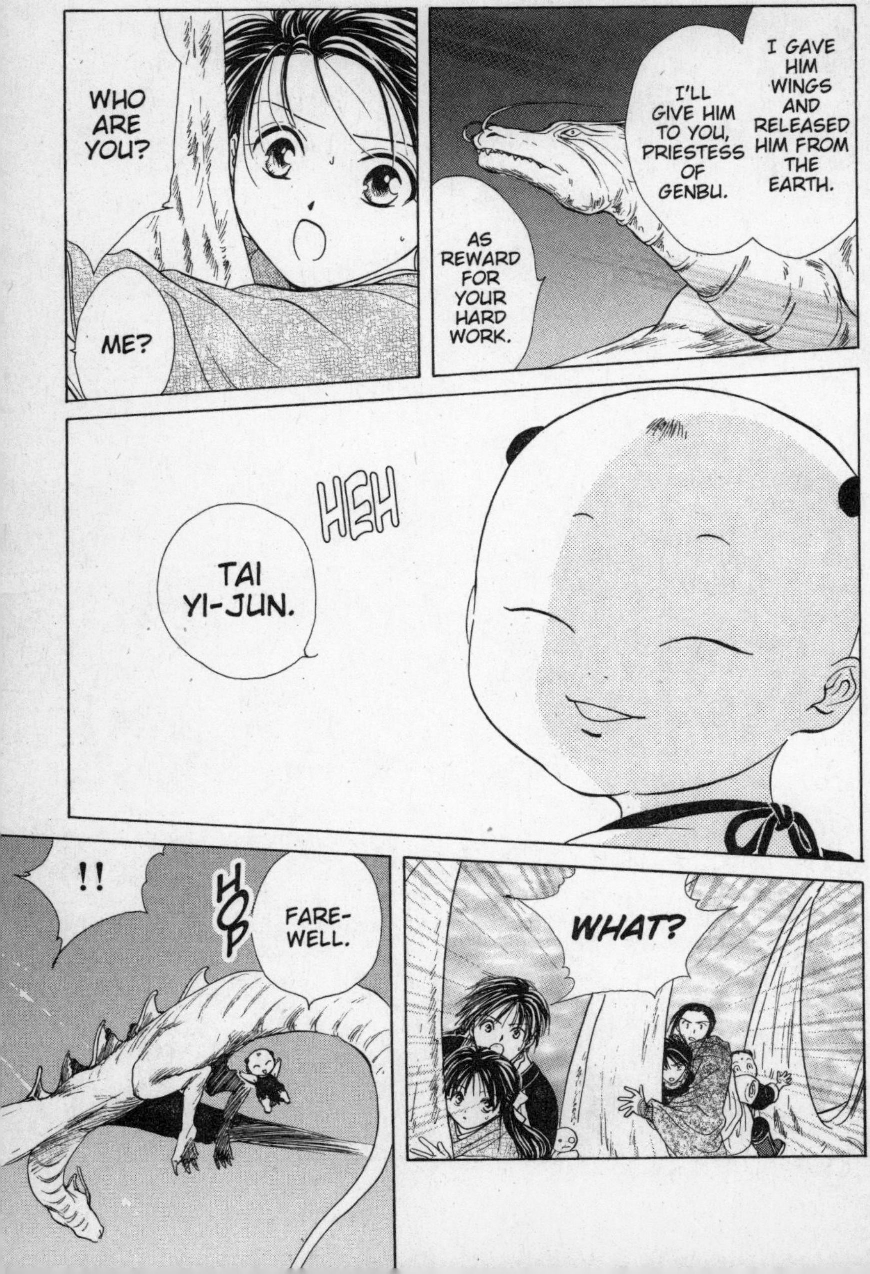
I GAVE HIM WINGS AND RELEASED HIM FROM THE EARTH.
I'LL GIVE HIM TO YOU, PRIESTESS OF GENBU.
AS REWARD FOR YOUR HARD WORK.
WHO ARE YOU?
ME?
HEH
TAI YI-JUN.
WHAT?
FARE-WELL.
HOP
!!

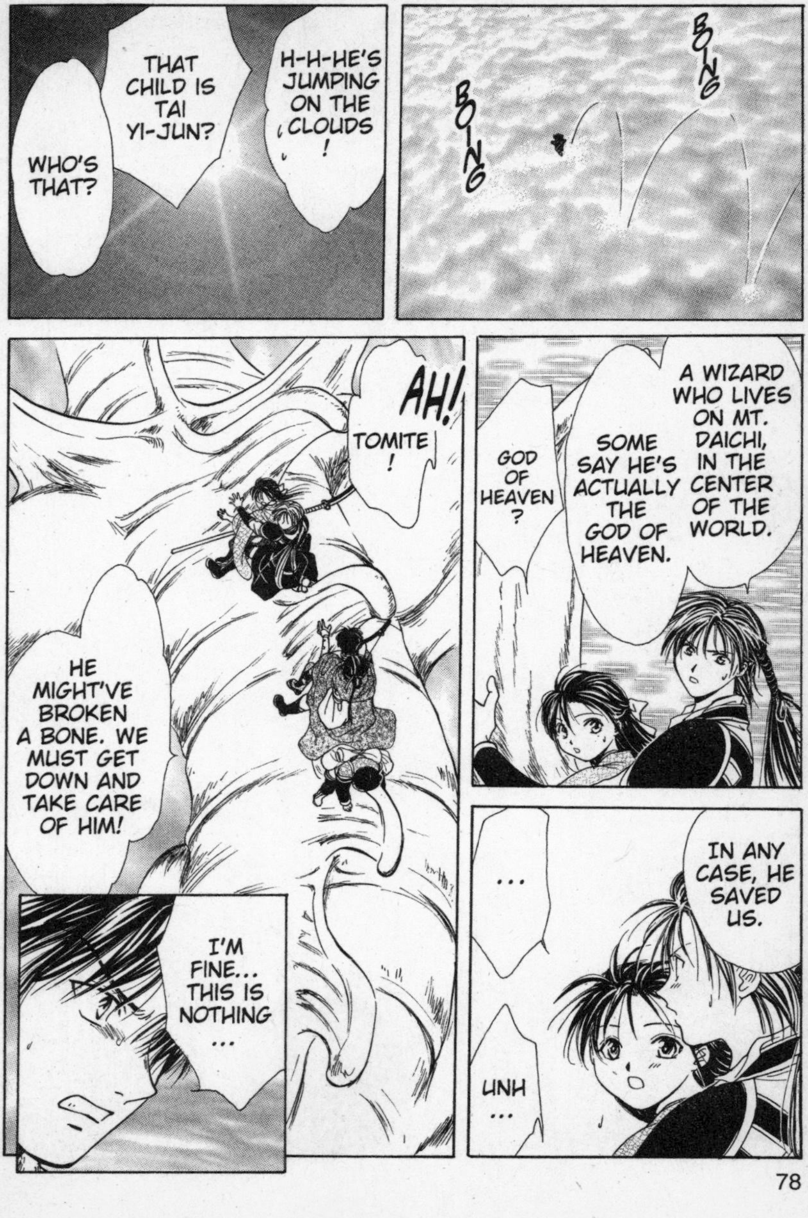
BOING
BOING
H-H-HE'S JUMPING ON THE CLOUDS!
THAT CHILD IS TAI YI-JUN?
WHO'S THAT?
A WIZARD WHO LIVES ON MT. DAICHI, IN THE CENTER OF THE WORLD.
SOME SAY HE'S ACTUALLY THE GOD OF HEAVEN.
GOD OF HEAVEN?
IN ANY CASE, HE SAVED US.
...
UNH...
AH!
TOMITE!
HE MIGHT'VE BROKEN A BONE. WE MUST GET DOWN AND TAKE CARE OF HIM!
I'M FINE... THIS IS NOTHING...

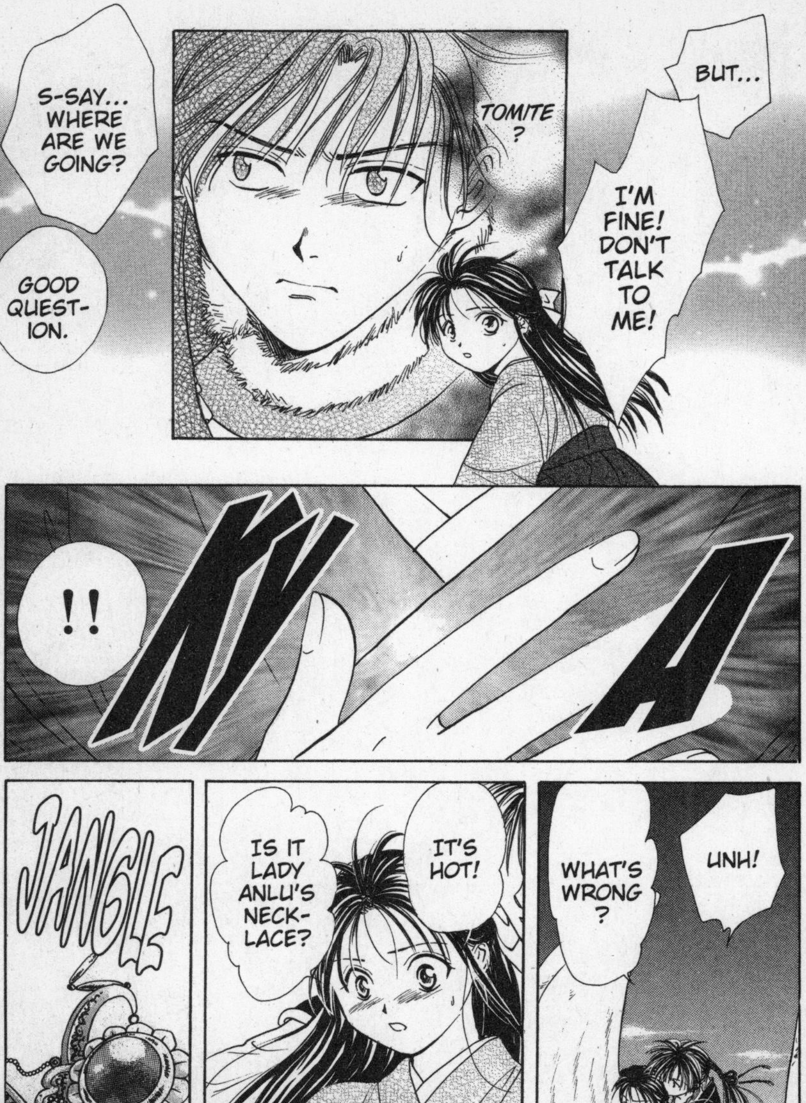
BUT...
I'M FINE! DON'T TALK TO ME!
TOMITE?
S-SAY... WHERE ARE WE GOING?
GOOD QUESTION.
KYA
!!
UNH!
WHAT'S WRONG?
IT'S HOT!
IS IT LADY ANLU'S NECKLACE?
JANGLE

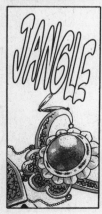

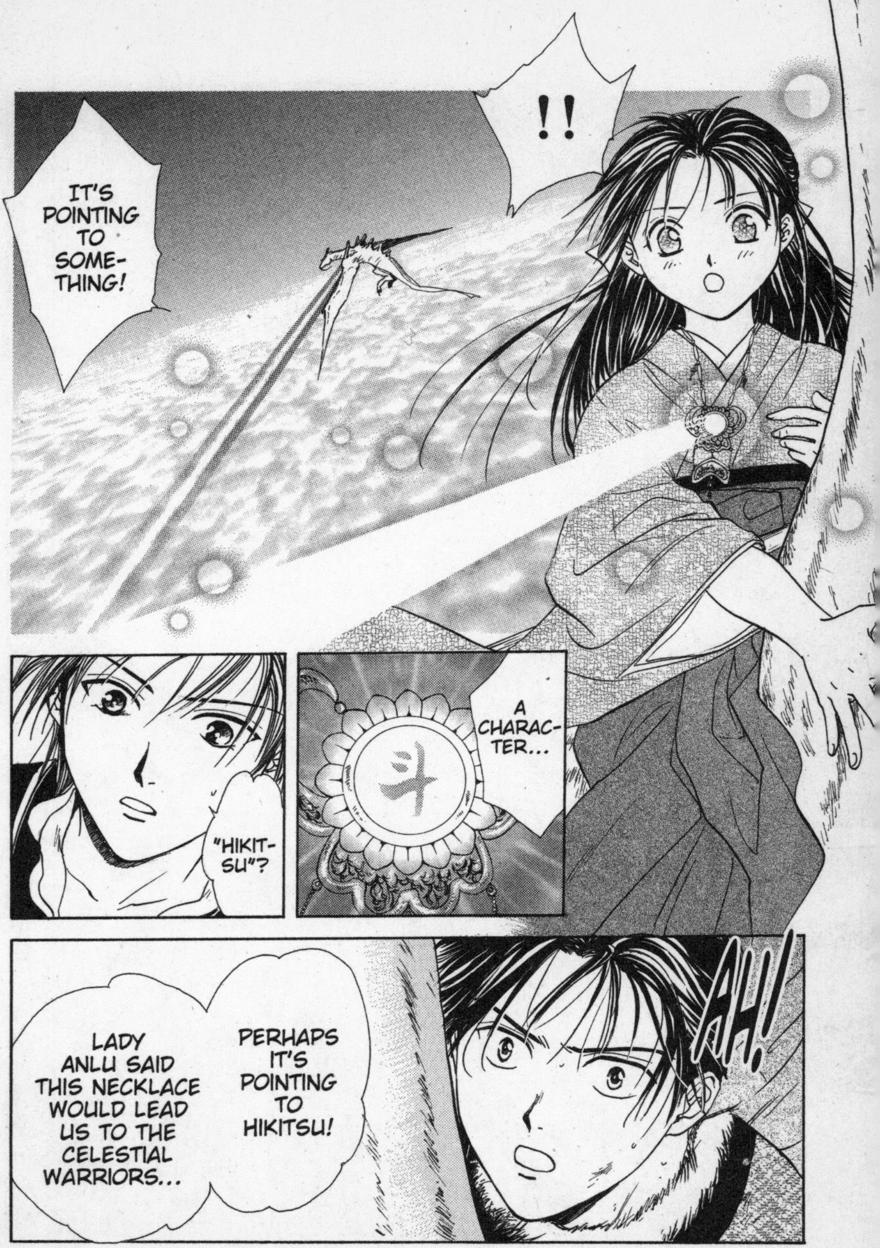
!!
IT'S POINTING TO SOME-THING!
A CHARACTER...
"HIKIT-SU"?
AH!
PERHAPS IT'S POINTING TO HIKITSU!
LADY ANLU SAID THIS NECKLACE WOULD LEAD US TO THE CELESTIAL WARRIORS...

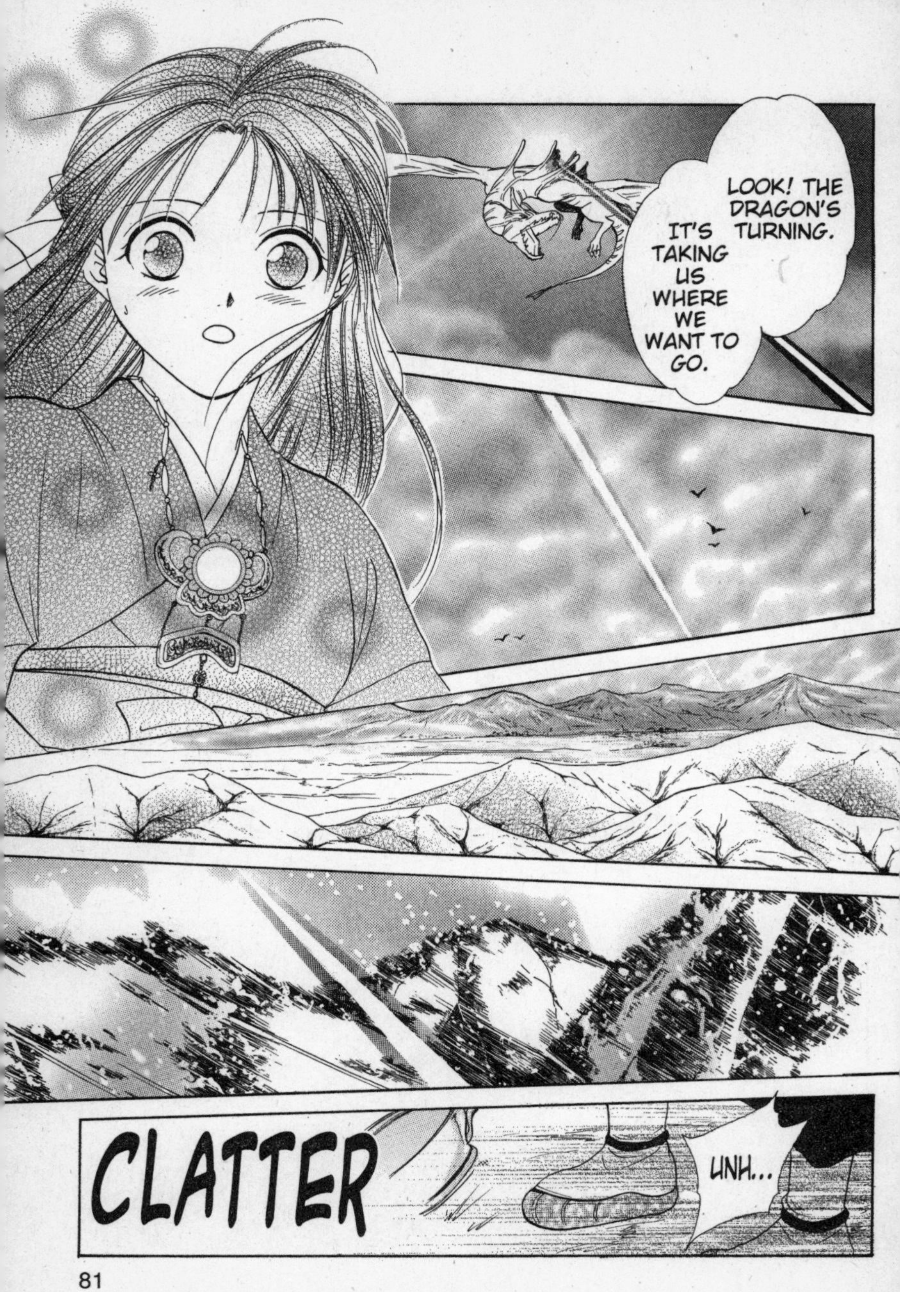
LOOK! THE DRAGON'S TURNING.
IT'S TAKING US WHERE WE WANT TO GO.
UNH...
CLATTER

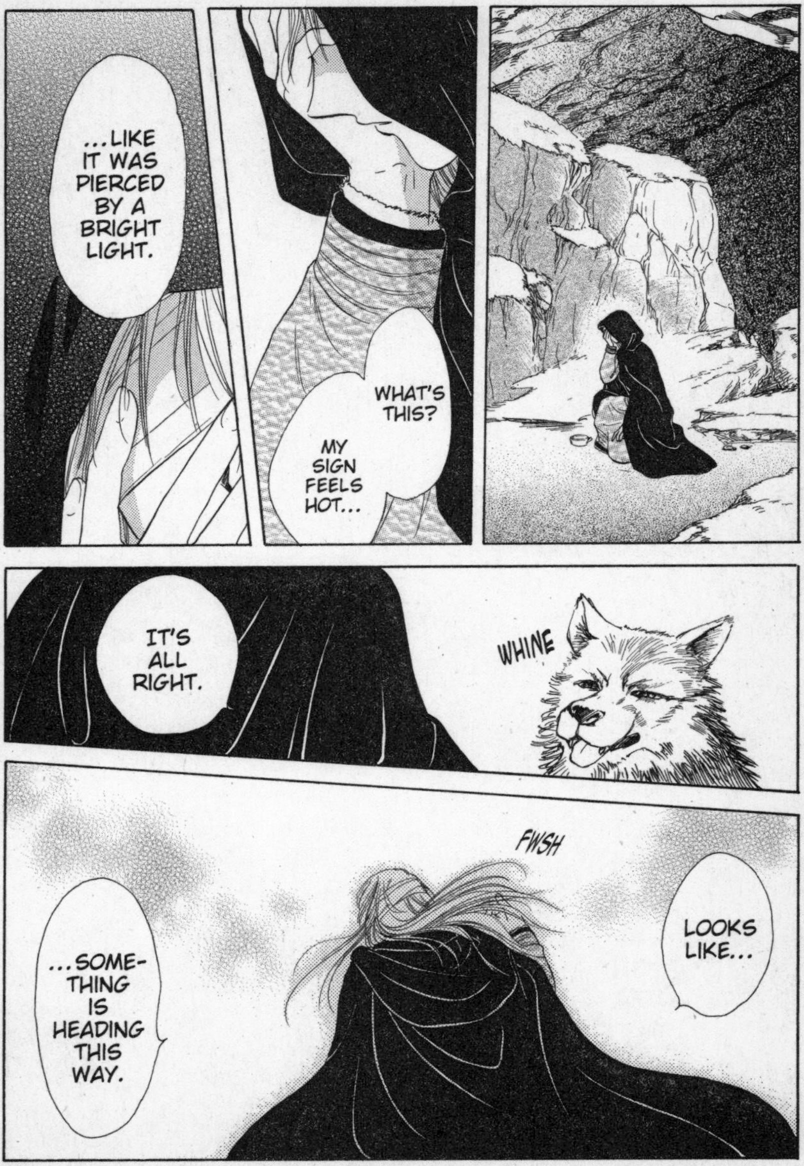
WHAT'S THIS?
MY SIGN FEELS HOT...
...LIKE IT WAS PIERCED BY A BRIGHT LIGHT.
WHINE
IT'S ALL RIGHT.
FWSH
LOOKS LIKE...
...SOME-THING IS HEADING THIS WAY.

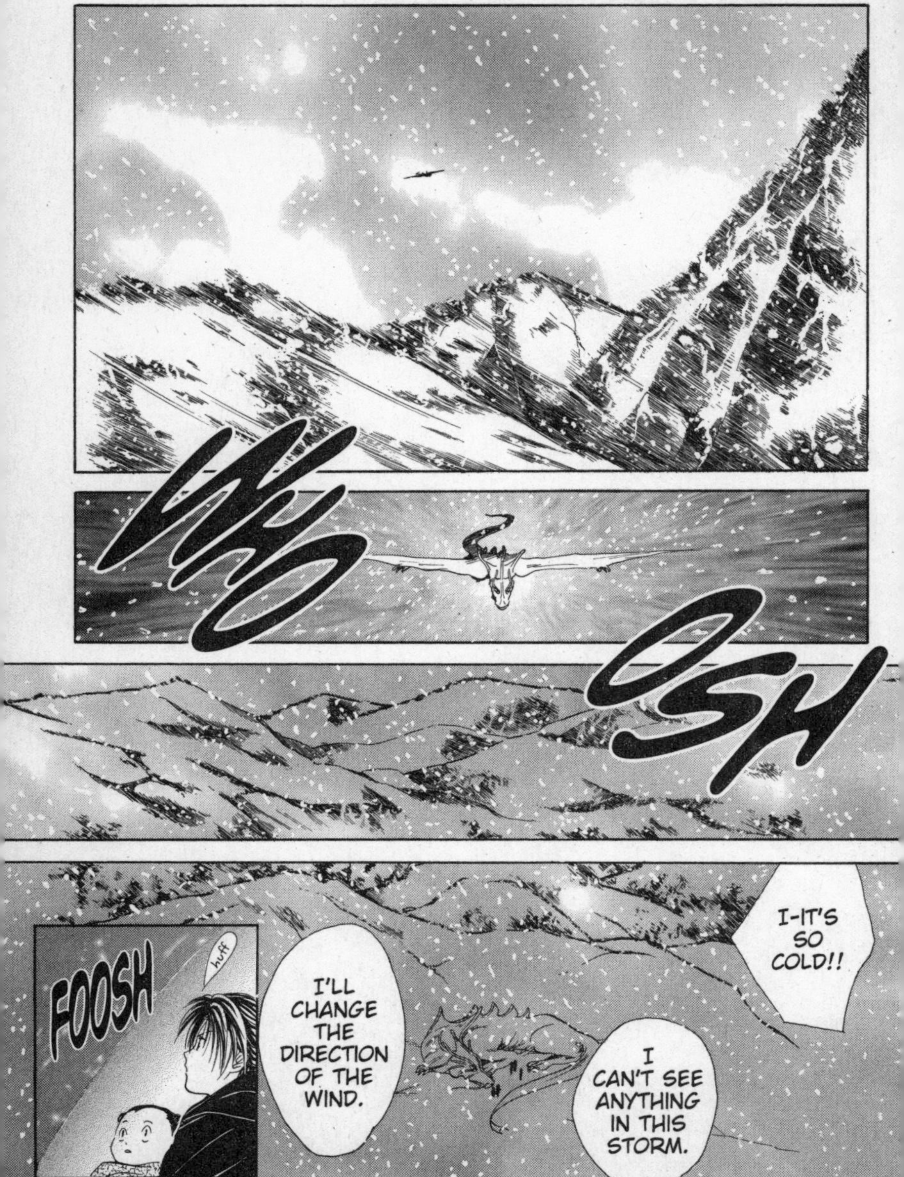
WHOOSH
I-IT'S SO COLD!!
I CAN'T SEE ANYTHING IN THIS STORM.
I'LL CHANGE THE DIRECTION OF THE WIND.
FOOSH
huff

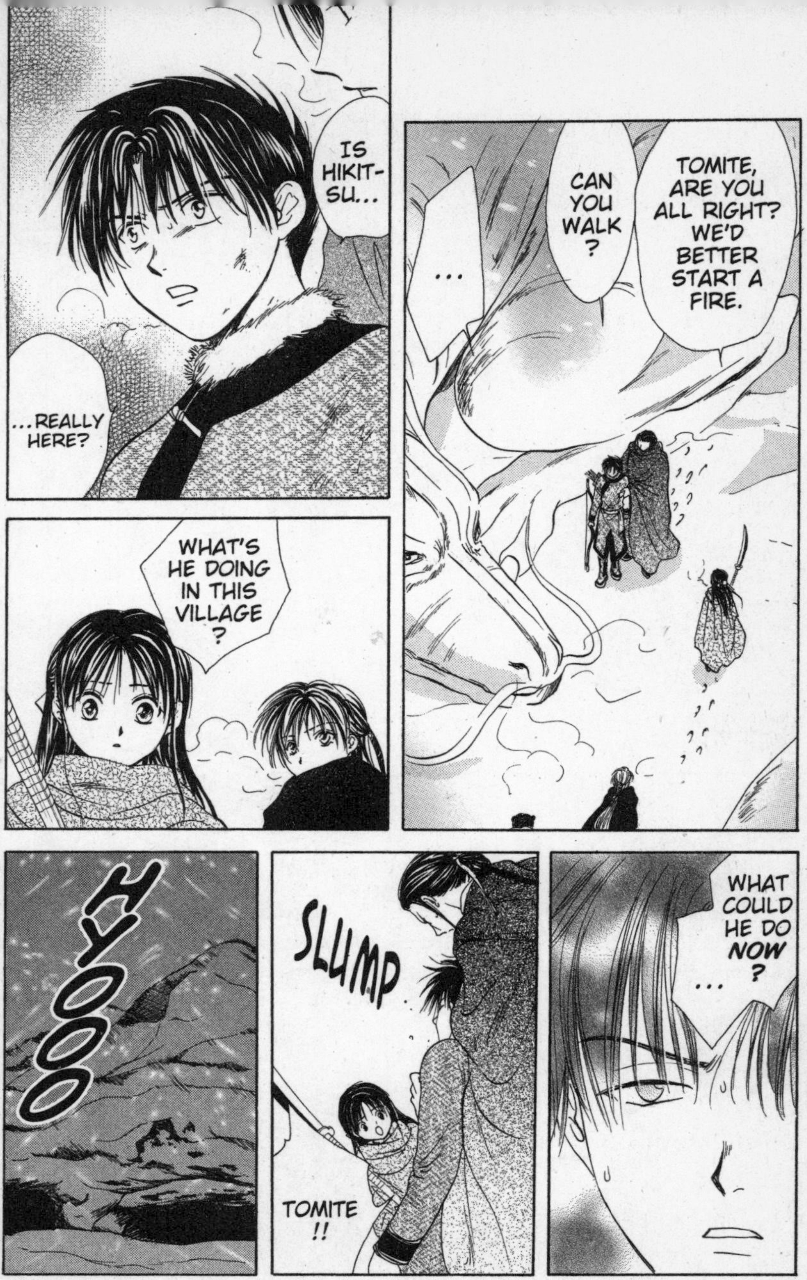
TOMITE, ARE YOU ALL RIGHT? WE'D BETTER START A FIRE.
CAN YOU WALK?
...
IS HIKIT-SU...
...REALLY HERE?
WHAT'S HE DOING IN THIS VILLAGE?
WHAT COULD HE DO NOW?
...
SLUMP
TOMITE!!
HYOOO

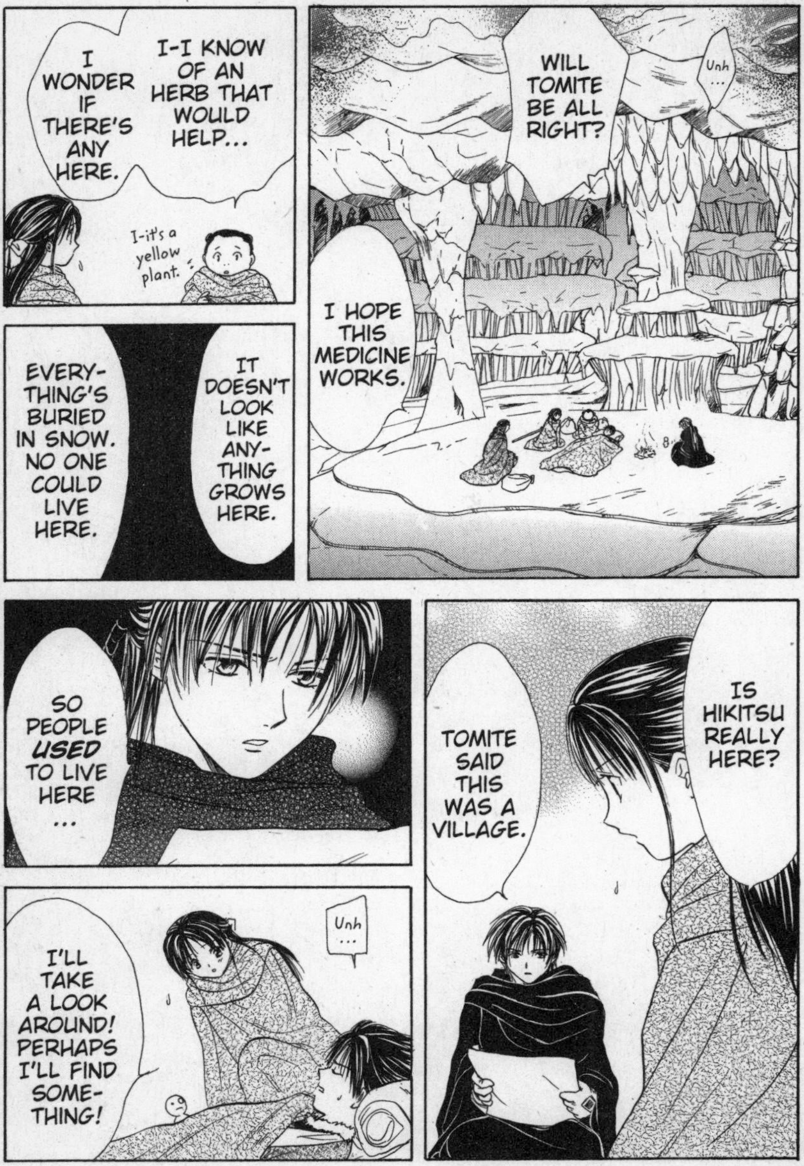
Unh...
WILL TOMITE BE ALL RIGHT?
I HOPE THIS MEDICINE WORKS.
I-I KNOW OF AN HERB THAT WOULD HELP...
I WONDER IF THERE'S ANY HERE.
I-it's a yellow plant.
IT DOESN'T LOOK LIKE ANYTHING GROWS HERE.
EVERYTHING'S BURIED IN SNOW. NO ONE COULD LIVE HERE.
IS HIKITSU REALLY HERE?
TOMITE SAID THIS WAS A VILLAGE.
SO PEOPLE *USED* TO LIVE HERE...
Unh...
I'LL TAKE A LOOK AROUND! PERHAPS I'LL FIND SOMETHING!

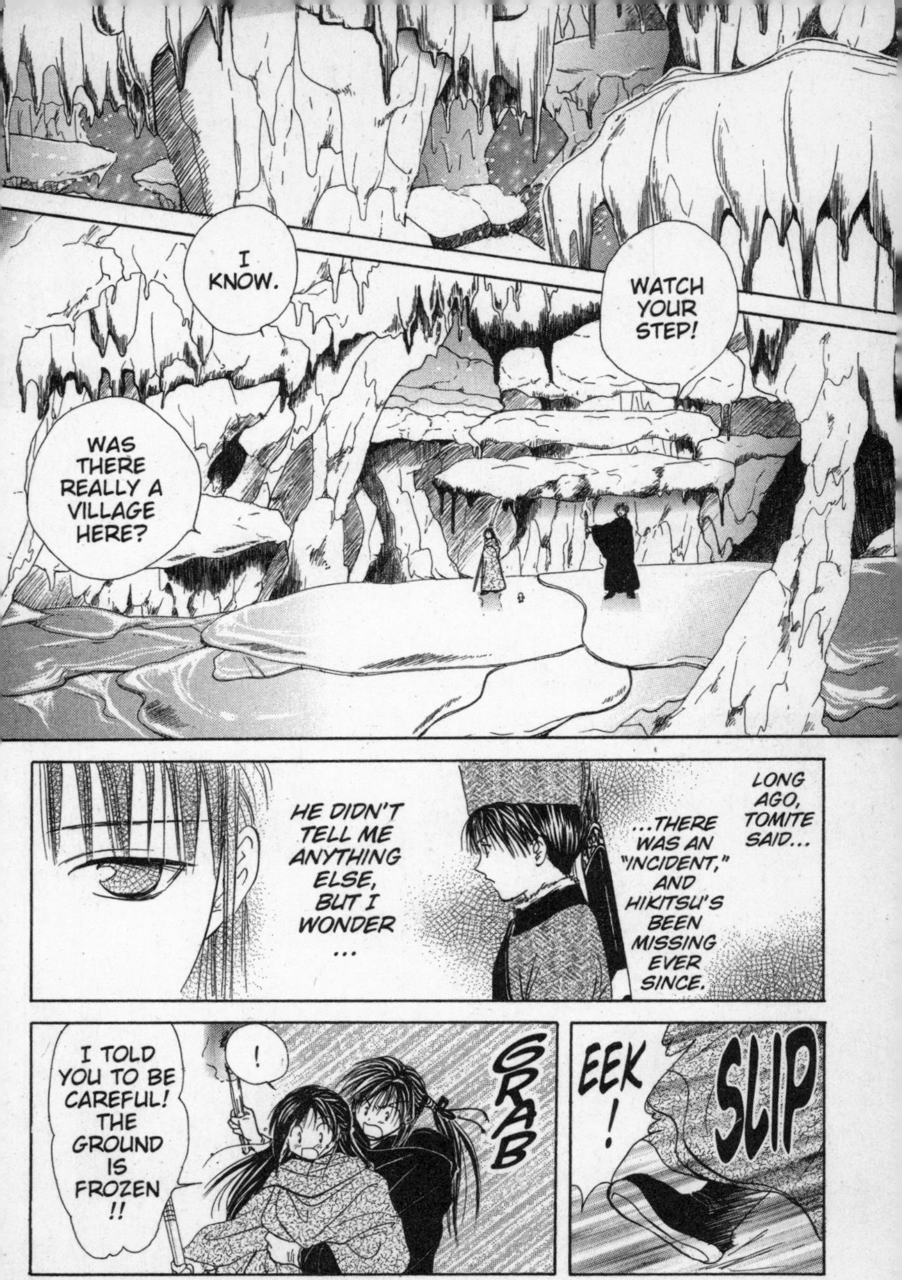
WATCH YOUR STEP!
I KNOW.
WAS THERE REALLY A VILLAGE HERE?
LONG AGO, TOMITE SAID...
...THERE WAS AN "INCIDENT," AND HIKITSU'S BEEN MISSING EVER SINCE.
HE DIDN'T TELL ME ANYTHING ELSE, BUT I WONDER...
SLIP
EEK!
GRAB
!
I TOLD YOU TO BE CAREFUL! THE GROUND IS FROZEN!!

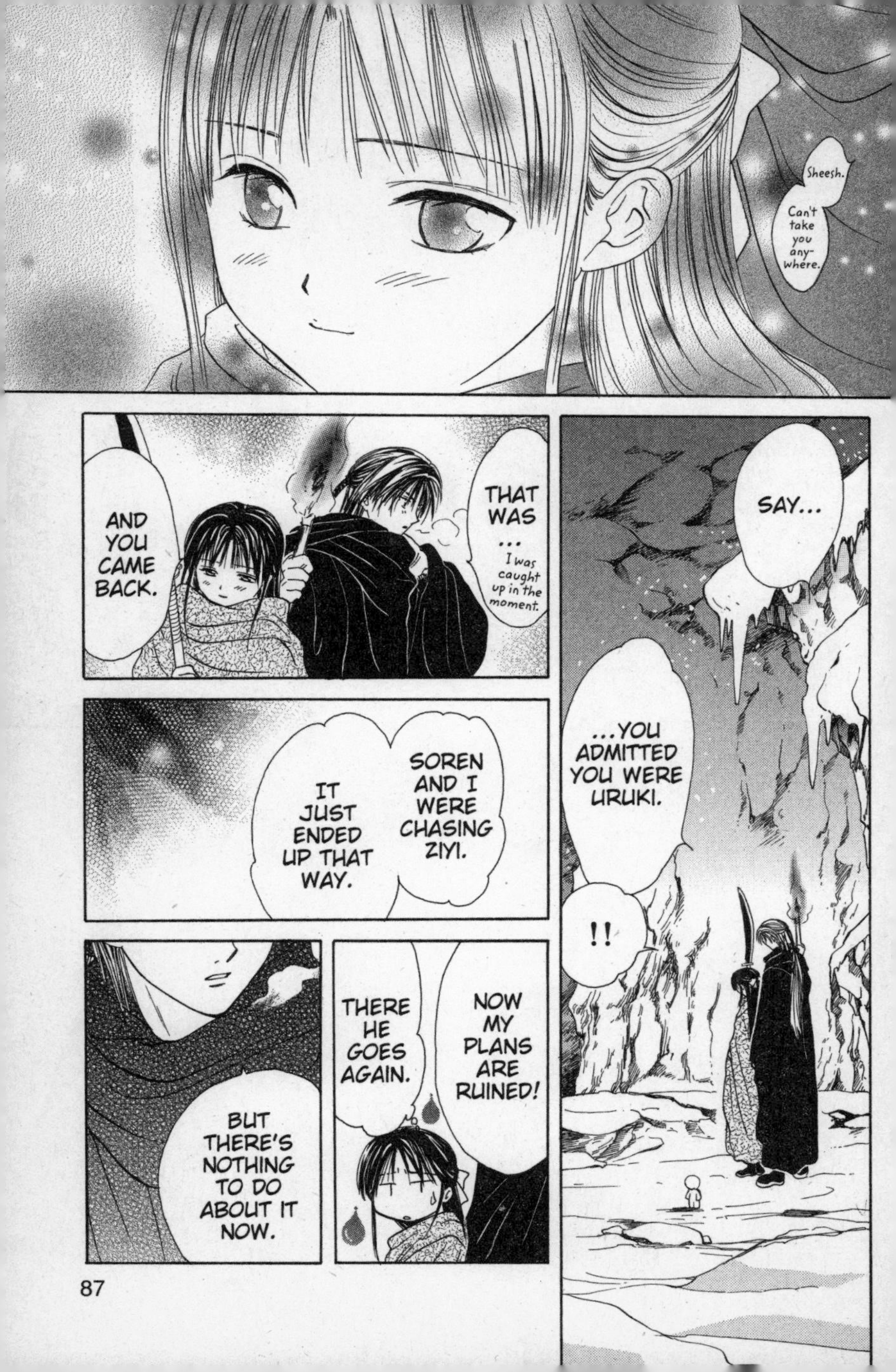
Sheesh.
Can't take you anywhere.
SAY...
...YOU ADMITTED YOU WERE URUKI.
!!
THAT WAS ...
I was caught up in the moment.
AND YOU CAME BACK.
SOREN AND I WERE CHASING ZIYI.
IT JUST ENDED UP THAT WAY.
NOW MY PLANS ARE RUINED!
THERE HE GOES AGAIN.
BUT THERE'S NOTHING TO DO ABOUT IT NOW.

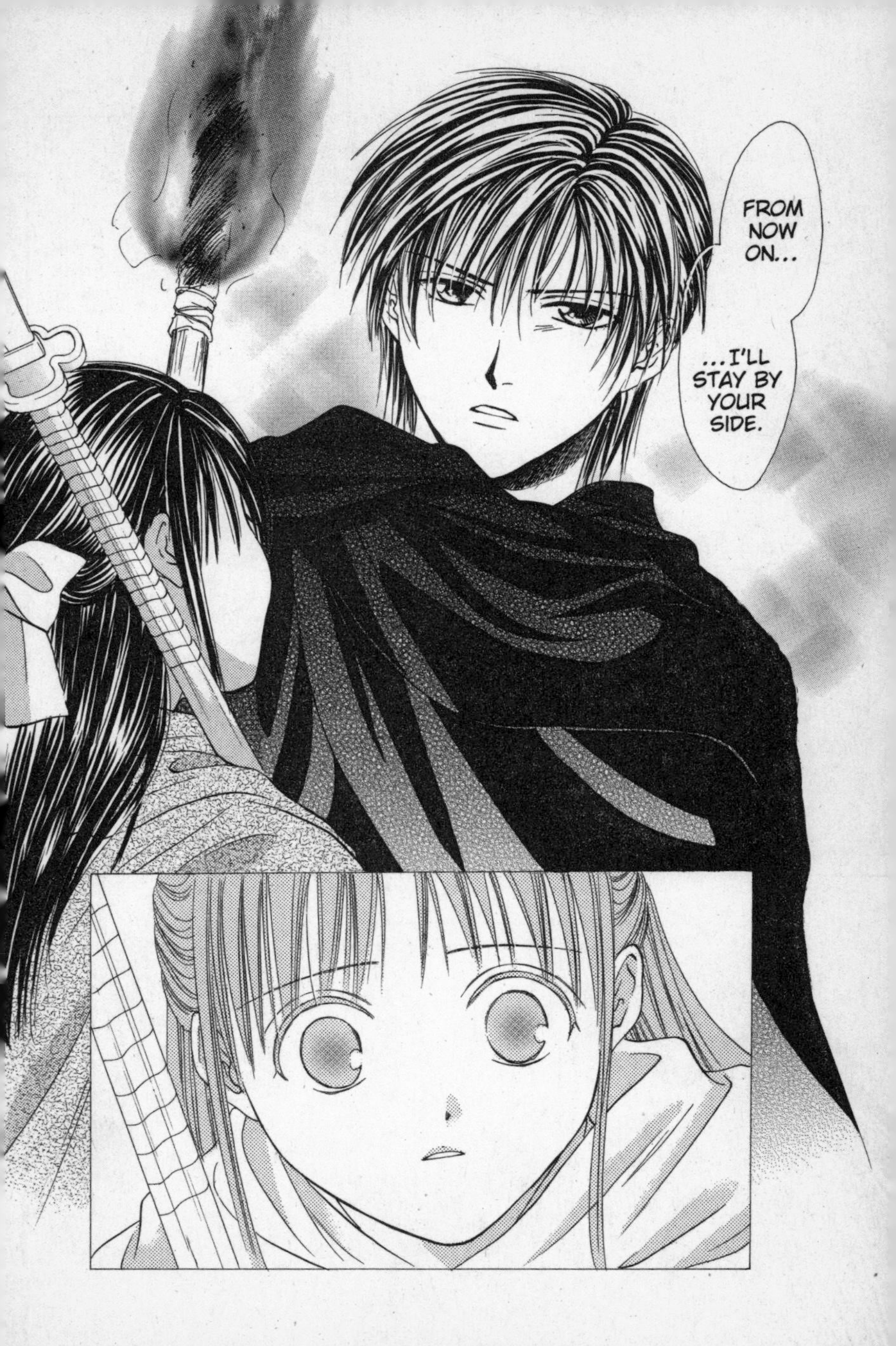
FROM NOW ON...
...I'LL STAY BY YOUR SIDE.

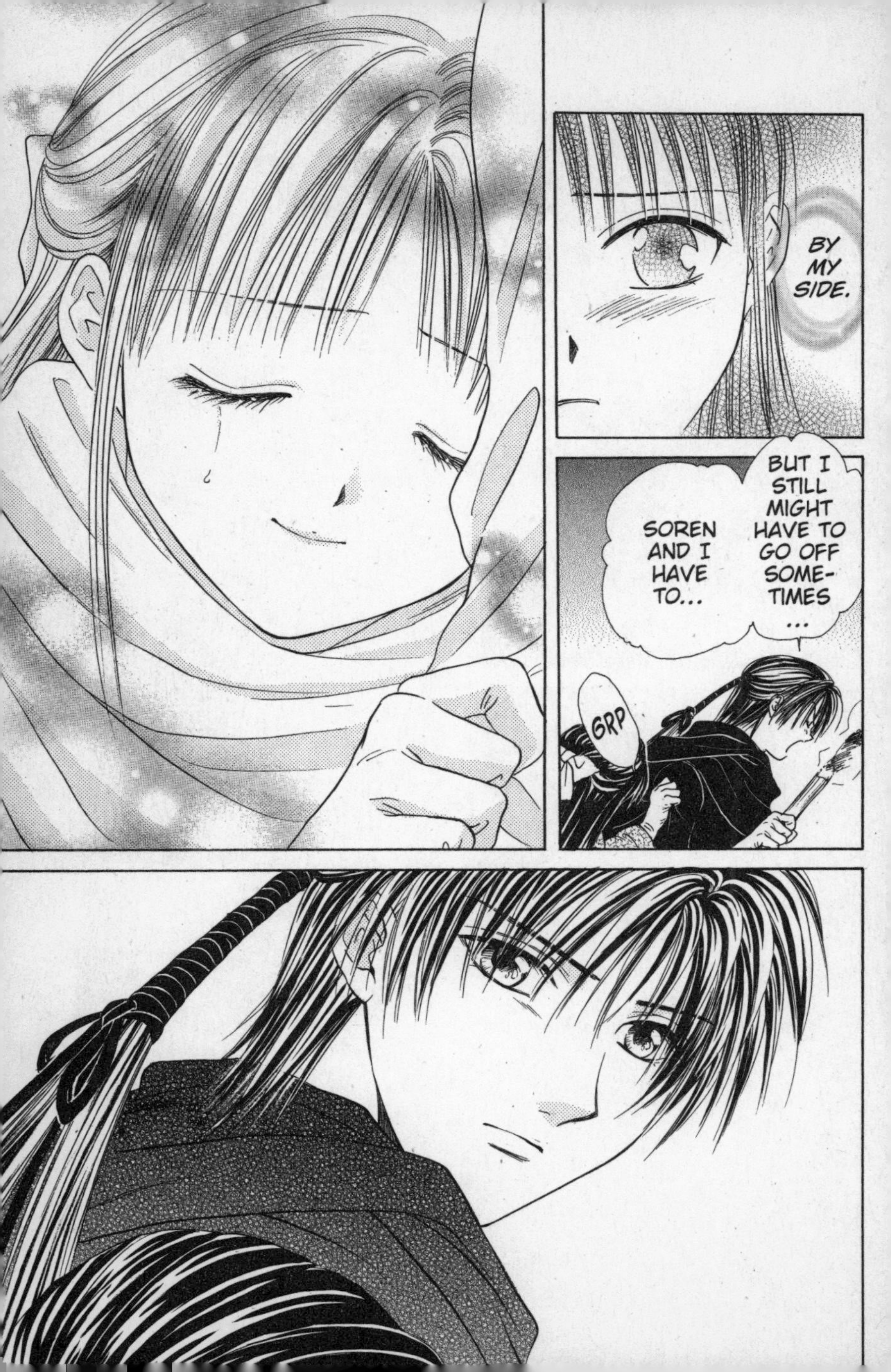
BY MY SIDE.
BUT I STILL MIGHT HAVE TO GO OFF SOME-TIMES ...
SOREN AND I HAVE TO...
GRP

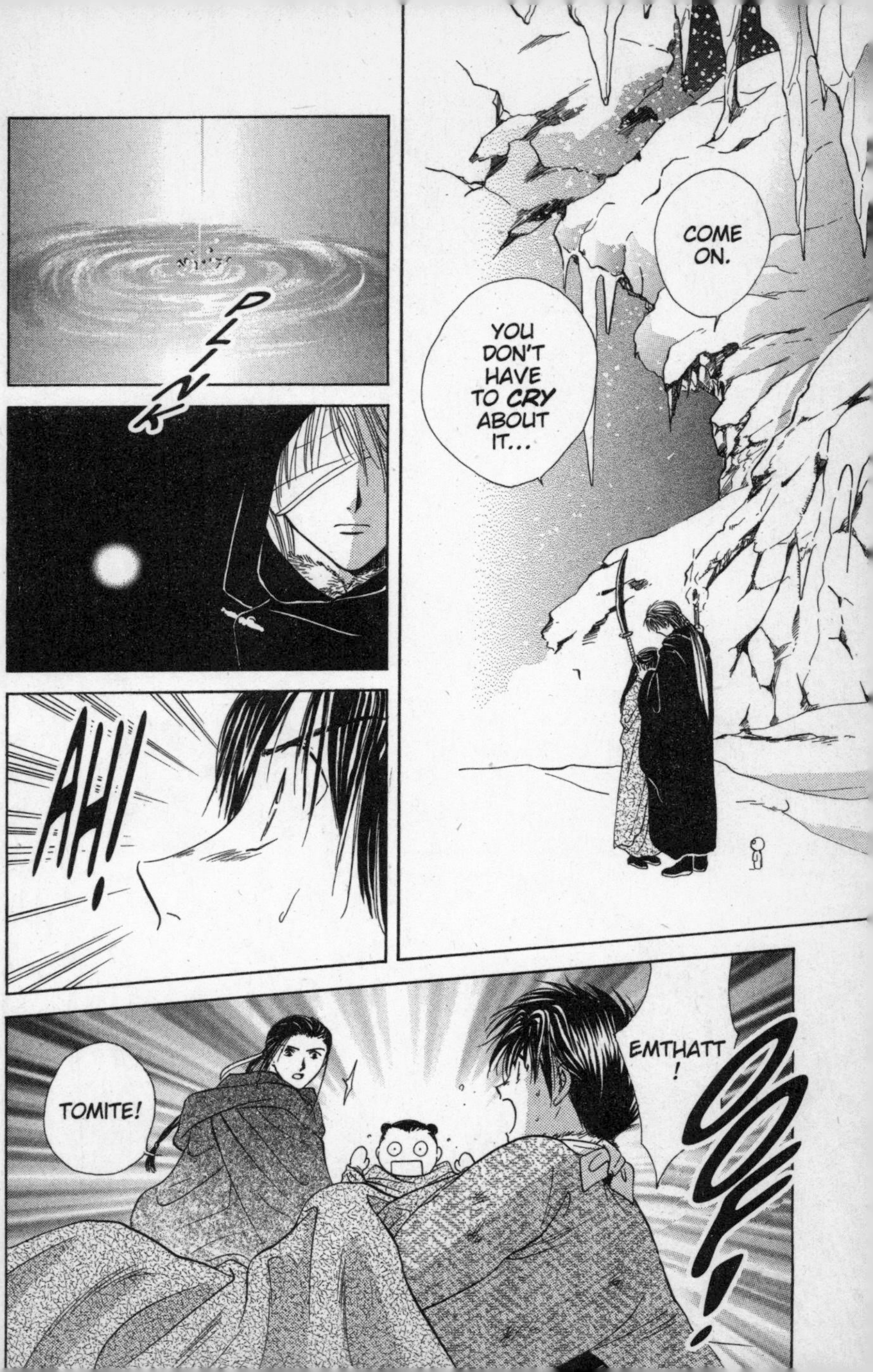
COME ON.
YOU DON'T HAVE TO **CRY** ABOUT IT...
PLINK
AH!
EMTHATT!
OOOH!
TOMITE!

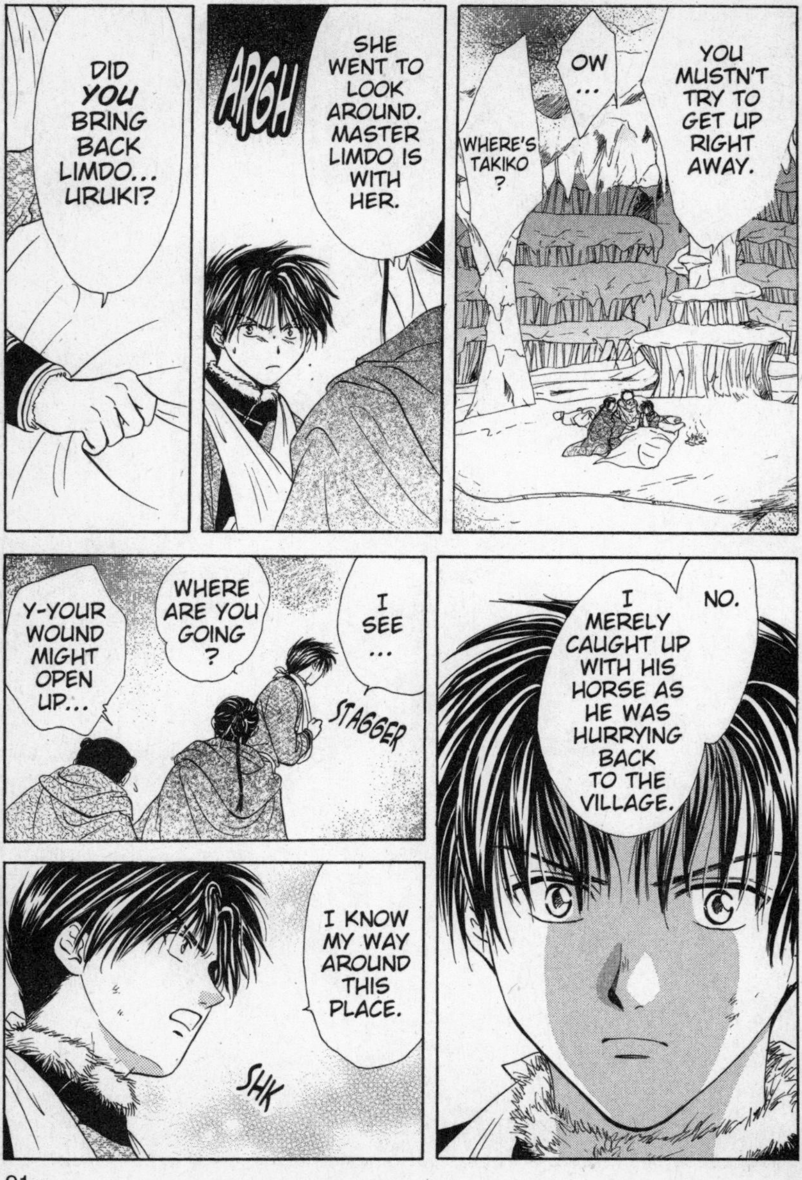
YOU MUSTN'T TRY TO GET UP RIGHT AWAY.
OW ...
WHERE'S TAKIKO ?
ARGH
SHE WENT TO LOOK AROUND. MASTER LIMDO IS WITH HER.
DID YOU BRING BACK LIMDO... URUKI?
NO.
I MERELY CAUGHT UP WITH HIS HORSE AS HE WAS HURRYING BACK TO THE VILLAGE.
I SEE ...
STAGGER
WHERE ARE YOU GOING ?
Y-YOUR WOUND MIGHT OPEN UP...
I KNOW MY WAY AROUND THIS PLACE.
SHK

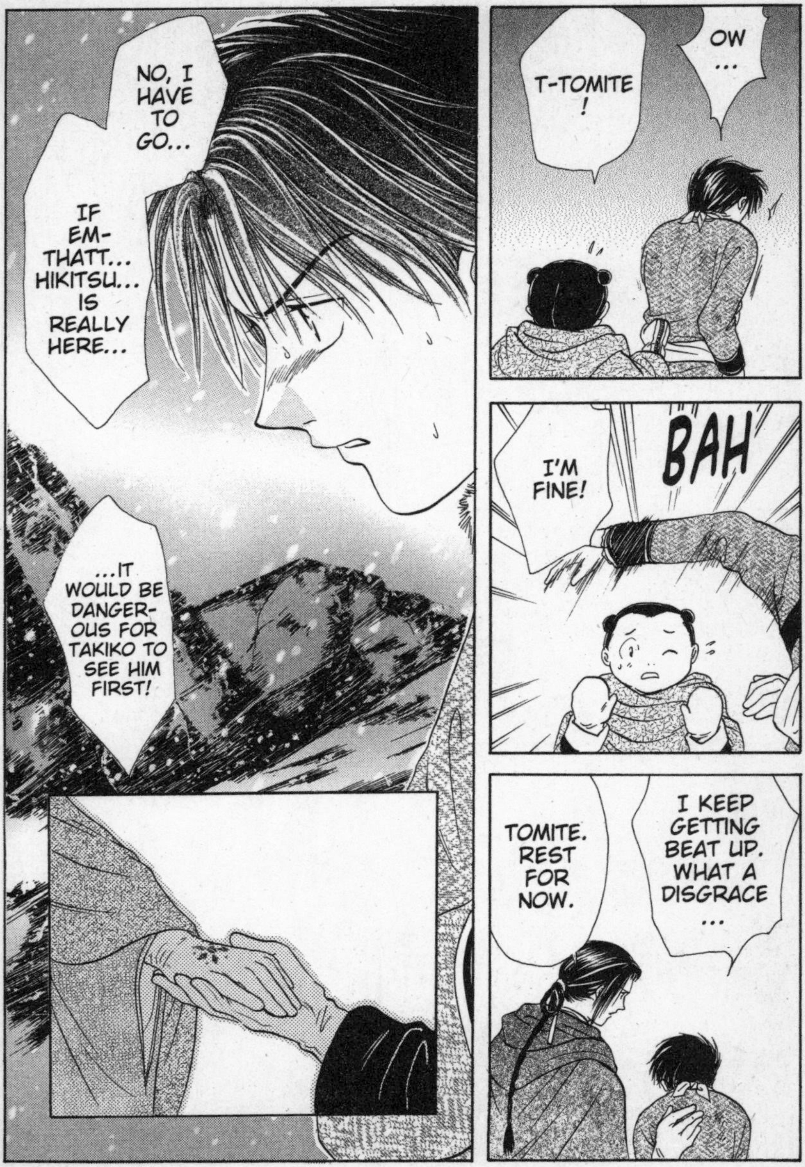
OW ...
T-TOMITE!
BAH
I'M FINE!
I KEEP GETTING BEAT UP. WHAT A DISGRACE ...
TOMITE. REST FOR NOW.
NO, I HAVE TO GO...
IF EMTHATT... HIKITSU... IS REALLY HERE...
...IT WOULD BE DANGEROUS FOR TAKIKO TO SEE HIM FIRST!

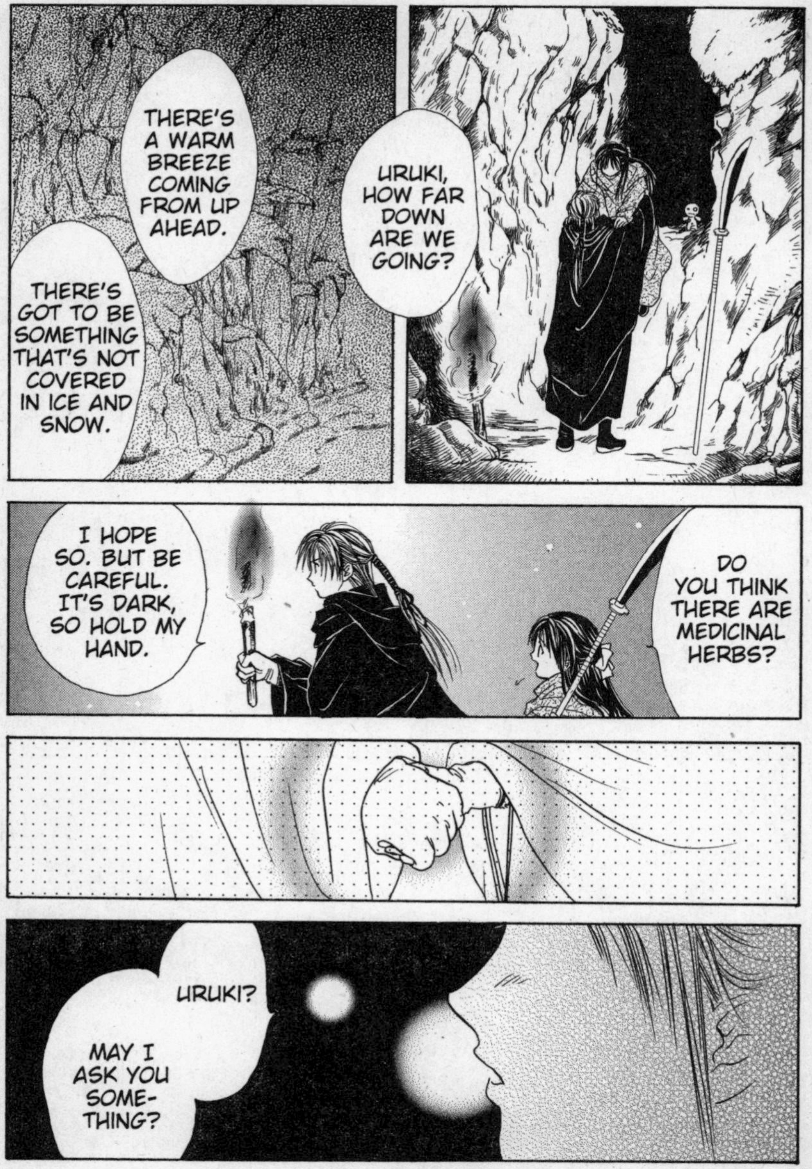
URUKI, HOW FAR DOWN ARE WE GOING?
THERE'S A WARM BREEZE COMING FROM UP AHEAD.
THERE'S GOT TO BE SOMETHING THAT'S NOT COVERED IN ICE AND SNOW.
DO YOU THINK THERE ARE MEDICINAL HERBS?
I HOPE SO. BUT BE CAREFUL. IT'S DARK, SO HOLD MY HAND.
URUKI?
MAY I ASK YOU SOME-THING?

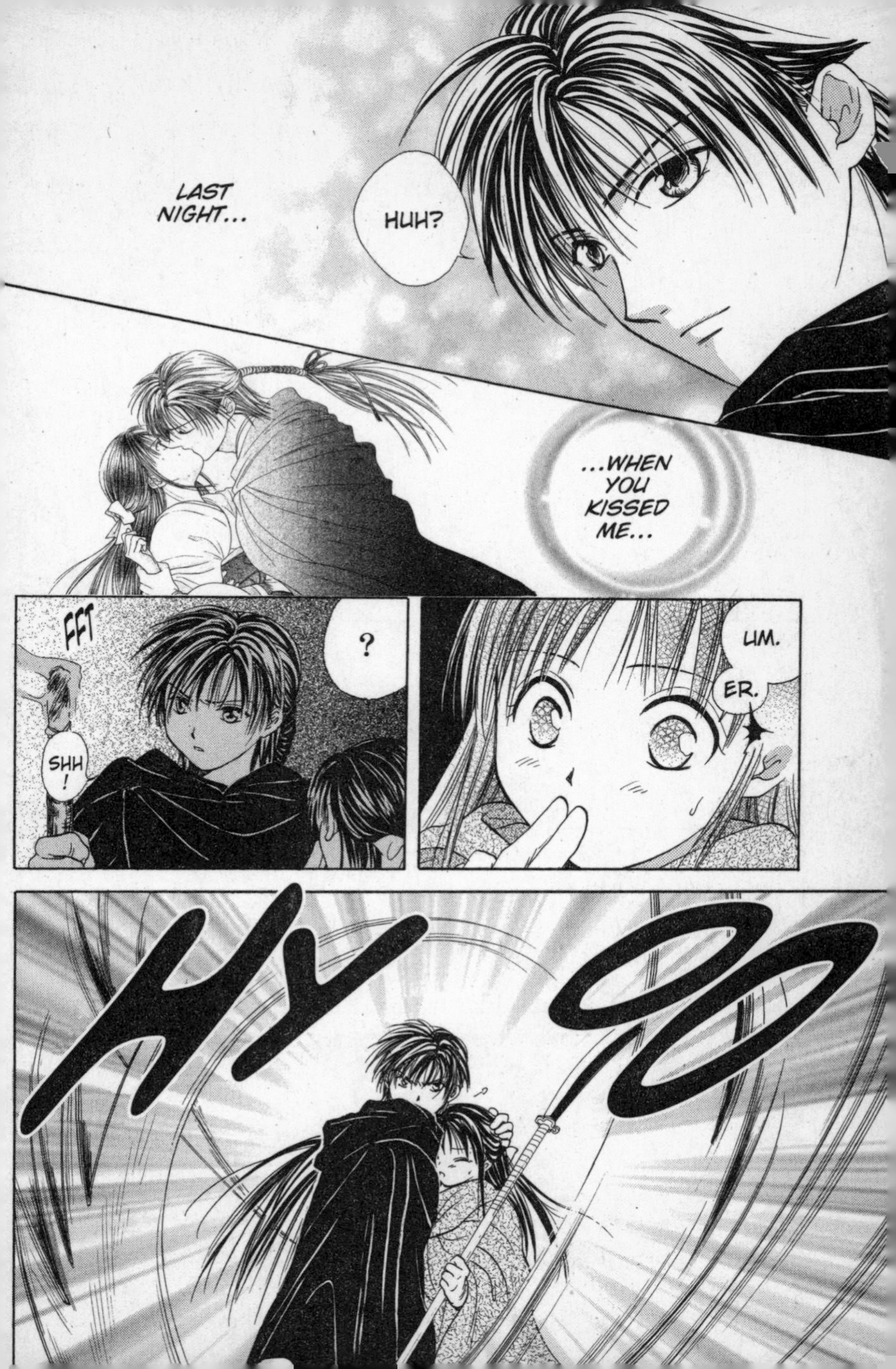
HUH?
LAST NIGHT...
...WHEN YOU KISSED ME...
UM.
ER.
?
FFT
SHH!
HYOO

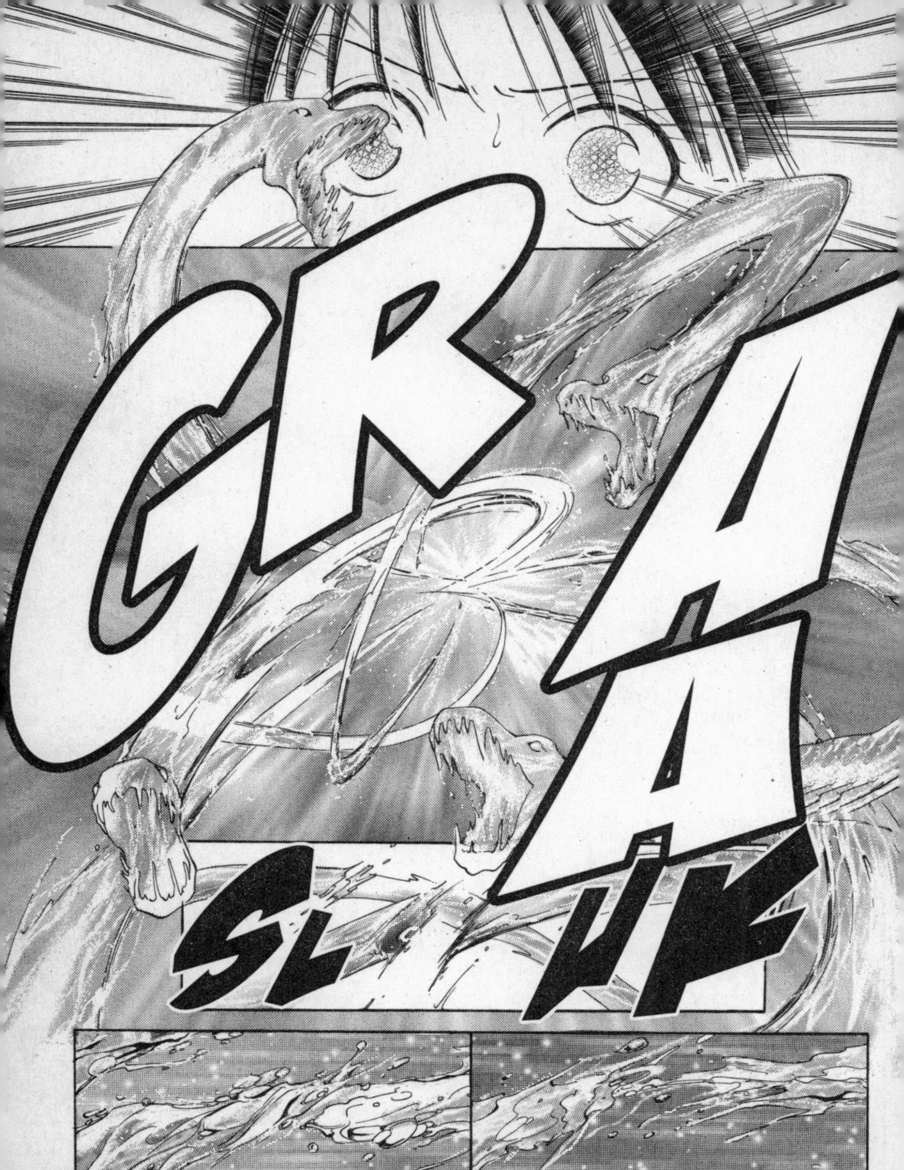
CRAA
SL

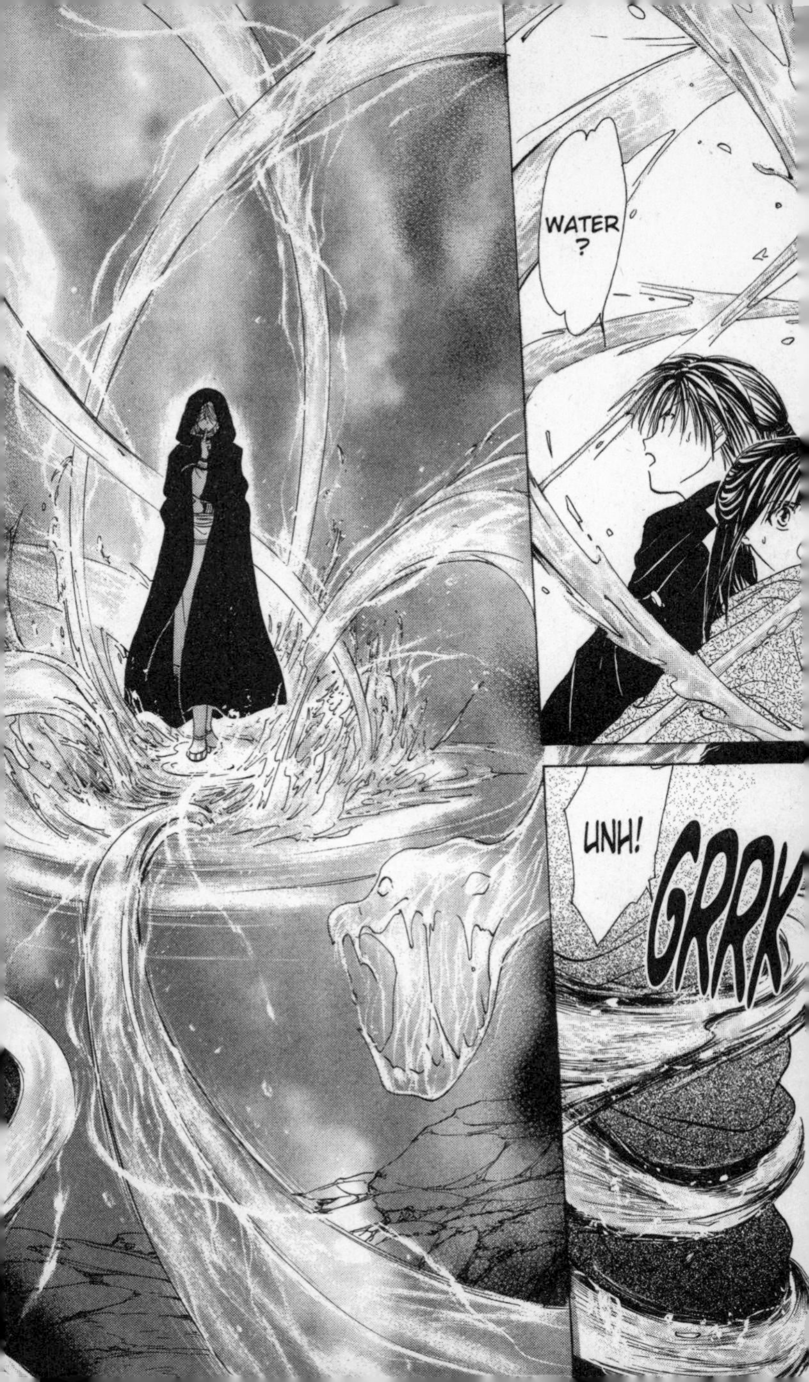
WATER ?
UNH!
GRRK

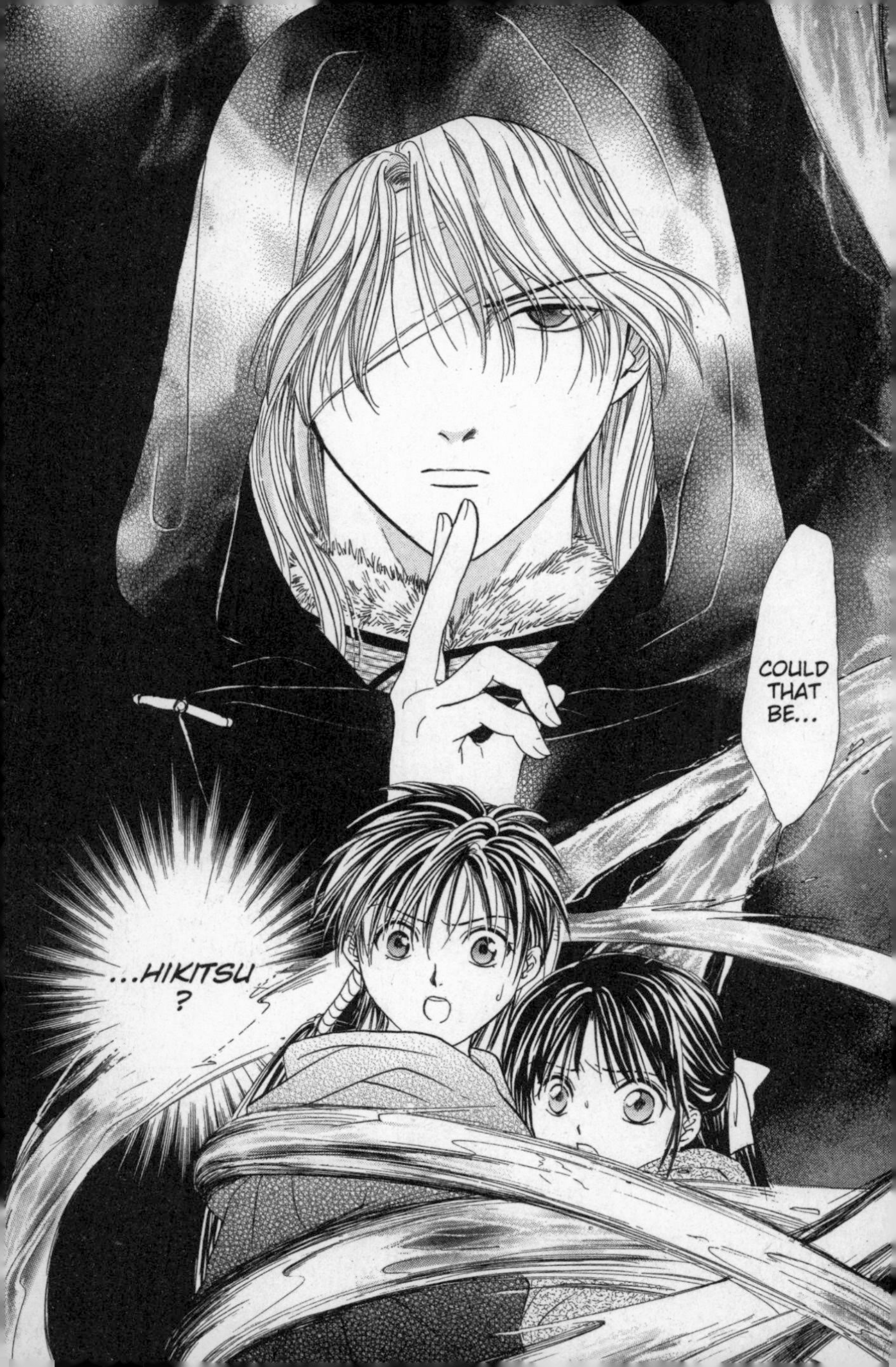
COULD THAT BE...
...HIKITSU ?

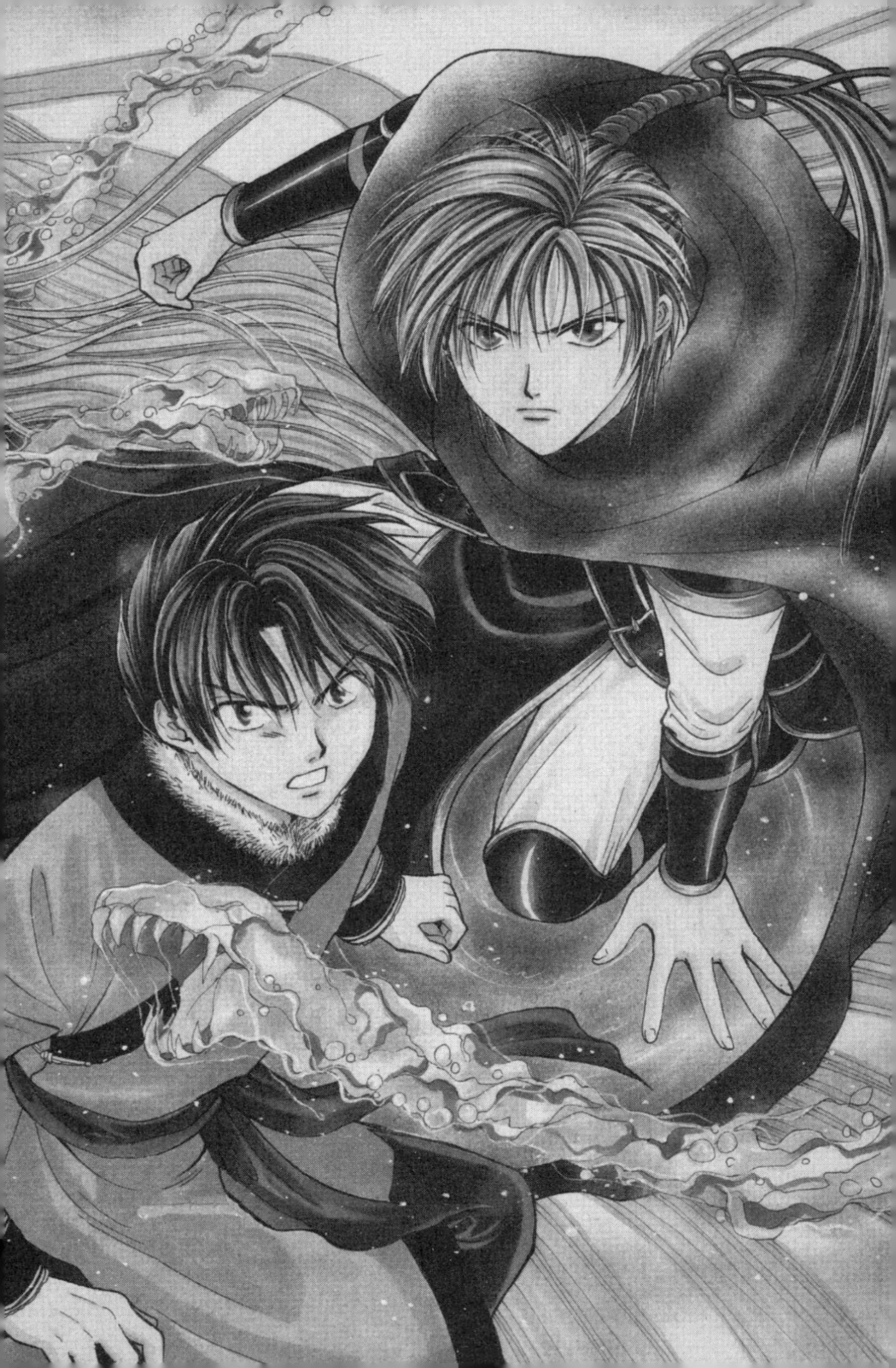

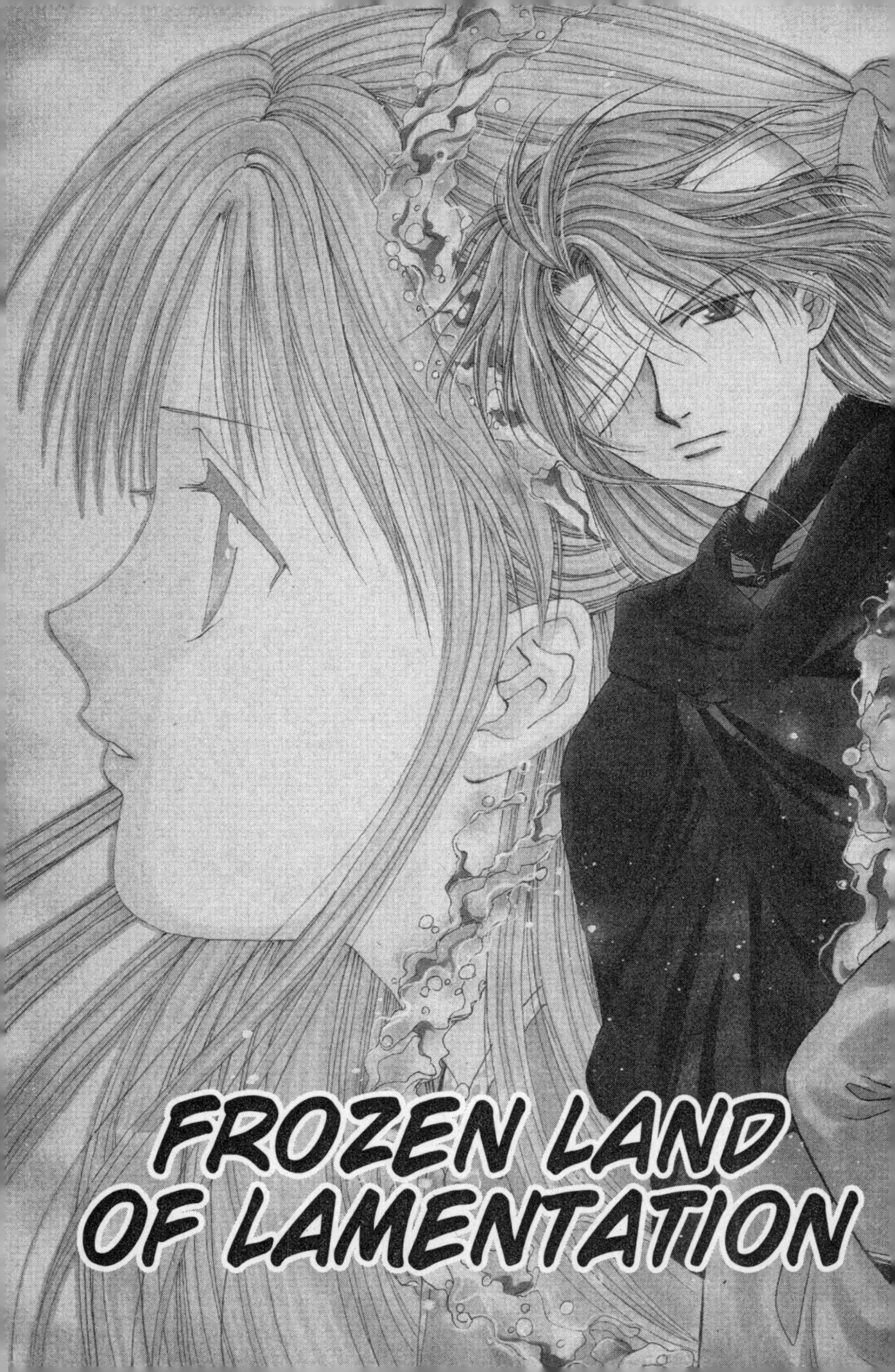
FROZEN LAND
OF LAMENTATION

Hello! Here we are at Volume 4! Finally.

The magazine *Fushigi Yugi: Perfect World* is now up to its fifth issue, all thanks to your support. We did a character popularity poll in the third issue, and we have the results! Limdo (Uruki) won by a mile. I guess you can't beat the popularity of the leading man.

Personally? Of **course** I like him. 😊 It's cute how reticent he is. Heh heh. Or maybe he's just an easy love interest to draw. With Limdo comes Soren. Yes, **I love stories about the master-servant relationship.** I vowed to add a servant this time, since Limdo is a prince and all! Yes, I have lots of fun with this. Soren is 28 years old, by the way. So he's older than Limdo.

I find the profound trust between a master and his servant to be very inspiring.

Samwise Gamgee, you're awesome!

The same goes for teachers and disciples. Limdo and Soren are master and servant, brothers, and good friends all at once. I want a relationship like that. (People in real life can't be trusted so easily. △) It's harder for women. No, that's not true. I have good friends. But that perfect relationship is something to admire and fantasize about. I mean...Soren has led a vagabond life since he was 12, all for Limdo's sake. There's been so much sacrifice. 😢 He couldn't even get married. If only Limdo were a real woman. Uh-oh! **Takiko, work harder!**

Speaking of working harder: Tomite! Actually, Takiko is more like a big sister to him. He's that way with Limdo, too. Tomite feels a bit of fondness for Takiko. Limdo keeps stealing the good scenes, but I like Tomite, too. He's easy to draw. But maybe he's not cut out for a romantic role. (I'm sorry. △) And that's **not** because of Hikitsu's presence, just so you know. Well, I was never really a big fan of romance. I'll keep it to a minimum this time (even though that's a no-no for shojo manga).

I want Tomite to focus on his path to becoming a man. He tries to be competent and strong. Hikitsu understands that. He's his honorary big brother, after all. Limdo & Soren may be similar in some ways.

Here we go again!

Men are perpetually at war with the world. Hmm...Tomite might be the boy I'd want to be if I were male.

I thought people would rag on me △ about how he seems so different from the Tomite who appeared in the first FY, but people have been nice about it. 😊 The ghost that Miaka and the Suzaku Warriors met was of a fully mature Tomite. But I'm glad he has his current personality. He was so full of life in the drama CD, and his voice was perfect: Mr. Tetsuya Iwanaga, the same guy who played him in the FY anime series. He also did the voices for Amiboshi and Suboshi in the previous CD. Seiryu Celestial Warriors, and now a Genbu Celestial Warrior. :) Actually, people were impatient to see Hikitsu show up. △ It's hard to imagine Tomite without Hikitsu. I tried to reflect that in the cover of *Perfect World* issue 3. And I'm glad Hikitsu showed up just in time to be included in the videogame. 😊

Yes, there's a videogame! Good thing I own a PS2. △ The CG artwork is stunning. I feasted my eyes on the bonus calendar that came with it. :) It's so nice that the characters are fully voiced. Please give it a try! 😊 And speaking of voices, another drama CD featuring the main story will be out soon as well!

They've committed to making a third one, too!

All this is possible through your support! Sniff. Thank you for all your letters. They give me the will to go on! Please be on the lookout for Volume 5.

Personally, I want to "befriend" Ziyi in the game. :)

See you in the next volume!!

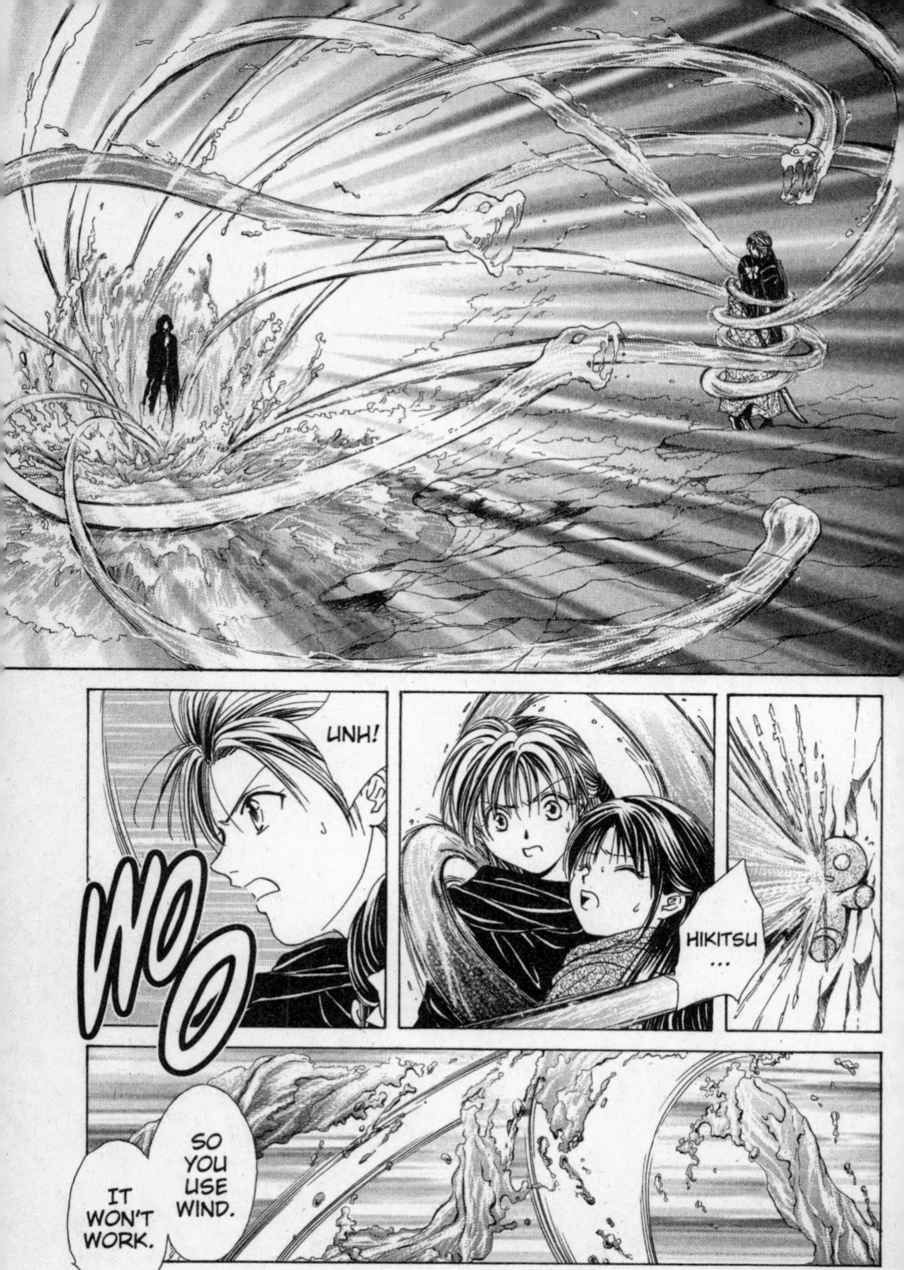
HIKITSU ...
UNH!
WOO
SO YOU USE WIND.
IT WON'T WORK.

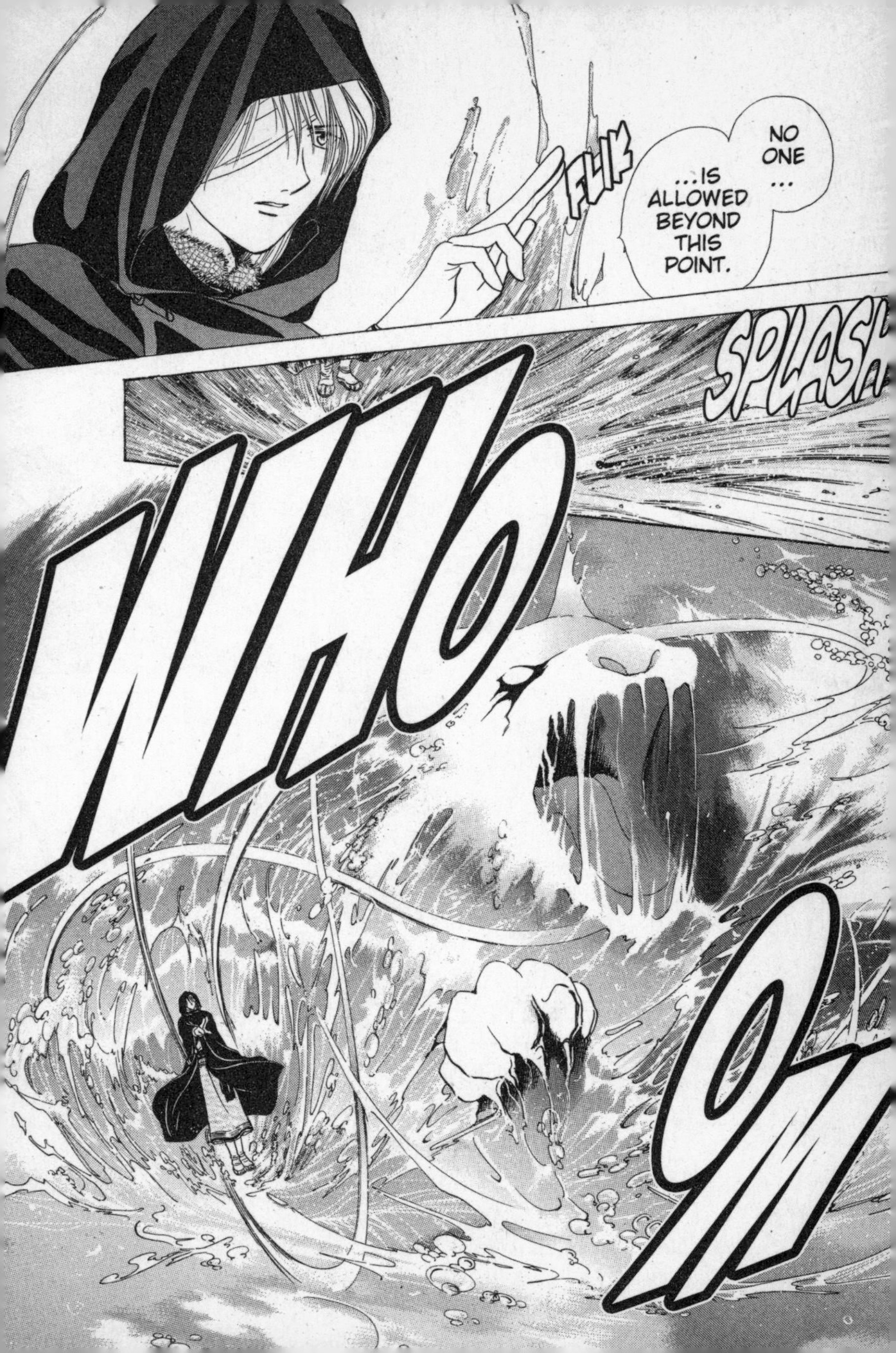
FLIK
NO ONE...
...IS ALLOWED BEYOND THIS POINT.
SPLASH

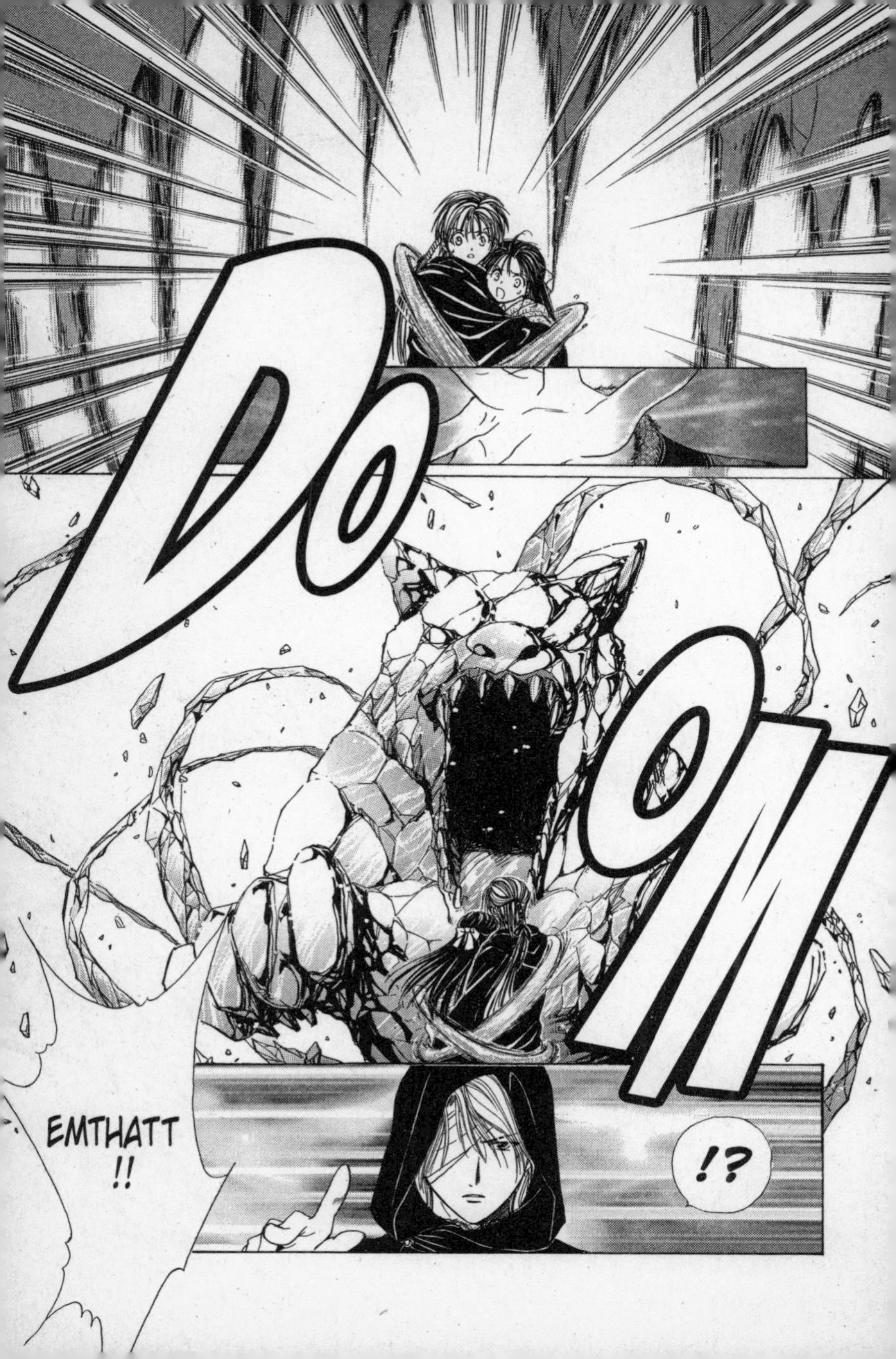
DOOM
!?
EMTHATT !!

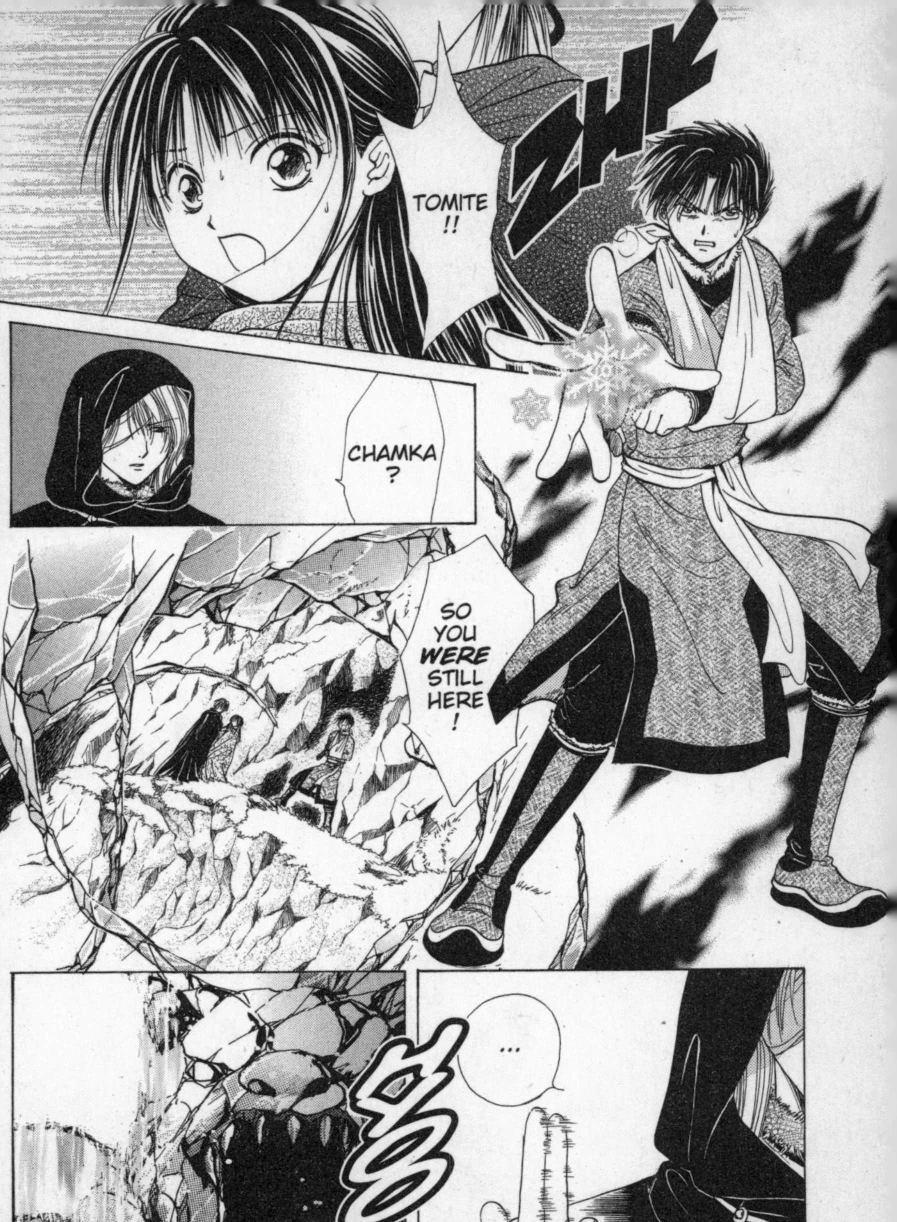
ZHK
TOMITE !!
CHAMKA ?
SO YOU WERE STILL HERE !
...

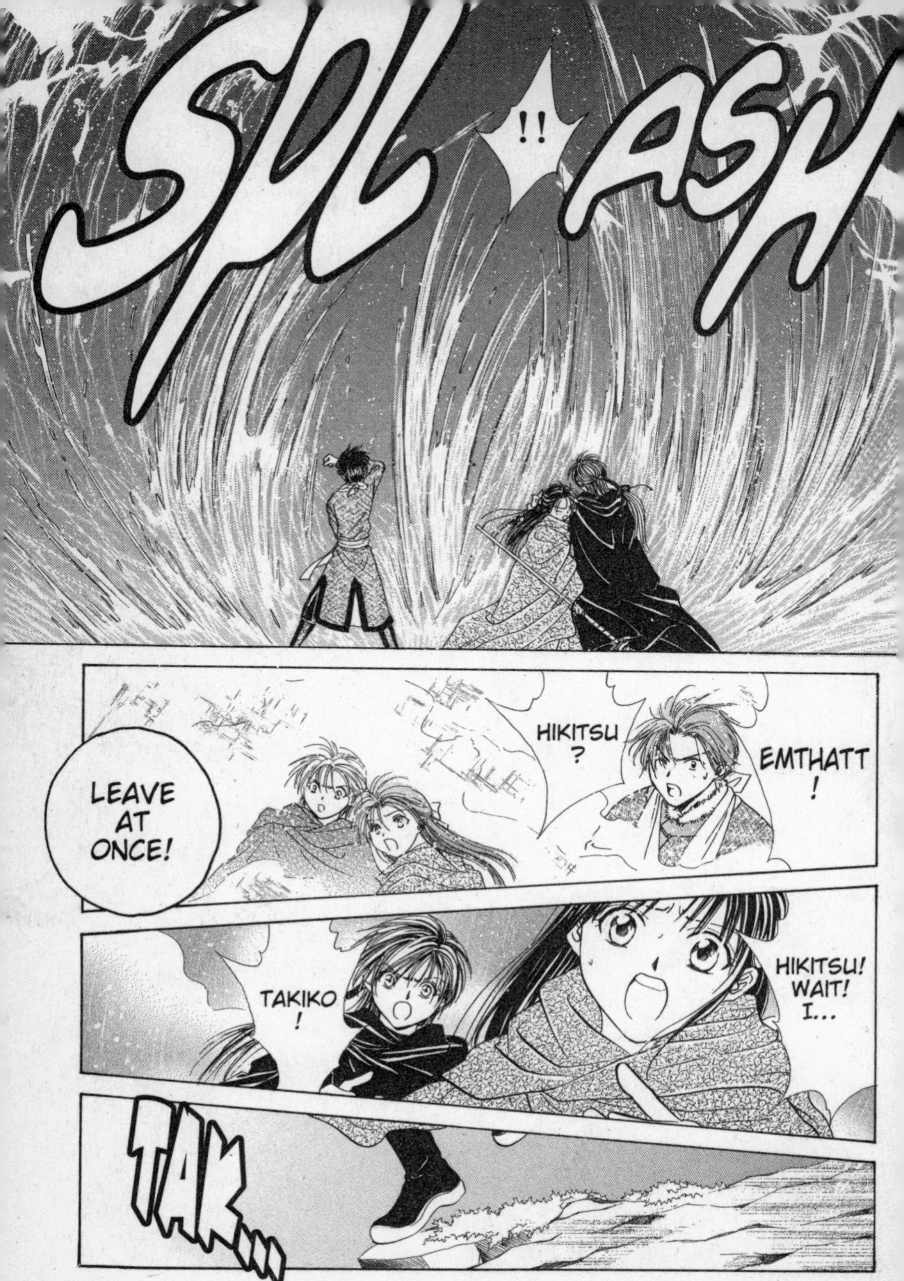
SPLASH
!!
EMTHATT!
HIKITSU?
LEAVE AT ONCE!
HIKITSU! WAIT! I...
TAKIKO!
TAK...

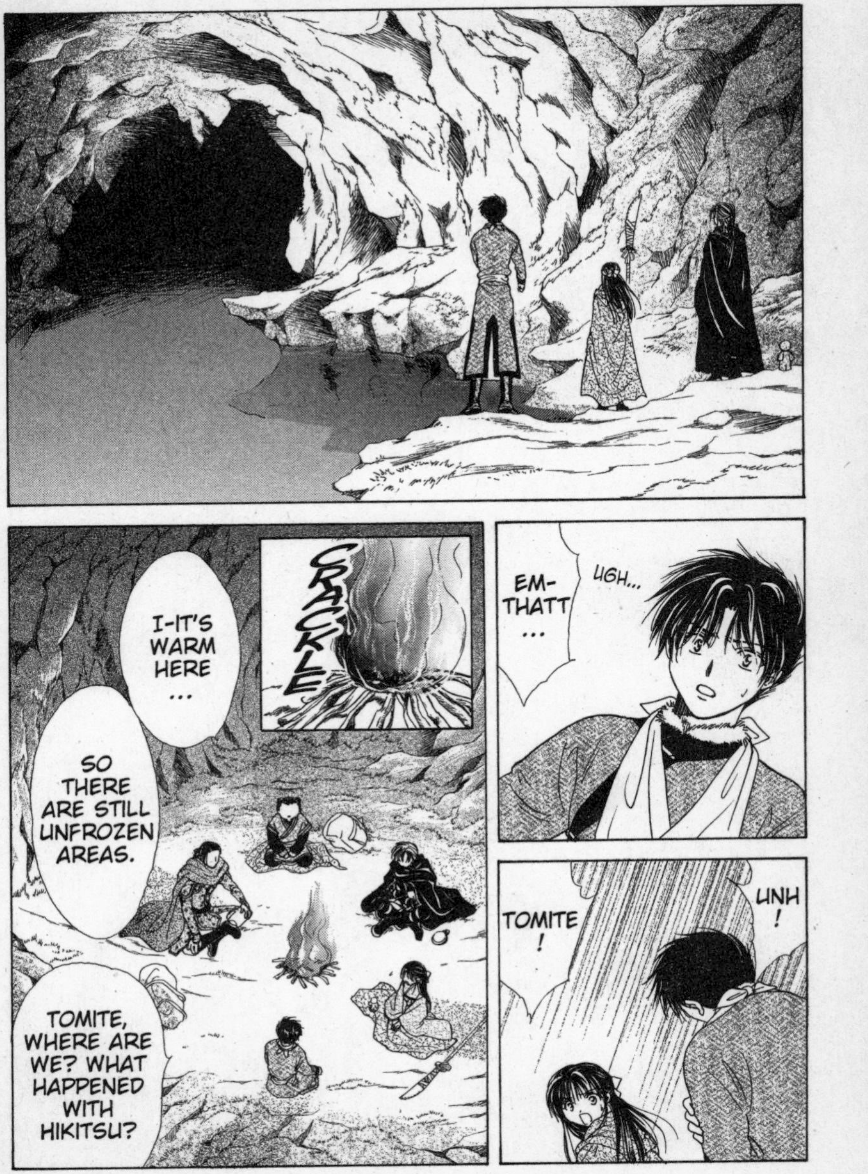
UGH...
EM-THATT ...
UNH!
TOMITE!
CRACKLE
I-IT'S WARM HERE ...
SO THERE ARE STILL UNFROZEN AREAS.
TOMITE, WHERE ARE WE? WHAT HAPPENED WITH HIKITSU?

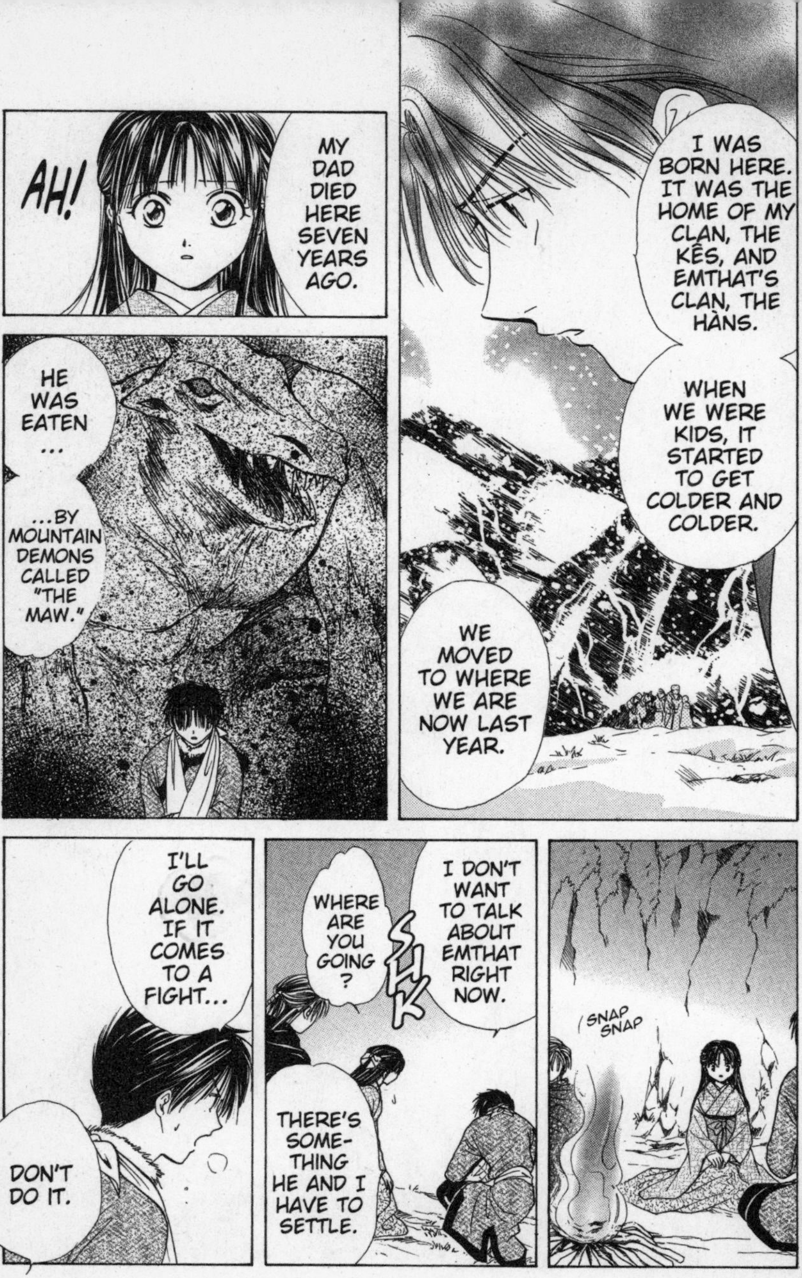
I WAS BORN HERE. IT WAS THE HOME OF MY CLAN, THE KÊS, AND EMTHAT'S CLAN, THE HÀNS.
WHEN WE WERE KIDS, IT STARTED TO GET COLDER AND COLDER.
WE MOVED TO WHERE WE ARE NOW LAST YEAR.
AH!
MY DAD DIED HERE SEVEN YEARS AGO.
HE WAS EATEN ...
...BY MOUNTAIN DEMONS CALLED "THE MAW."
SNAP SNAP
I DON'T WANT TO TALK ABOUT EMTHAT RIGHT NOW.
WHERE ARE YOU GOING?
SHK
THERE'S SOME-THING HE AND I HAVE TO SETTLE.
I'LL GO ALONE. IF IT COMES TO A FIGHT...
DON'T DO IT.

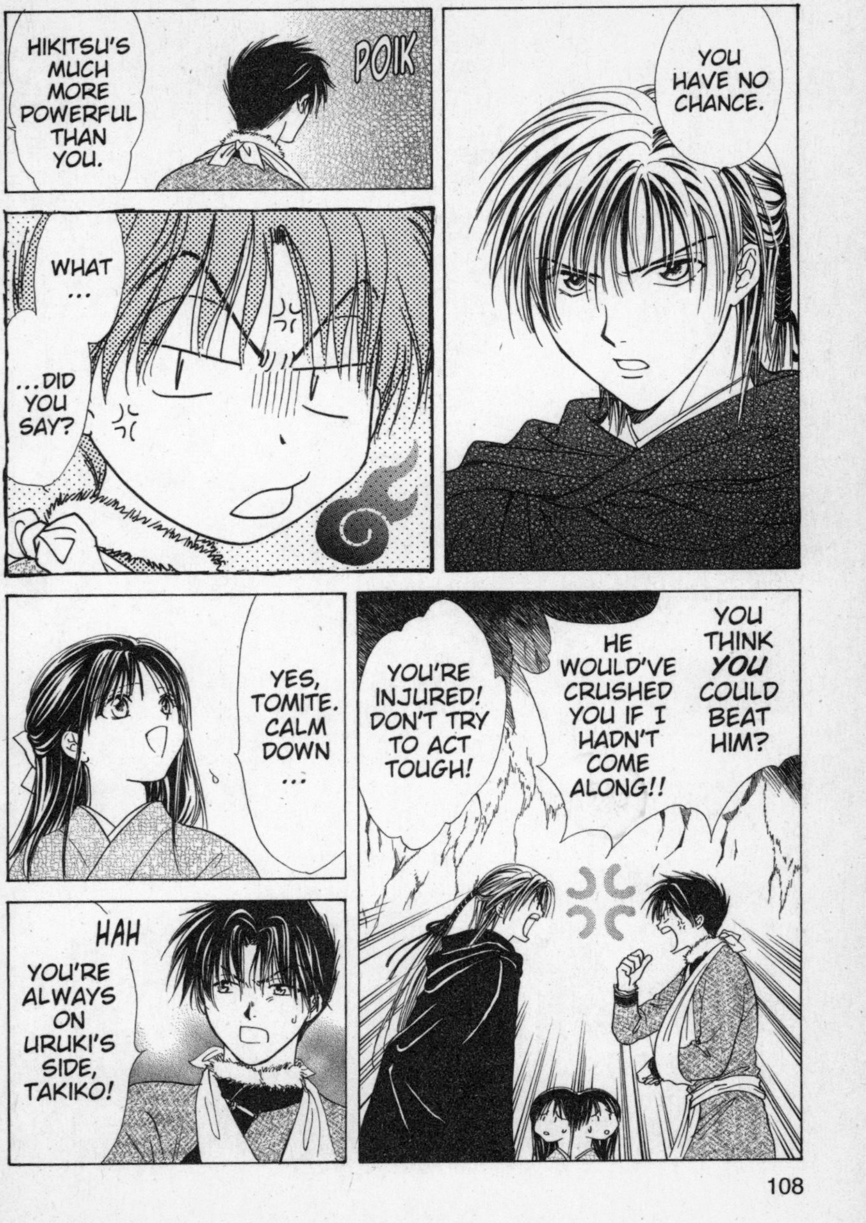
YOU HAVE NO CHANCE.
HIKITSU'S MUCH MORE POWERFUL THAN YOU.
POIK
WHAT ...
...DID YOU SAY?
YOU THINK *YOU* COULD BEAT HIM?
HE WOULD'VE CRUSHED YOU IF I HADN'T COME ALONG!!
YOU'RE INJURED! DON'T TRY TO ACT TOUGH!
YES, TOMITE. CALM DOWN ...
HAH
YOU'RE ALWAYS ON URUKI'S SIDE, TAKIKO!

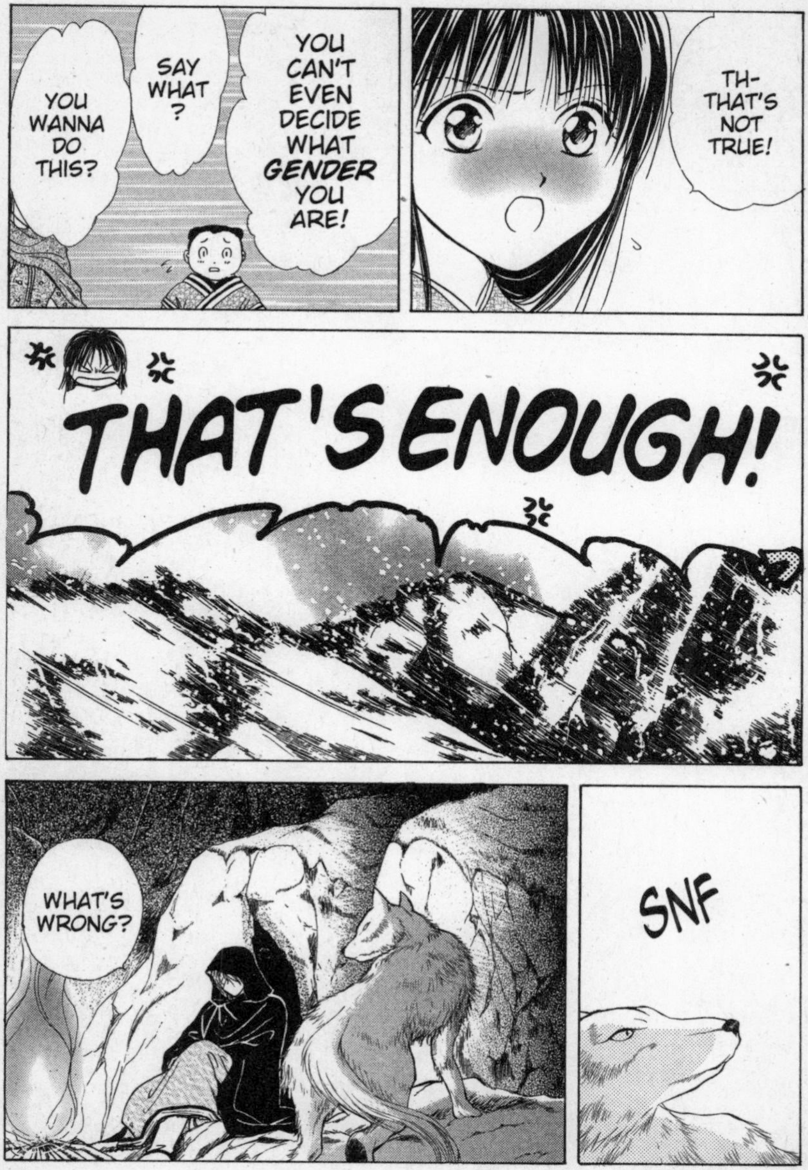
TH- THAT'S NOT TRUE!
YOU CAN'T EVEN DECIDE WHAT GENDER YOU ARE!
SAY WHAT?
YOU WANNA DO THIS?
THAT'S ENOUGH!
SNF
WHAT'S WRONG?

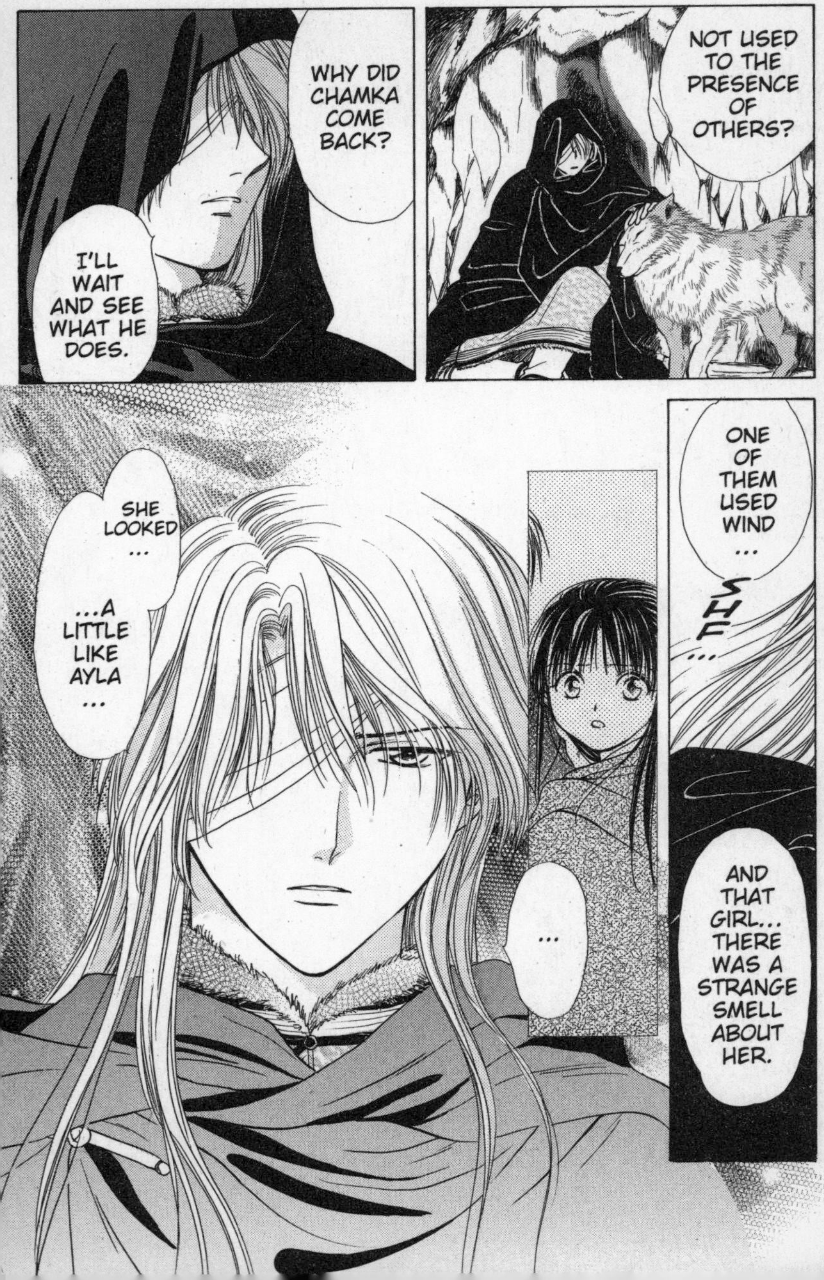
NOT USED TO THE PRESENCE OF OTHERS?
WHY DID CHAMKA COME BACK?
I'LL WAIT AND SEE WHAT HE DOES.
ONE OF THEM USED WIND...
SHF...
AND THAT GIRL... THERE WAS A STRANGE SMELL ABOUT HER.
...
SHE LOOKED...
...A LITTLE LIKE AYLA...

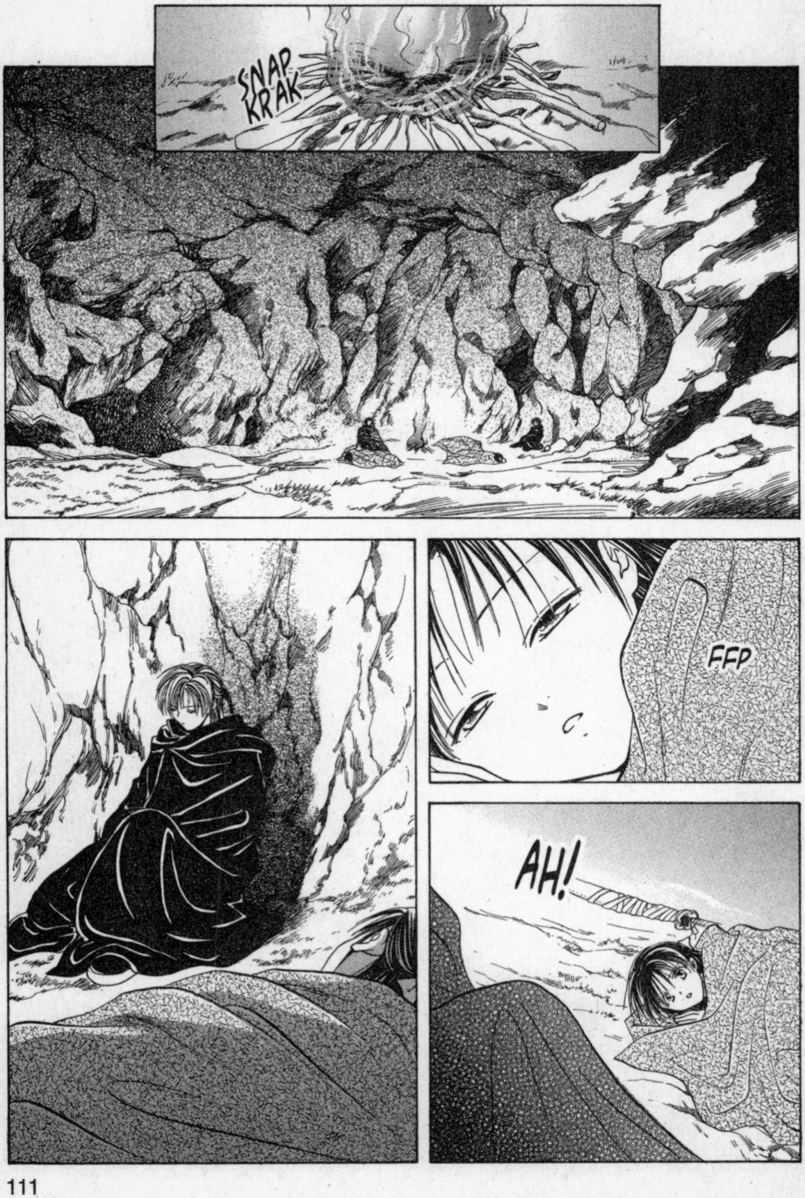
SNAP
KRAK
FFP
AH!

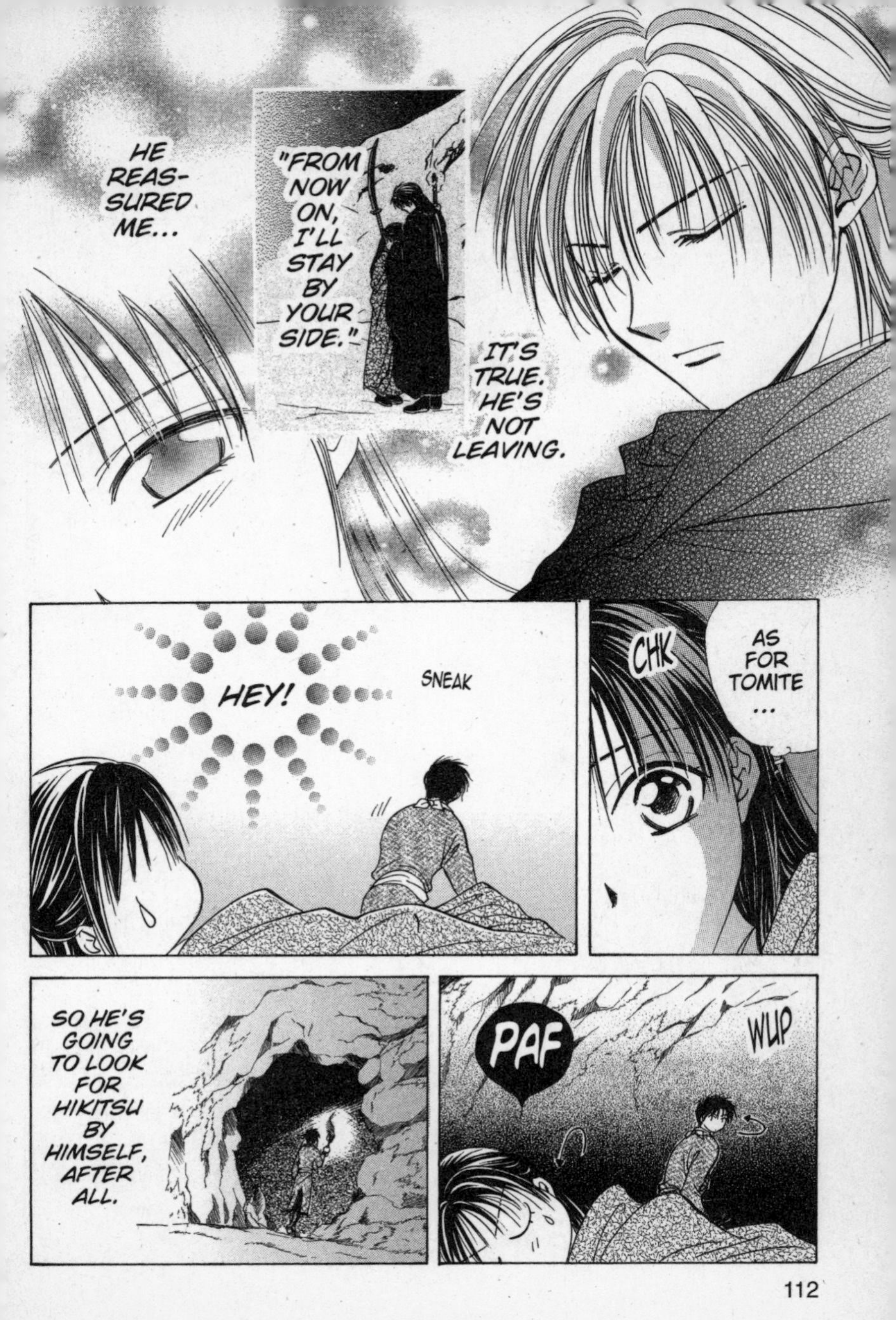
HE REASSURED ME...
"FROM NOW ON, I'LL STAY BY YOUR SIDE."
IT'S TRUE. HE'S NOT LEAVING.
CHK
AS FOR TOMITE...
SNEAK
HEY!
WUP
PAF
SO HE'S GOING TO LOOK FOR HIKITSU BY HIMSELF, AFTER ALL.

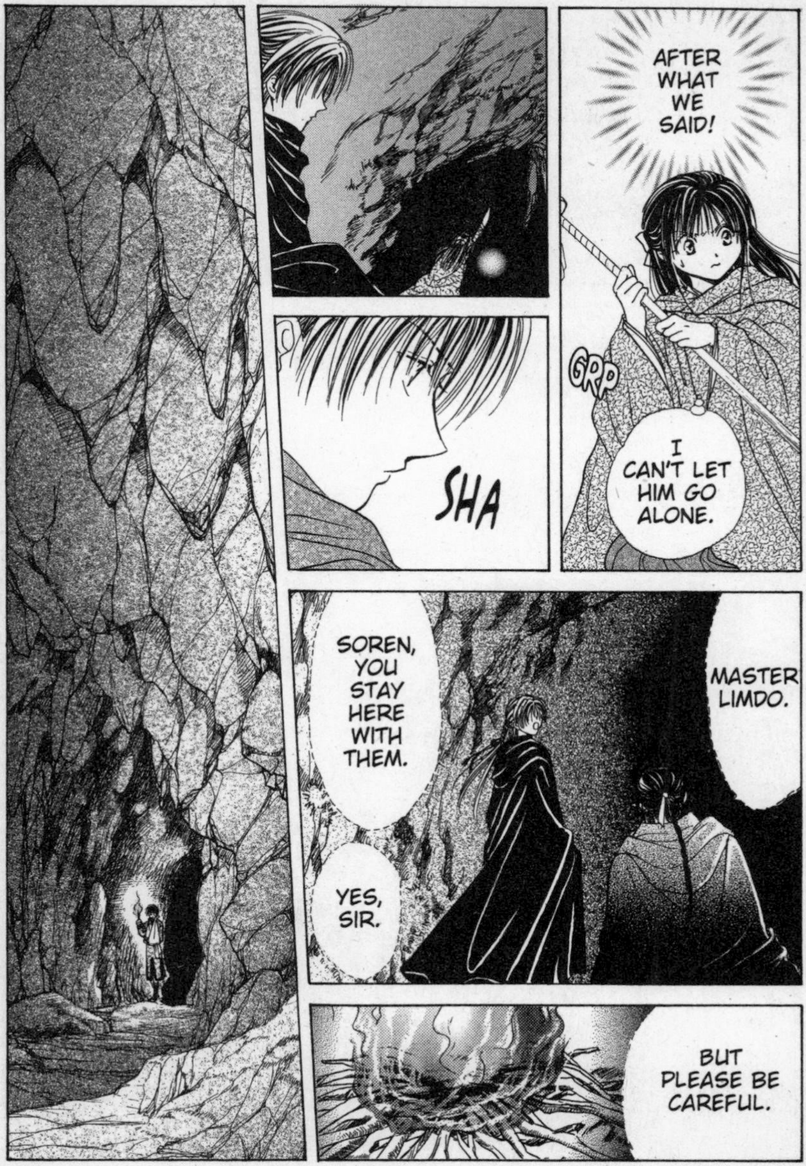
AFTER WHAT WE SAID!
GRP
I CAN'T LET HIM GO ALONE.
SHA
MASTER LIMDO.
SOREN, YOU STAY HERE WITH THEM.
YES, SIR.
BUT PLEASE BE CAREFUL.

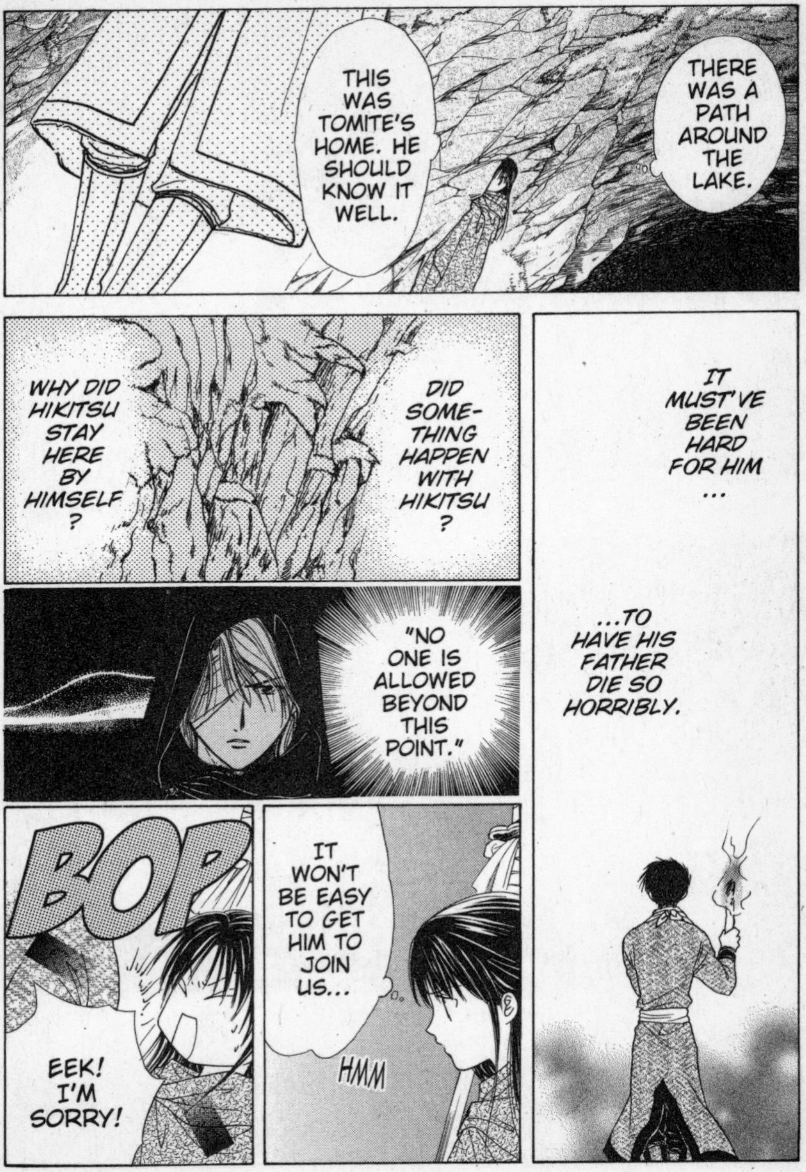
THERE WAS A PATH AROUND THE LAKE.
THIS WAS TOMITE'S HOME. HE SHOULD KNOW IT WELL.
IT MUST'VE BEEN HARD FOR HIM...
...TO HAVE HIS FATHER DIE SO HORRIBLY.
DID SOMETHING HAPPEN WITH HIKITSU?
WHY DID HIKITSU STAY HERE BY HIMSELF?
"NO ONE IS ALLOWED BEYOND THIS POINT."
IT WON'T BE EASY TO GET HIM TO JOIN US...
HMM
BOP
EEK! I'M SORRY!

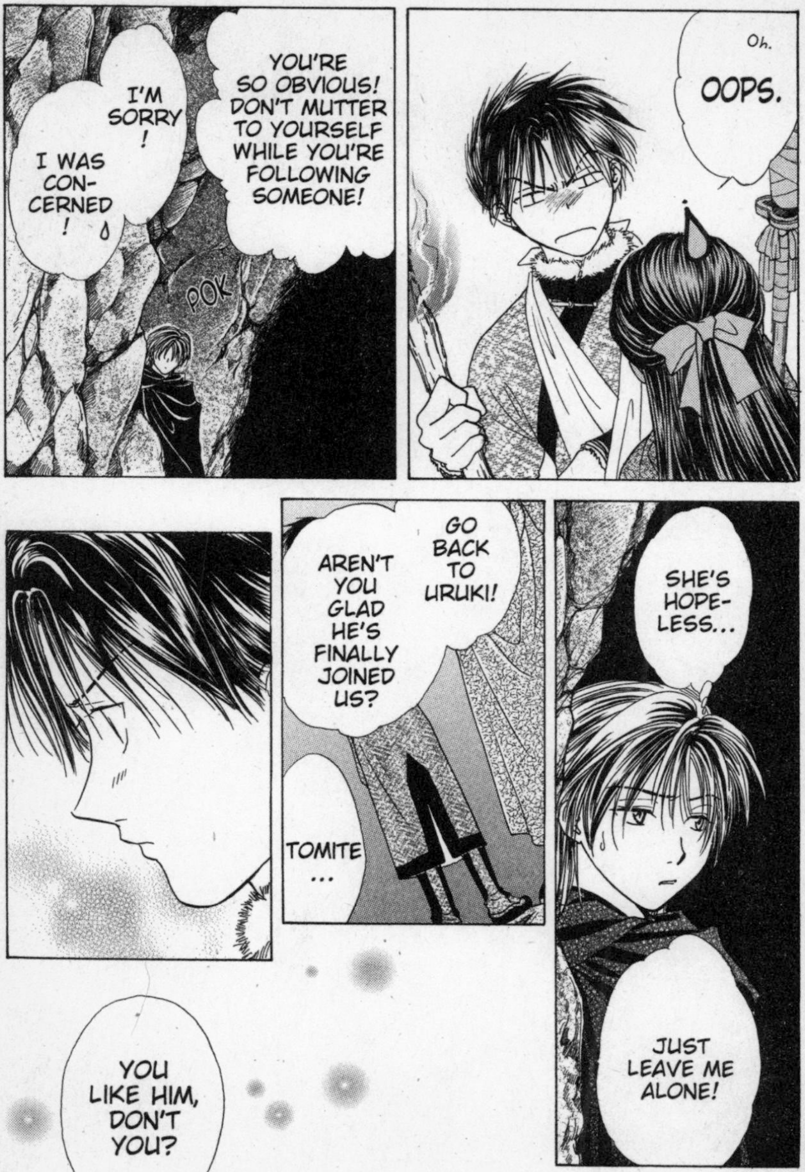
Oh.
OOPS.
YOU'RE SO OBVIOUS! DON'T MUTTER TO YOURSELF WHILE YOU'RE FOLLOWING SOMEONE!
I'M SORRY!
I WAS CON-CERNED!
POK
SHE'S HOPE-LESS...
JUST LEAVE ME ALONE!
GO BACK TO URUKI!
AREN'T YOU GLAD HE'S FINALLY JOINED US?
TOMITE...
YOU LIKE HIM, DON'T YOU?

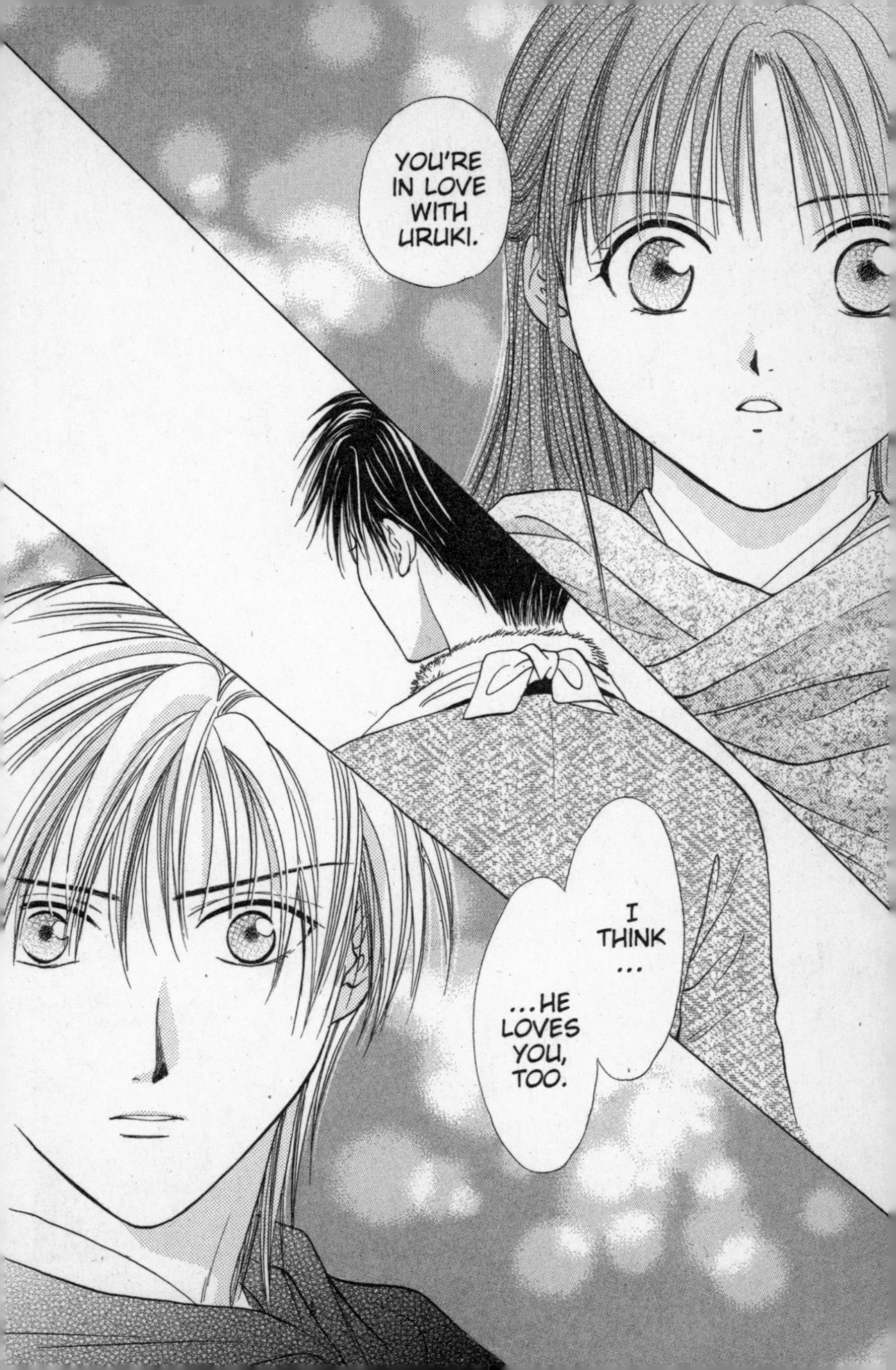
YOU'RE IN LOVE WITH URUKI.
I THINK...
...HE LOVES YOU, TOO.

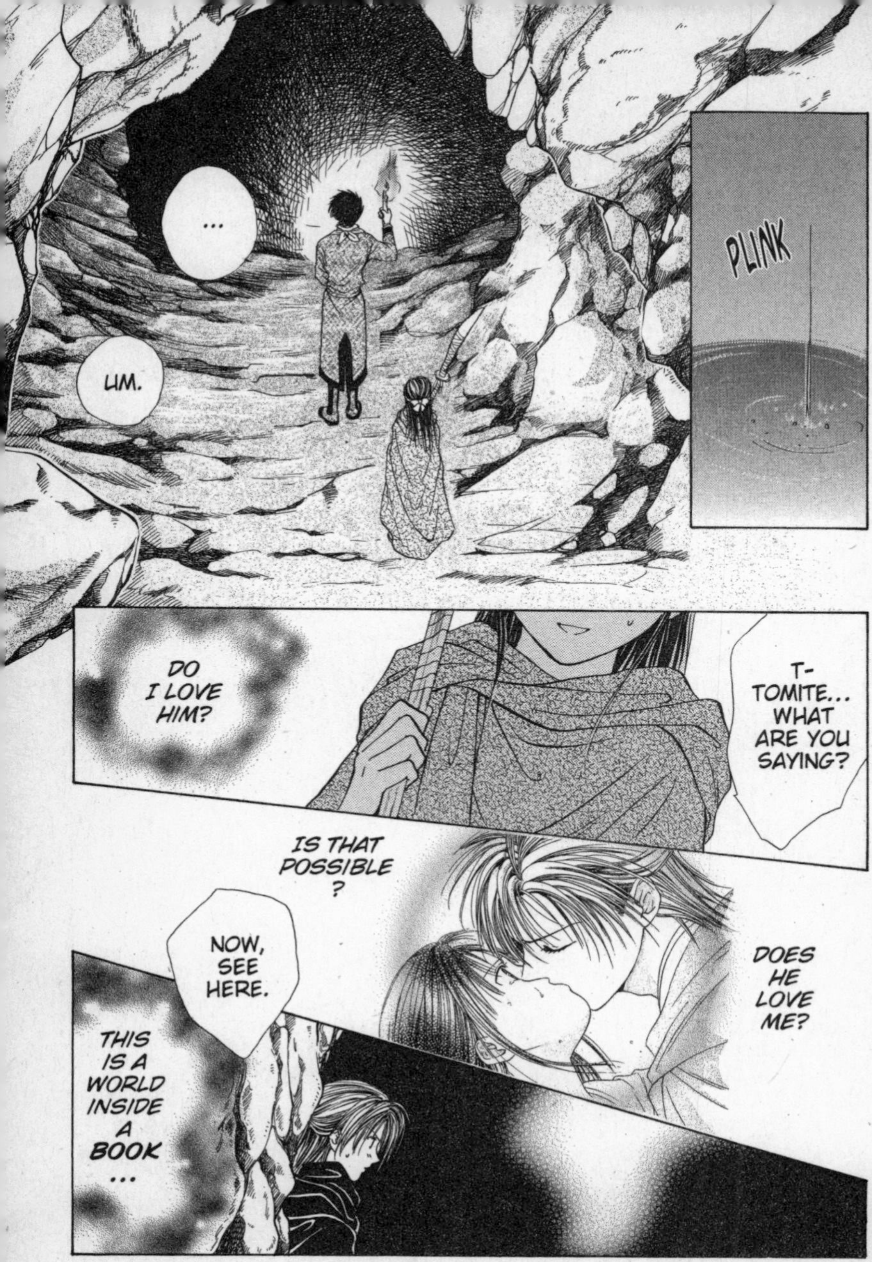
PLINK
...
UM.
T-TOMITE... WHAT ARE YOU SAYING?
DO I LOVE HIM?
DOES HE LOVE ME?
IS THAT POSSIBLE?
NOW, SEE HERE.
THIS IS A WORLD INSIDE A BOOK...

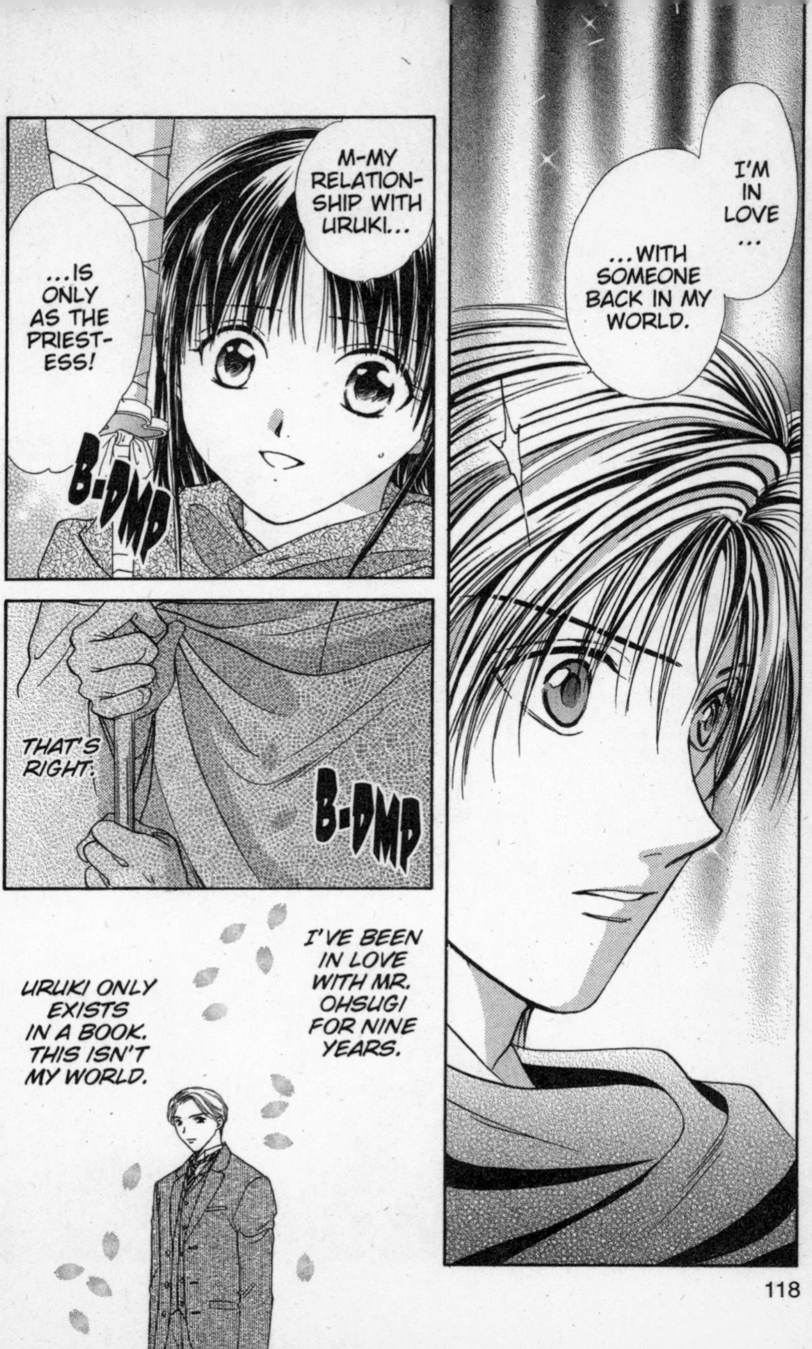
I'M IN LOVE ...
...WITH SOMEONE BACK IN MY WORLD.
M-MY RELATIONSHIP WITH URUKI...
...IS ONLY AS THE PRIESTESS!
B-DMP
B-DMP
THAT'S RIGHT.
I'VE BEEN IN LOVE WITH MR. OHSUGI FOR NINE YEARS.
URUKI ONLY EXISTS IN A BOOK. THIS ISN'T MY WORLD.

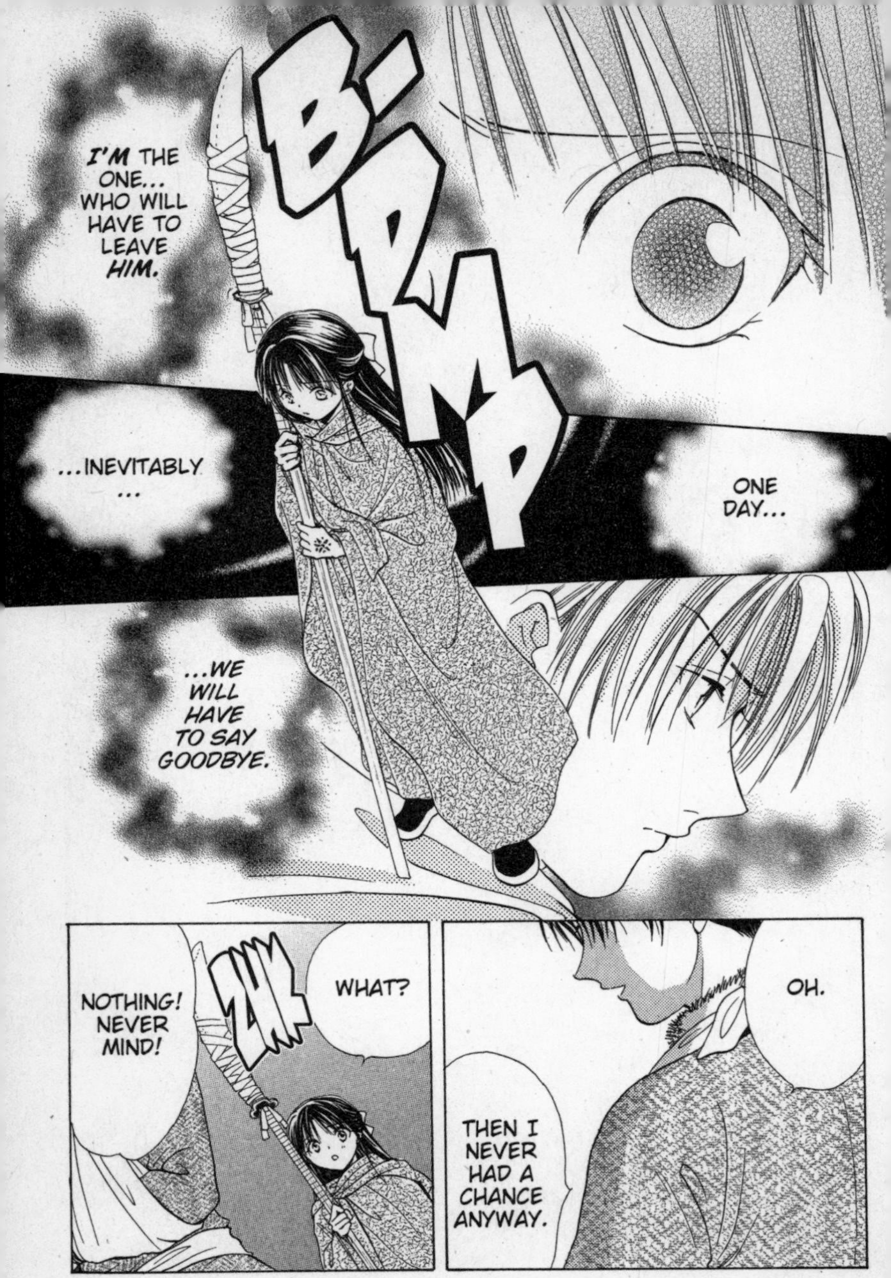
B-DMP
I'M THE ONE... WHO WILL HAVE TO LEAVE HIM.
ONE DAY...
...INEVITABLY ...
...WE WILL HAVE TO SAY GOODBYE.
OH.
THEN I NEVER HAD A CHANCE ANYWAY.
WHAT?
NOTHING! NEVER MIND!

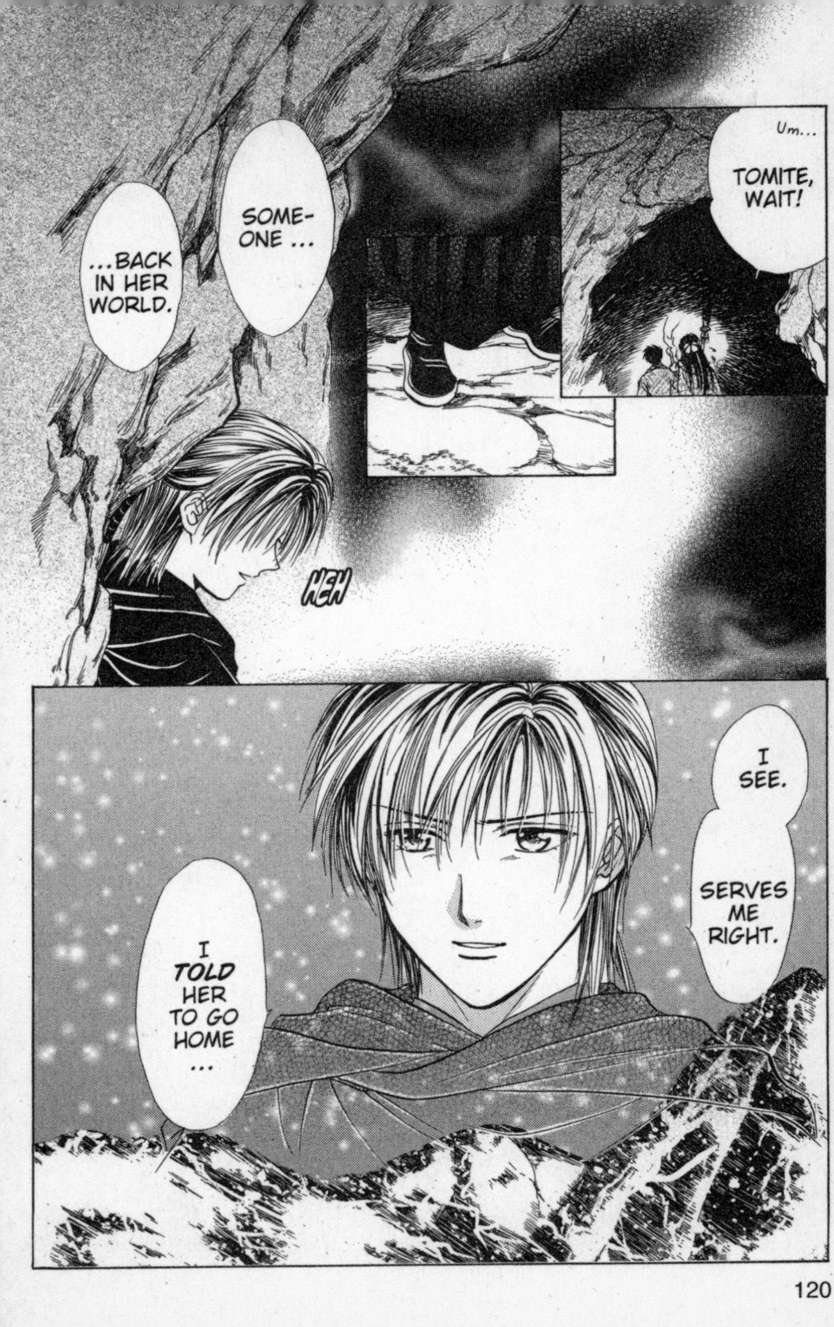
Um...
TOMITE, WAIT!
SOME-ONE ...
...BACK IN HER WORLD.
HEH
I SEE.
SERVES ME RIGHT.
I TOLD HER TO GO HOME ...

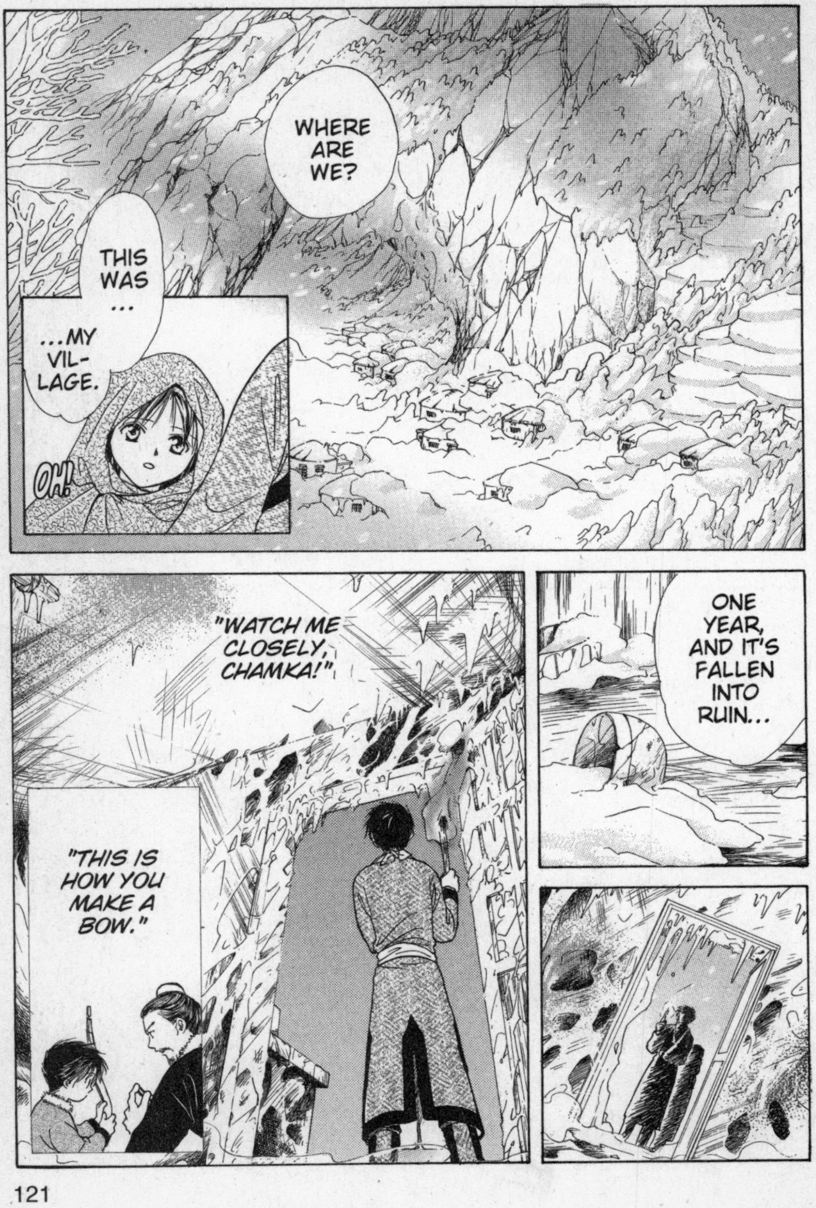
WHERE ARE WE?
THIS WAS...
...MY VIL-LAGE.
OH!
ONE YEAR, AND IT'S FALLEN INTO RUIN...
"WATCH ME CLOSELY, CHAMKA!"
"THIS IS HOW YOU MAKE A BOW."

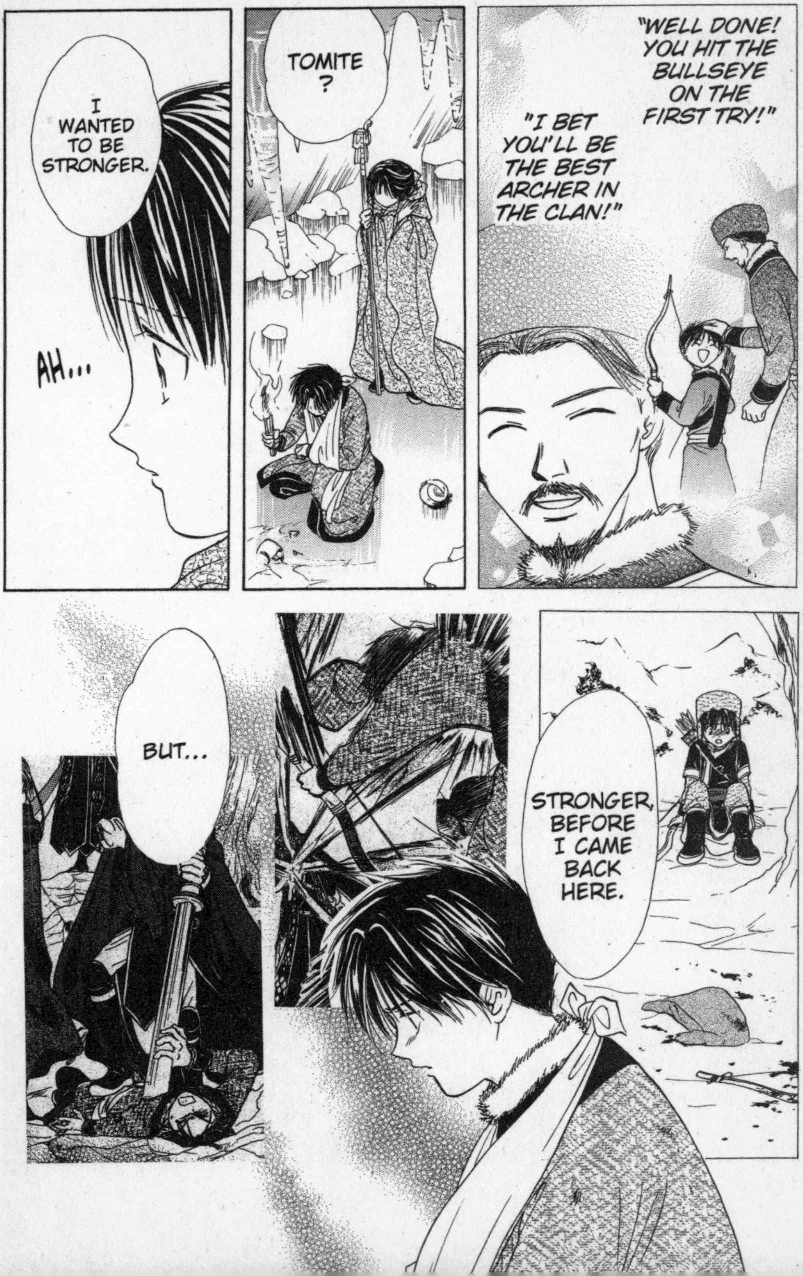
"WELL DONE! YOU HIT THE BULLSEYE ON THE FIRST TRY!"
"I BET YOU'LL BE THE BEST ARCHER IN THE CLAN!"
TOMITE ?
I WANTED TO BE STRONGER.
AH...
STRONGER, BEFORE I CAME BACK HERE.
BUT...

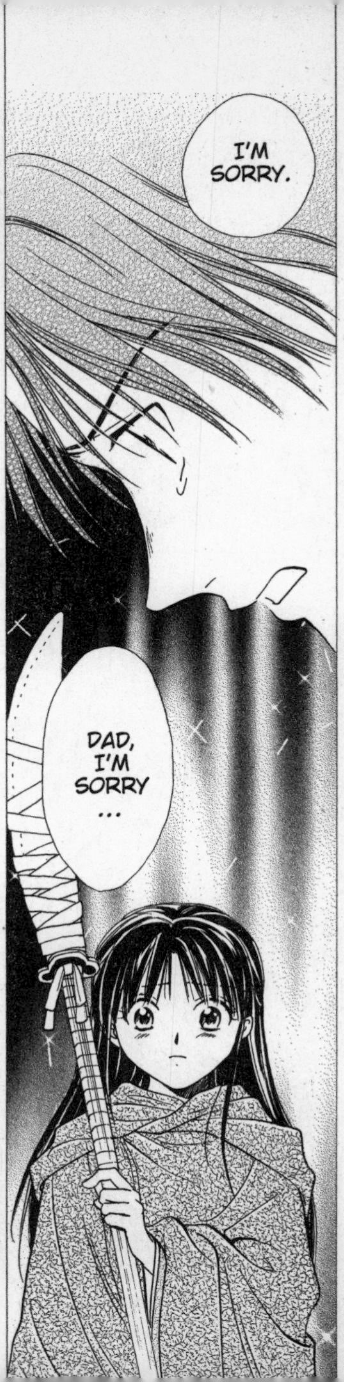
I'M SORRY.
DAD, I'M SORRY ...

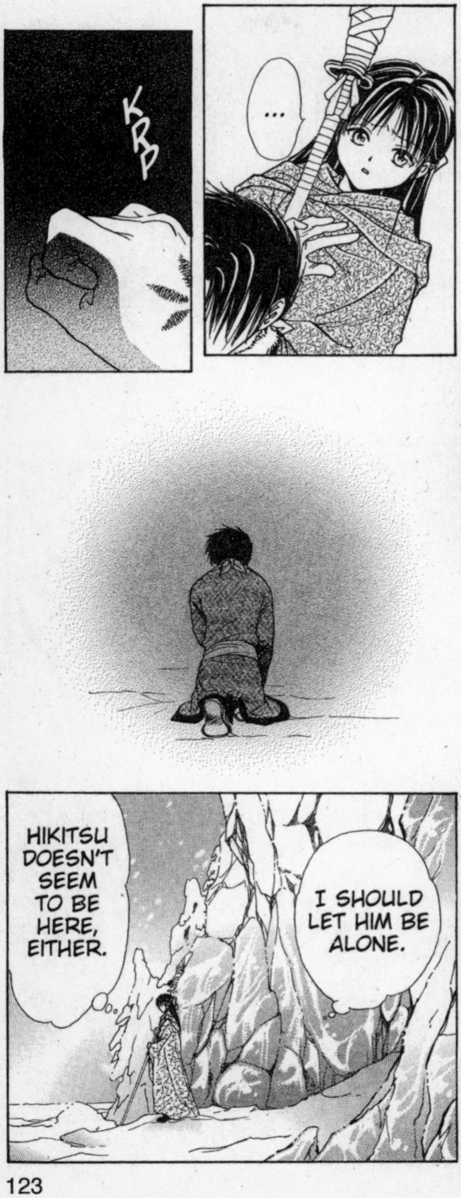
...
KRP
I SHOULD LET HIM BE ALONE.
HIKITSU DOESN'T SEEM TO BE HERE, EITHER.

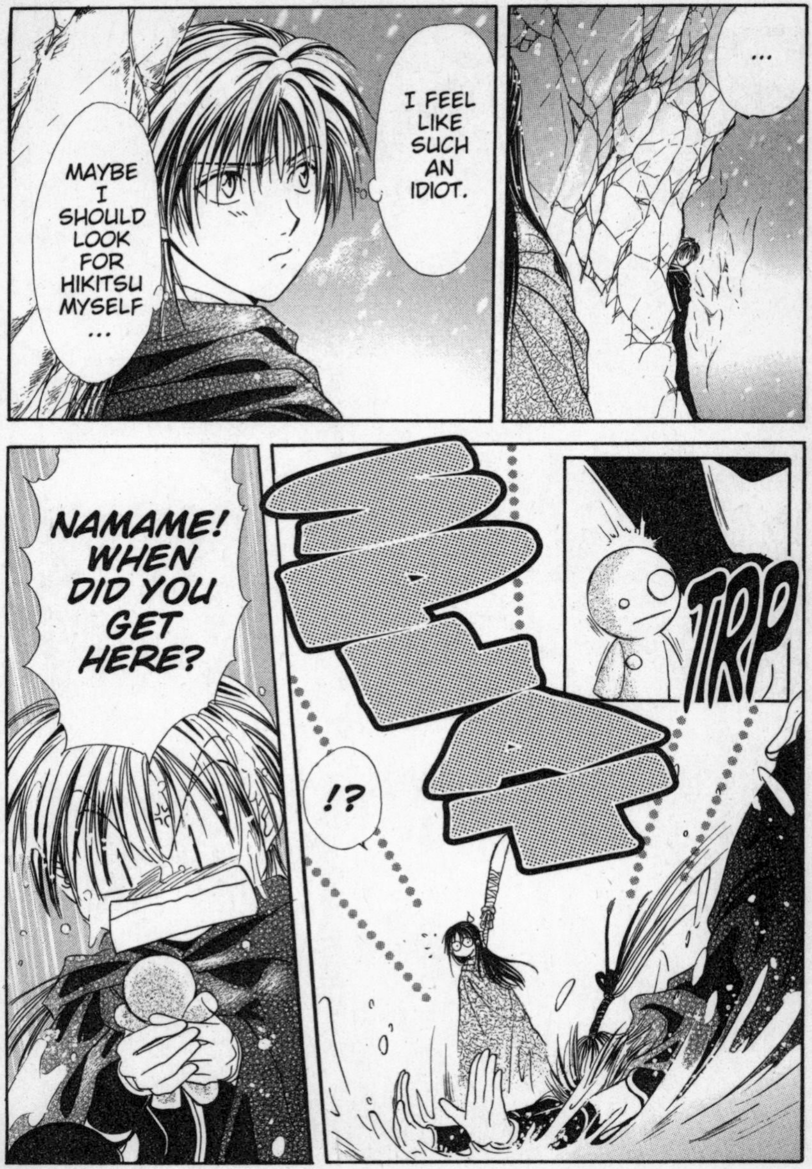
...
I FEEL LIKE SUCH AN IDIOT.
MAYBE I SHOULD LOOK FOR HIKITSU MYSELF ...
TRP
!?
NAMAME! WHEN DID YOU GET HERE?

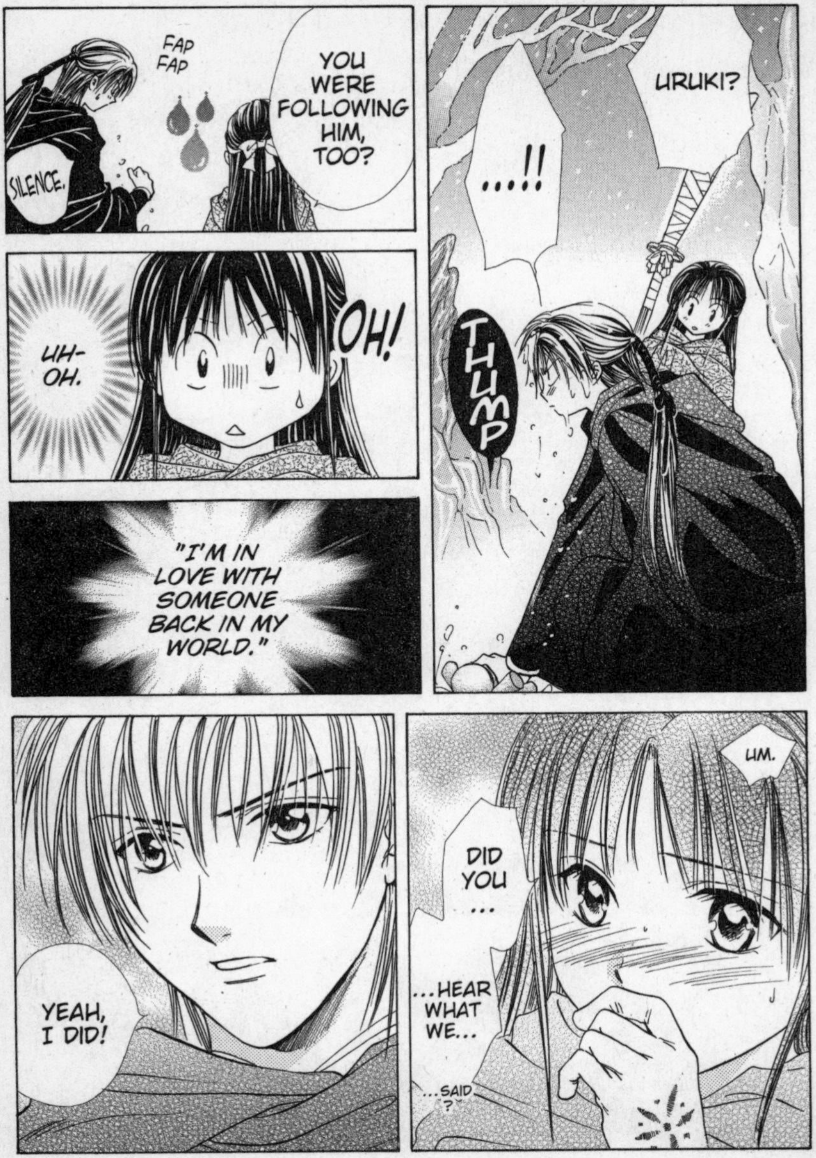
URUKI?
...!!
THUMP
YOU WERE FOLLOWING HIM, TOO?
FAP FAP
SILENCE.
OH!
UH-OH.
"I'M IN LOVE WITH SOMEONE BACK IN MY WORLD."
UM.
DID YOU ...
...HEAR WHAT WE...
...SAID?
YEAH, I DID!

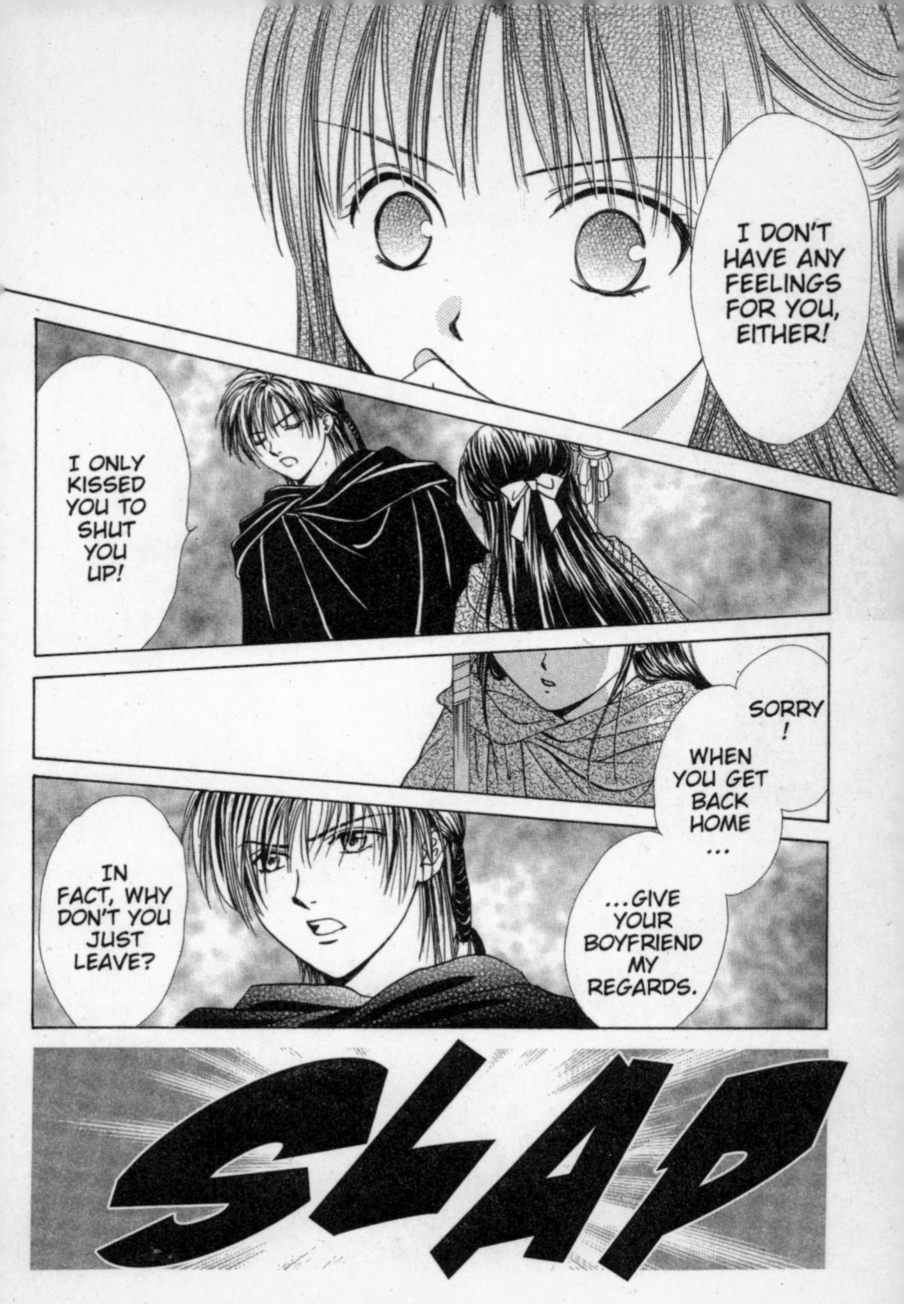
I DON'T HAVE ANY FEELINGS FOR YOU, EITHER!
I ONLY KISSED YOU TO SHUT YOU UP!
SORRY!
WHEN YOU GET BACK HOME...
...GIVE YOUR BOYFRIEND MY REGARDS.
IN FACT, WHY DON'T YOU JUST LEAVE?
SLAP

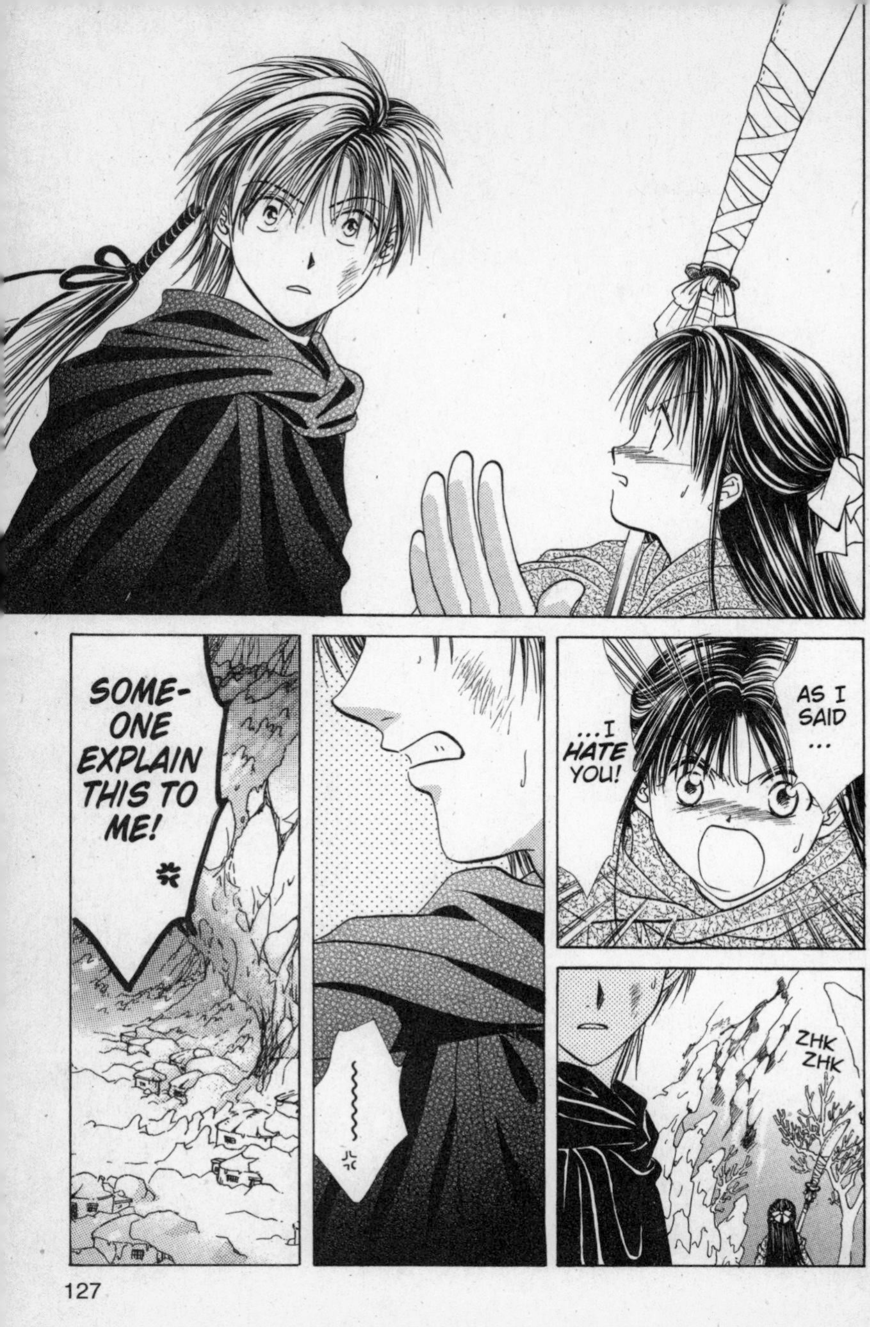
AS I SAID ...
...I HATE YOU!
ZHK ZHK
SOME-ONE EXPLAIN THIS TO ME!

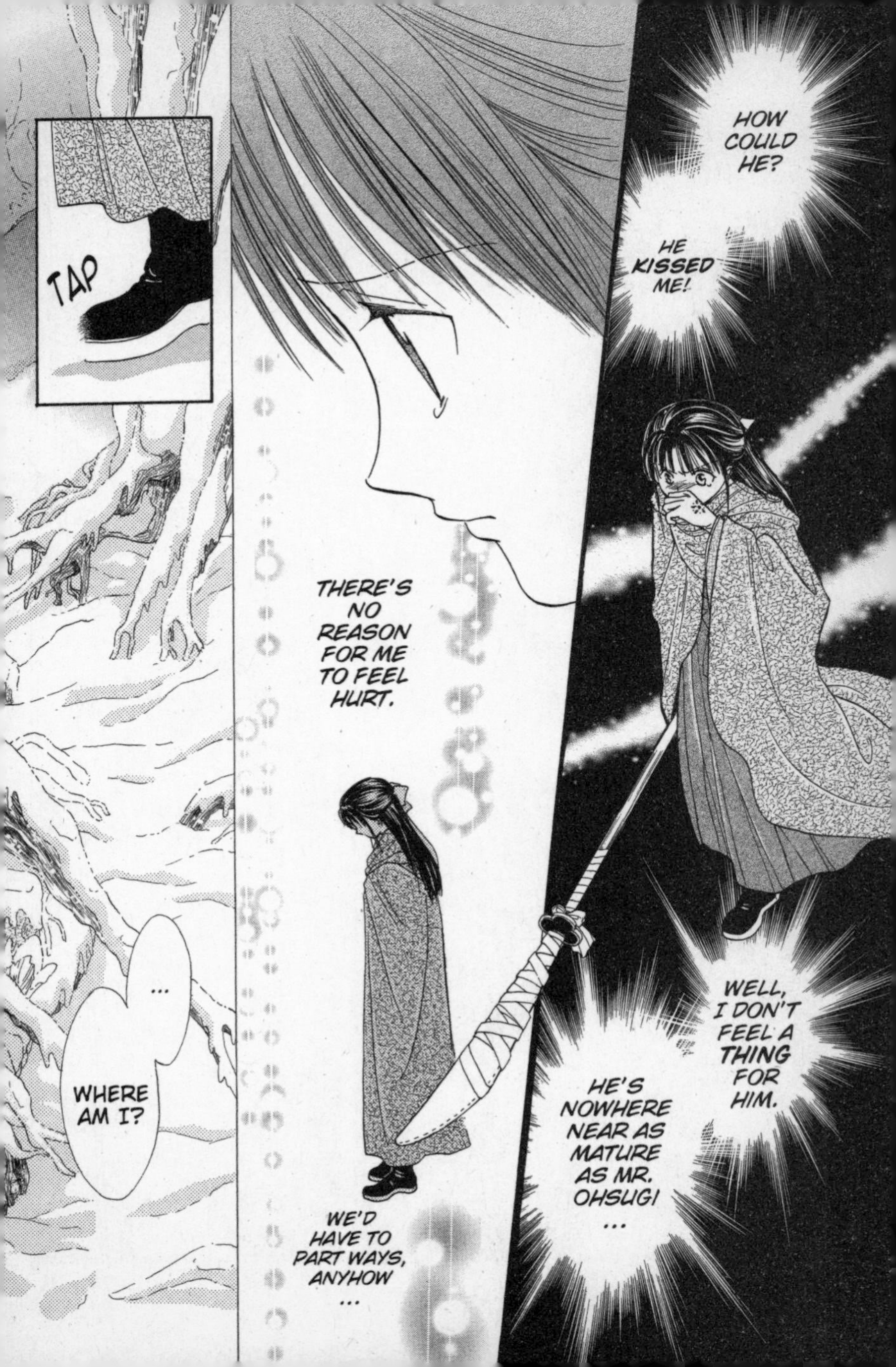
HOW COULD HE?
HE KISSED ME!
WELL, I DON'T FEEL A THING FOR HIM.
HE'S NOWHERE NEAR AS MATURE AS MR. OHSUGI ...
THERE'S NO REASON FOR ME TO FEEL HURT.
WE'D HAVE TO PART WAYS, ANYHOW ...
TAP
...
WHERE AM I?

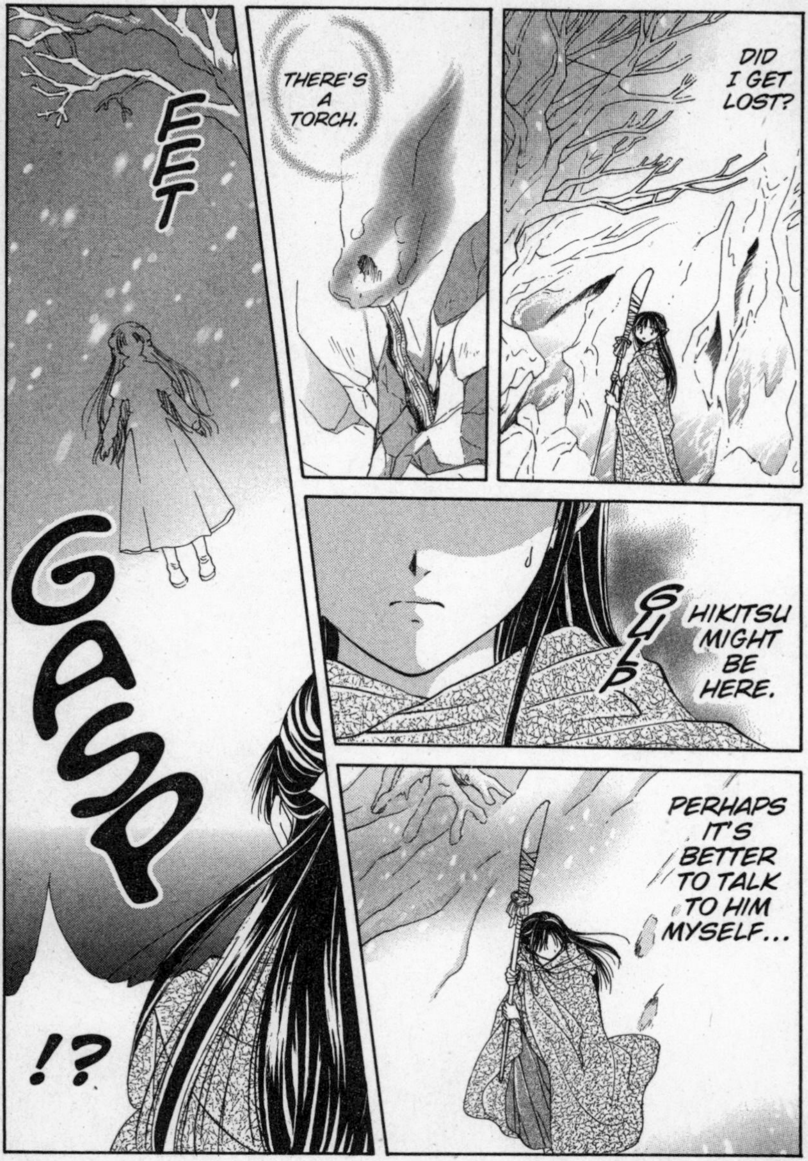
DID I GET LOST?
THERE'S A TORCH.
GULP
HIKITSU MIGHT BE HERE.
PERHAPS IT'S BETTER TO TALK TO HIM MYSELF...
FFT
GASP
!?

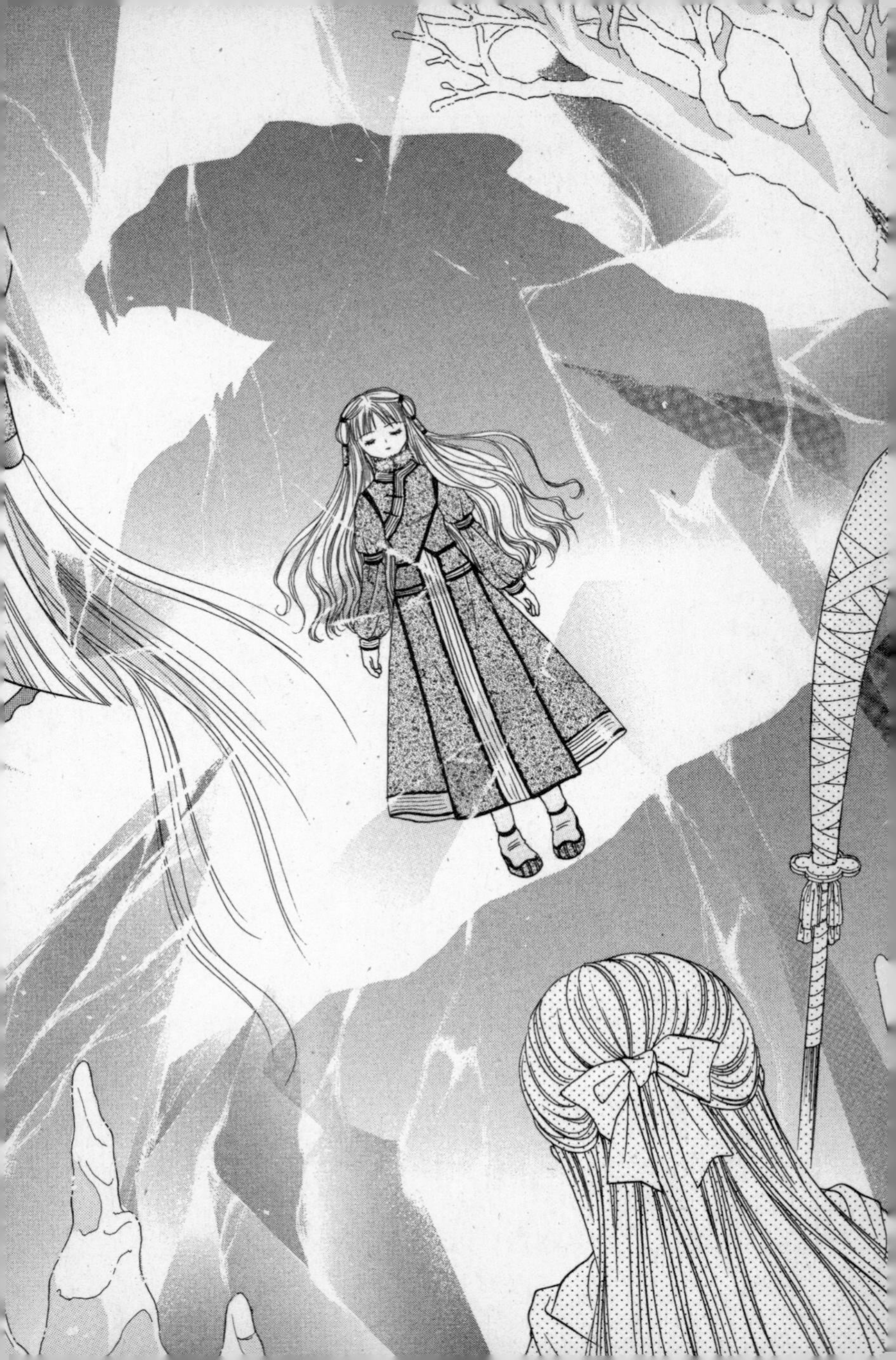

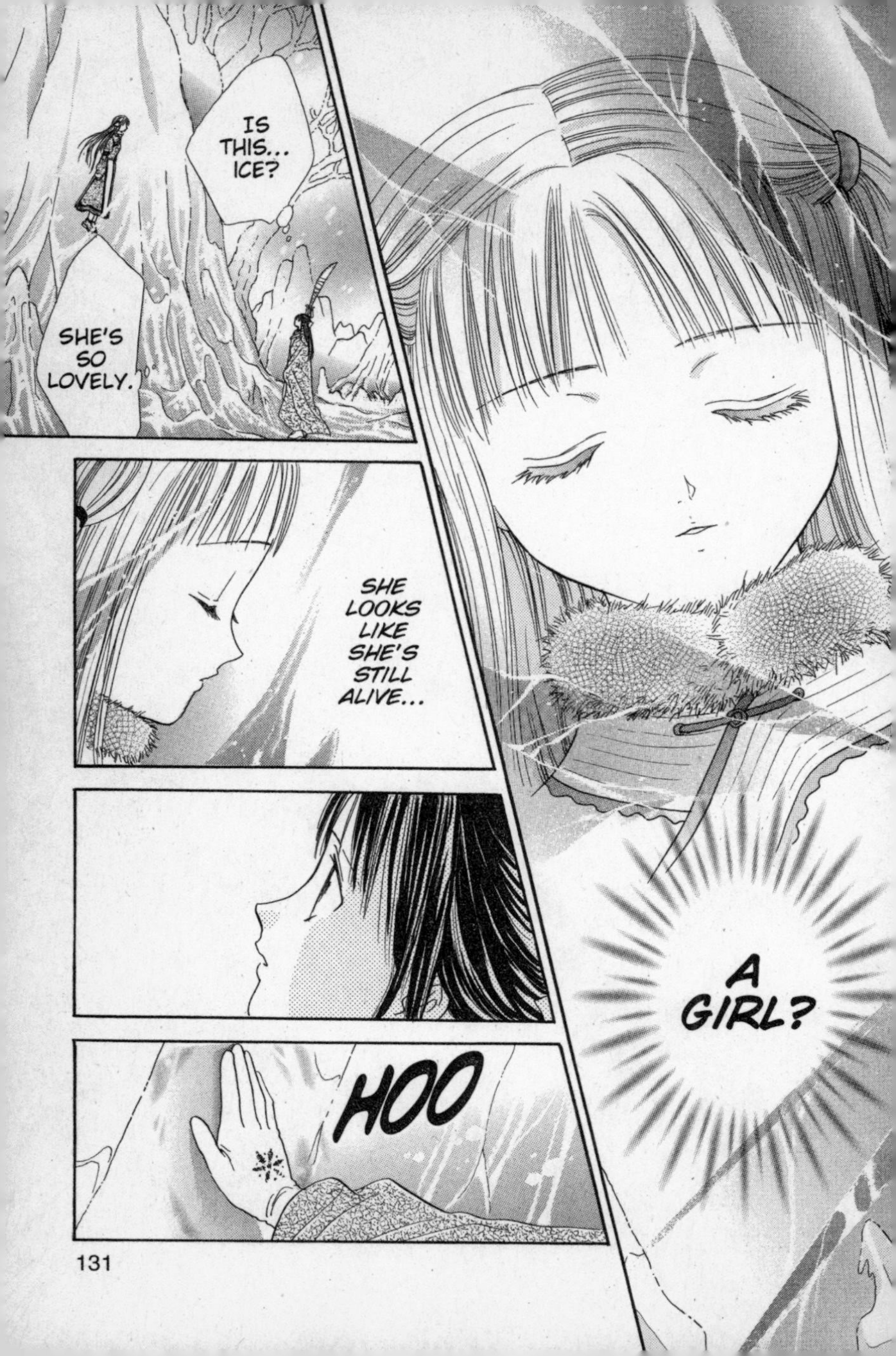
A GIRL?
IS THIS... ICE?
SHE'S SO LOVELY.
SHE LOOKS LIKE SHE'S STILL ALIVE...
HOO

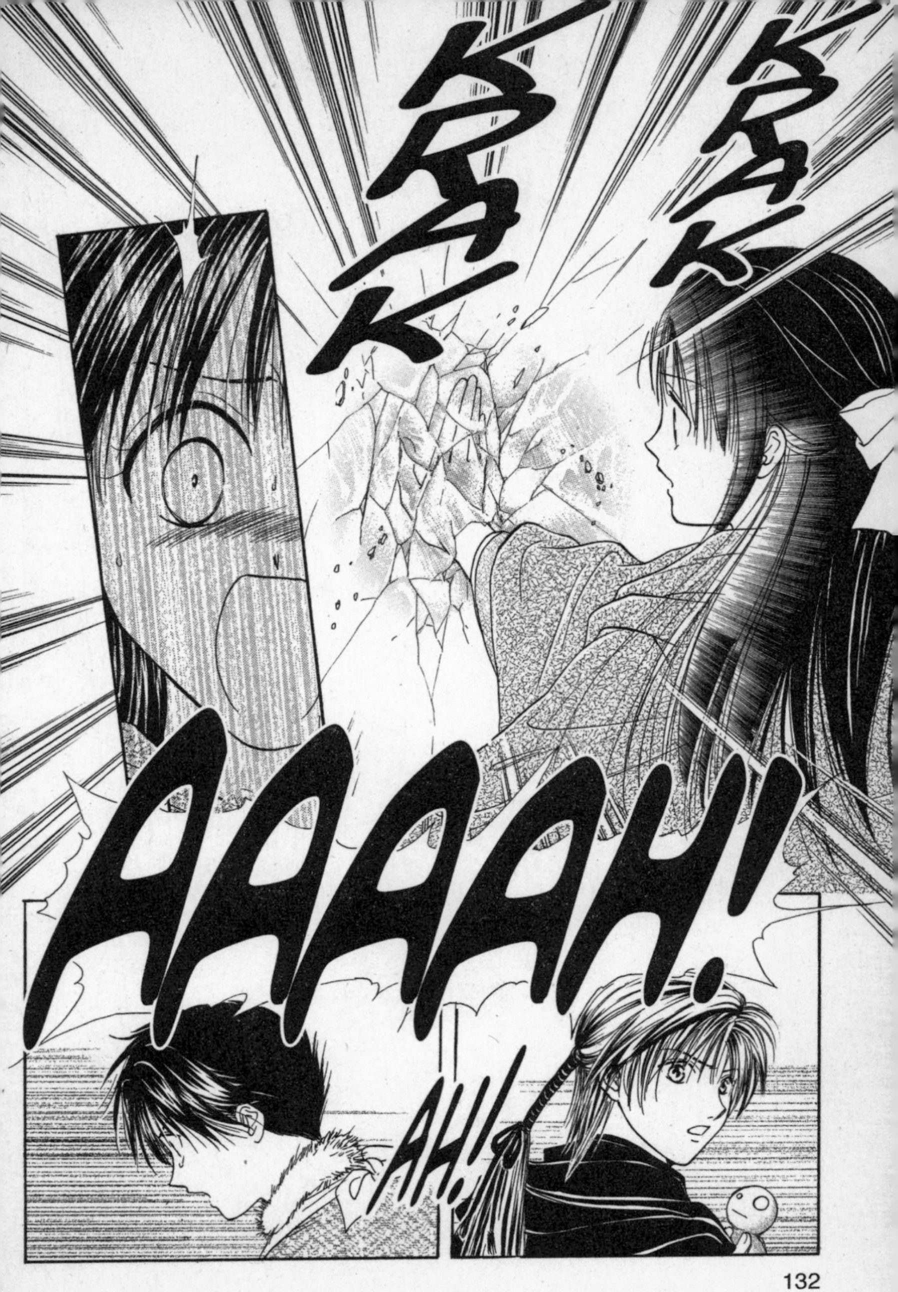
KRAK
KRAK
AAAAH!
AH!!

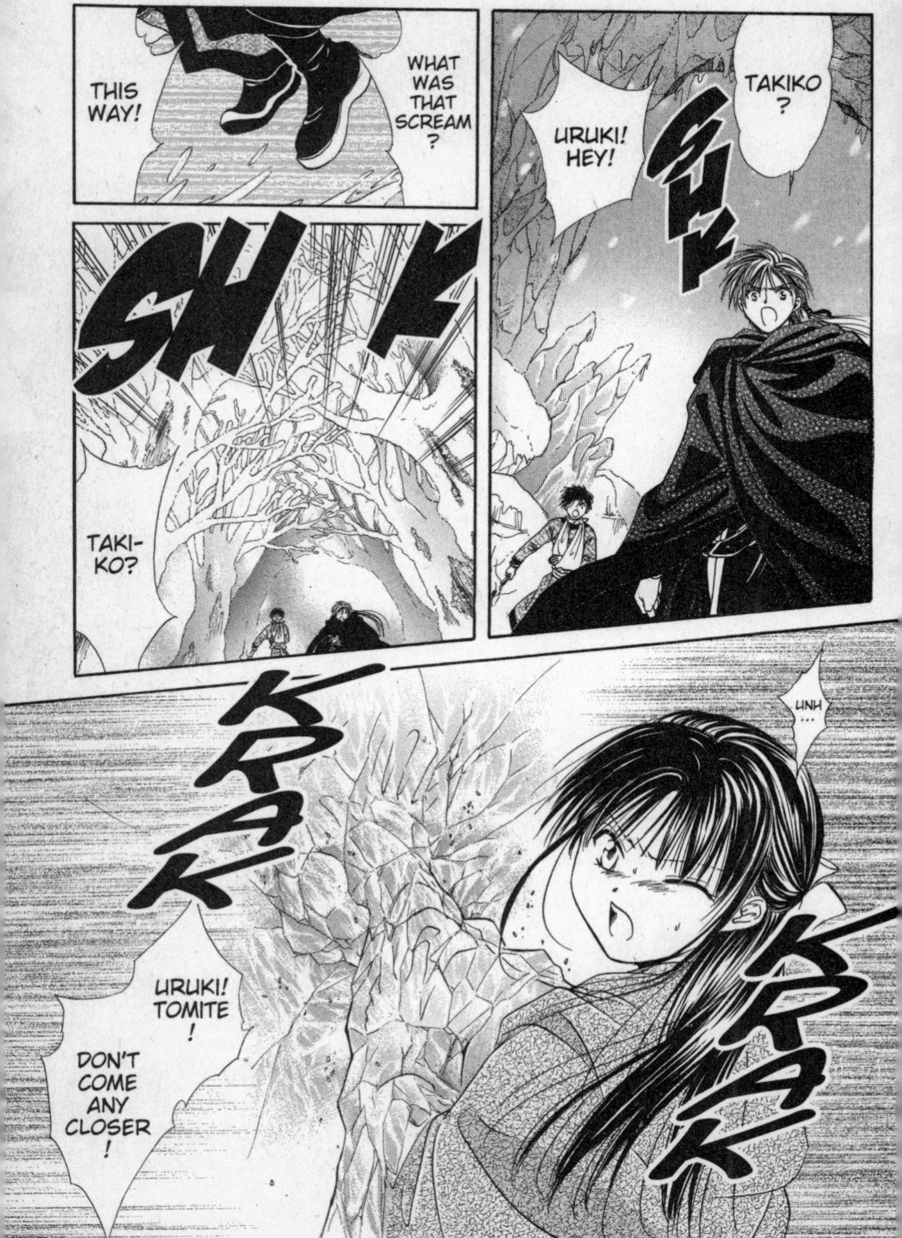
TAKIKO ?
URUKI! HEY!
SHK
WHAT WAS THAT SCREAM ?
THIS WAY!
SHK
TAKI-KO?
UNH ...
KRAK
KRAK
URUKI! TOMITE !
DON'T COME ANY CLOSER !

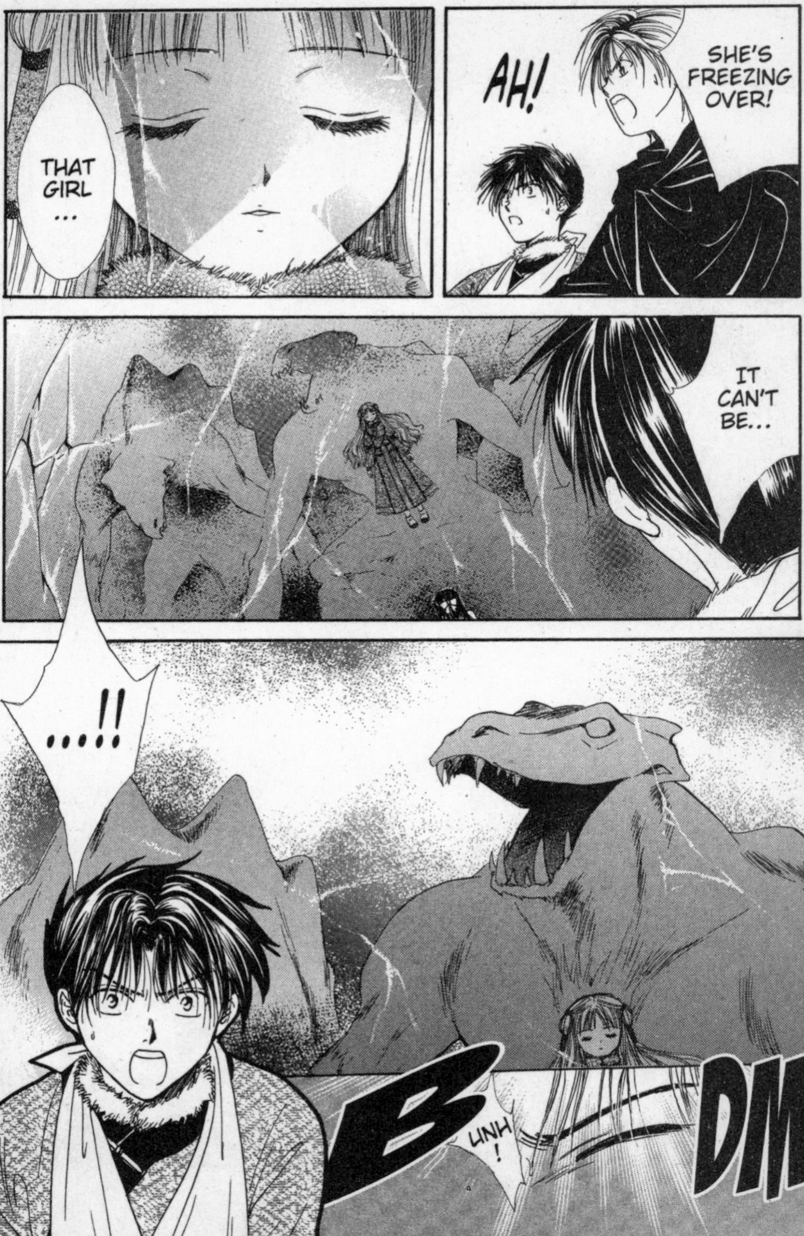

AH!
SHE'S FREEZING OVER!
THAT GIRL ...
IT CAN'T BE...
...!!
B
UNH!
DMP

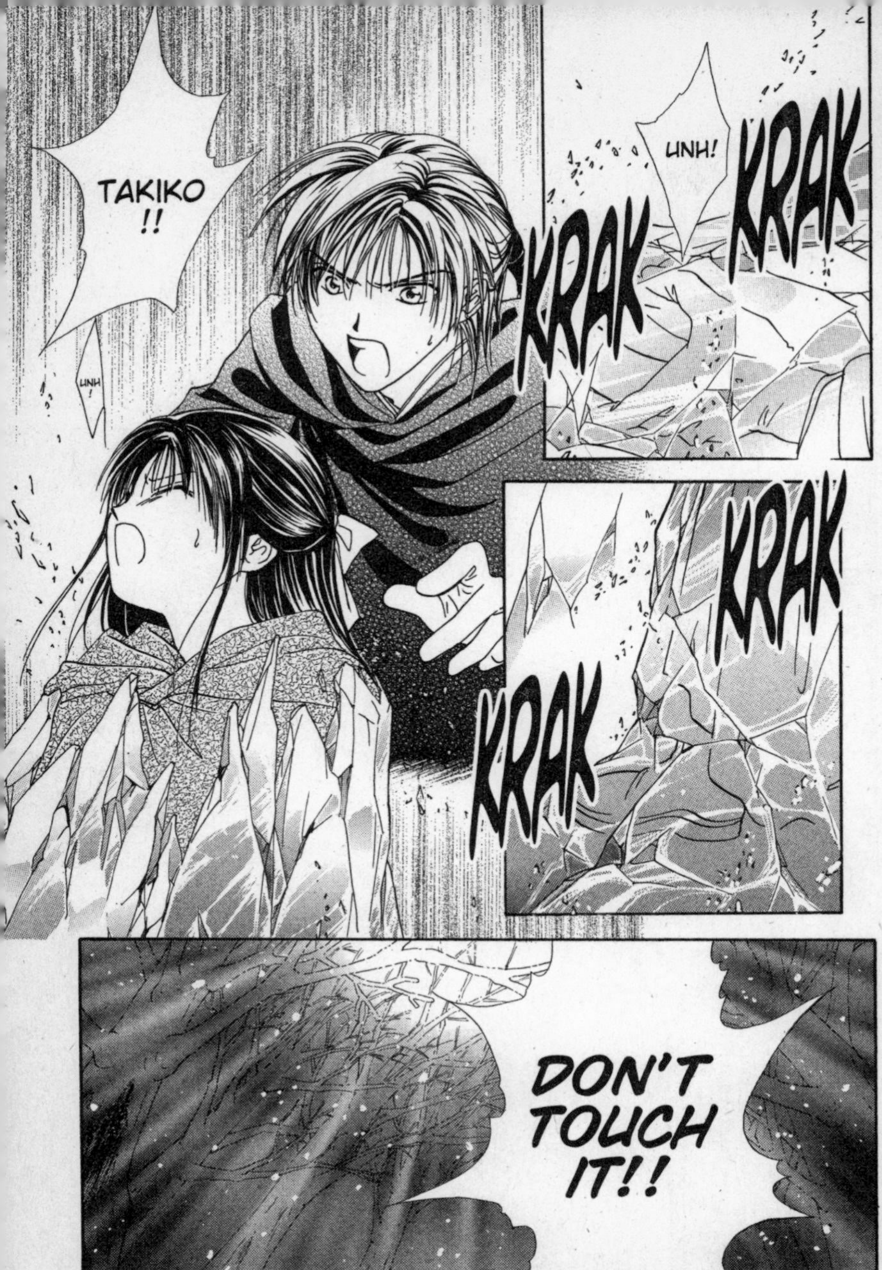
KRAK
UNH!
KRAK
KRAK
KRAK
TAKIKO!!
UNH!
DON'T TOUCH IT!!

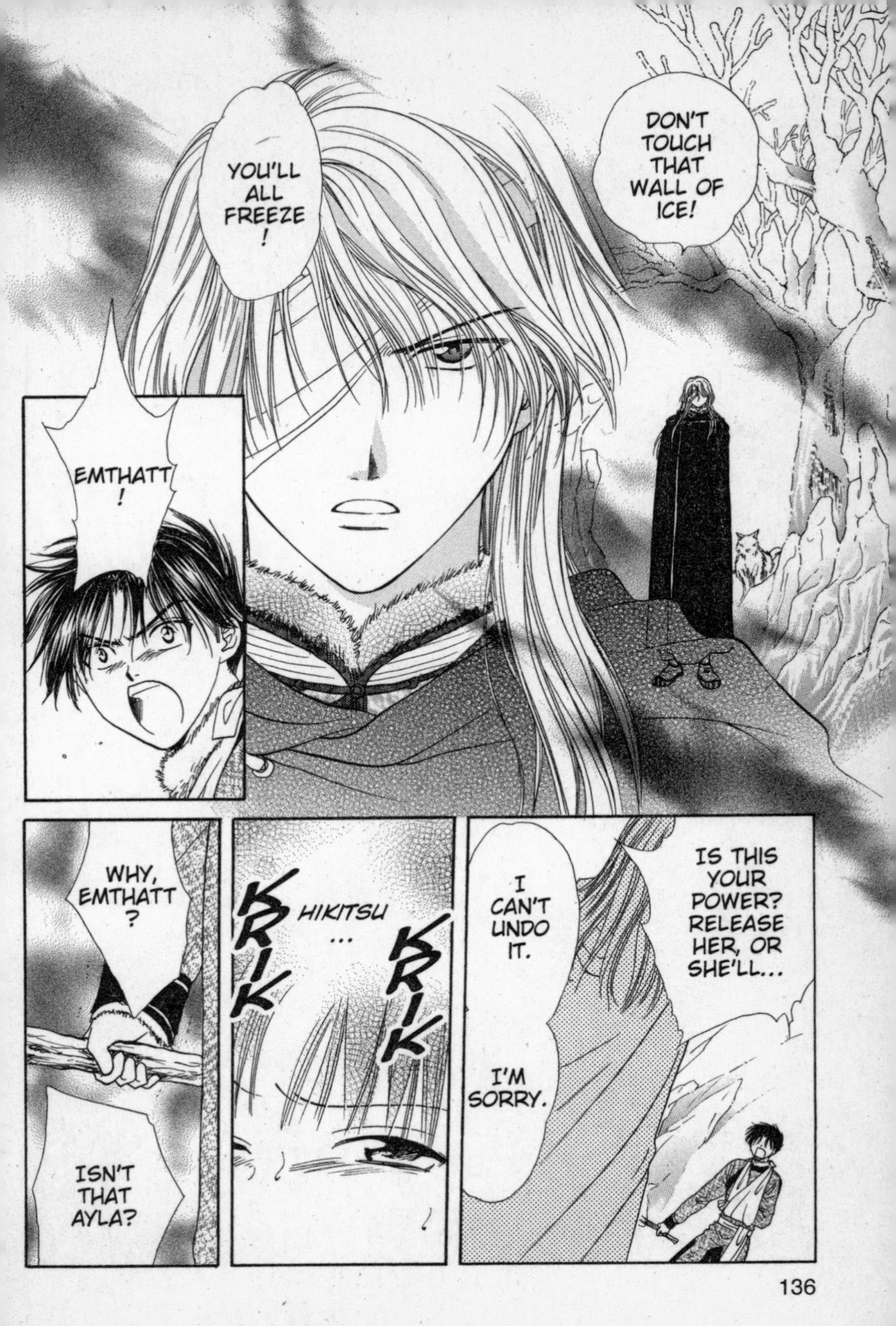
DON'T TOUCH THAT WALL OF ICE!
YOU'LL ALL FREEZE!
EMTHATT!
IS THIS YOUR POWER? RELEASE HER, OR SHE'LL...
I CAN'T UNDO IT.
I'M SORRY.
KRIK
HIKITSU...
KRIK
WHY, EMTHATT?
ISN'T THAT AYLA?

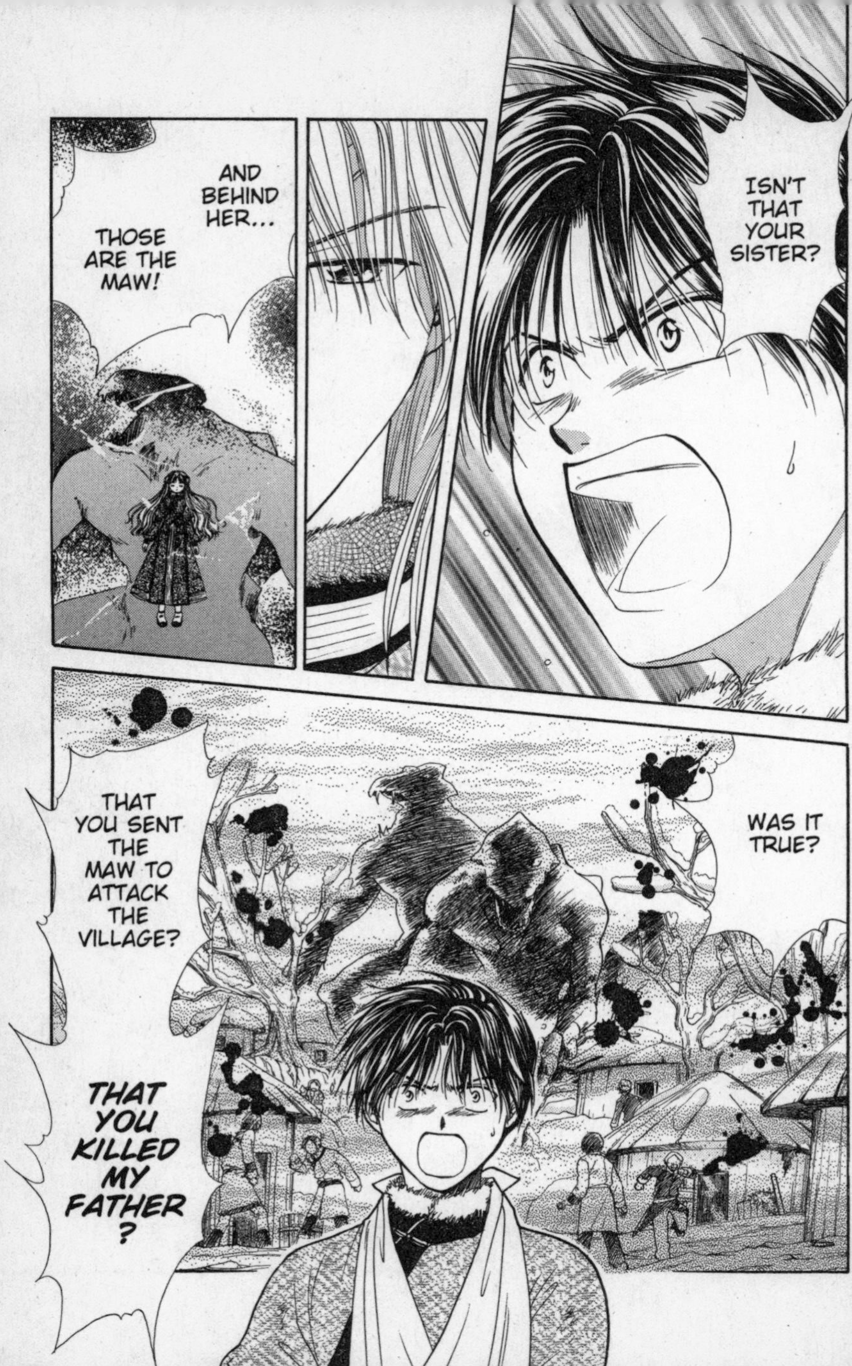
ISN'T THAT YOUR SISTER?
AND BEHIND HER...
THOSE ARE THE MAW!
WAS IT TRUE?
THAT YOU SENT THE MAW TO ATTACK THE VILLAGE?
THAT YOU KILLED MY FATHER?

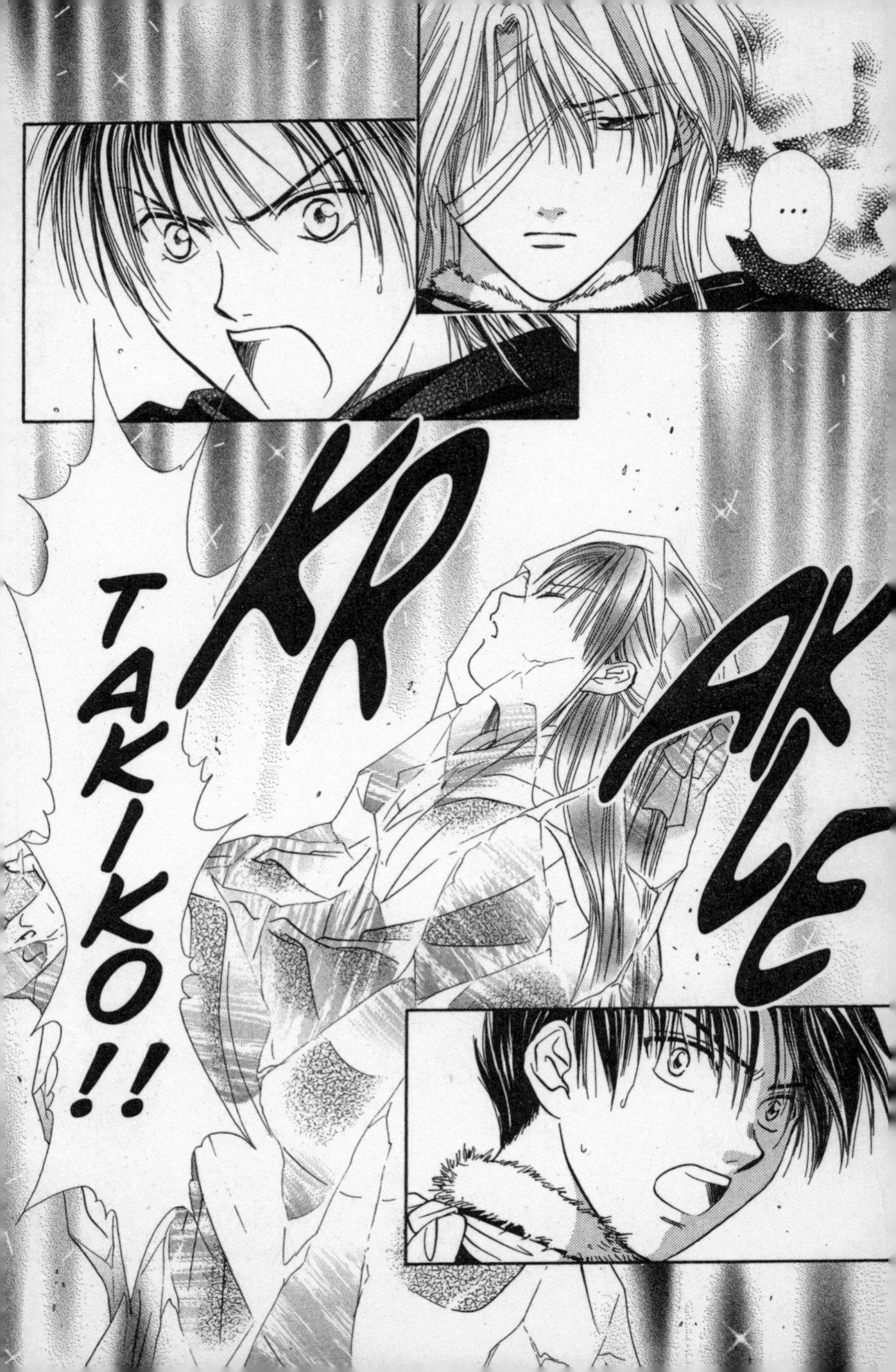
...
TAKIKO!!
KRRAKLE

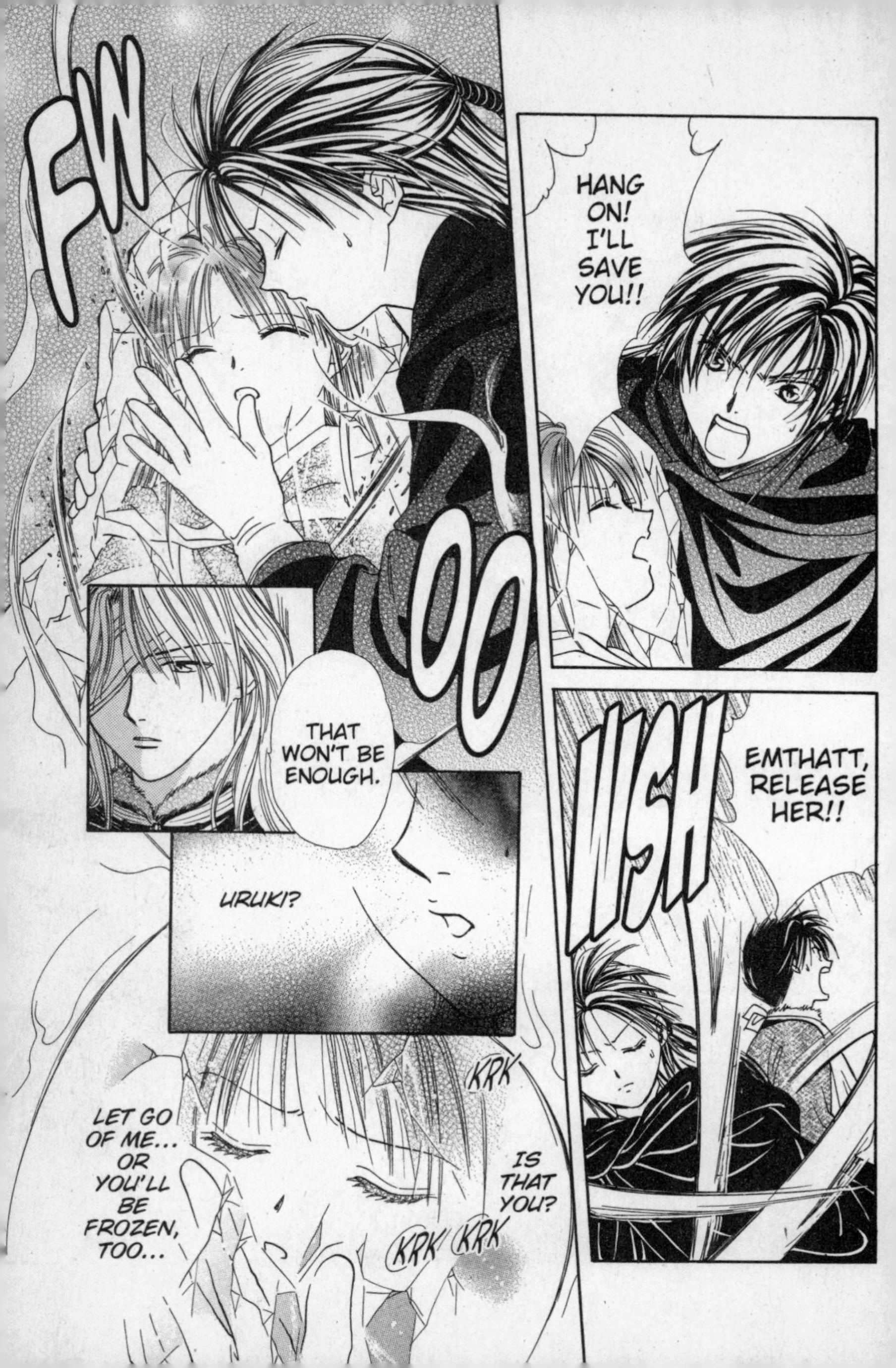
HANG ON! I'LL SAVE YOU!!
FWN
WOOO
WSH
EMTHATT, RELEASE HER!!
THAT WON'T BE ENOUGH.
URUKI?
IS THAT YOU?
KRK
KRK KRK
LET GO OF ME... OR YOU'LL BE FROZEN, TOO...

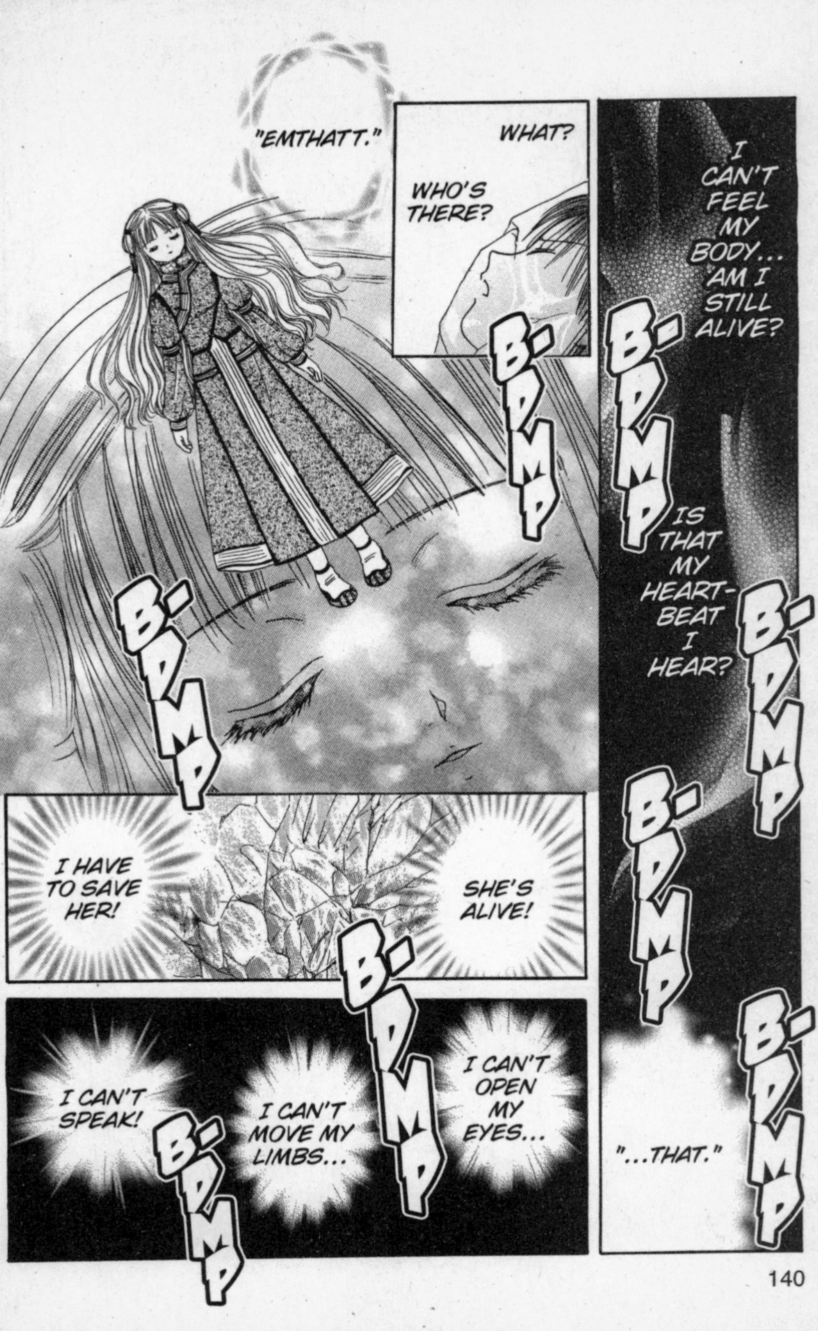
I CAN'T FEEL MY BODY... AM I STILL ALIVE?
B-DMP
IS THAT MY HEART-BEAT I HEAR?
B-DMP
B-DMP
B-DMP
"...THAT."
WHAT?
WHO'S THERE?
B-DMP
"EMTHATT."
B-DMP
SHE'S ALIVE!
I HAVE TO SAVE HER!
B-DMP
I CAN'T OPEN MY EYES...
I CAN'T MOVE MY LIMBS...
I CAN'T SPEAK!
B-DMP

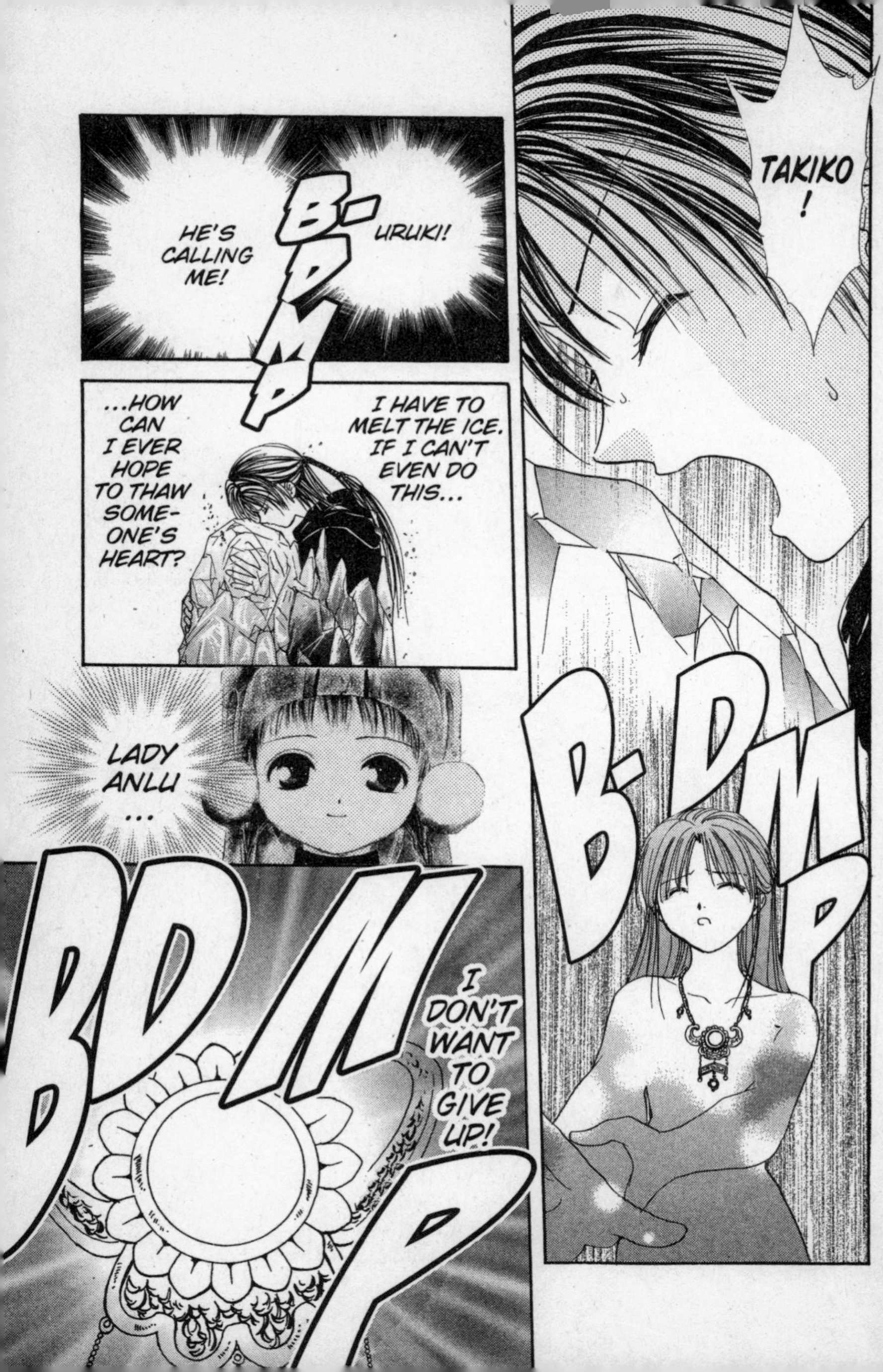
TAKIKO!
B-DMP
URUKI!
B-DMP
HE'S CALLING ME!
I HAVE TO MELT THE ICE. IF I CAN'T EVEN DO THIS...
...HOW CAN I EVER HOPE TO THAW SOME-ONE'S HEART?
LADY ANLU ...
I DON'T WANT TO GIVE UP!
BDMP

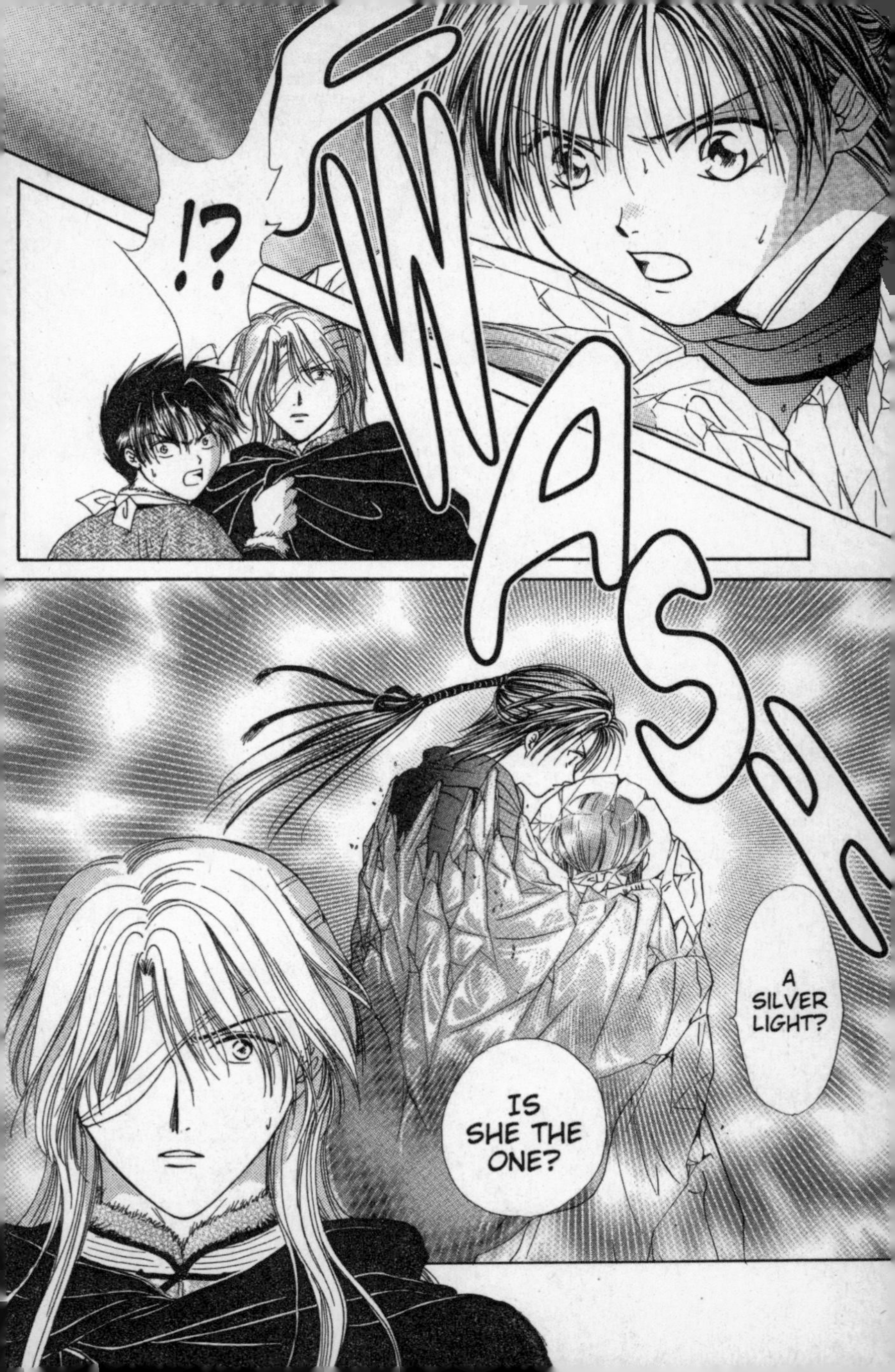
!?
SWASH
A SILVER LIGHT?
IS SHE THE ONE?

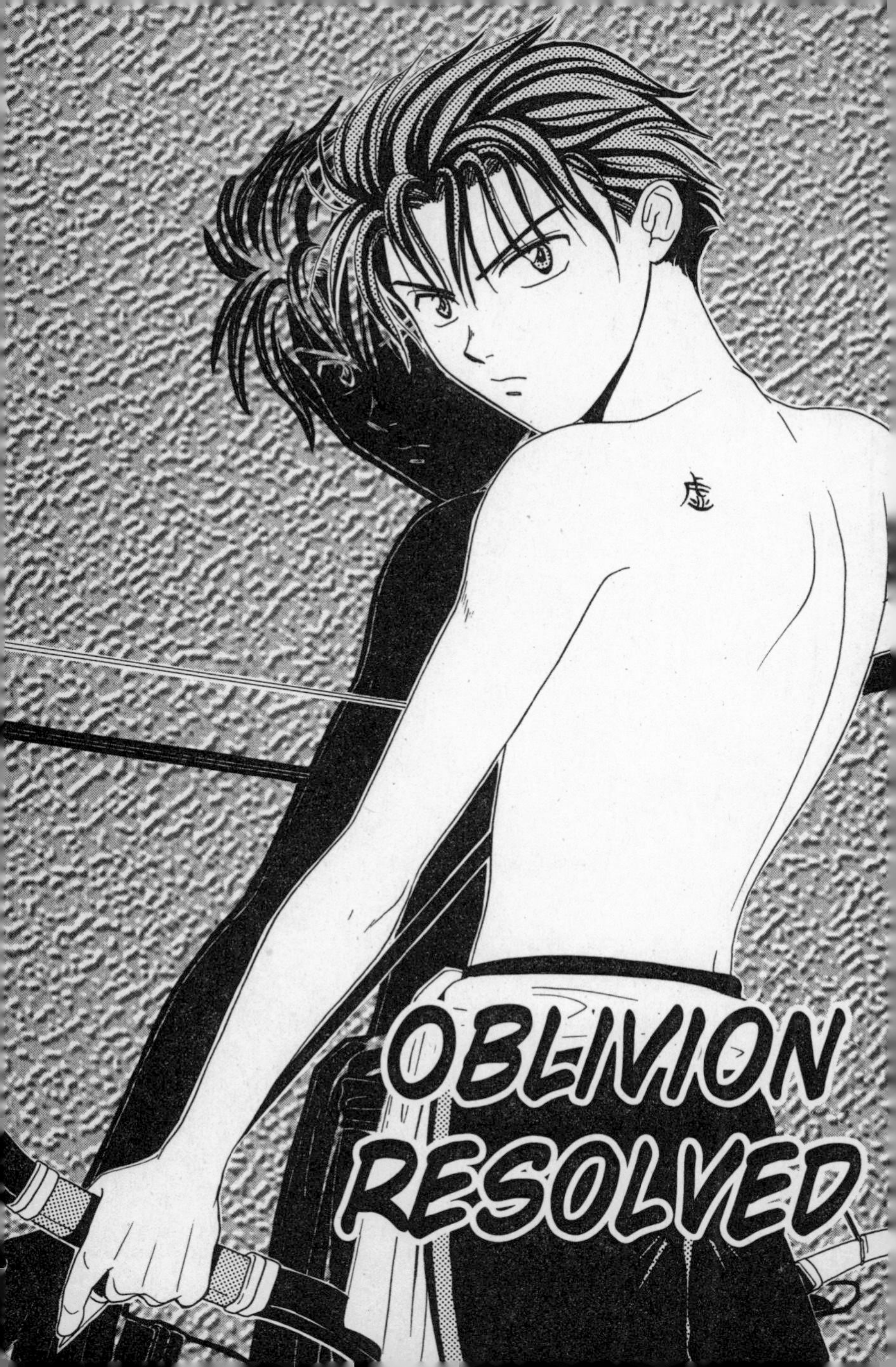
OBLIVION
RESOLVED

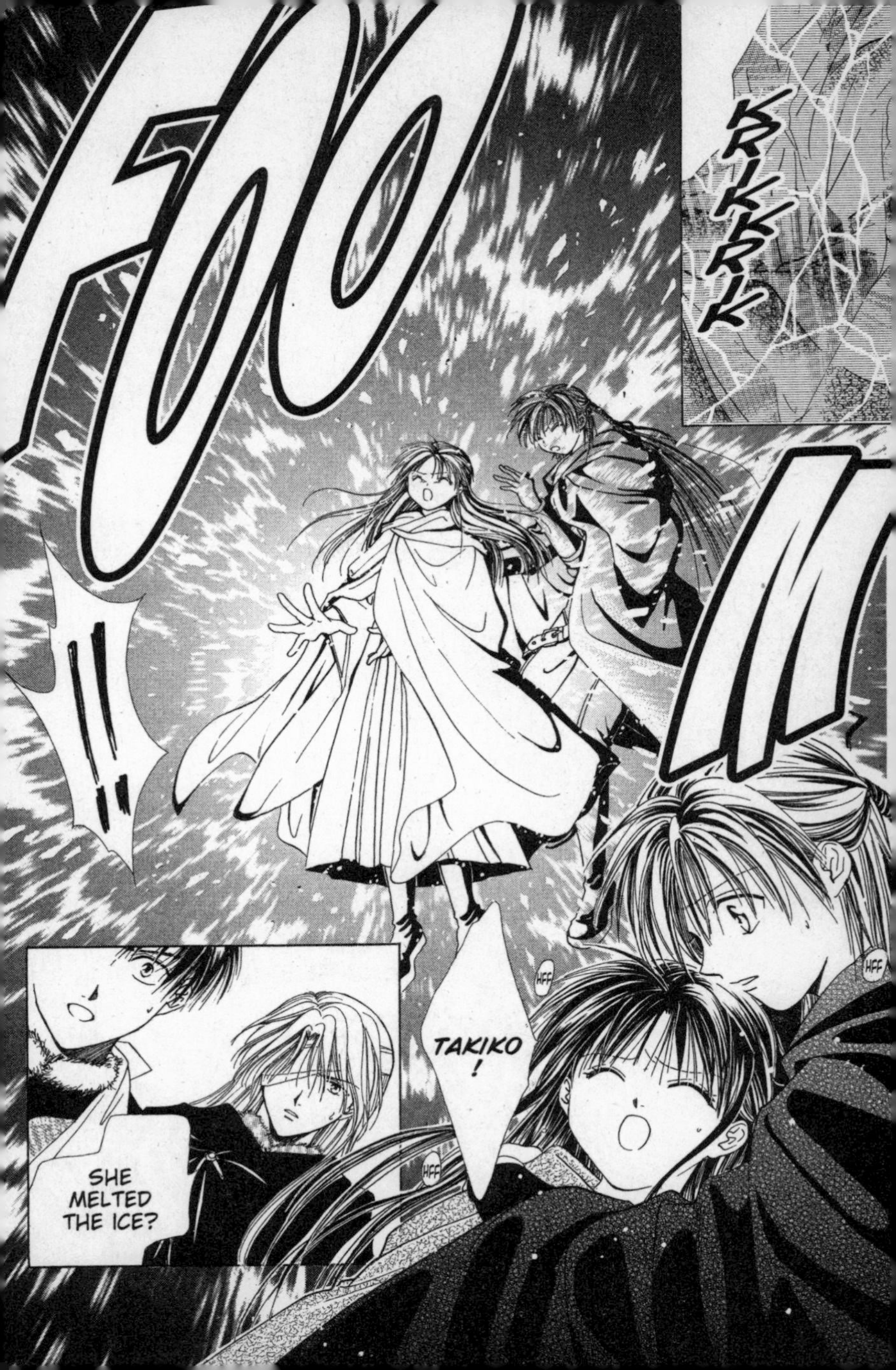
KRIKKRIK
!!
TAKIKO!
HFF
HFF
HFF
SHE MELTED THE ICE?

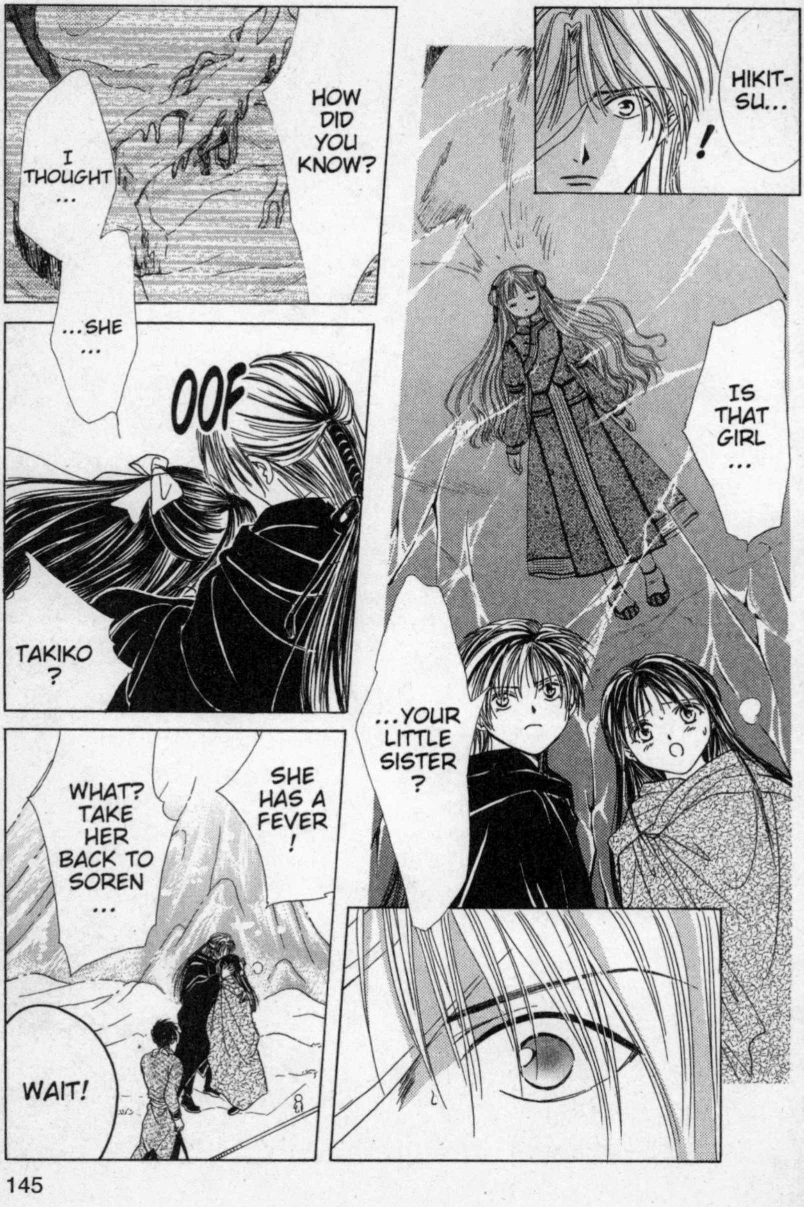
HIKIT-SU...
!
IS THAT GIRL...
...YOUR LITTLE SISTER?
HOW DID YOU KNOW?
I THOUGHT...
...SHE...
OOF
TAKIKO?
SHE HAS A FEVER!
WHAT? TAKE HER BACK TO SOREN...
WAIT!

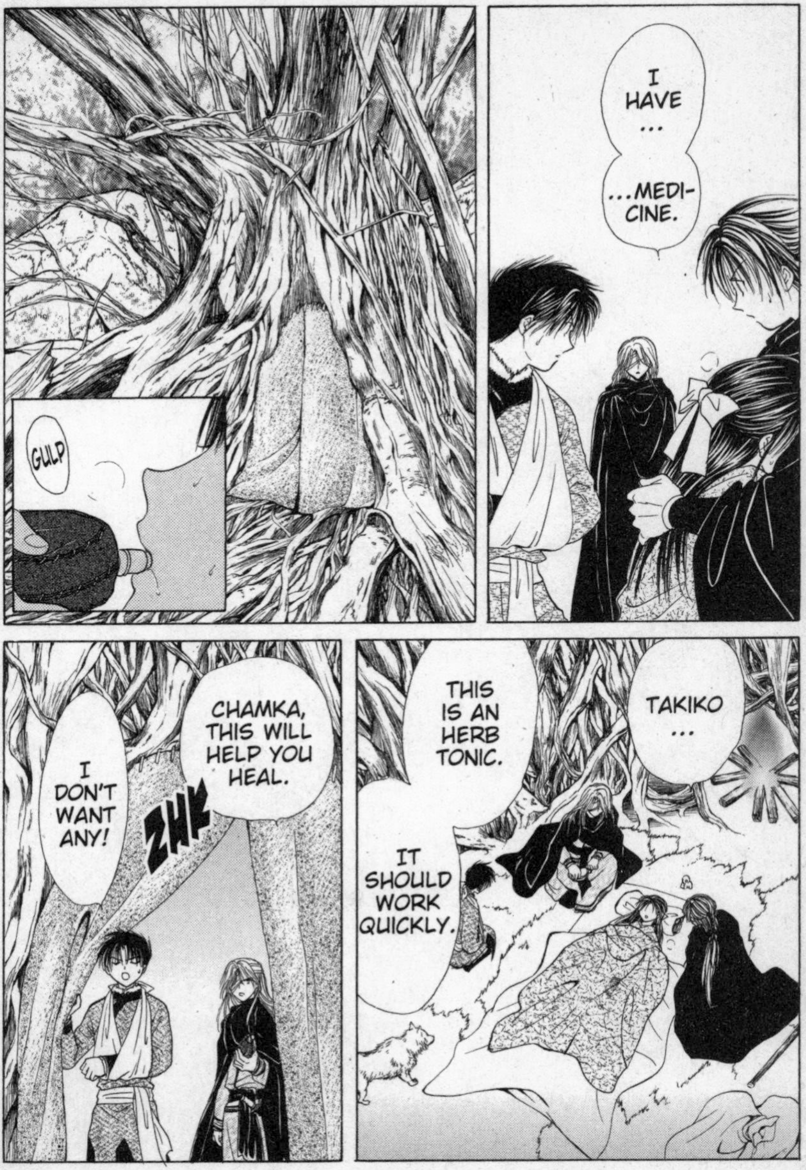
I HAVE ...
...MEDICINE.
GULP
TAKIKO ...
THIS IS AN HERB TONIC.
IT SHOULD WORK QUICKLY.
CHAMKA, THIS WILL HELP YOU HEAL.
ZHK
I DON'T WANT ANY!

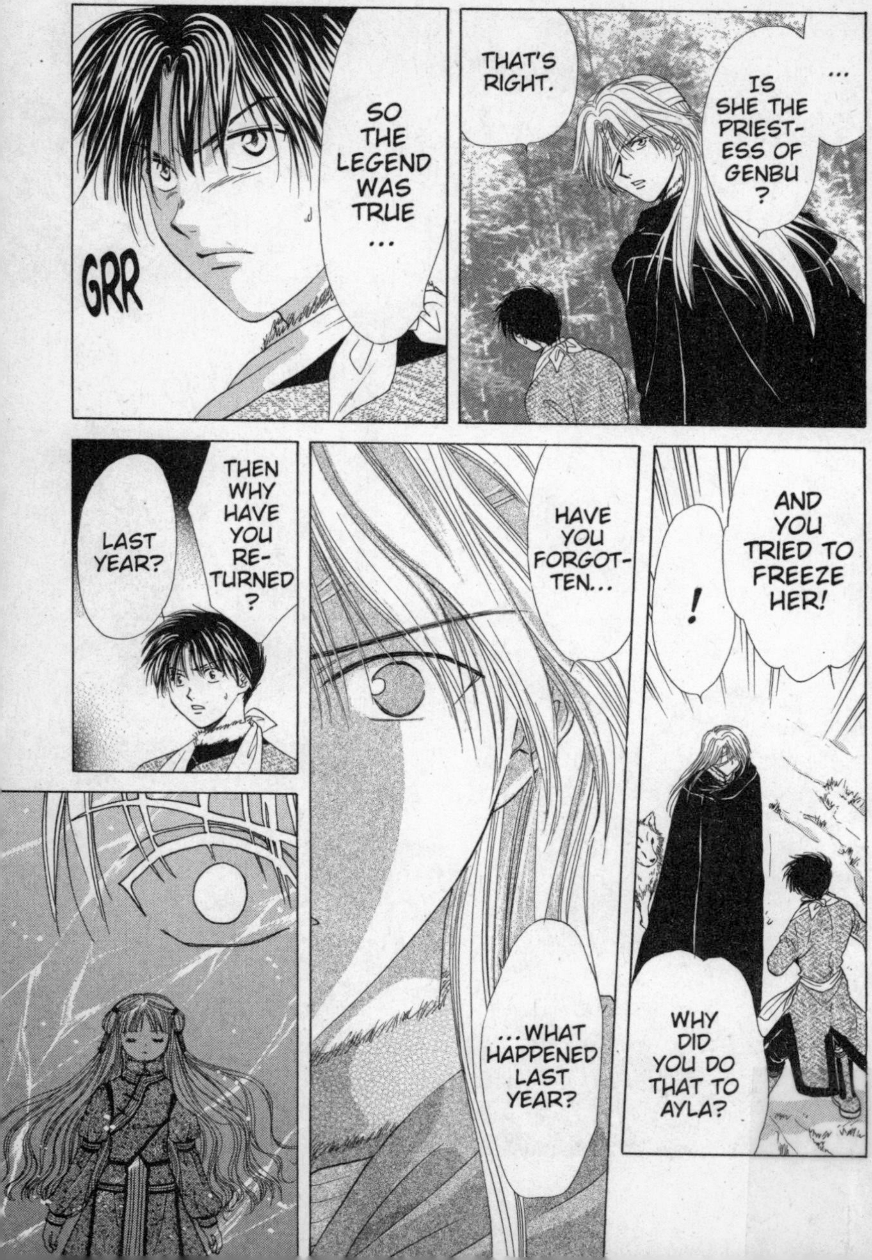
...
IS SHE THE PRIESTESS OF GENBU?
THAT'S RIGHT.
SO THE LEGEND WAS TRUE ...
GRR
AND YOU TRIED TO FREEZE HER!
!
WHY DID YOU DO THAT TO AYLA?
HAVE YOU FORGOTTEN...
...WHAT HAPPENED LAST YEAR?
THEN WHY HAVE YOU RE-TURNED?
LAST YEAR?

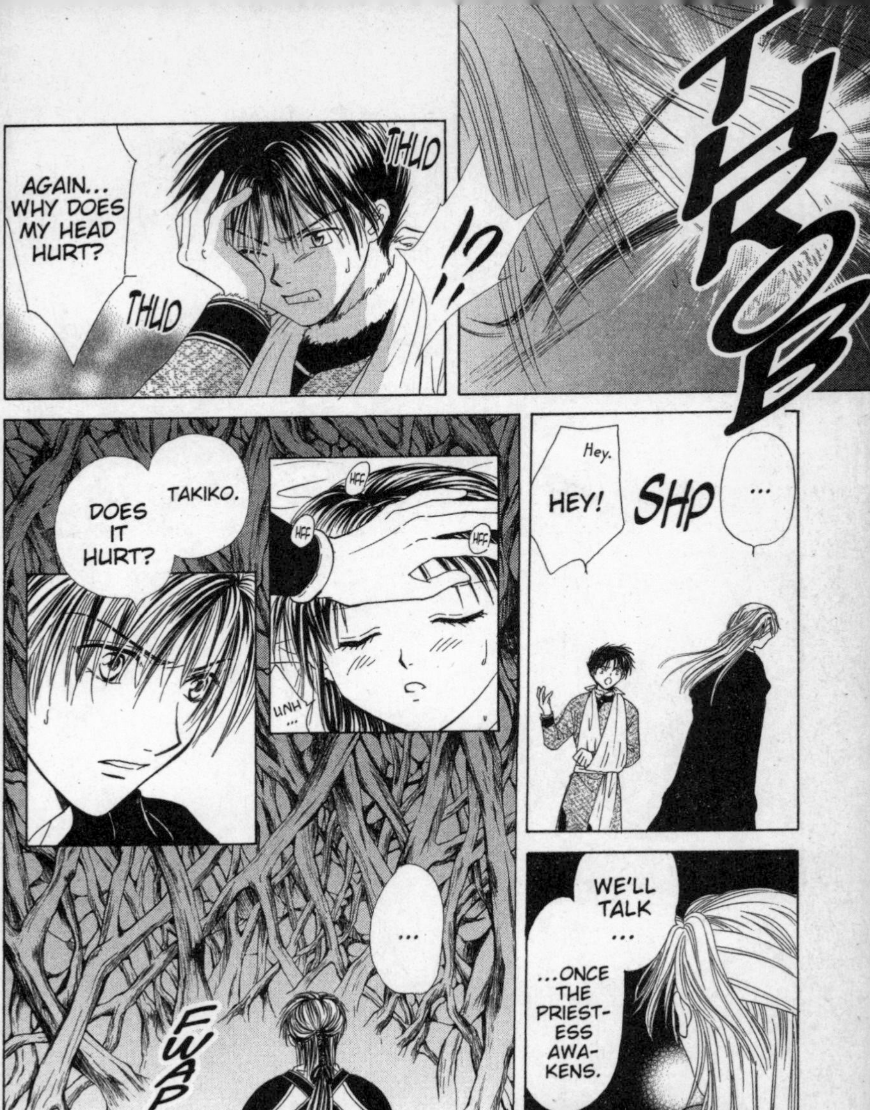
THROB
!?
THUD
AGAIN... WHY DOES MY HEAD HURT?
THUD
...
SHP
Hey.
HEY!
WE'LL TALK ...
...ONCE THE PRIEST-ESS AWA-KENS.
TAKIKO.
DOES IT HURT?
HFF
HFF
HFF
UNH ...
...
FWAP

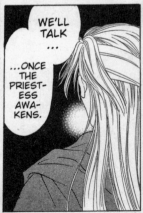

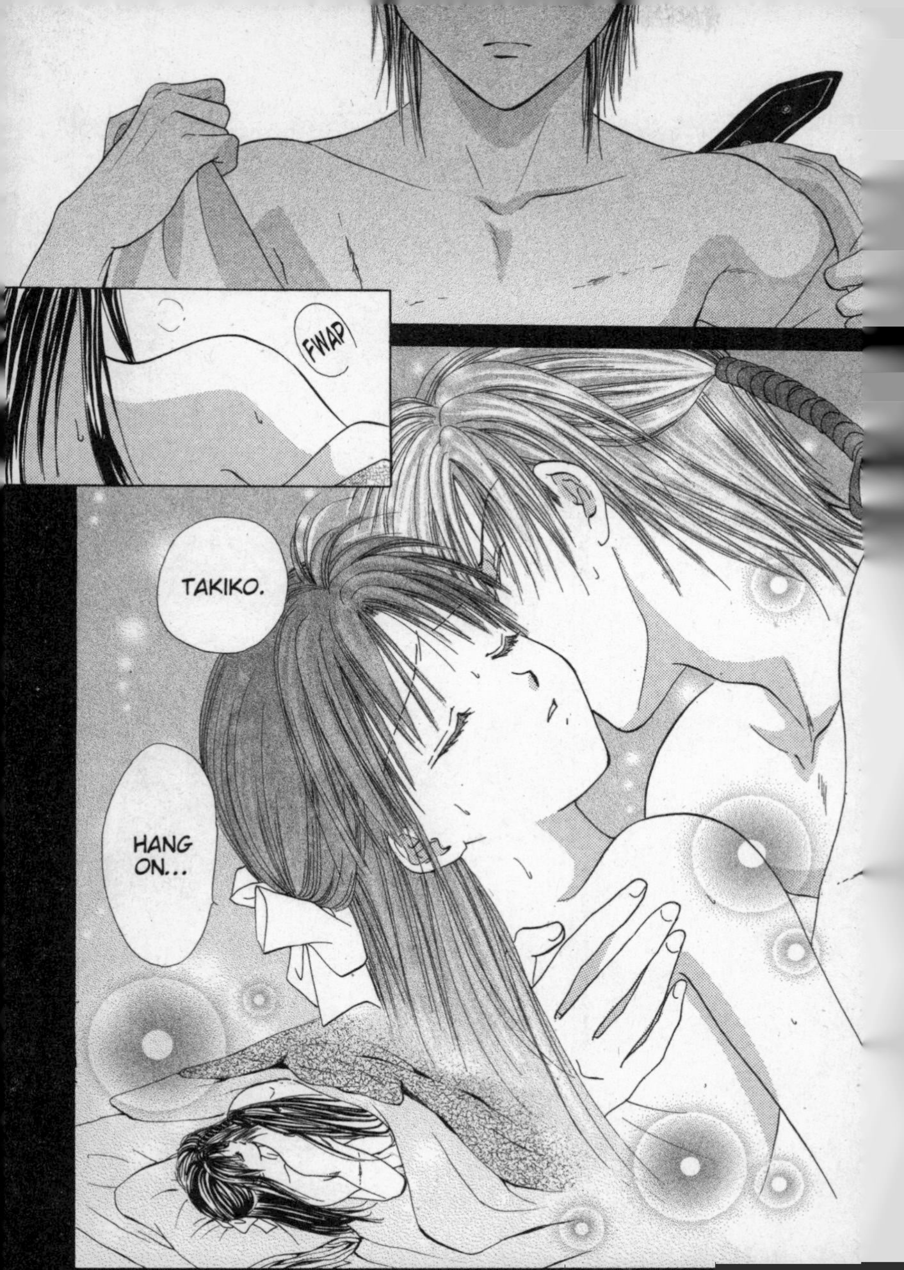
FWAP
TAKIKO.
HANG ON...

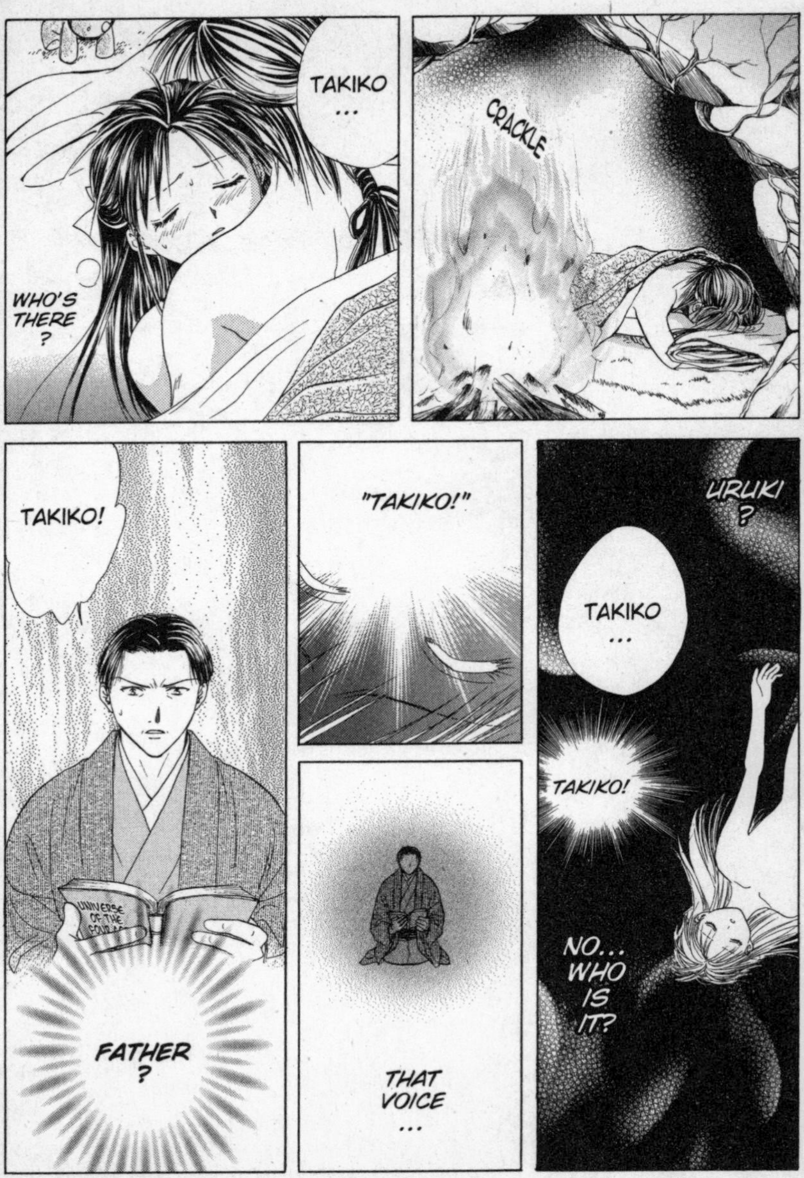
CRACKLE
TAKIKO ...
WHO'S THERE ?
URUKI ?
TAKIKO ...
TAKIKO!
NO... WHO IS IT?
"TAKIKO!"
THAT VOICE ...
TAKIKO!
UNIVERSE OF THE
FATHER ?

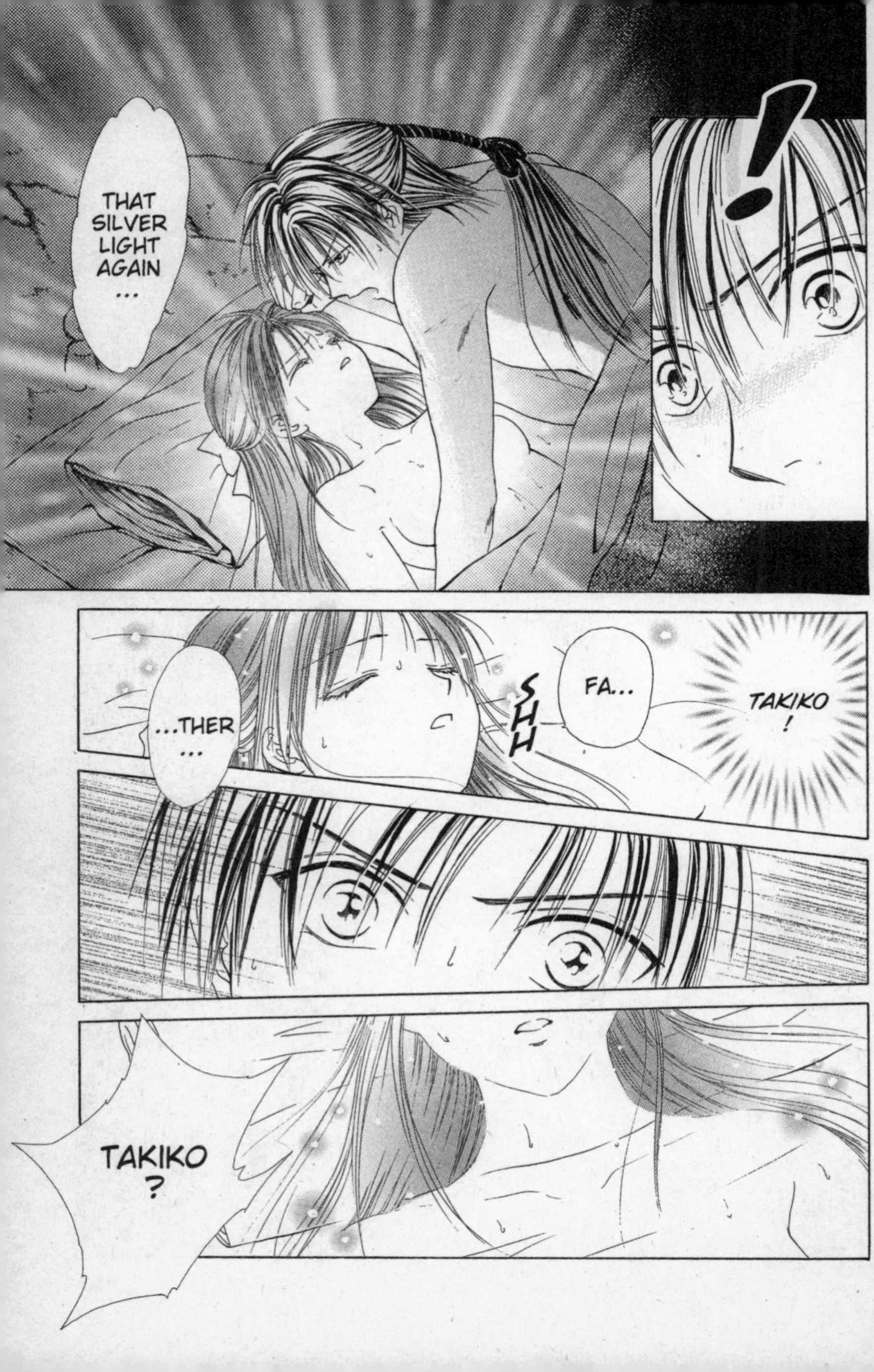
!
THAT SILVER LIGHT AGAIN ...
TAKIKO!
FA...
SHH
...THER ...
TAKIKO?

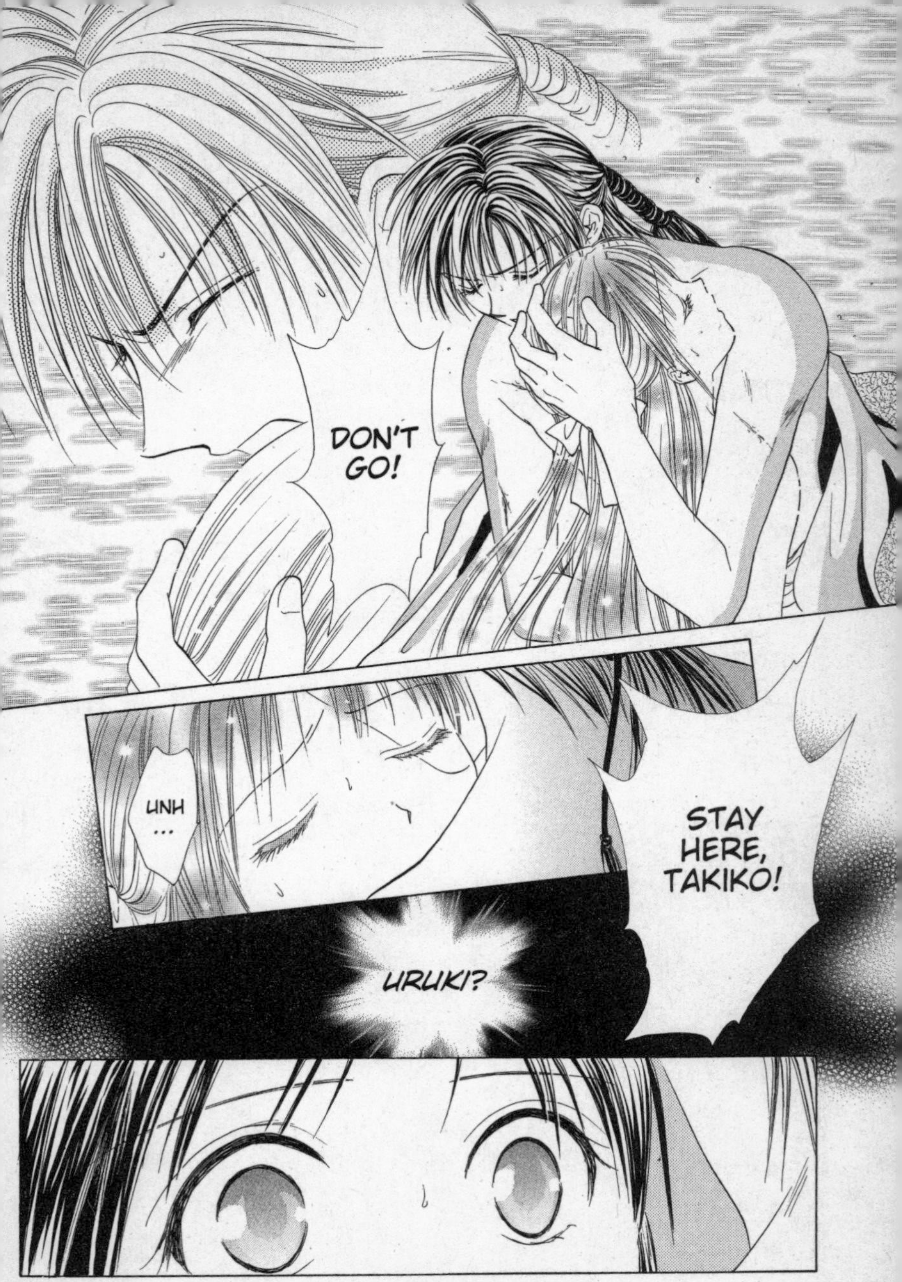
DON'T GO!
STAY HERE, TAKIKO!
UNH ...
URUKI?

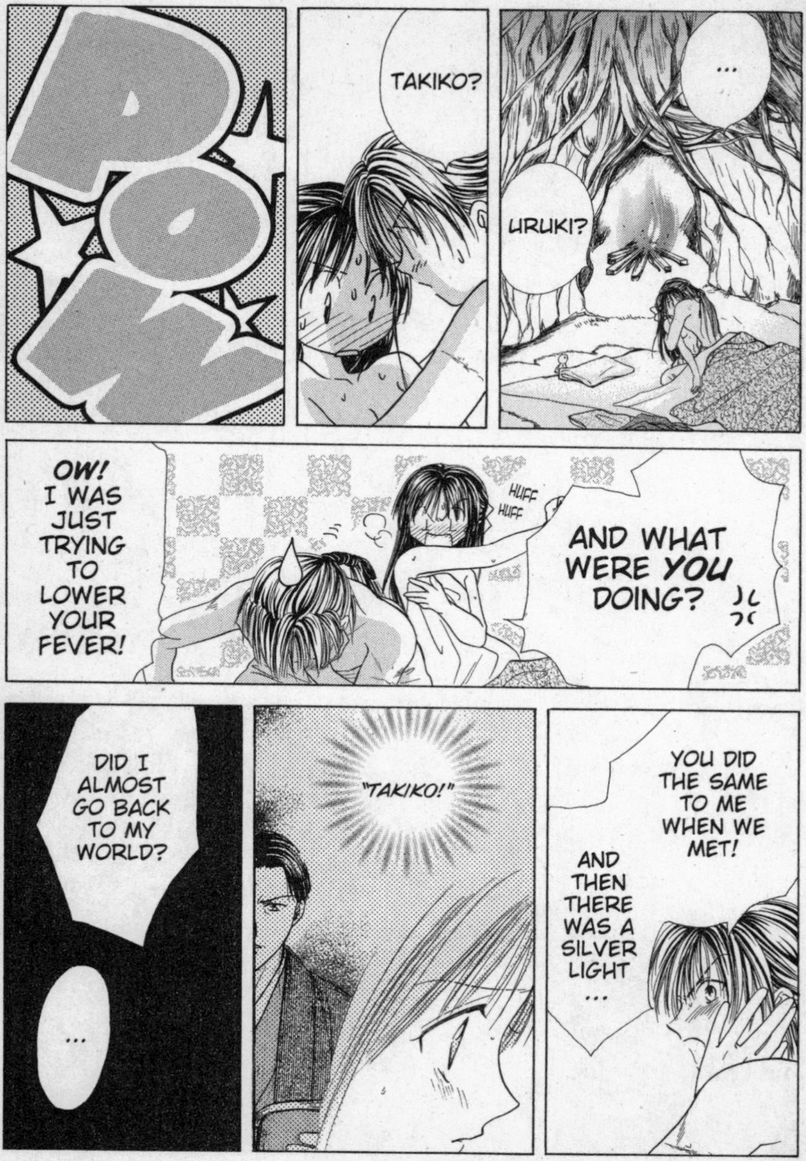
...
URUKI?
TAKIKO?
POW
AND WHAT WERE *YOU* DOING?
HUFF HUFF
OW! I WAS JUST TRYING TO LOWER YOUR FEVER!
YOU DID THE SAME TO ME WHEN WE MET!
AND THEN THERE WAS A SILVER LIGHT ...
"TAKIKO!"
DID I ALMOST GO BACK TO MY WORLD?
...

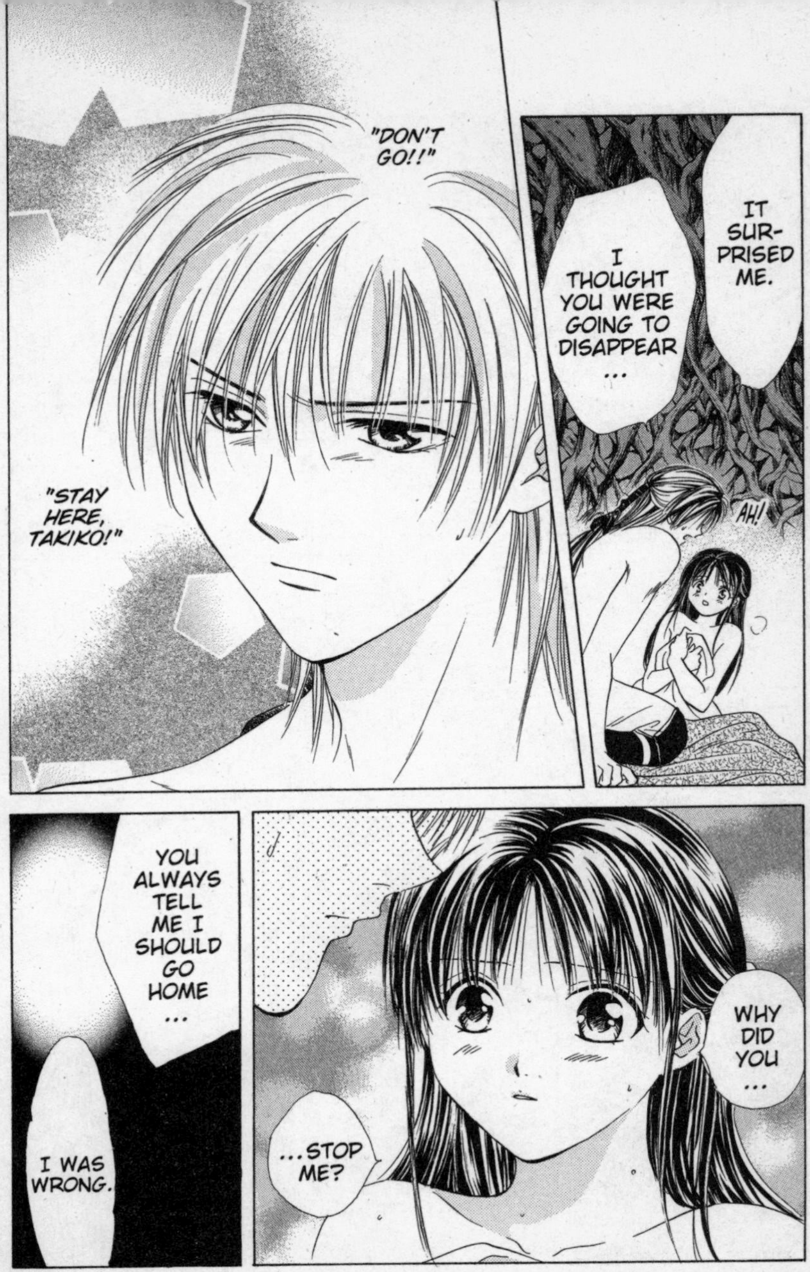
IT SUR-PRISED ME.
I THOUGHT YOU WERE GOING TO DISAPPEAR ...
AH!
"DON'T GO!!"
"STAY HERE, TAKIKO!"
WHY DID YOU ...
...STOP ME?
YOU ALWAYS TELL ME I SHOULD GO HOME ...
I WAS WRONG.

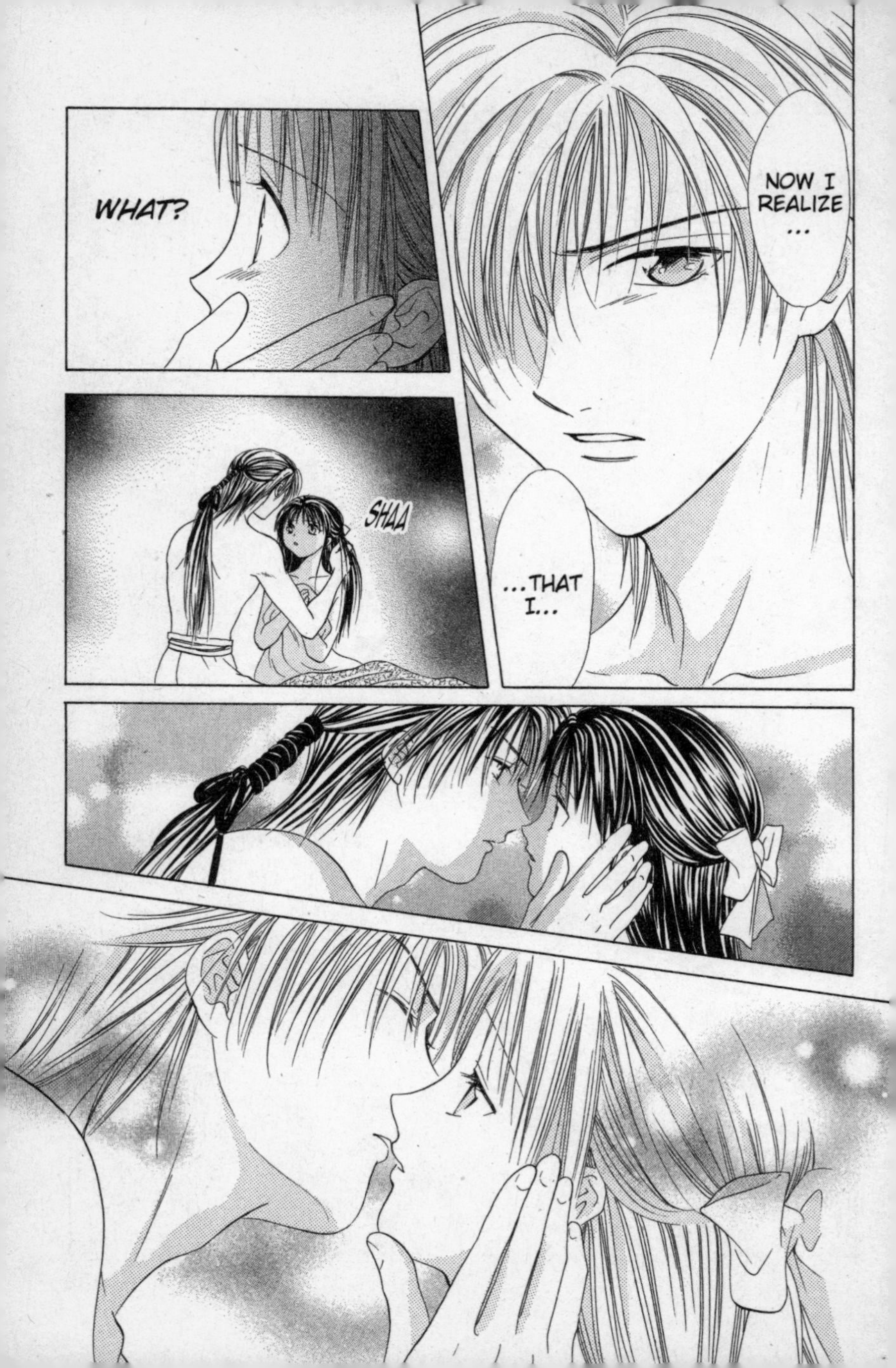
NOW I REALIZE ...
...THAT I...
WHAT?
SHAA

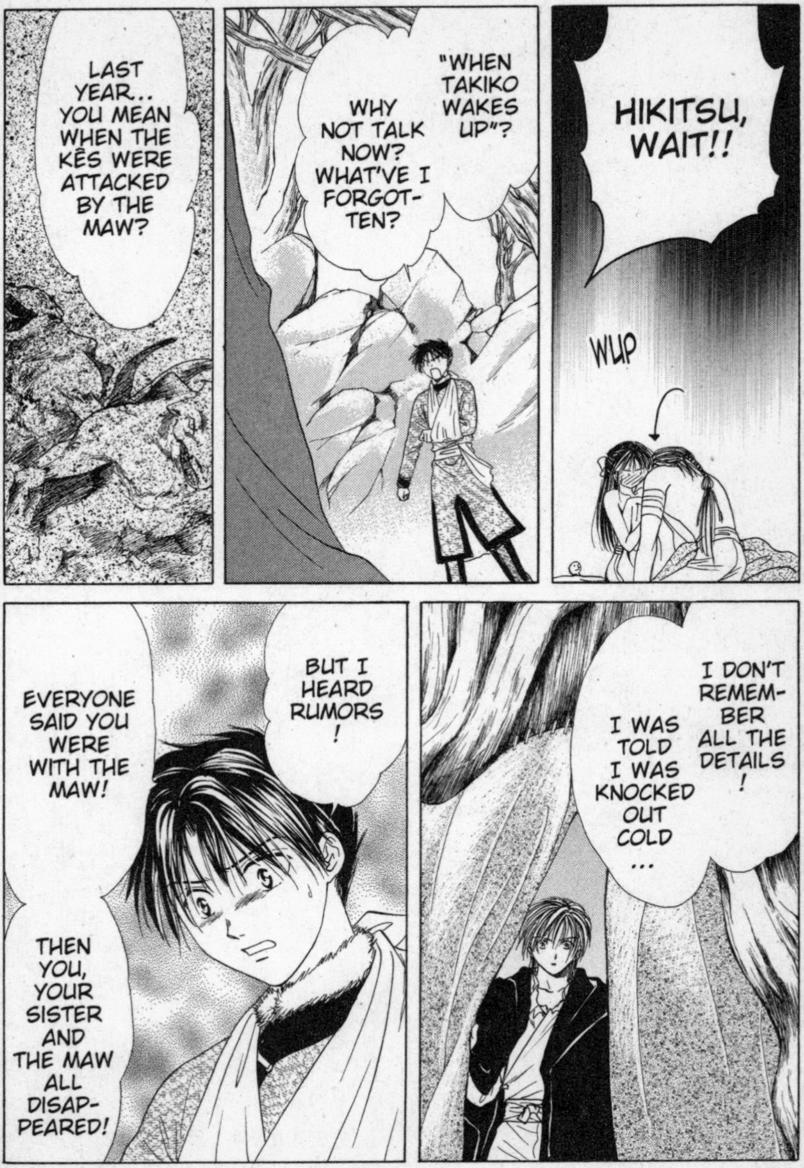
HIKITSU, WAIT!!
WUP
"WHEN TAKIKO WAKES UP"?
WHY NOT TALK NOW? WHAT'VE I FORGOT-TEN?
LAST YEAR... YOU MEAN WHEN THE KÊS WERE ATTACKED BY THE MAW?
I DON'T REMEM-BER ALL THE DETAILS!
I WAS TOLD I WAS KNOCKED OUT COLD...
BUT I HEARD RUMORS!
EVERYONE SAID YOU WERE WITH THE MAW!
THEN YOU, YOUR SISTER AND THE MAW ALL DISAP-PEARED!

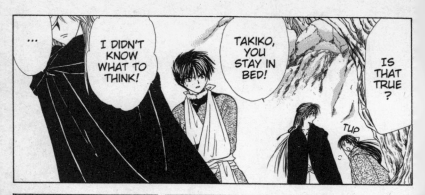

IS THAT TRUE?
TUP
TAKIKO, YOU STAY IN BED!
I DIDN'T KNOW WHAT TO THINK!
...
WHEN THE MAW ATTACKED US SEVEN YEARS AGO...
"CHAMKA, RUN!"

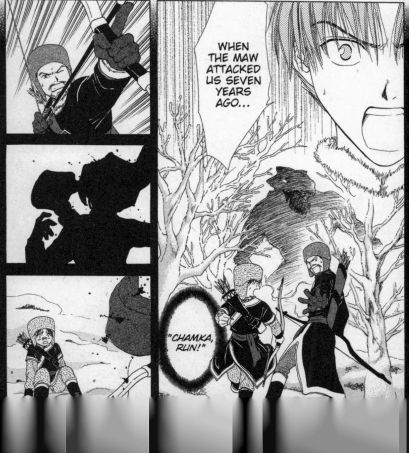

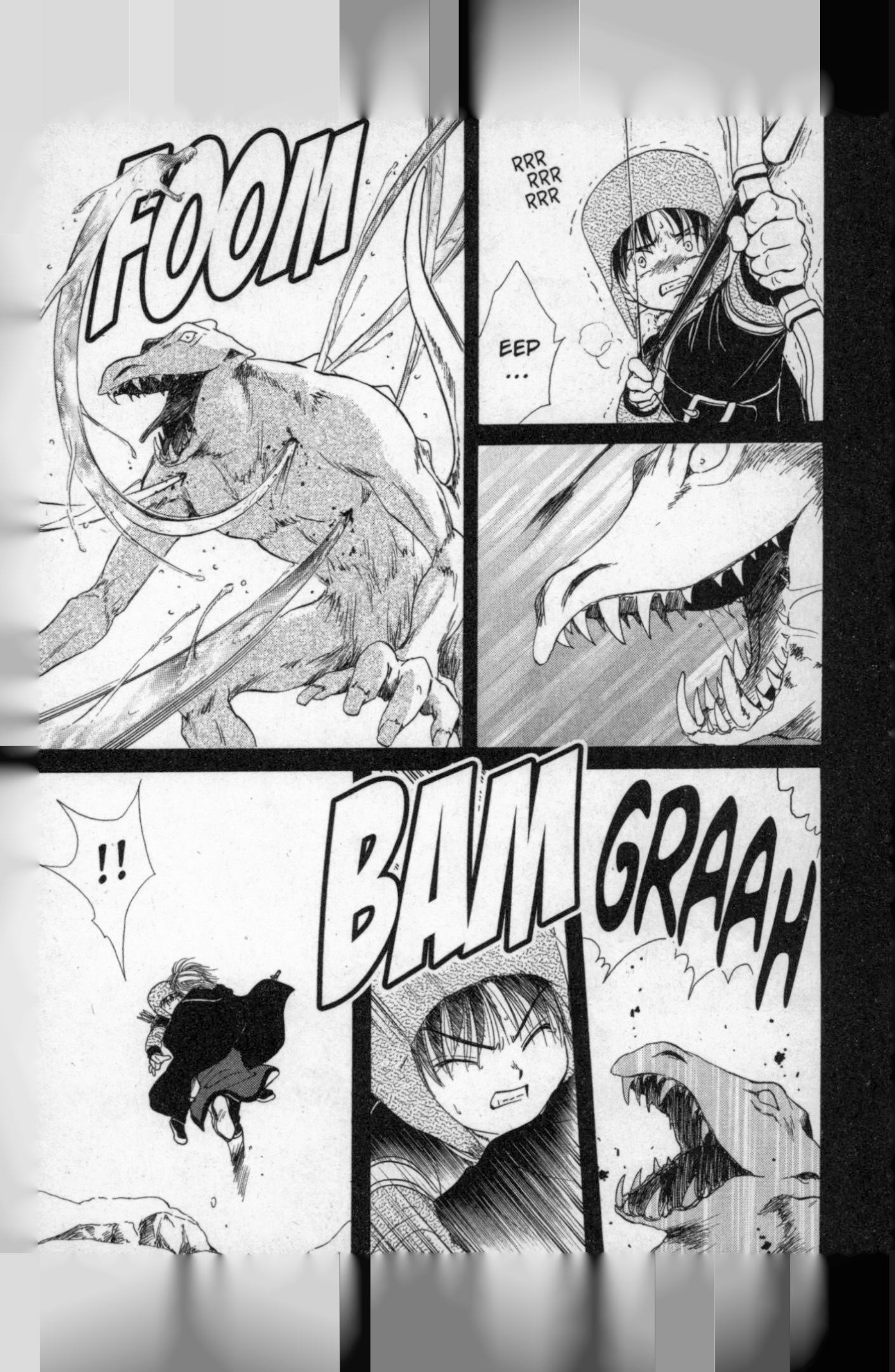
RRR RRR RRR
EEP ...
FOOM
GRAAH
BAM
!!

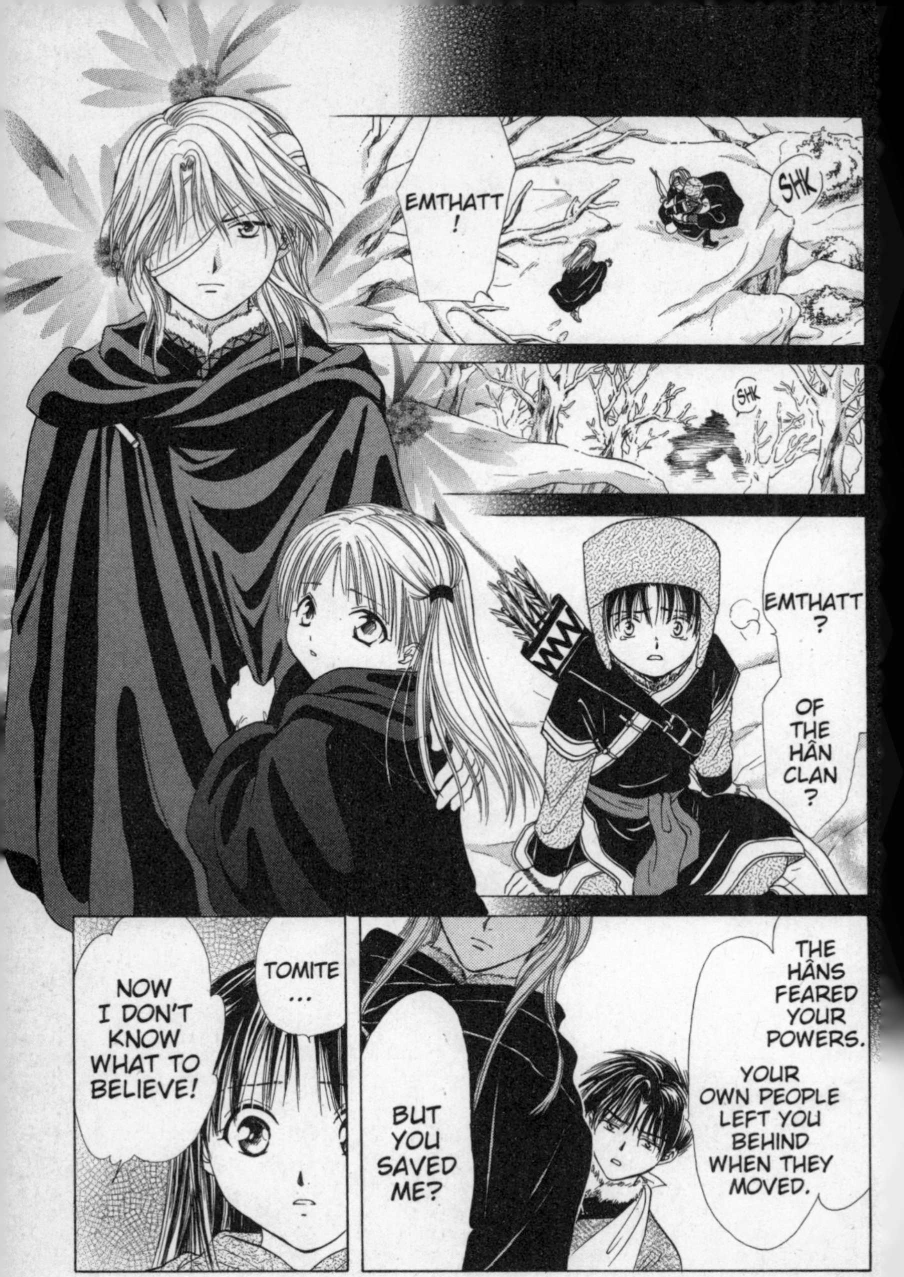
SHK
EMTHATT!
SHK
EMTHATT?
OF THE HÂN CLAN?
THE HÂNS FEARED YOUR POWERS.
YOUR OWN PEOPLE LEFT YOU BEHIND WHEN THEY MOVED.
BUT YOU SAVED ME?
TOMITE...
NOW I DON'T KNOW WHAT TO BELIEVE!

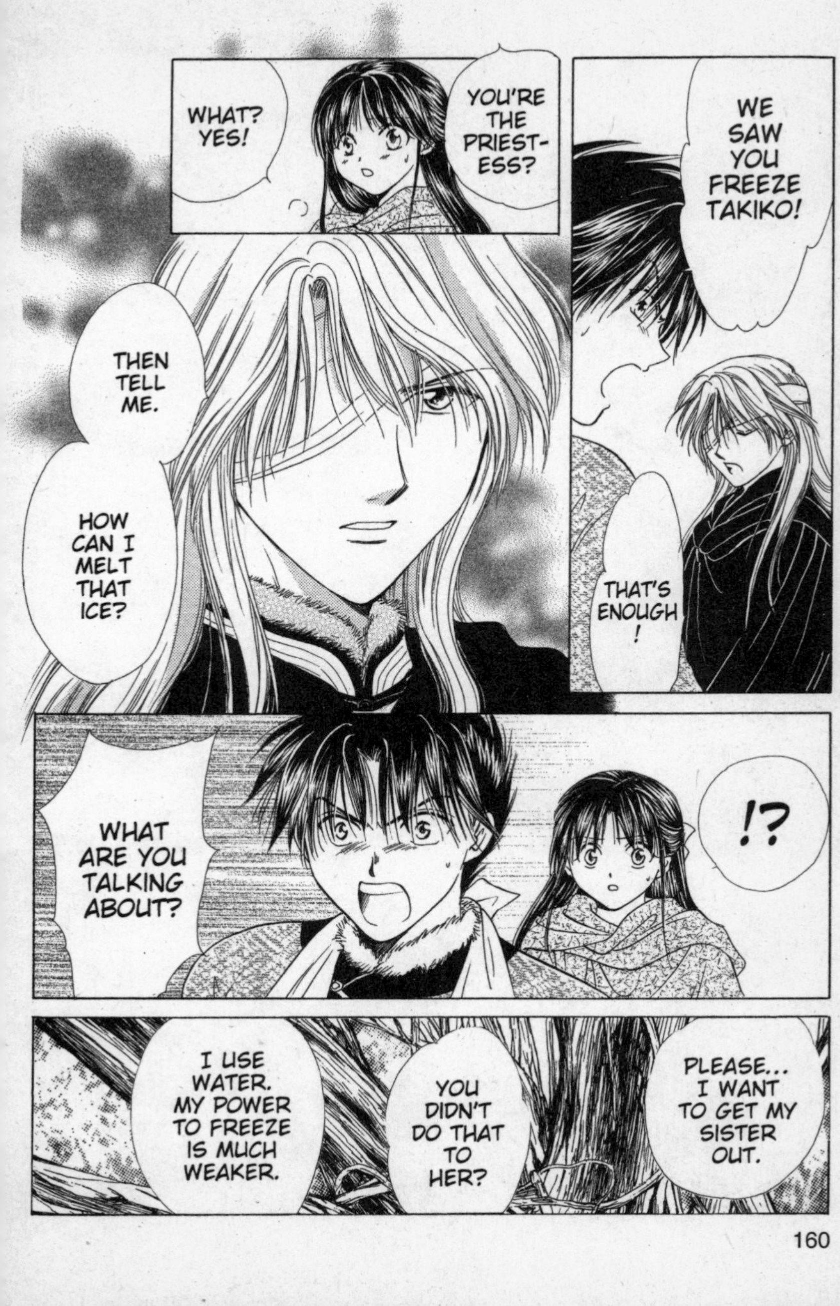
WE SAW YOU FREEZE TAKIKO!
THAT'S ENOUGH!
YOU'RE THE PRIEST-ESS?
WHAT? YES!
THEN TELL ME.
HOW CAN I MELT THAT ICE?
!?
WHAT ARE YOU TALKING ABOUT?
PLEASE... I WANT TO GET MY SISTER OUT.
YOU DIDN'T DO THAT TO HER?
I USE WATER. MY POWER TO FREEZE IS MUCH WEAKER.

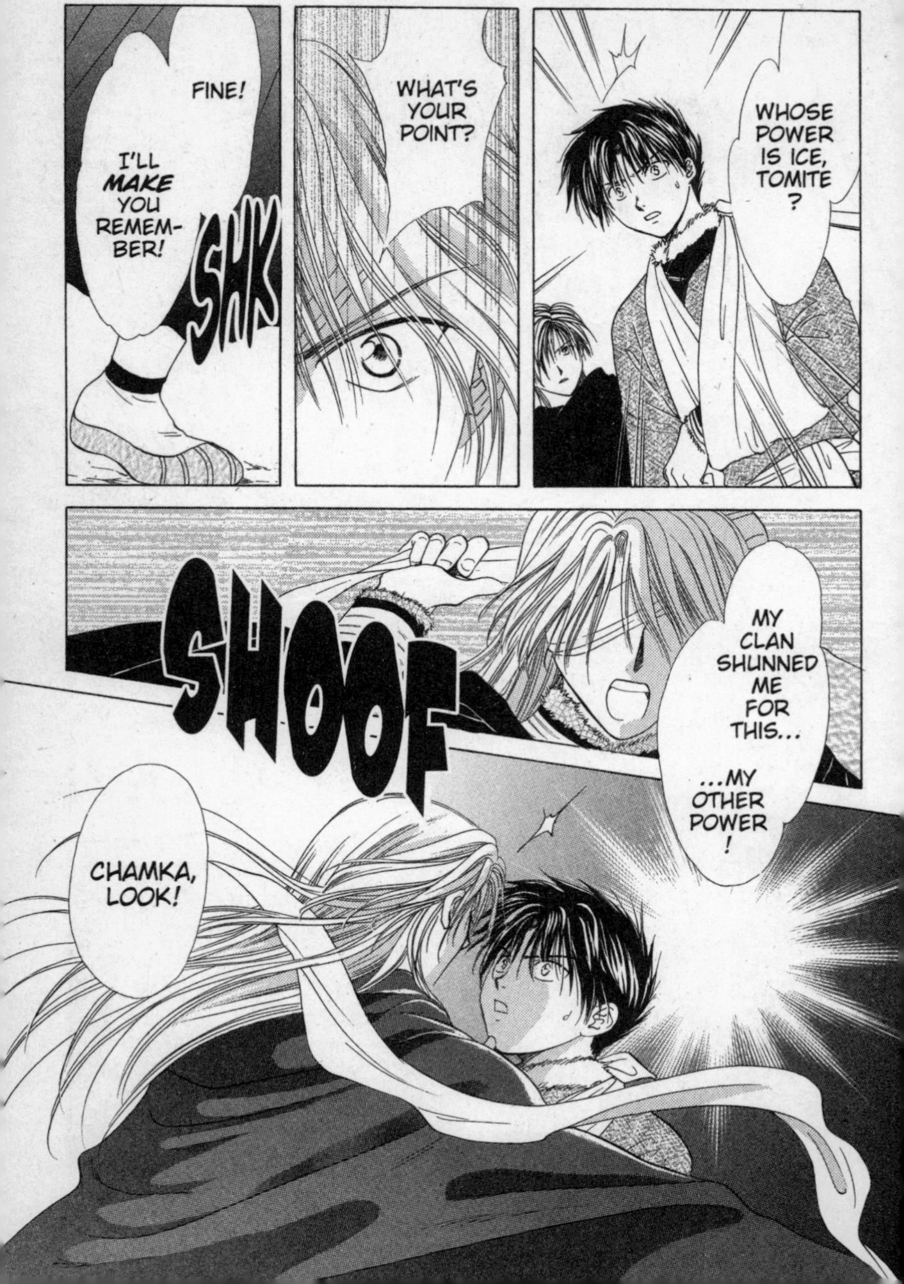
WHOSE POWER IS ICE, TOMITE?
WHAT'S YOUR POINT?
FINE!
I'LL *MAKE* YOU REMEMBER!
SHK
MY CLAN SHUNNED ME FOR THIS...
...MY OTHER POWER!
SHOOF
CHAMKA, LOOK!

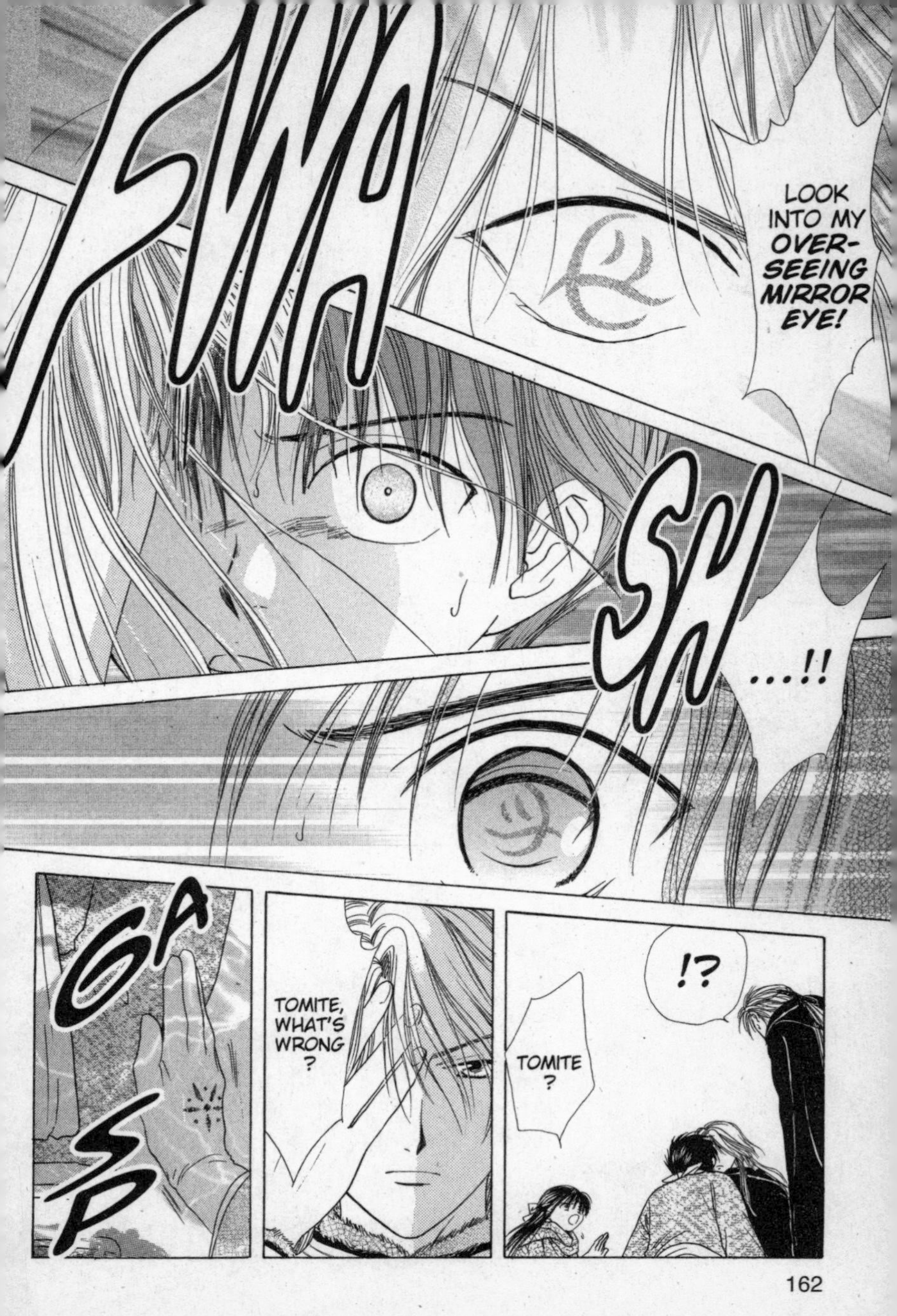
SWA
LOOK INTO MY OVER-SEEING MIRROR EYE!
SH
...!!
!?
TOMITE ?
TOMITE, WHAT'S WRONG ?
GA
SP

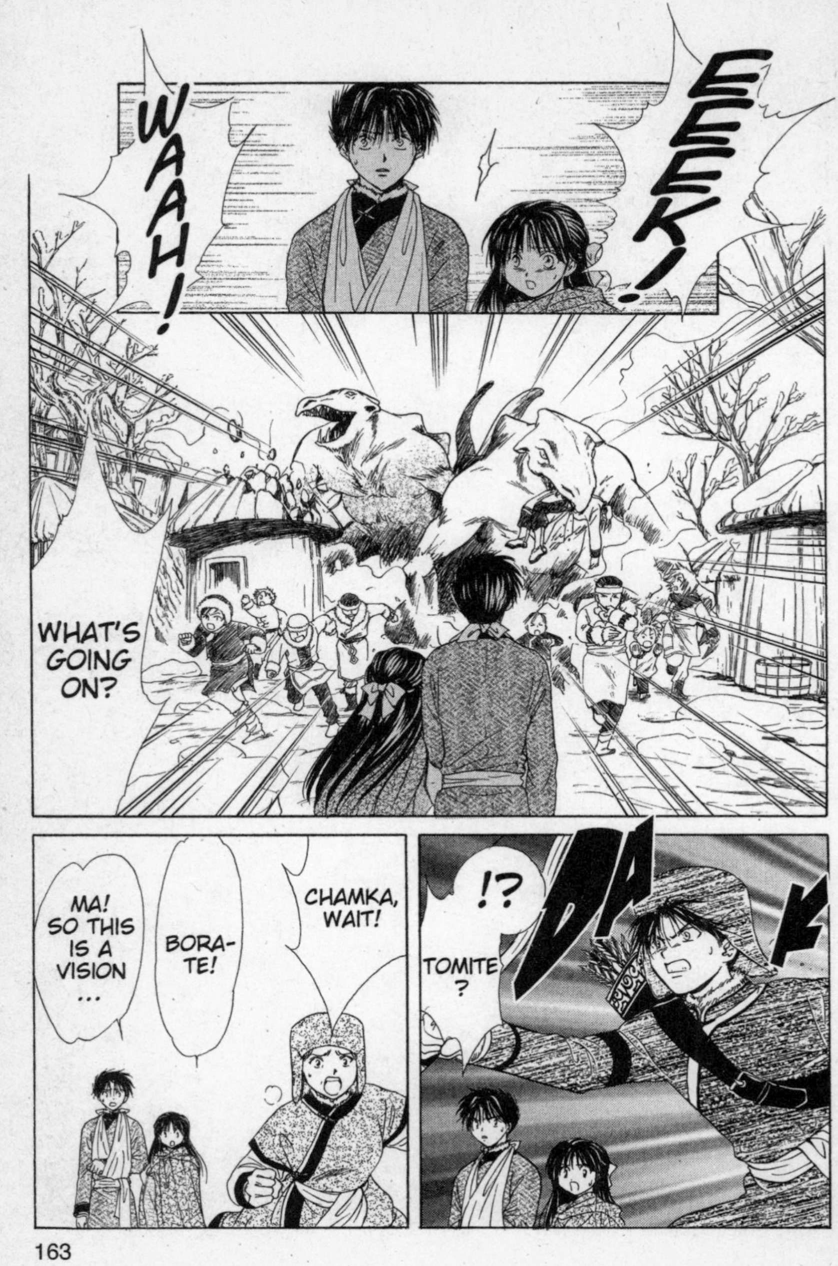
EEEEK!
WAAH!
WHAT'S GOING ON?
DAK
!?
TOMITE?
CHAMKA, WAIT!
BORA-TE!
MA! SO THIS IS A VISION...

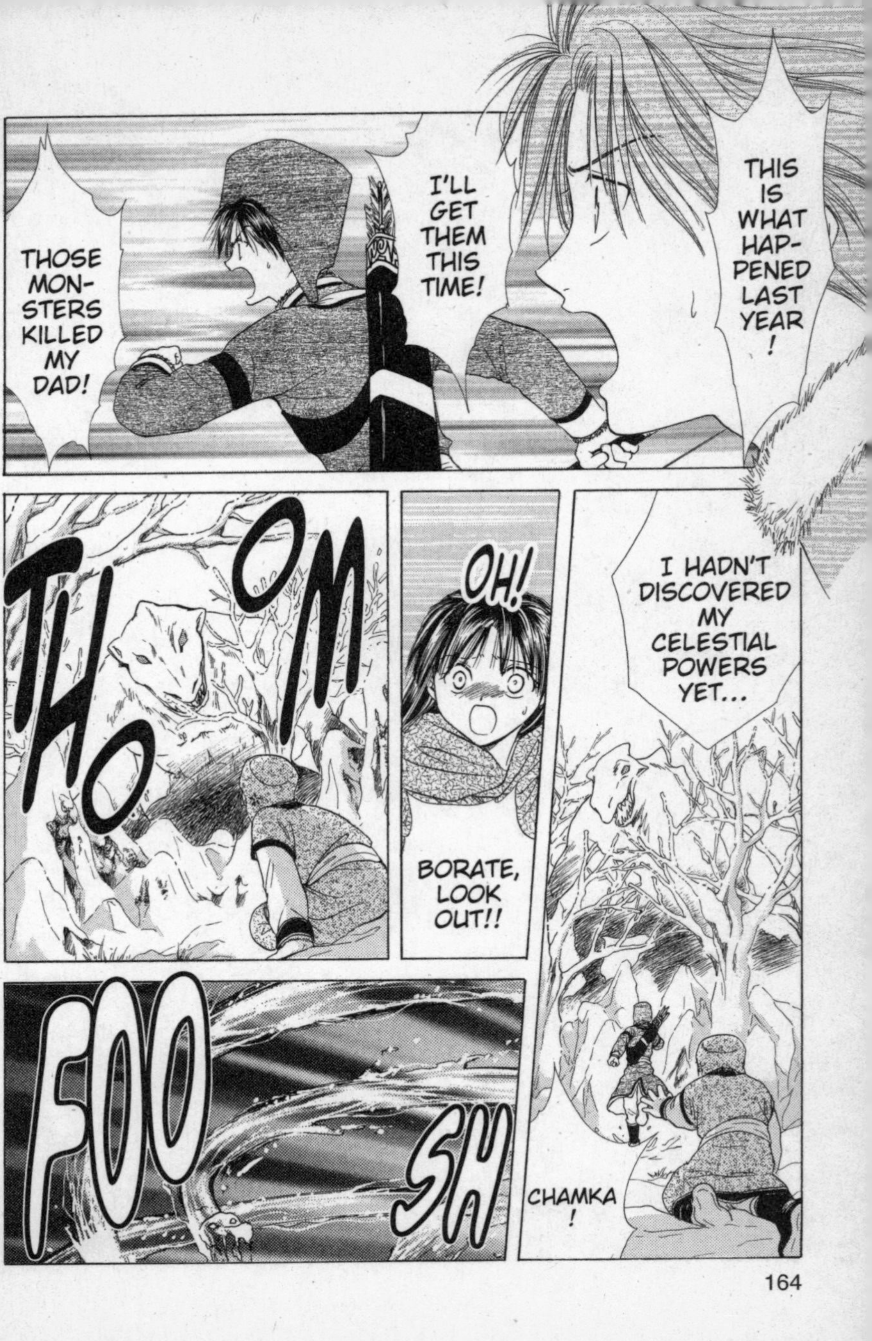
THIS IS WHAT HAP-PENED LAST YEAR!
I'LL GET THEM THIS TIME!
THOSE MON-STERS KILLED MY DAD!
I HADN'T DISCOVERED MY CELESTIAL POWERS YET...
CHAMKA!
OH!
BORATE, LOOK OUT!!
THOOM
FOOSH

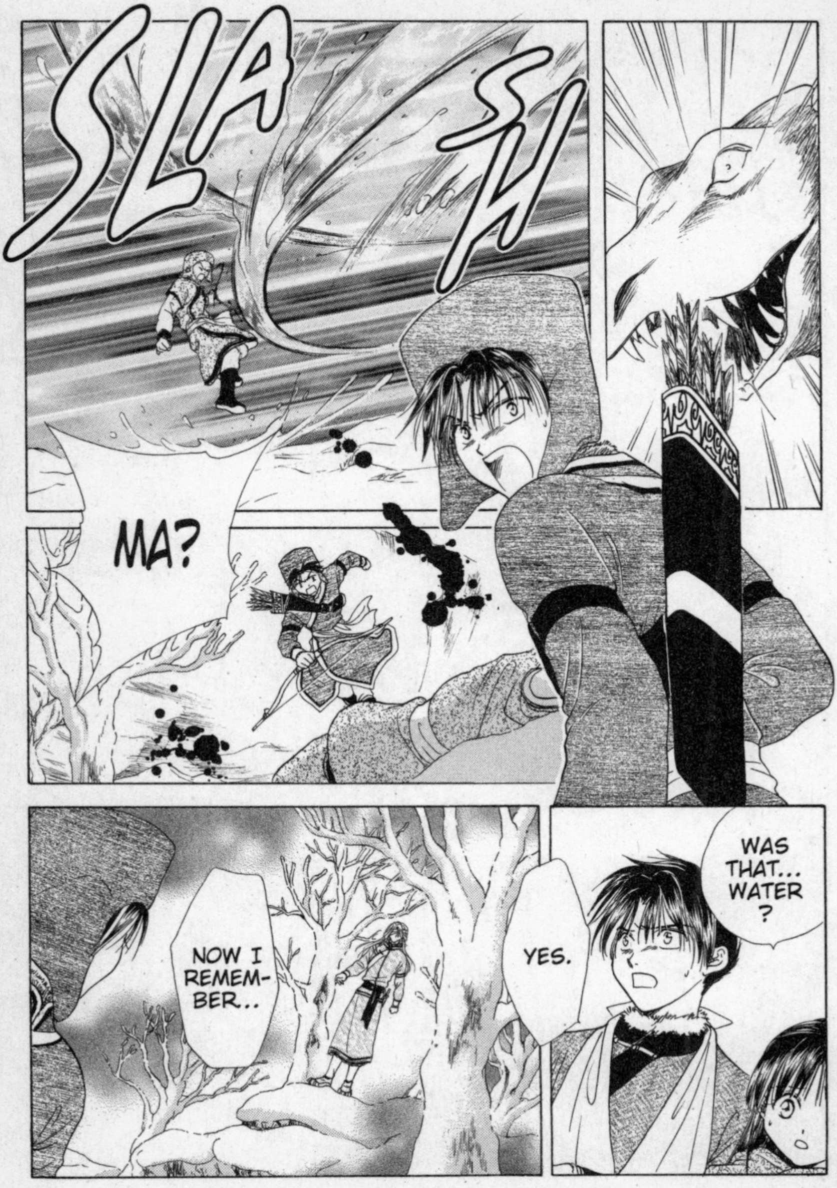
SLASH
MA?
WAS THAT... WATER?
YES.
NOW I REMEMBER...

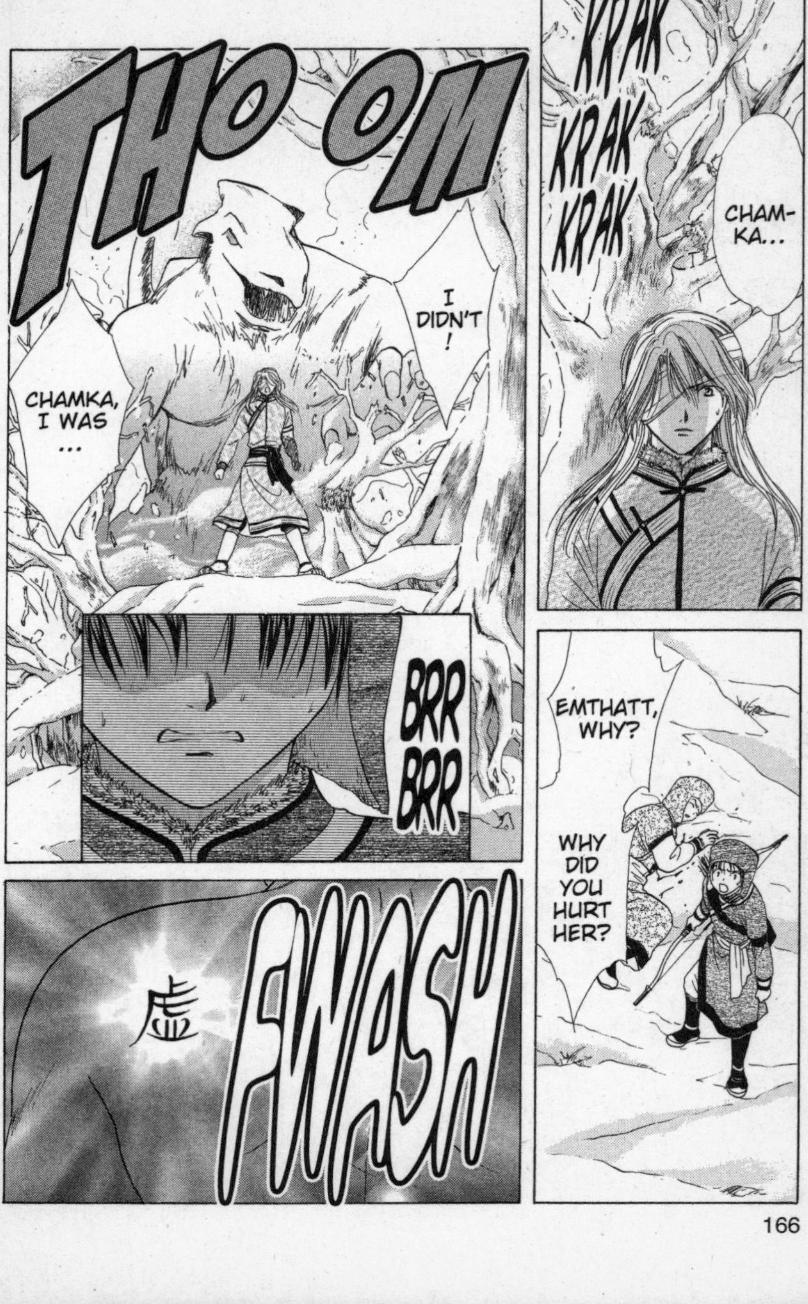
KRAK KRAK KRAK
CHAM-KA...
THOOM
I DIDN'T!
CHAMKA, I WAS...
EMTHATT, WHY?
WHY DID YOU HURT HER?
BRR BRR
虚
FWASH

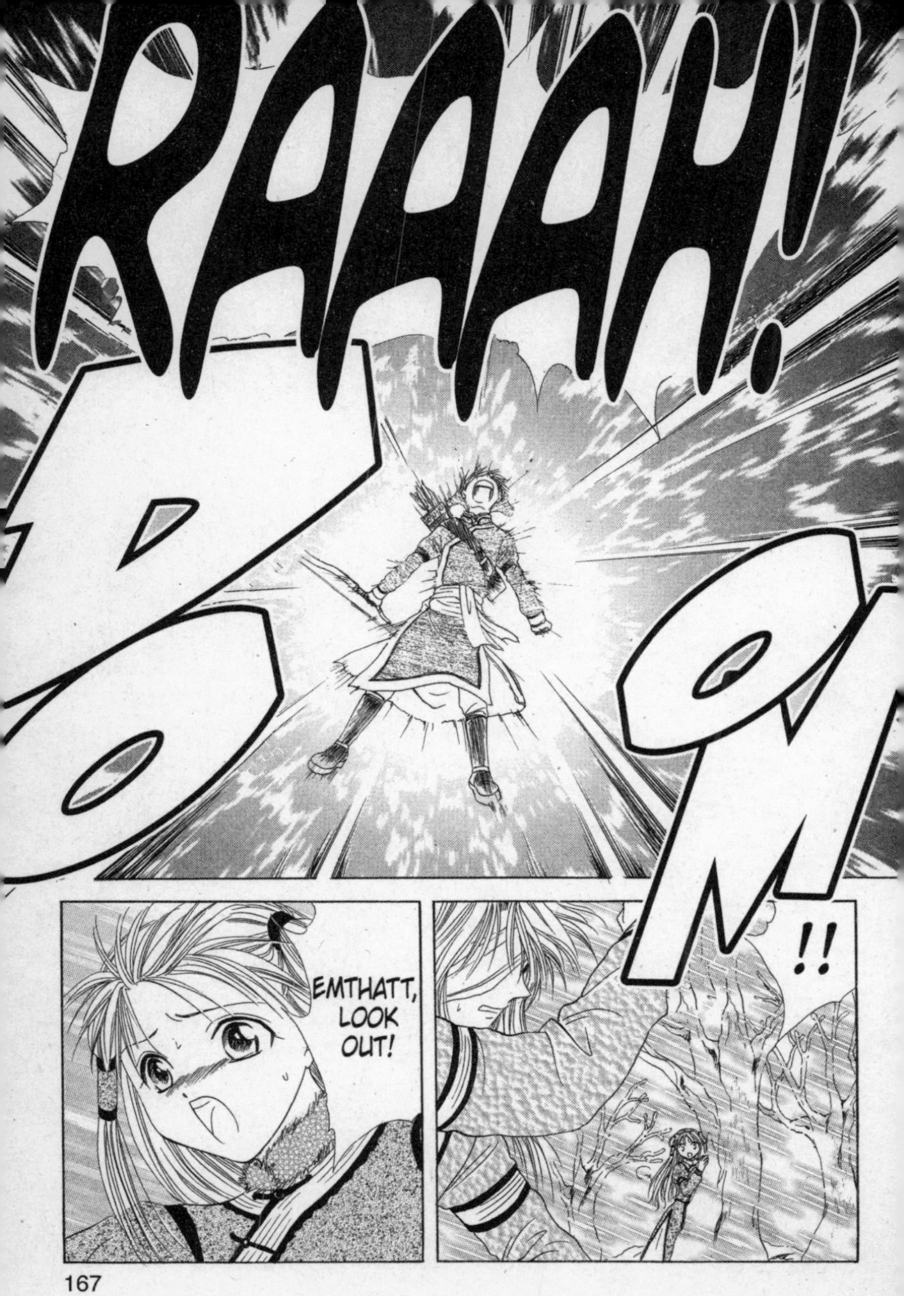
RAAAH!
!!
EMTHATT, LOOK OUT!

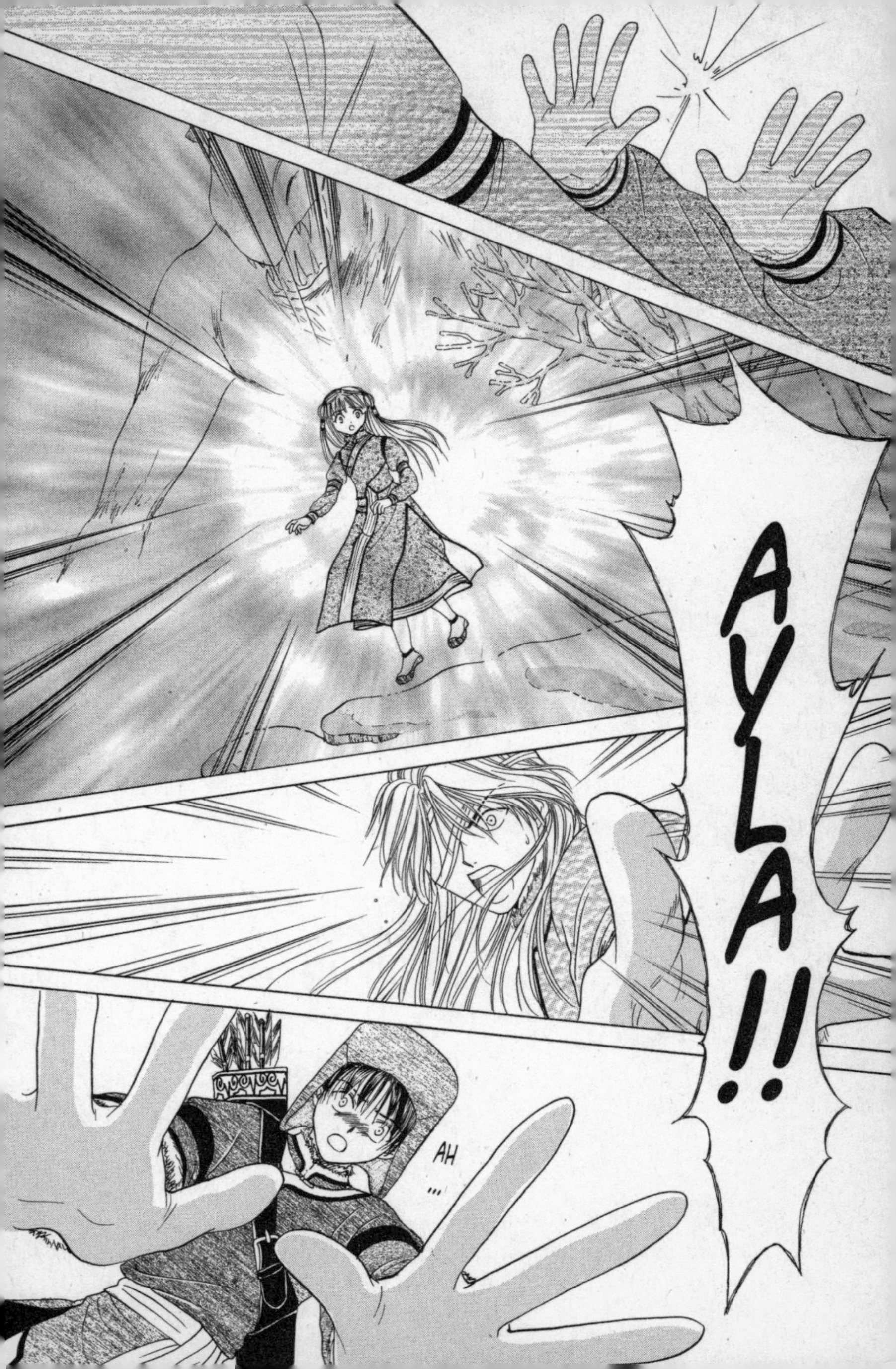
AYLA!!
AH
...

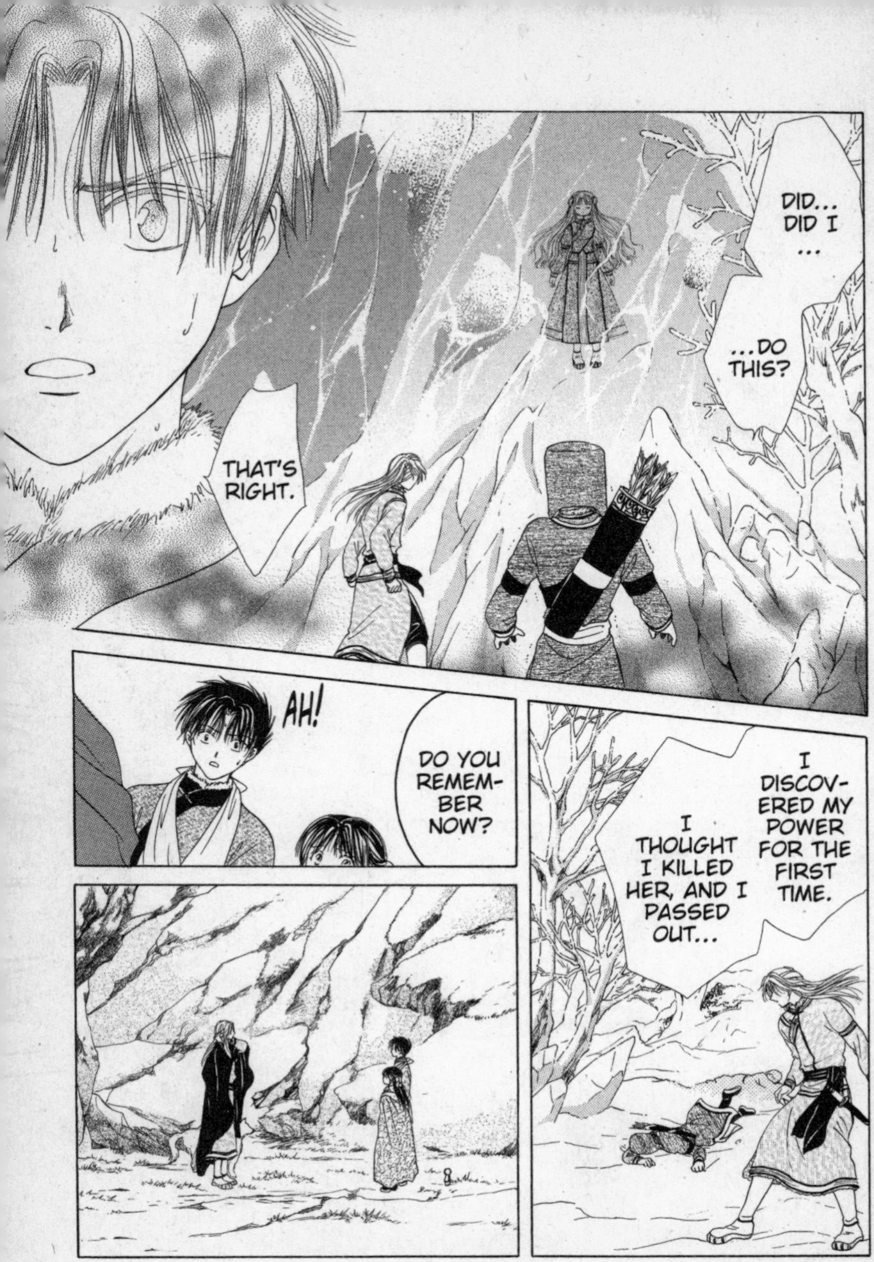
DID... DID I ...
...DO THIS?
THAT'S RIGHT.
I DISCOVERED MY POWER FOR THE FIRST TIME.
I THOUGHT I KILLED HER, AND I PASSED OUT...
DO YOU REMEMBER NOW?
AH!

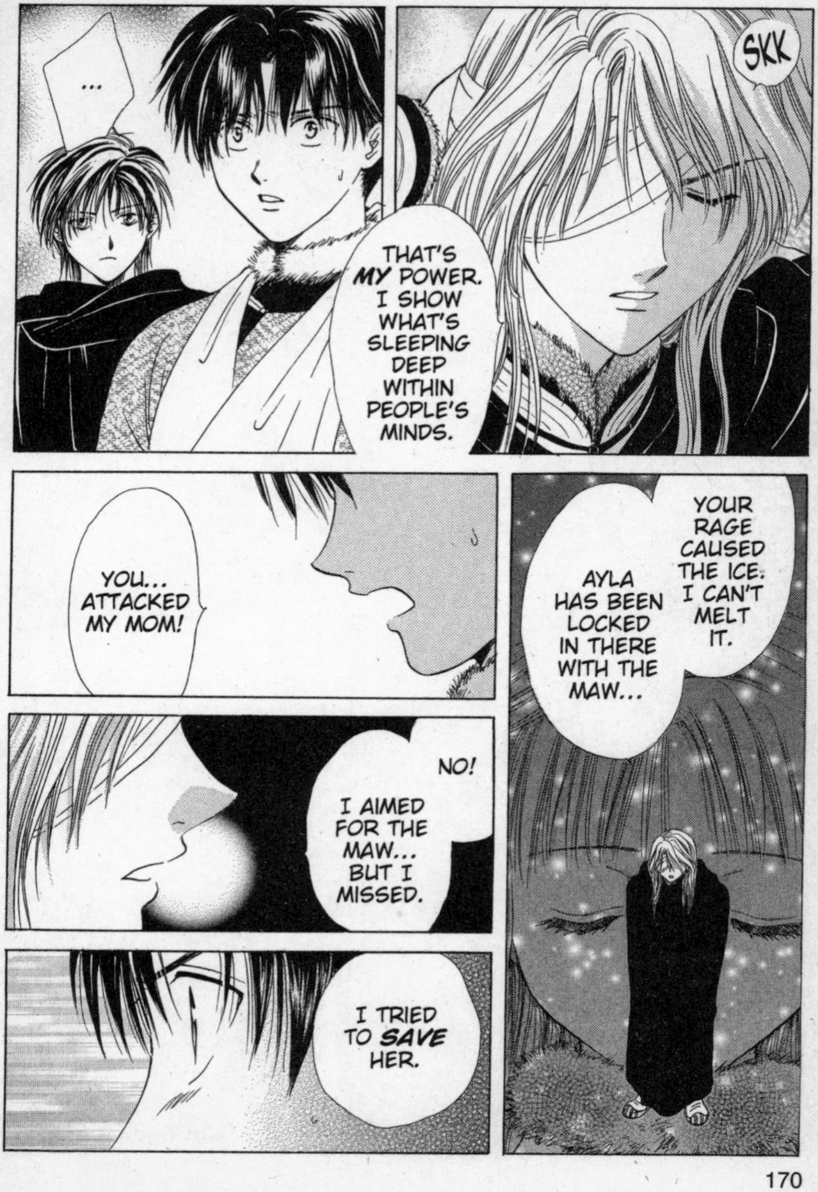
SKK
THAT'S *MY* POWER. I SHOW WHAT'S SLEEPING DEEP WITHIN PEOPLE'S MINDS.
...
YOUR RAGE CAUSED THE ICE. I CAN'T MELT IT.
AYLA HAS BEEN LOCKED IN THERE WITH THE MAW...
YOU... ATTACKED MY MOM!
NO!
I AIMED FOR THE MAW... BUT I MISSED.
I TRIED TO *SAVE* HER.

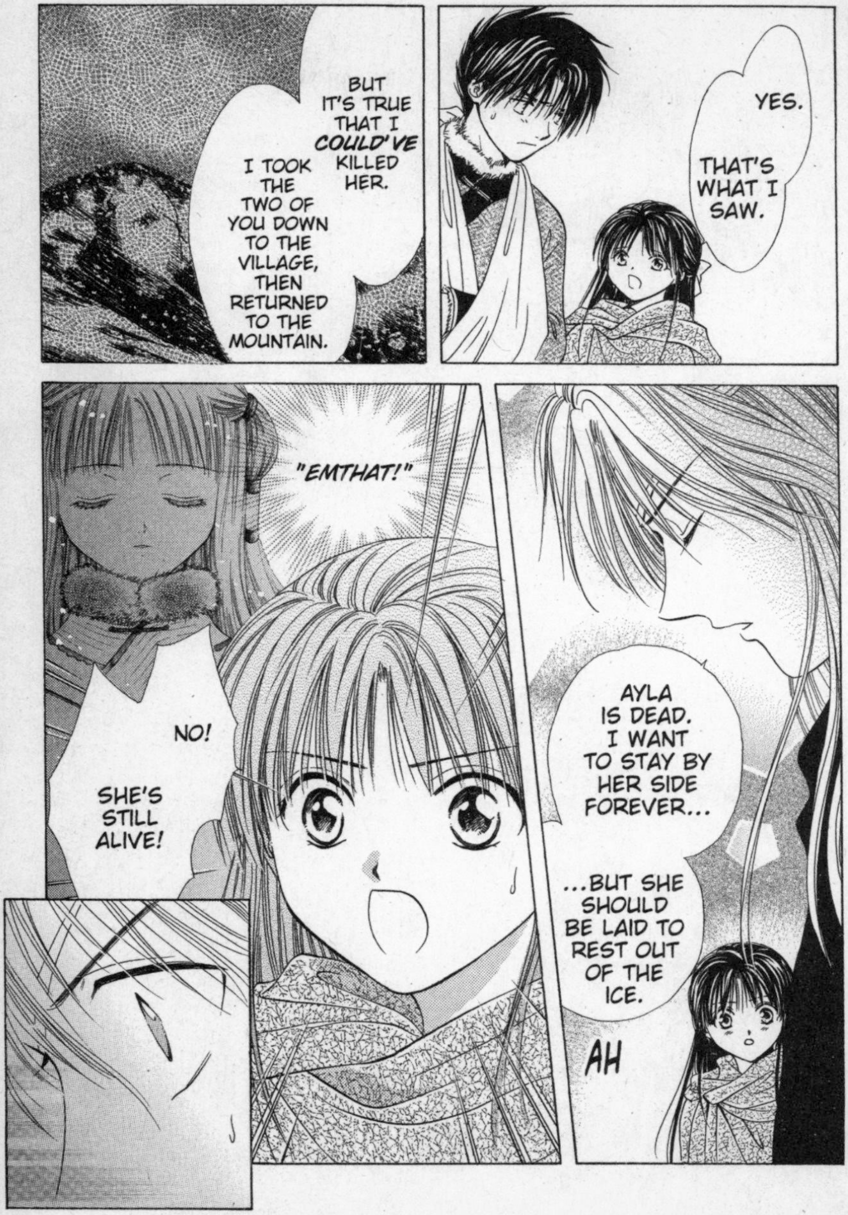
YES.
THAT'S WHAT I SAW.
BUT IT'S TRUE THAT I *COULD'VE* KILLED HER.
I TOOK THE TWO OF YOU DOWN TO THE VILLAGE, THEN RETURNED TO THE MOUNTAIN.
AYLA IS DEAD. I WANT TO STAY BY HER SIDE FOREVER...
...BUT SHE SHOULD BE LAID TO REST OUT OF THE ICE.
AH
"EMTHAT!"
NO!
SHE'S STILL ALIVE!

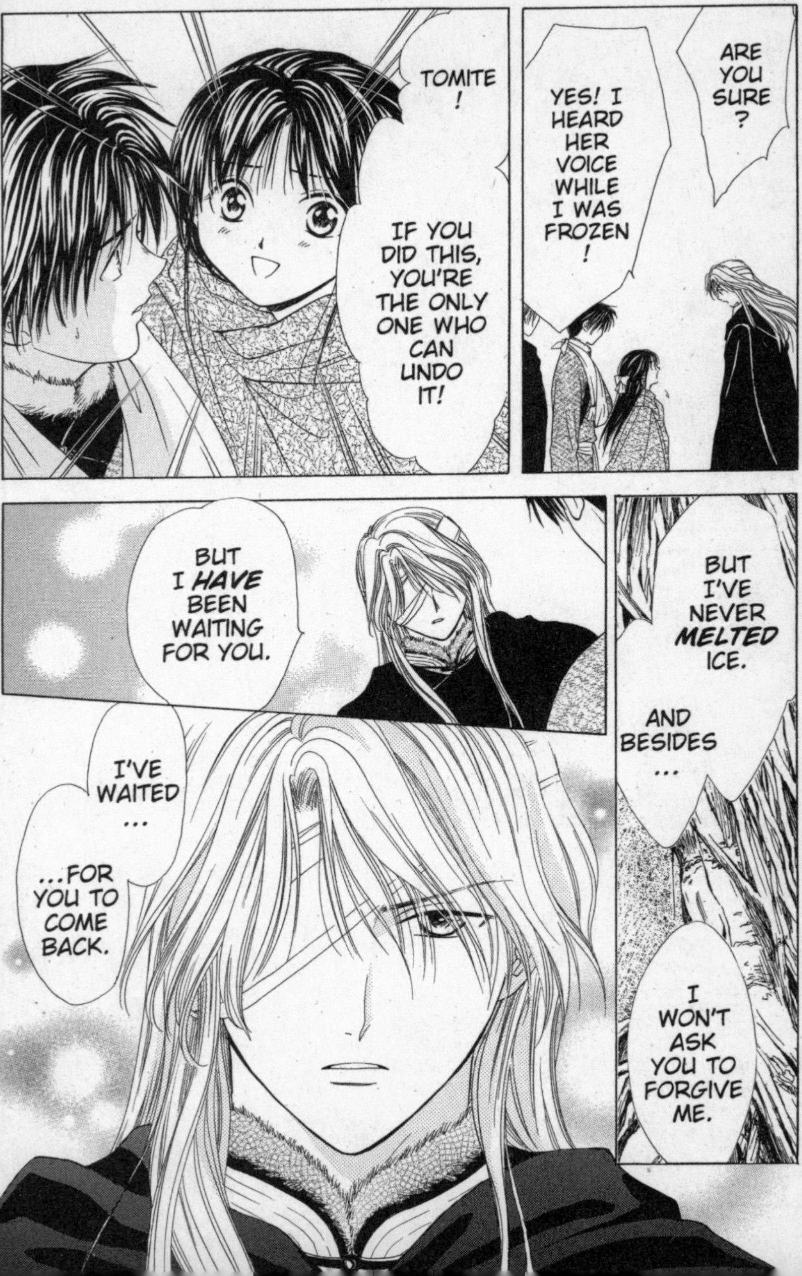
ARE YOU SURE?
YES! I HEARD HER VOICE WHILE I WAS FROZEN!
TOMITE!
IF YOU DID THIS, YOU'RE THE ONLY ONE WHO CAN UNDO IT!
BUT I'VE NEVER *MELTED* ICE.
AND BESIDES...
I WON'T ASK YOU TO FORGIVE ME.
BUT I *HAVE* BEEN WAITING FOR YOU.
I'VE WAITED...
...FOR YOU TO COME BACK.

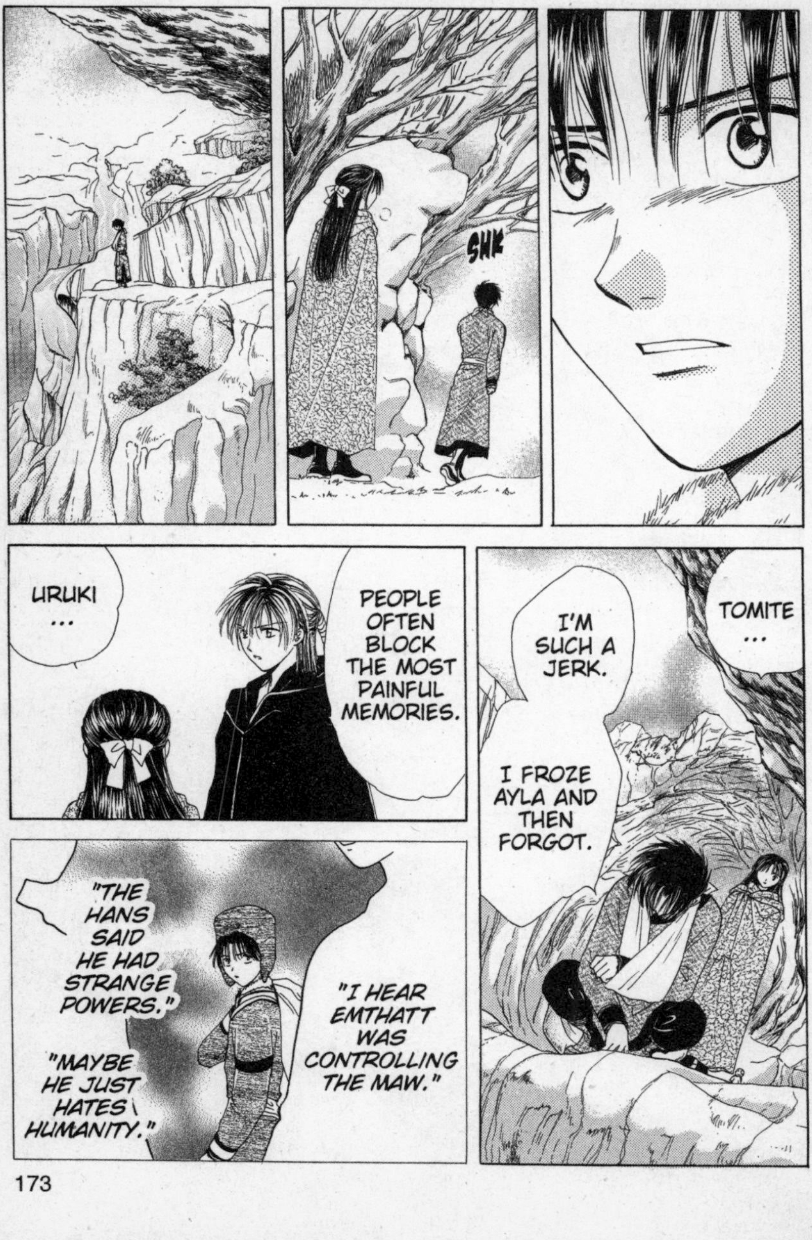
SHK
TOMITE ...
I'M SUCH A JERK.
I FROZE AYLA AND THEN FORGOT.
PEOPLE OFTEN BLOCK THE MOST PAINFUL MEMORIES.
URUKI ...
"THE HANS SAID HE HAD STRANGE POWERS."
"I HEAR EMTHATT WAS CONTROLLING THE MAW."
"MAYBE HE JUST HATES HUMANITY."

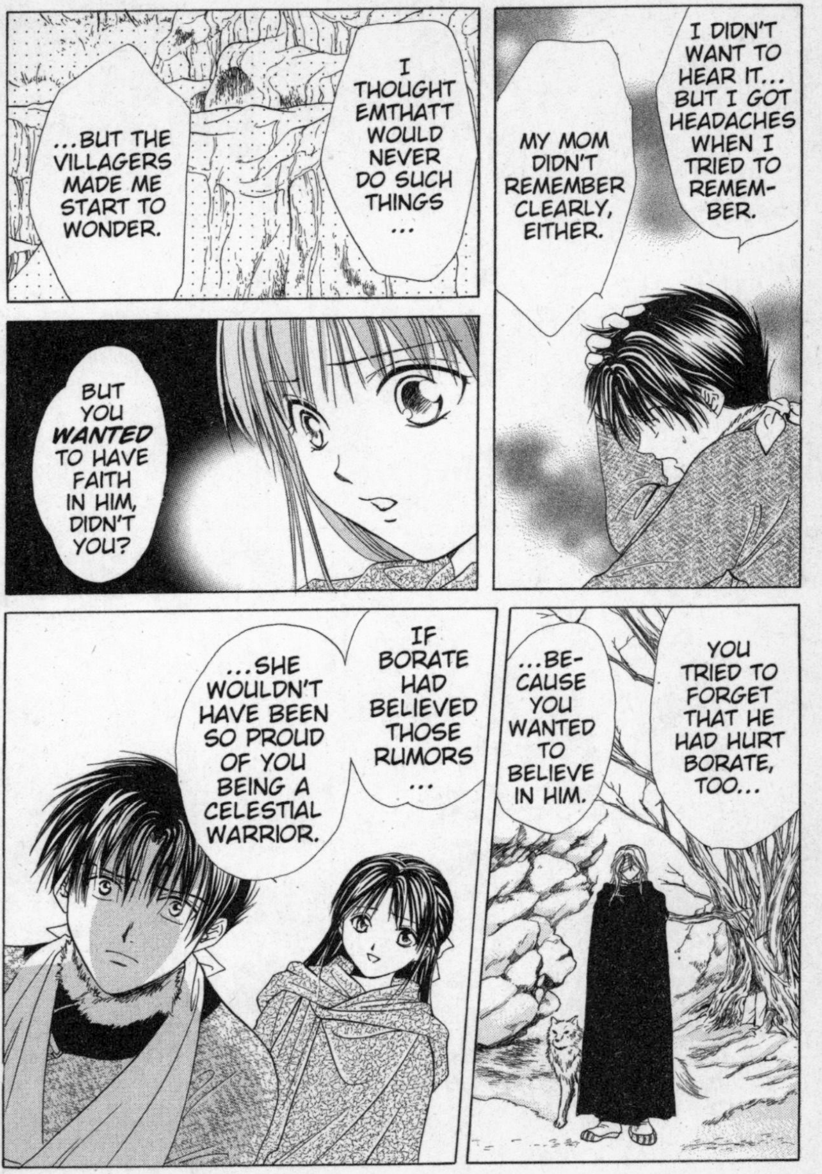
I DIDN'T WANT TO HEAR IT... BUT I GOT HEADACHES WHEN I TRIED TO REMEM-BER.
MY MOM DIDN'T REMEMBER CLEARLY, EITHER.
I THOUGHT EMTHATT WOULD NEVER DO SUCH THINGS...
...BUT THE VILLAGERS MADE ME START TO WONDER.
BUT YOU *WANTED* TO HAVE FAITH IN HIM, DIDN'T YOU?
YOU TRIED TO FORGET THAT HE HAD HURT BORATE, TOO...
...BE-CAUSE YOU WANTED TO BELIEVE IN HIM.
IF BORATE HAD BELIEVED THOSE RUMORS...
...SHE WOULDN'T HAVE BEEN SO PROUD OF YOU BEING A CELESTIAL WARRIOR.

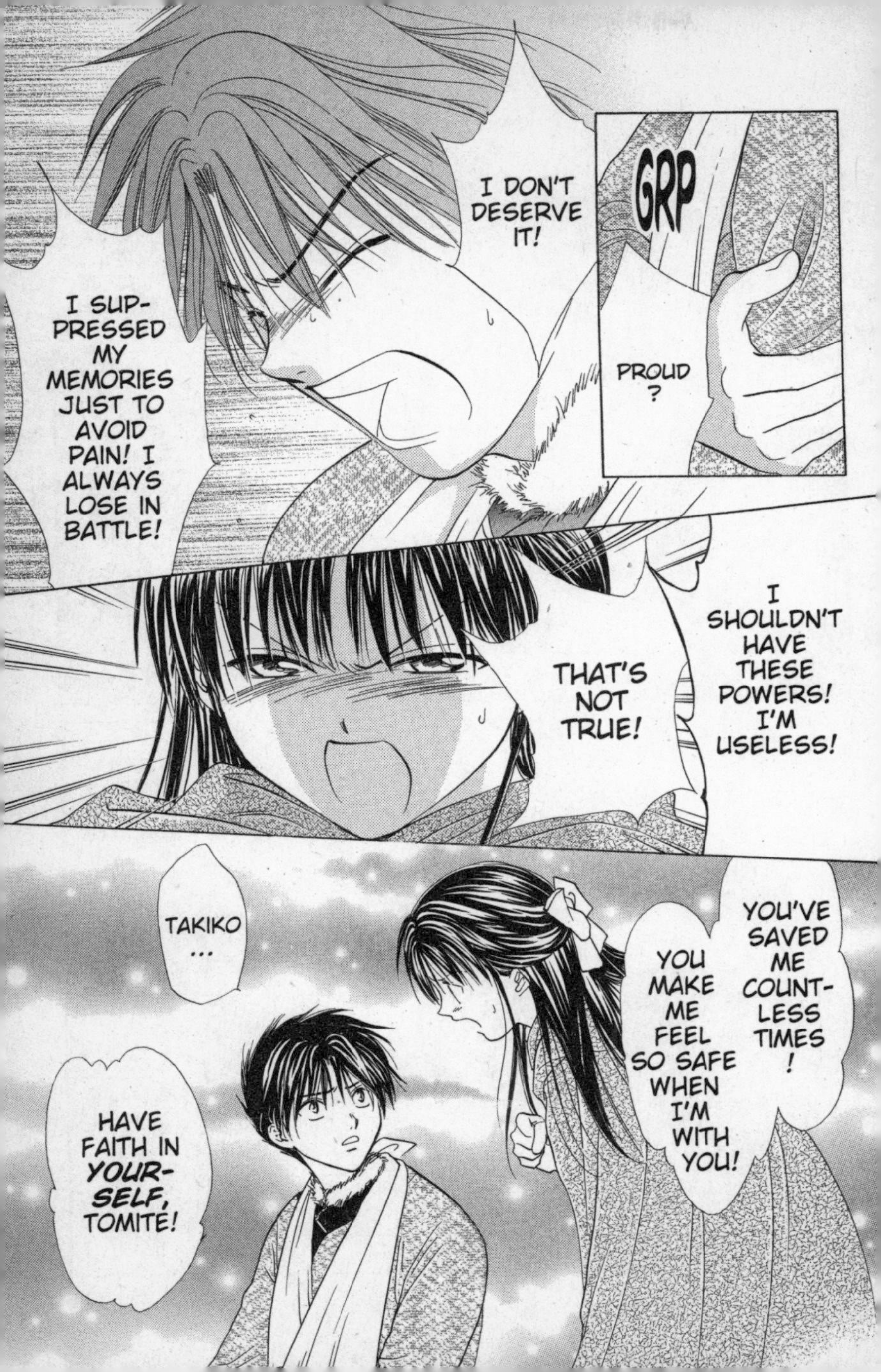
GRP
PROUD?
I DON'T DESERVE IT!
I SUP-PRESSED MY MEMORIES JUST TO AVOID PAIN! I ALWAYS LOSE IN BATTLE!
I SHOULDN'T HAVE THESE POWERS! I'M USELESS!
THAT'S NOT TRUE!
YOU'VE SAVED ME COUNT-LESS TIMES!
YOU MAKE ME FEEL SO SAFE WHEN I'M WITH YOU!
TAKIKO...
HAVE FAITH IN ***YOUR-SELF***, TOMITE!

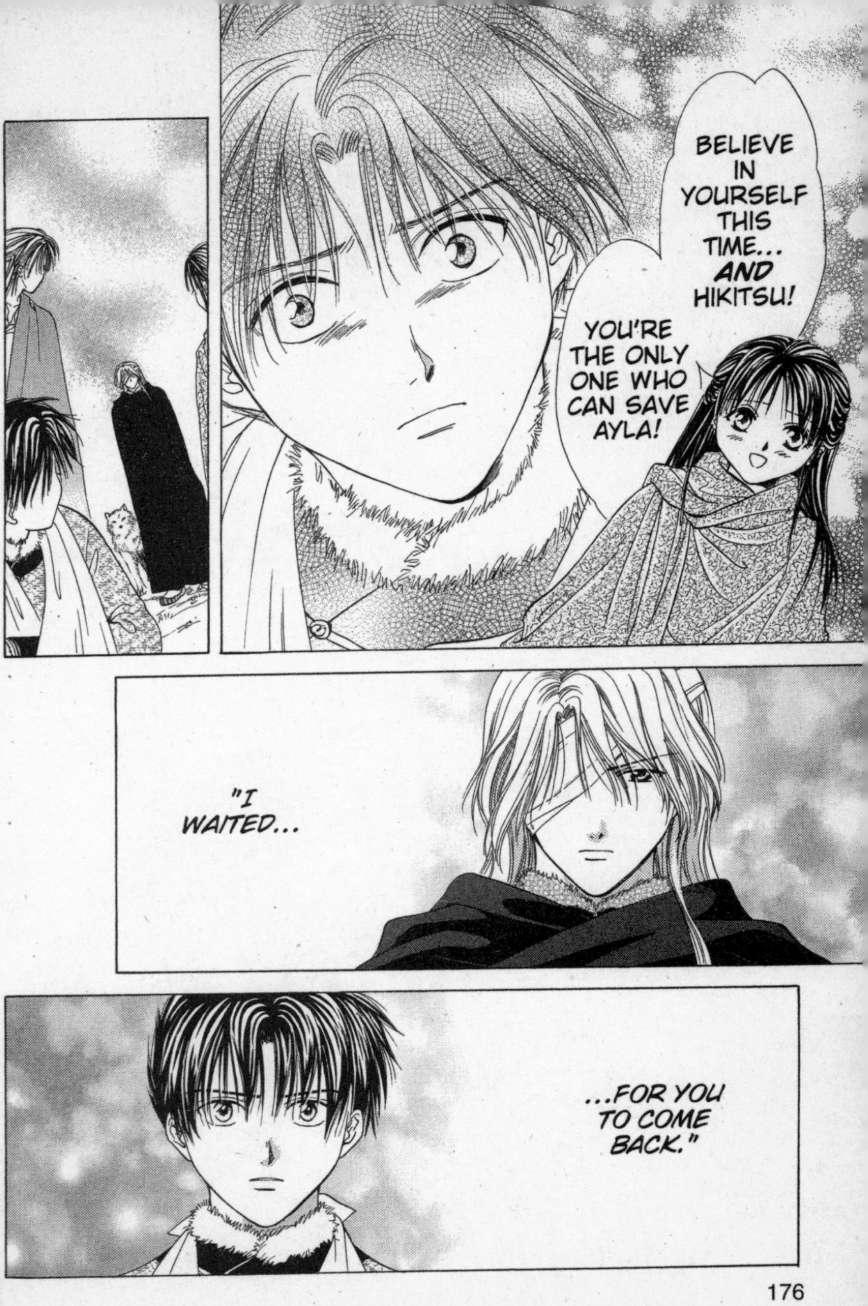
BELIEVE IN YOURSELF THIS TIME... AND HIKITSU!
YOU'RE THE ONLY ONE WHO CAN SAVE AYLA!
"I WAITED...
...FOR YOU TO COME BACK."

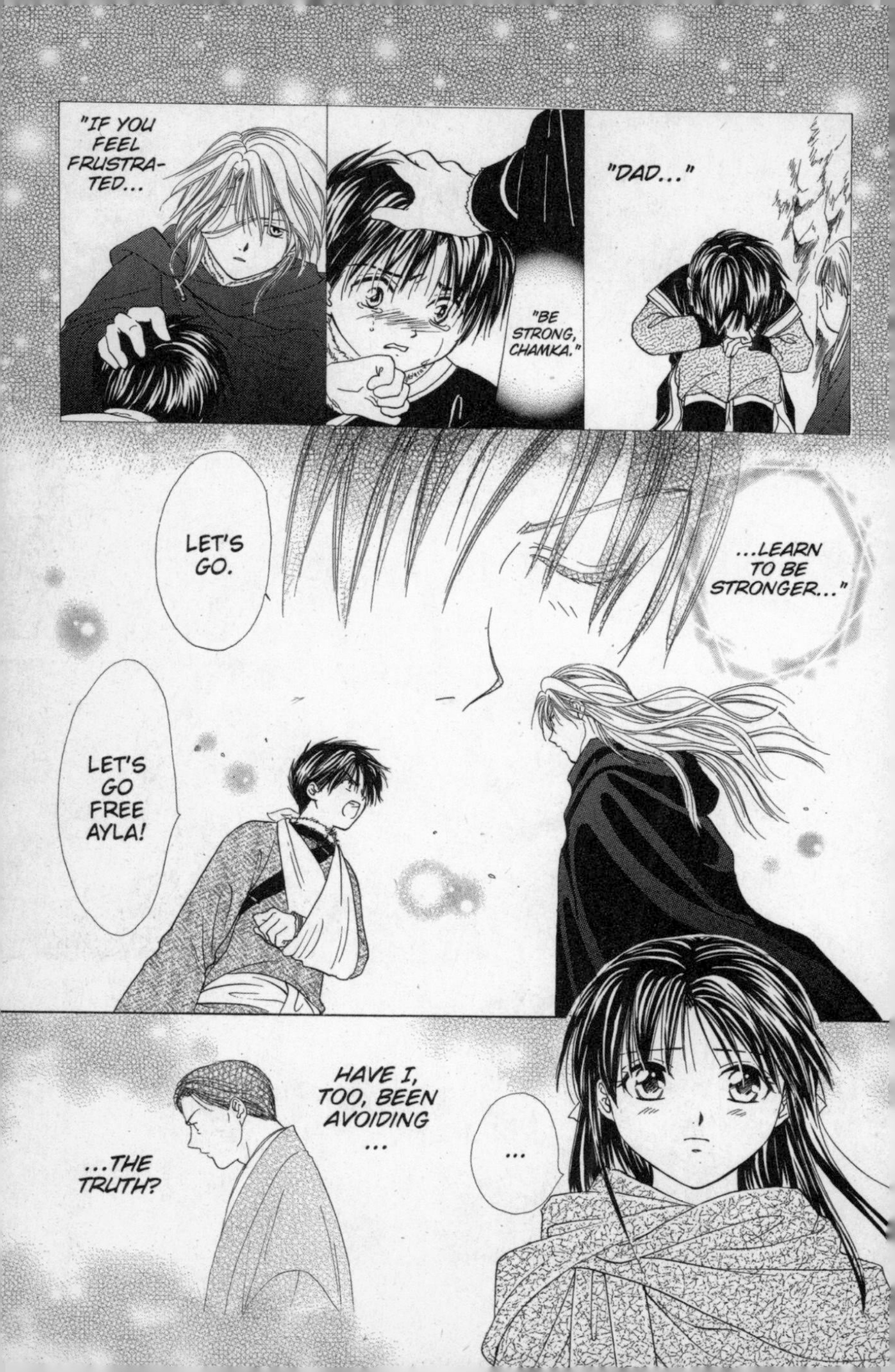
"DAD..."
"BE STRONG, CHAMKA."
"IF YOU FEEL FRUSTRATED...
...LEARN TO BE STRONGER..."
LET'S GO.
LET'S GO FREE AYLA!
...
HAVE I, TOO, BEEN AVOIDING ...
...THE TRUTH?

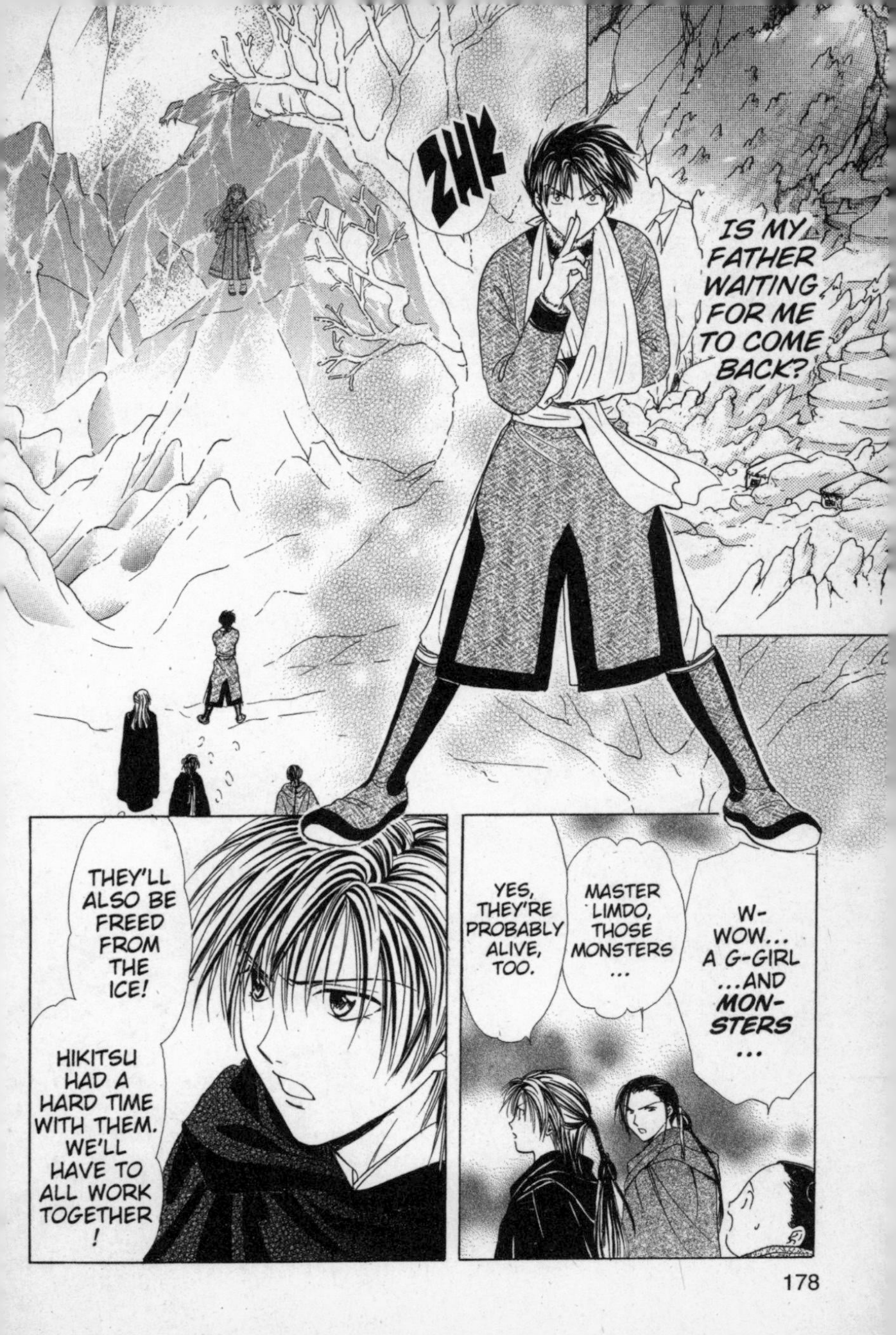
IS MY FATHER WAITING FOR ME TO COME BACK?
ZHK
W- WOW... A G-GIRL ...AND MON-STERS ...
MASTER LIMDO, THOSE MONSTERS ...
YES, THEY'RE PROBABLY ALIVE, TOO.
THEY'LL ALSO BE FREED FROM THE ICE!
HIKITSU HAD A HARD TIME WITH THEM. WE'LL HAVE TO ALL WORK TOGETHER!

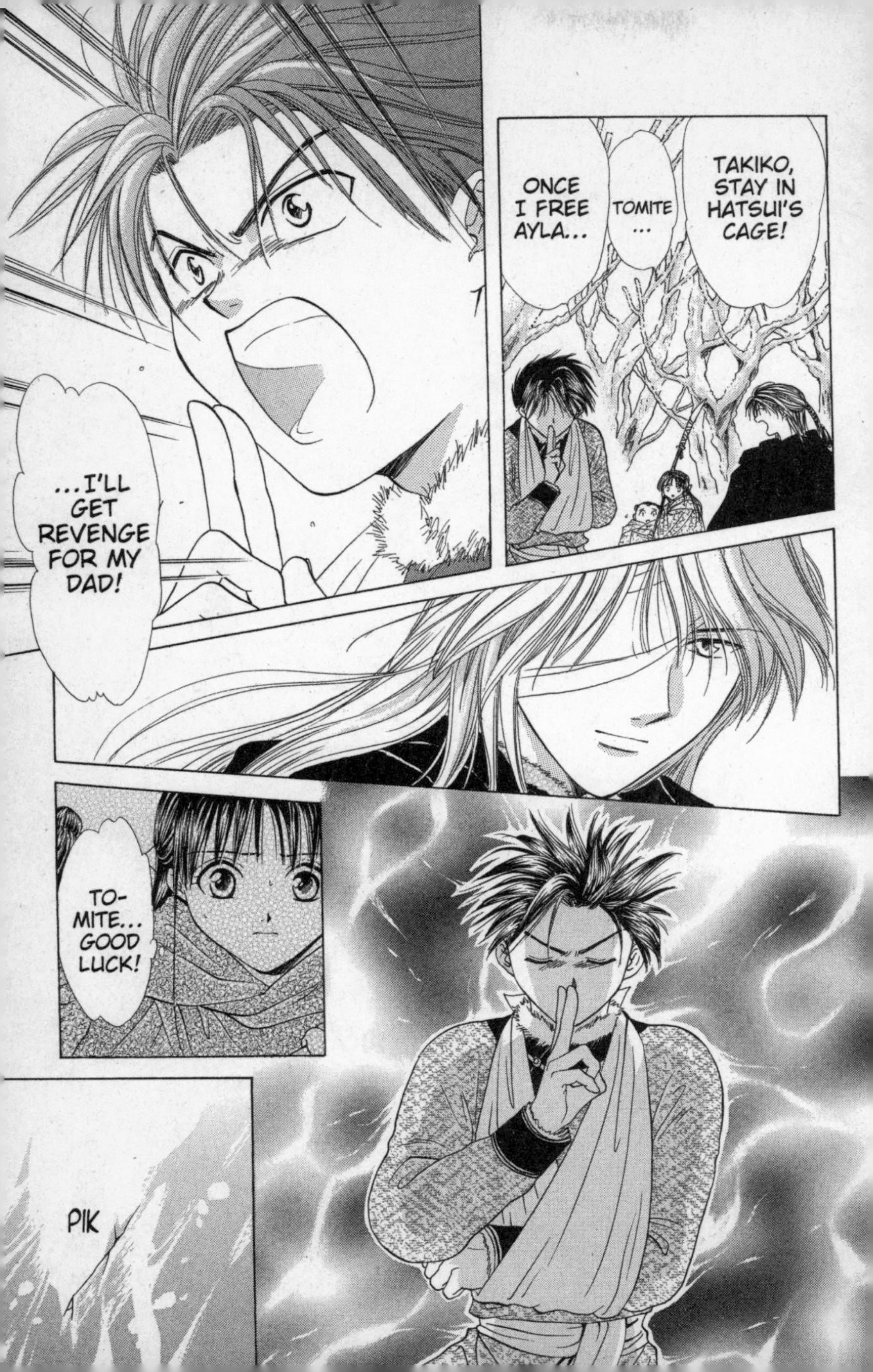
TAKIKO, STAY IN HATSUI'S CAGE!
TOMITE ...
ONCE I FREE AYLA...
...I'LL GET REVENGE FOR MY DAD!
TO-MITE... GOOD LUCK!
PIK

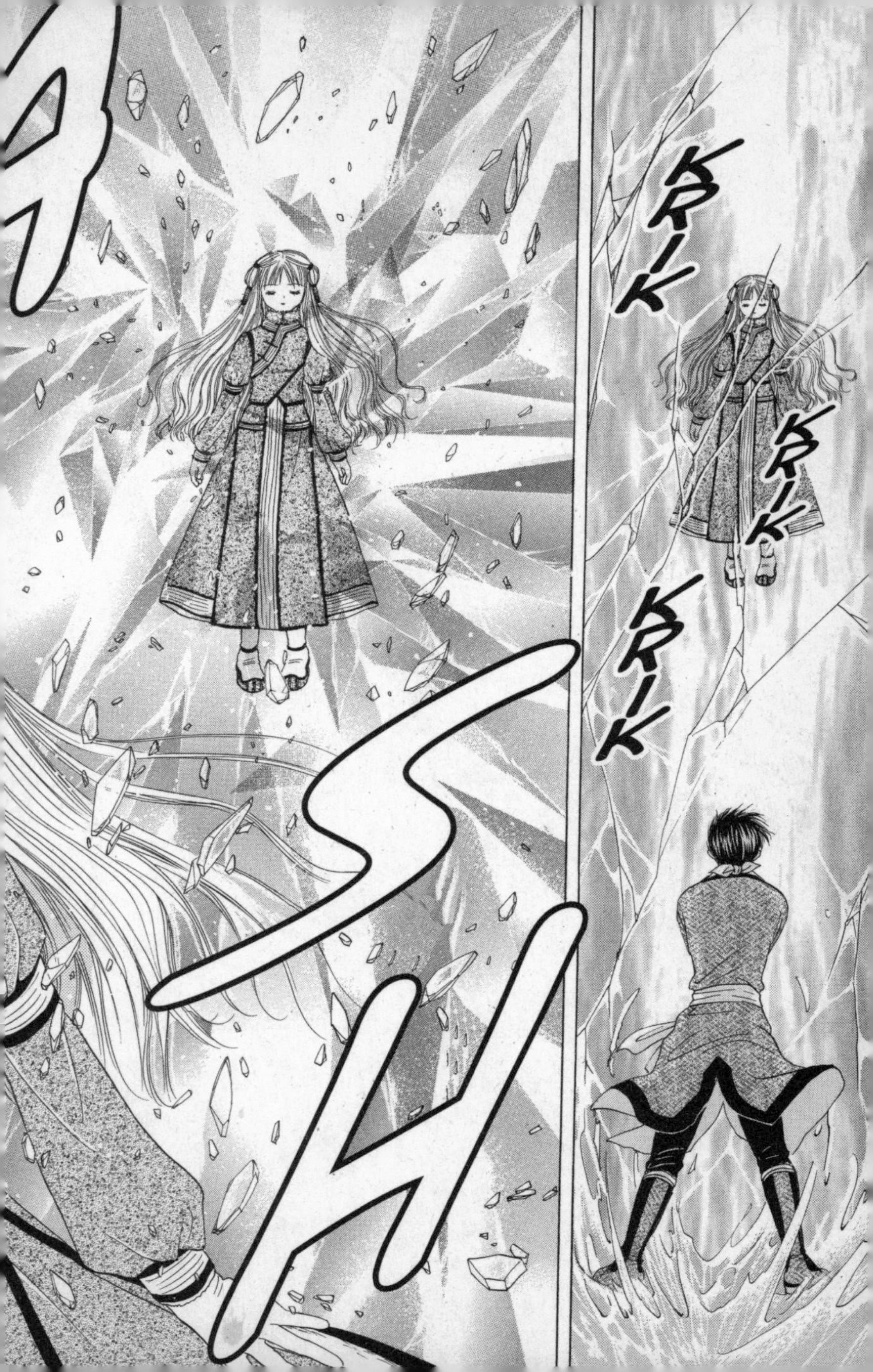
KRIK
KRIK
KRIK
SH

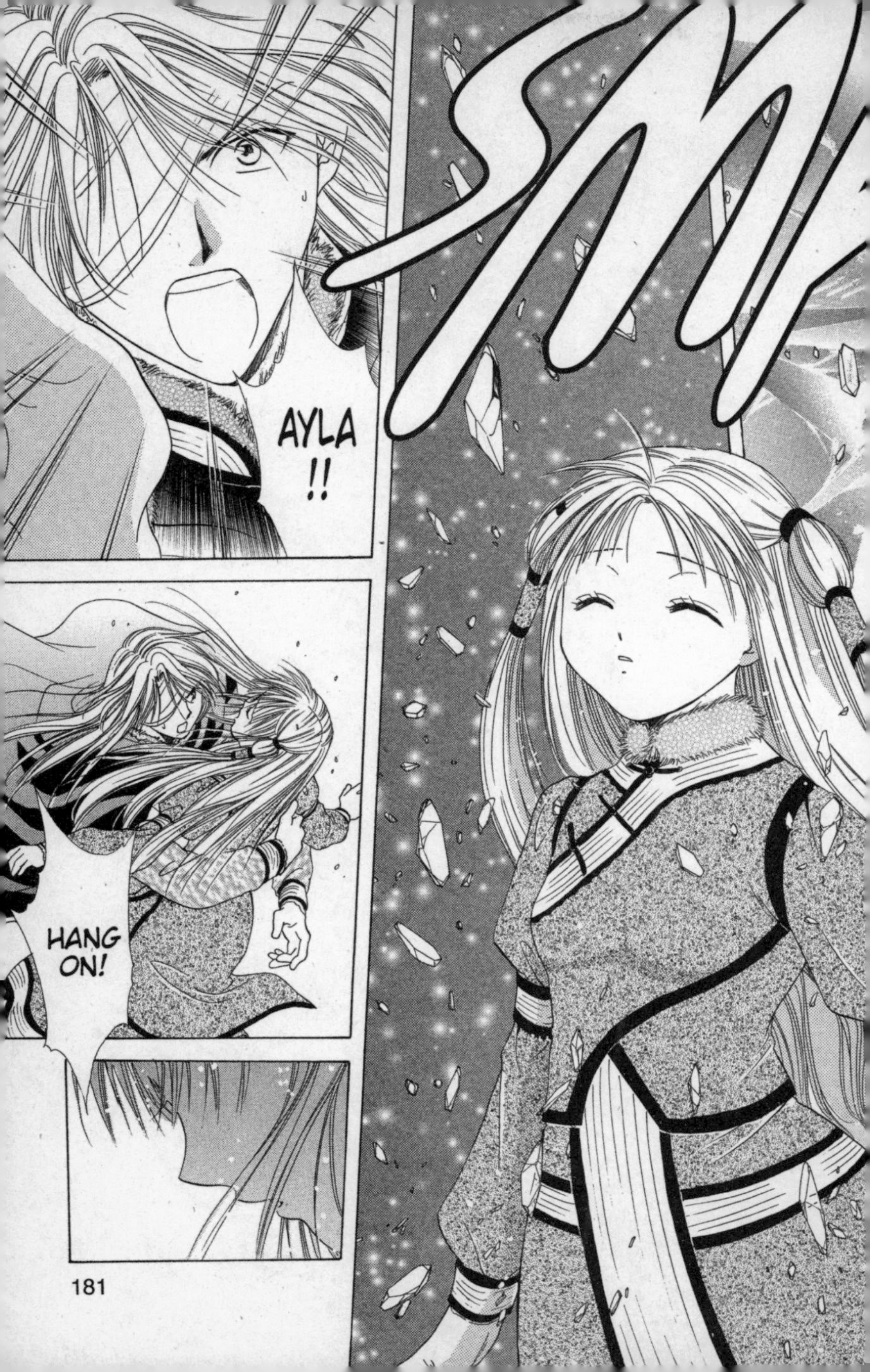
AYLA !!
HANG ON!

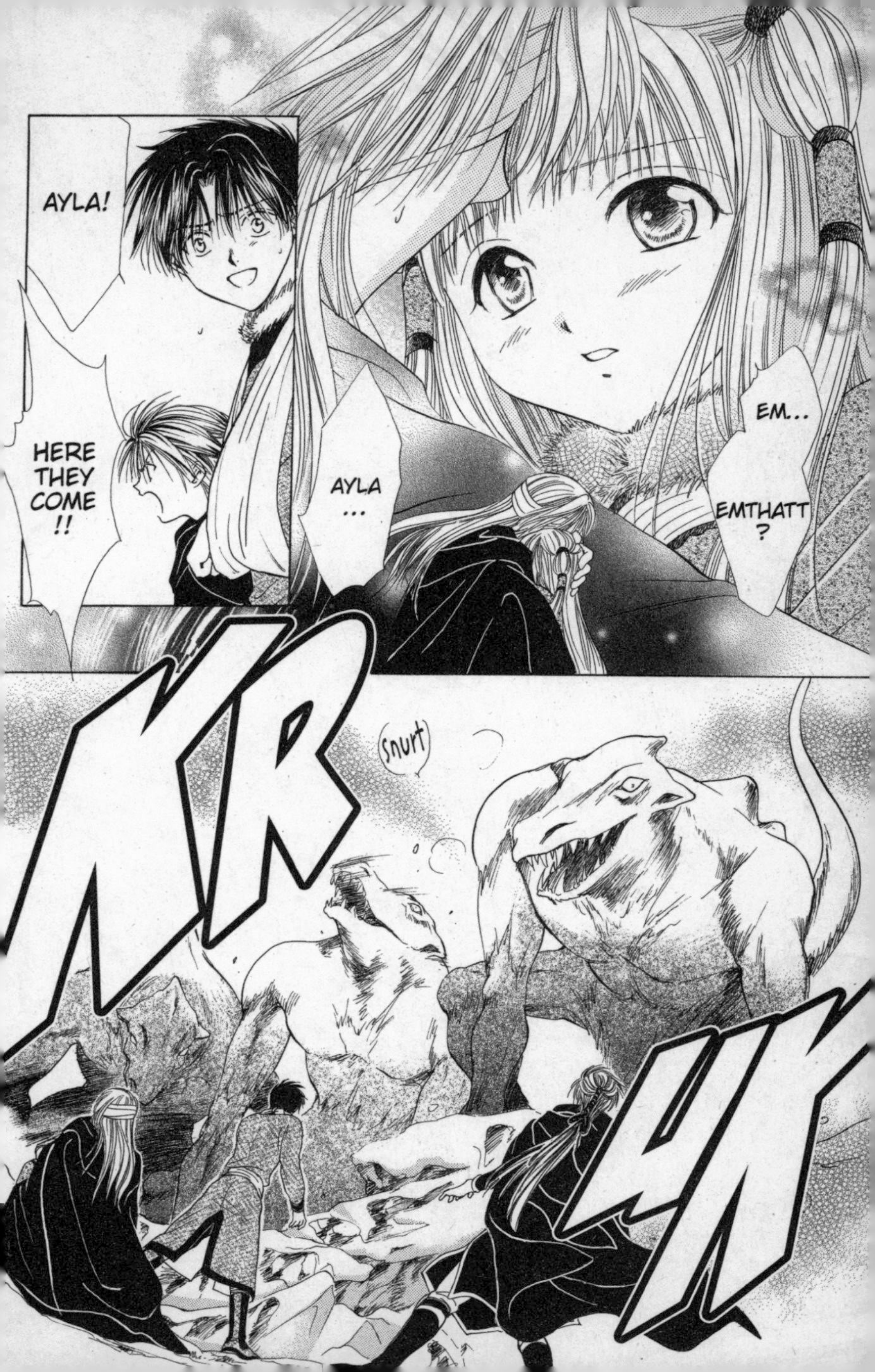
EM...
EMTHATT?
AYLA...
AYLA!
HERE THEY COME!!
snurt
KRAH

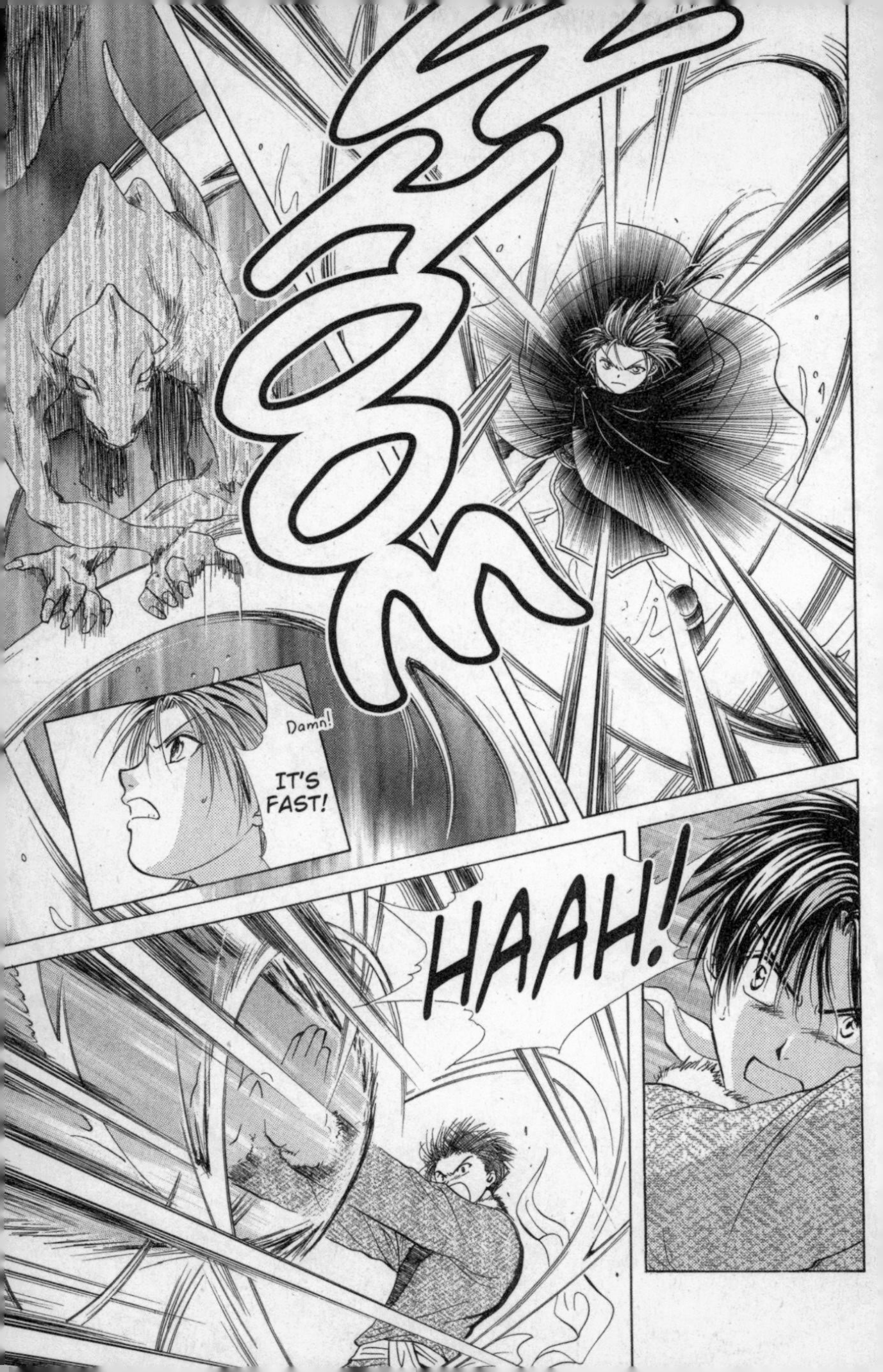
Damn!
IT'S FAST!
HAAH!

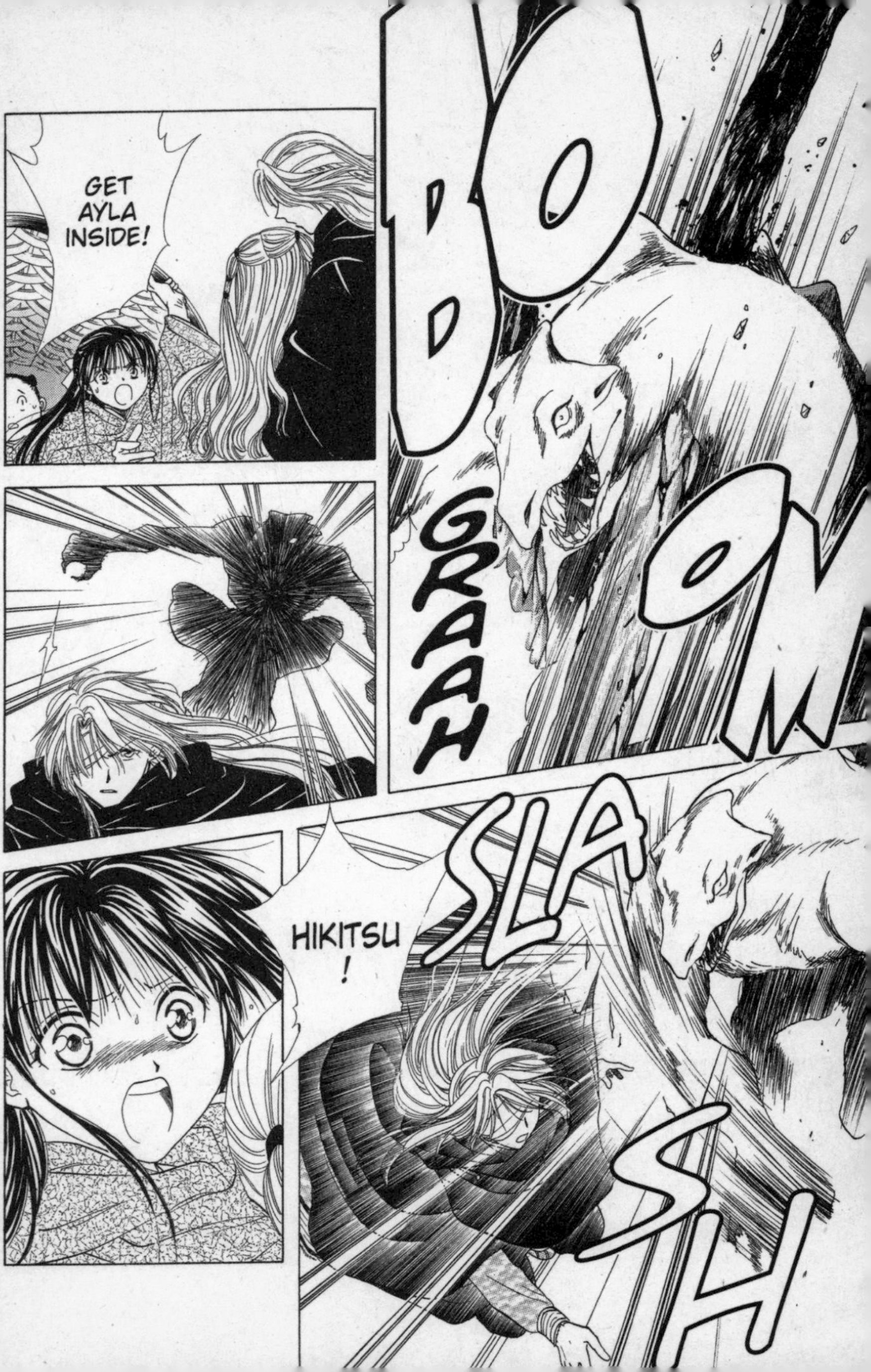
BOOM
GRAAAH
GET AYLA INSIDE!
SLASH
HIKITSU!

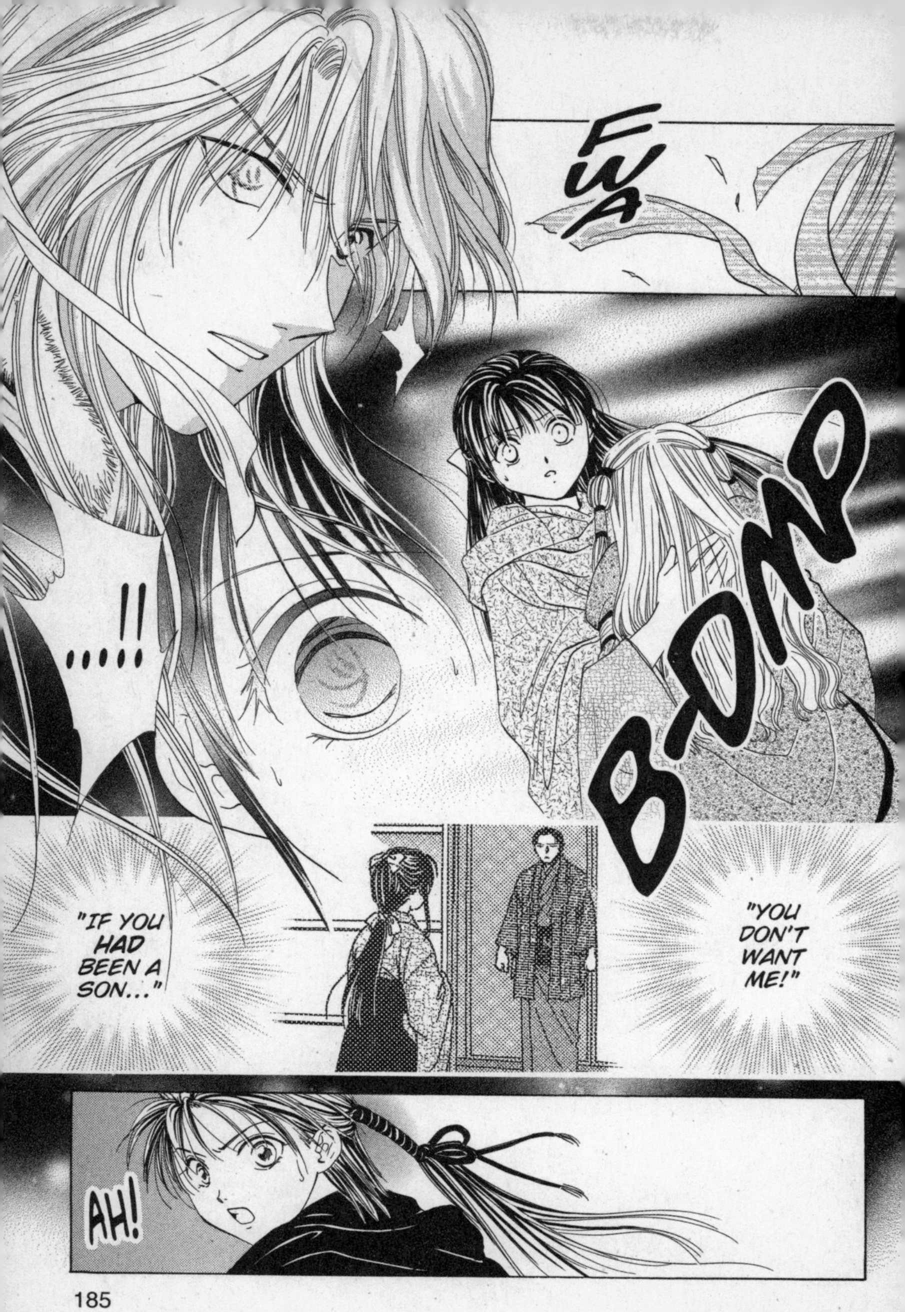
FWA
B-DMP
...!!
"YOU DON'T WANT ME!"
"IF YOU HAD BEEN A SON..."
AH!

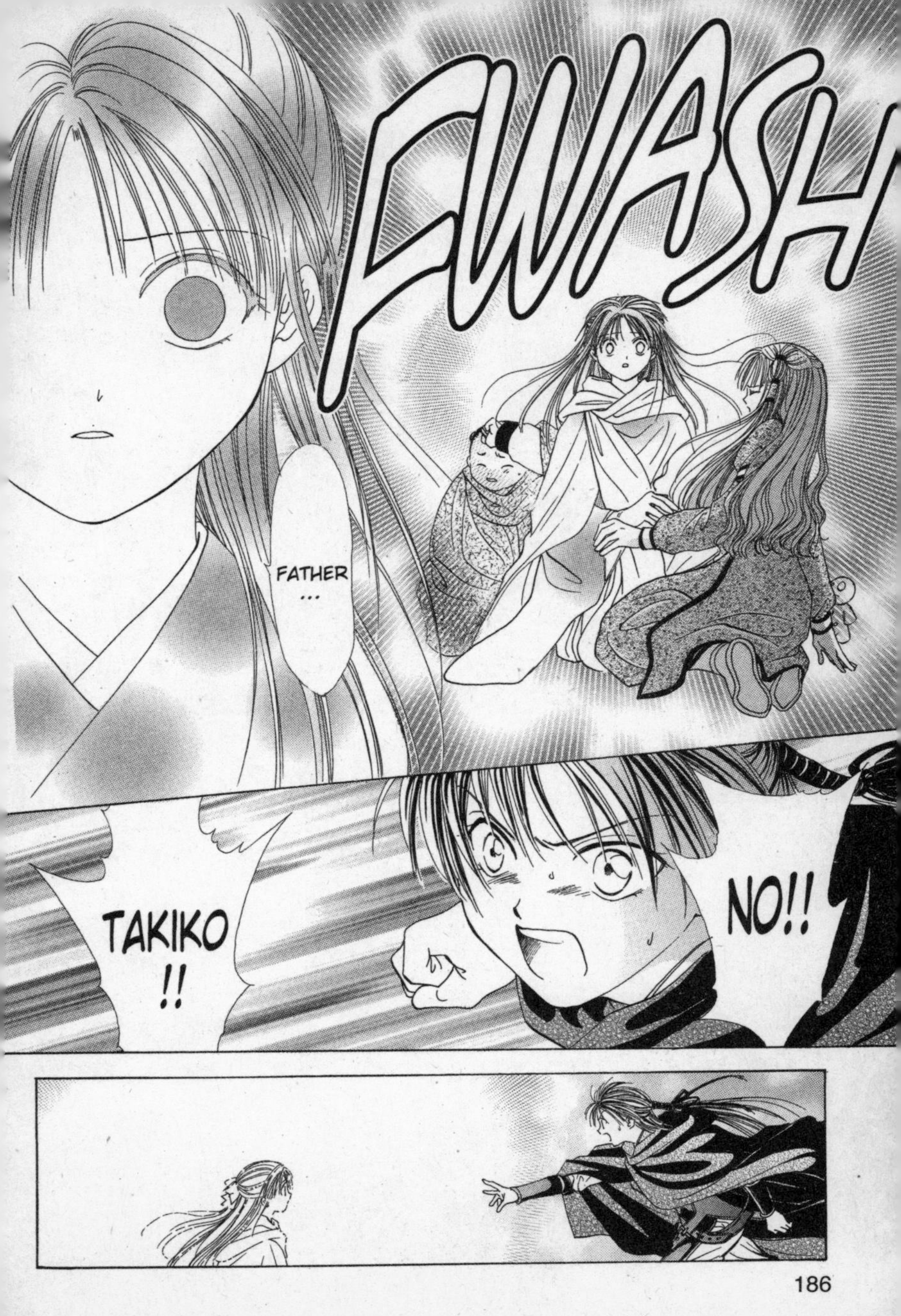
FWASH
FATHER ...
NO!!
TAKIKO !!

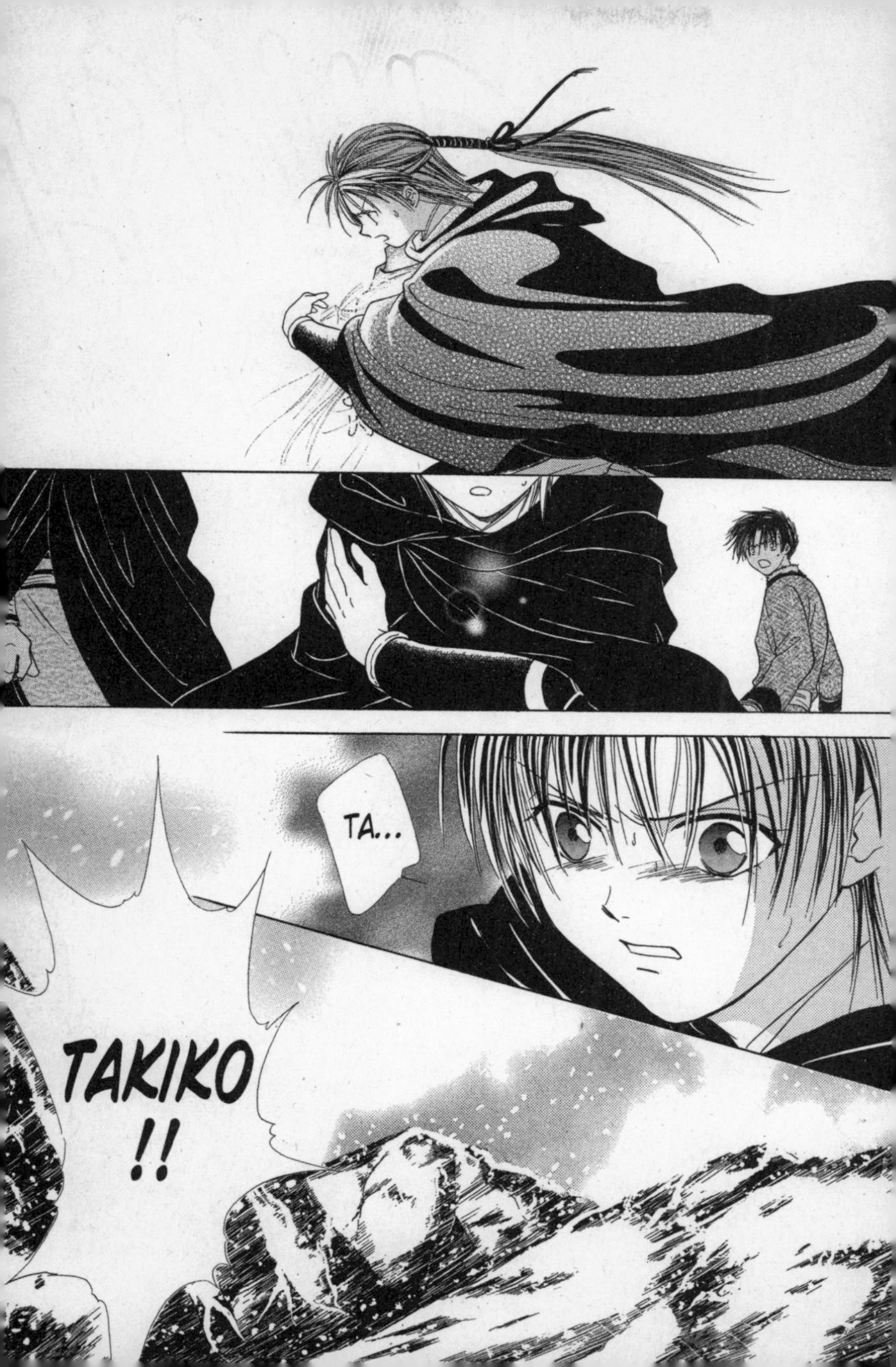
TA...
TAKIKO !!

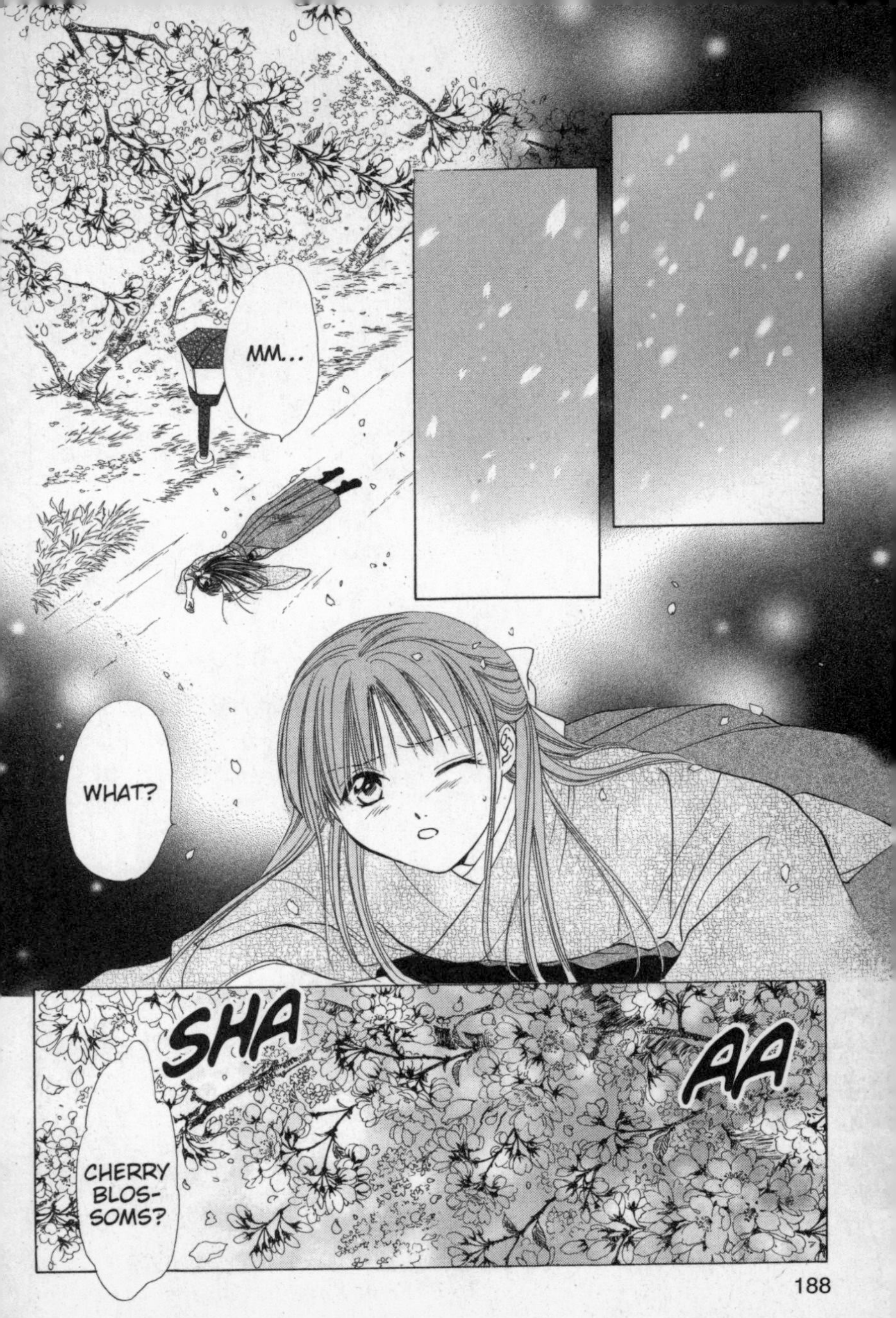
MM...
WHAT?
SHA
AA
CHERRY BLOS-SOMS?

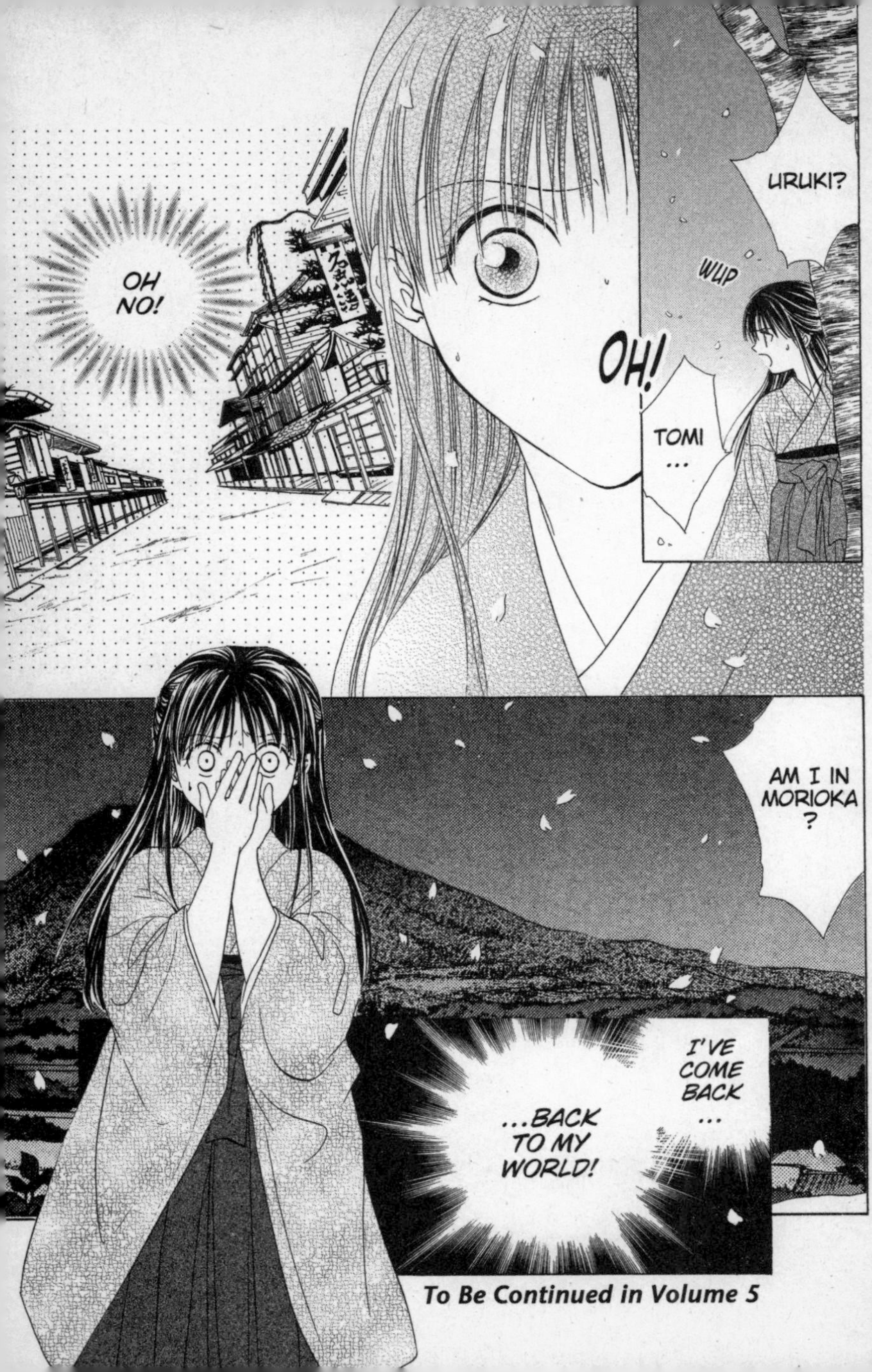
URUKI?
WUP
TOMI ...
OH!
OH NO!
AM I IN MORIOKA ?
I'VE COME BACK ...
...BACK TO MY WORLD!

To Be Continued in Volume 5

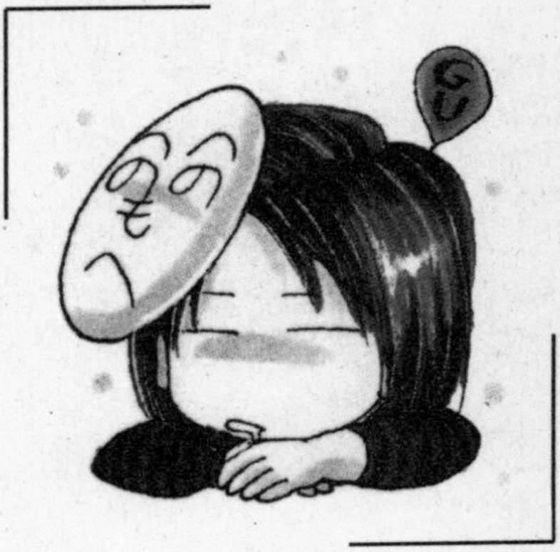
GU

Yuu Watase was born on March 5 in a town near Osaka, Japan. She was raised there before moving to Tokyo to follow her dream of creating manga. In the decade since her debut short story, *Pajama De Ojama* (An Intrusion in Pajamas), she has produced more than 50 volumes of short stories and continuing series. Her latest work, *Absolute Boyfriend*, appeared in Japan in the anthology magazine *Shôjo Comic* and is currently serialized in English in *Shojo Beat* magazine. Watase's other beloved series, *Alice 19th*, *Imadoki!*, and *Ceres: Celestial Legend*, are available in North America in English editions published by VIZ Media.

Fushigi Yûgi:
Genbu Kaiden Vol. 4

The Shojo Beat Manga Edition
STORY AND ART BY
YUU WATASE

Translation/Lillian Olsen
Touch-up Art & Lettering/Rina Mapa
Design/Amy Martin
Editor/Shaenon K. Garrity

Managing Editor/Megan Bates
Director of Production/Noboru Watanabe
Vice President of Publishing/Alvin Lu
Vice President & Editor in Chief/Yumi Hoashi
Sr. Director of Acquisitions/Rika Inouye
Vice President of Sales & Marketing/Liza Coppola
Publisher/Hyoe Narita

Printed in Canada

Published by VIZ Media, LLC
P.O. Box 77010
San Francisco, CA 94107

Shojo Beat Manga Edition
10 9 8 7 6 5 4 3 2 1
First printing, July 2006

store.viz.com

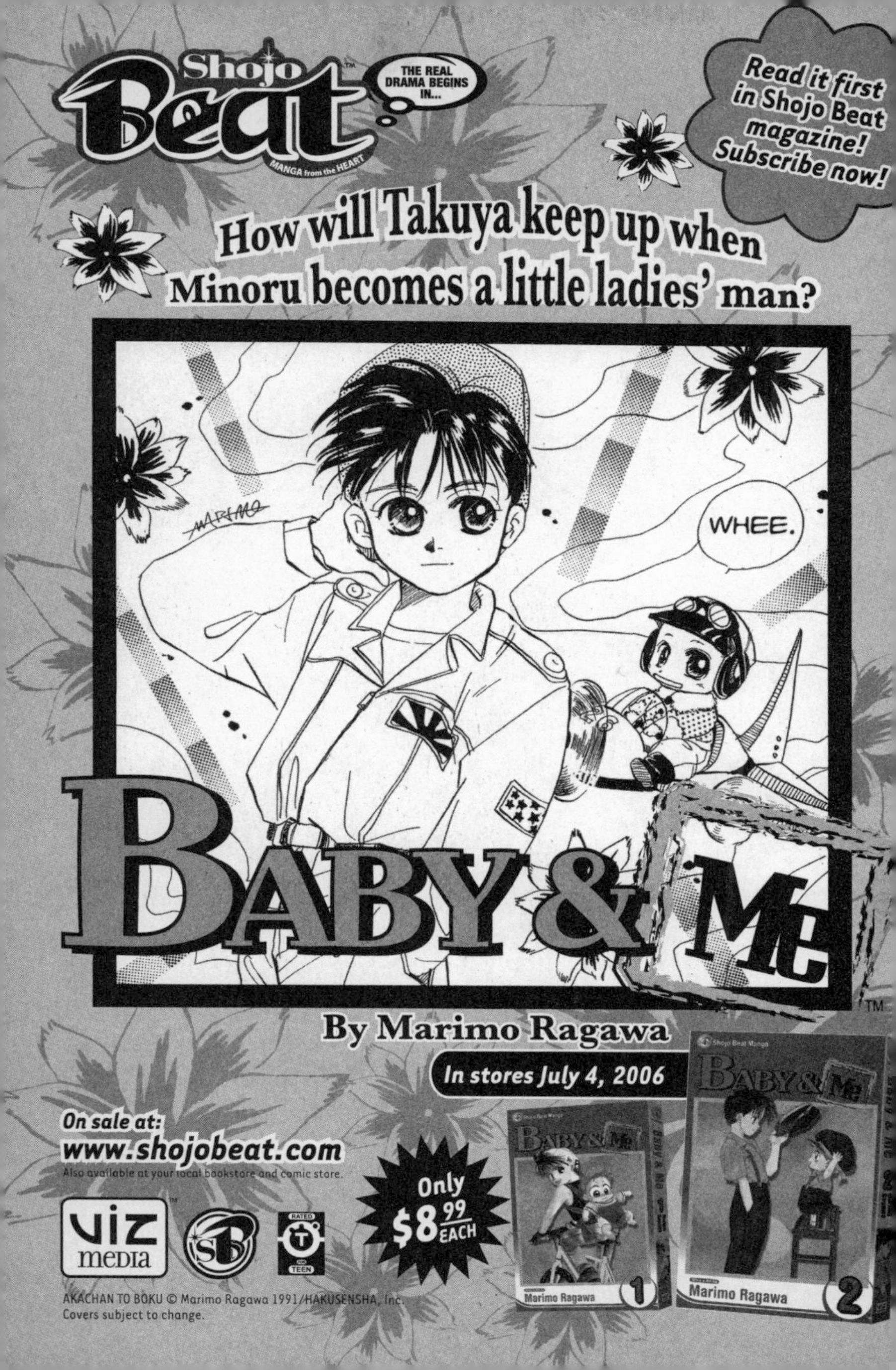
Shojo Beat™
THE REAL DRAMA BEGINS IN...
MANGA from the HEART
Read it first in Shojo Beat magazine! Subscribe now!
How will Takuya keep up when Minoru becomes a little ladies' man?
WHEE.
BABY & ME™
By Marimo Ragawa
In stores July 4, 2006
On sale at:
www.shojobeat.com
Also available at your local bookstore and comic store.
Only $8.99 EACH
VIZ media
RATED T TEEN
Marimo Ragawa 1
Marimo Ragawa 2
AKACHAN TO BOKU © Marimo Ragawa 1991/HAKUSENSHA, Inc.
Covers subject to change.

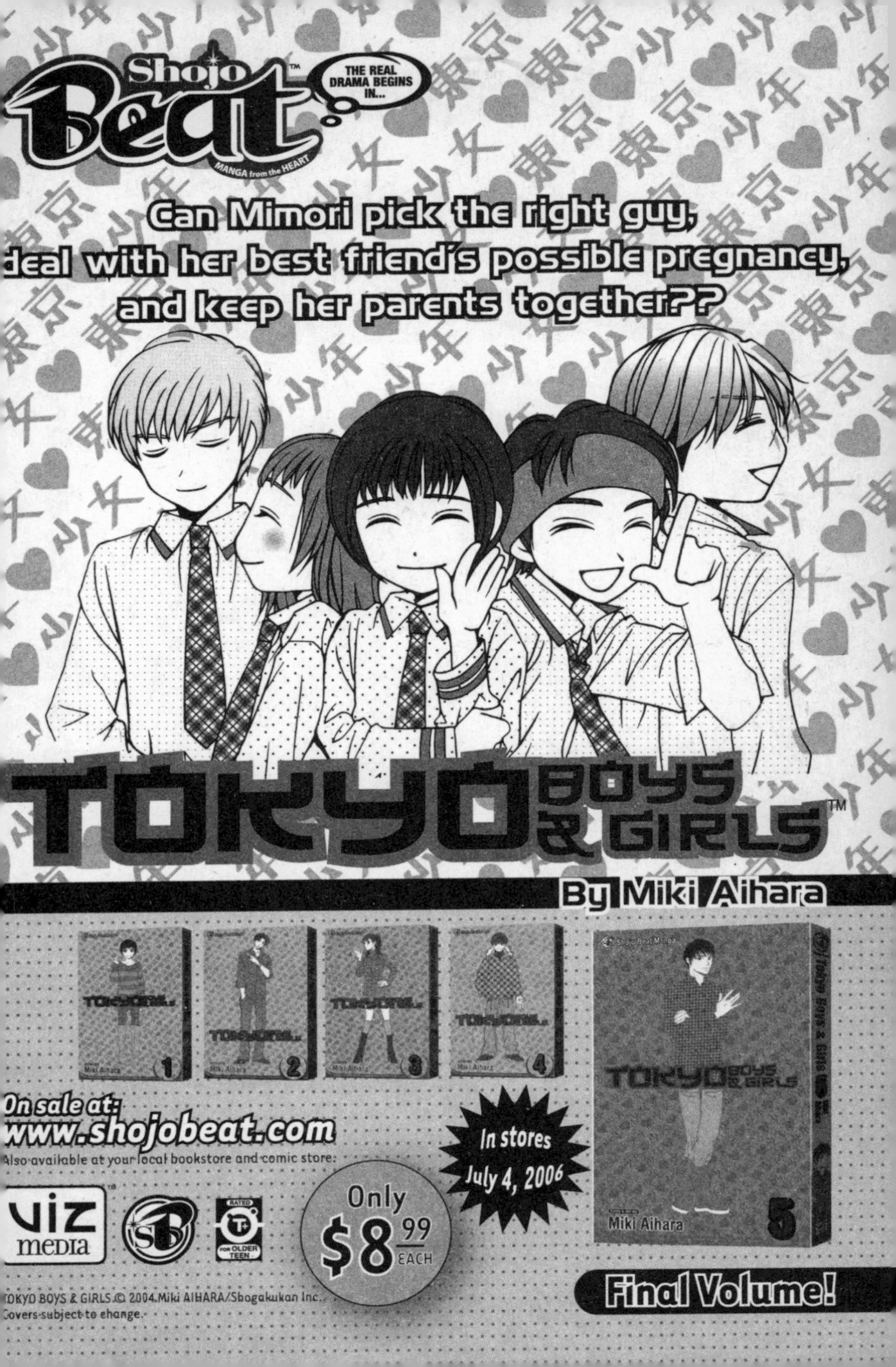
Shojo Beat
THE REAL DRAMA BEGINS IN...
MANGA from the HEART
Can Mimori pick the right guy,
deal with her best friend's possible pregnancy,
and keep her parents together??
TOKYO BOYS & GIRLS
By Miki Aihara
Miki Aihara
On sale at:
www.shojobeat.com
Also available at your local bookstore and comic store.
In stores
July 4, 2006
Only
$8.99
EACH
Final Volume!
viz media
RATED T+ FOR OLDER TEEN
TOKYO BOYS & GIRLS © 2004 Miki AIHARA/Shogakukan Inc.
Covers subject to change.

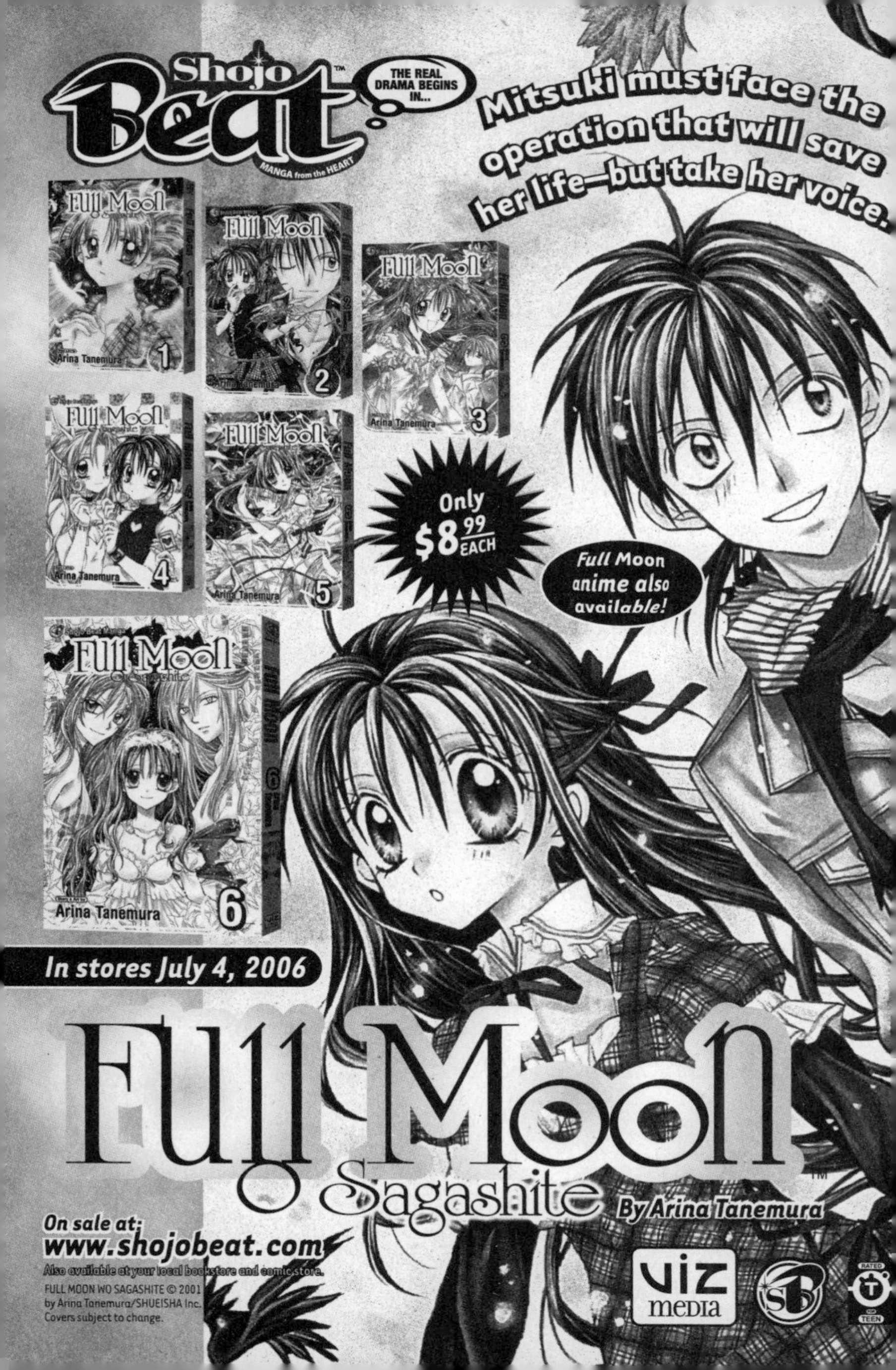
Shojo Beat™
MANGA from the HEART
THE REAL DRAMA BEGINS IN...
Mitsuki must face the operation that will save her life—but take her voice.
Full Moon
Arina Tanemura 1
Full Moon
Arina Tanemura 2
Full Moon
Arina Tanemura 3
Full Moon
Arina Tanemura 4
Full Moon
Arina Tanemura 5
Full Moon
Arina Tanemura 6
Only $8.99 EACH
Full Moon anime also available!
In stores July 4, 2006
Full Moon O Sagashite™
By Arina Tanemura
On sale at:
www.shojobeat.com
Also available at your local bookstore and comic store.
FULL MOON WO SAGASHITE © 2001 by Arina Tanemura/SHUEISHA Inc.
Covers subject to change.
VIZ media
RATED T FOR TEEN

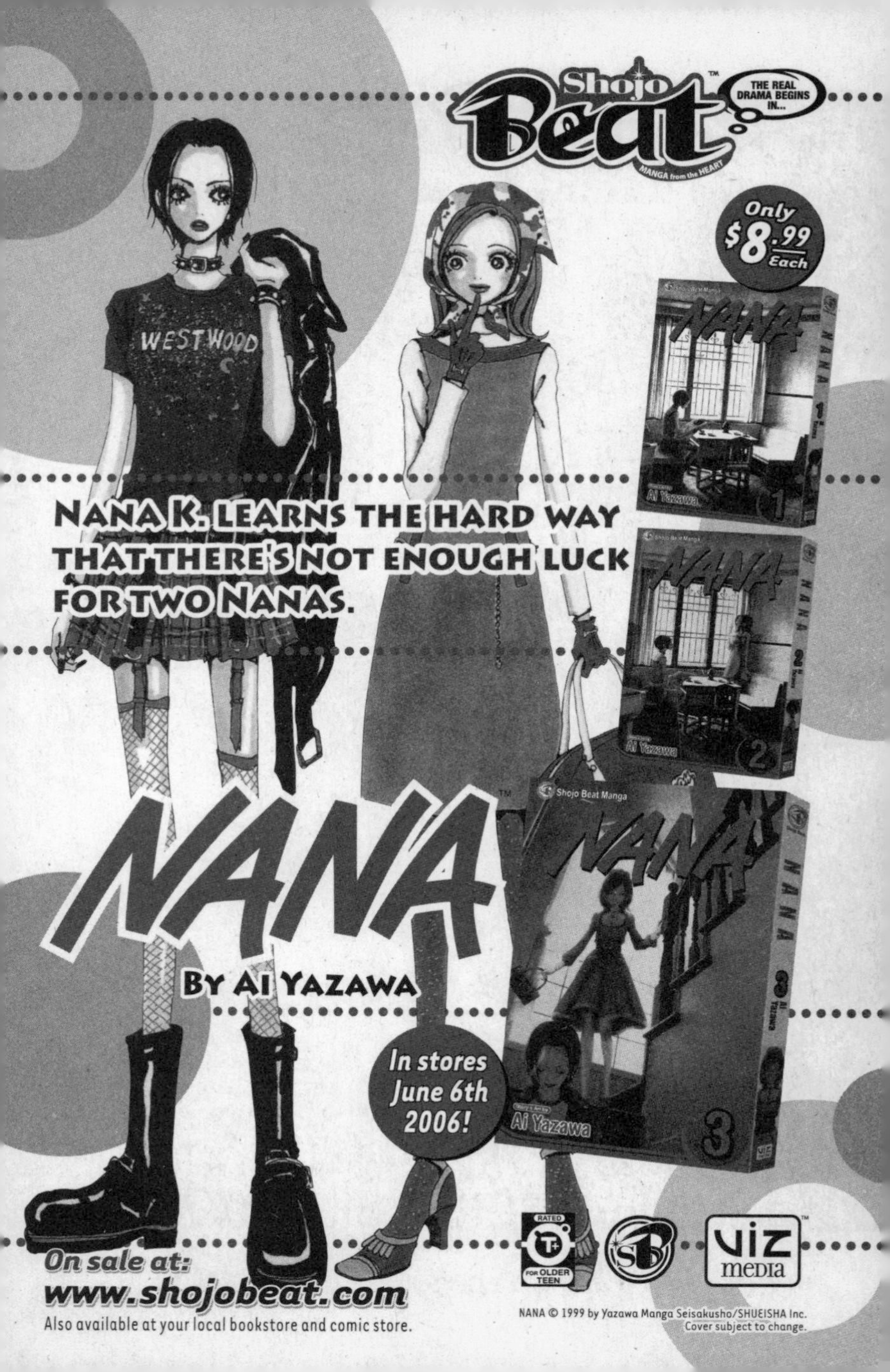

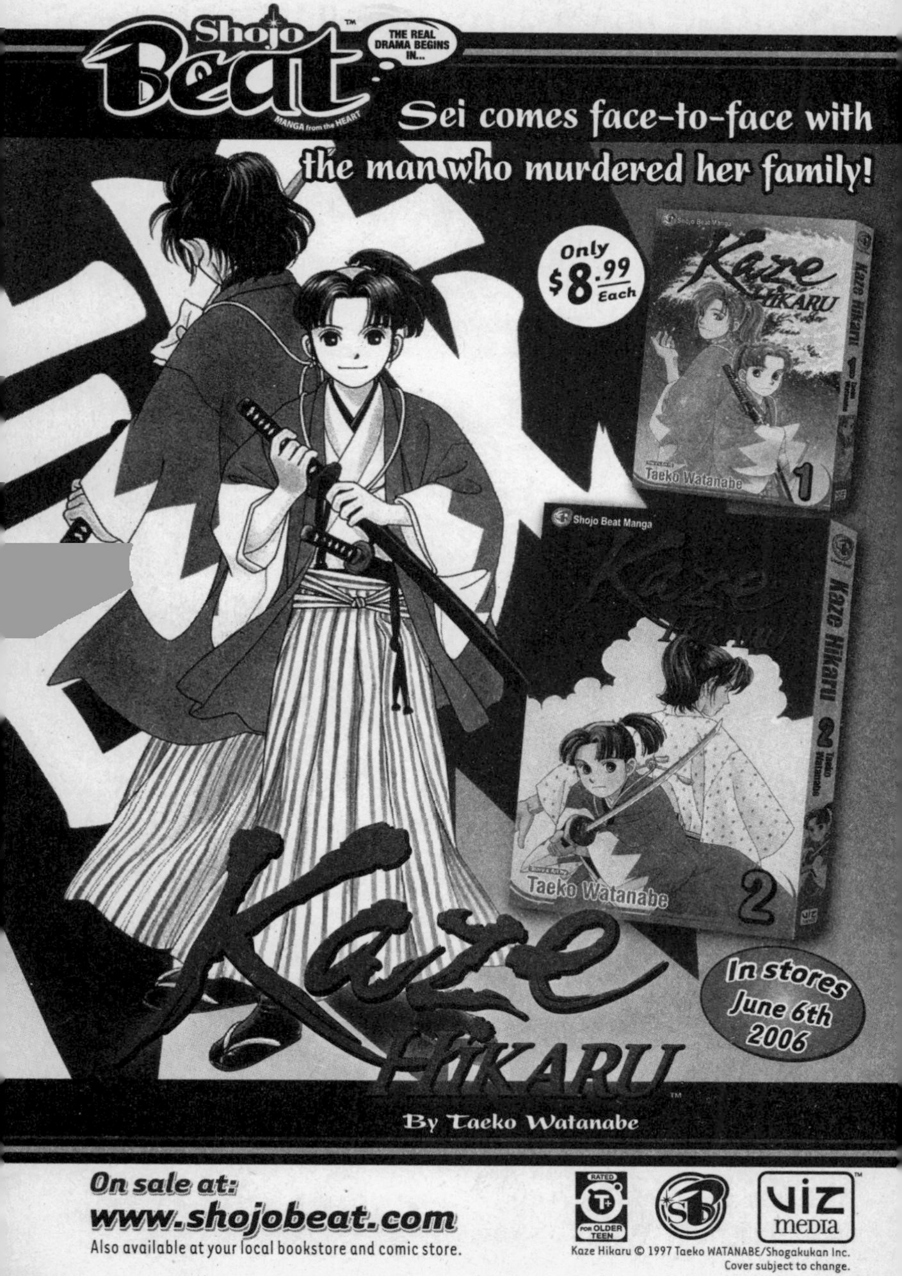
Shojo Beat
MANGA from the HEART
THE REAL DRAMA BEGINS IN...
Sei comes face-to-face with the man who murdered her family!
Only $8.99 Each
Shojo Beat Manga
Kaze Hikaru
Taeko Watanabe
1
Shojo Beat Manga
Kaze Hikaru
Taeko Watanabe
2
In stores June 6th 2006
Kaze Hikaru
By Taeko Watanabe
On sale at:
www.shojobeat.com
Also available at your local bookstore and comic store.
RATED T+ FOR OLDER TEEN
VIZ media
Kaze Hikaru © 1997 Taeko WATANABE/Shogakukan Inc.
Cover subject to change.

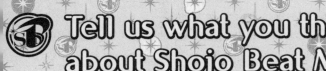

Tell us what you think about Shojo Beat Manga!

Our survey is now available online. Go to:

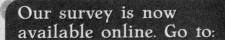

shojobeat.com/mangasurvey

Help us make our product offerings better!

Love. Laugh. Live.

In addition to hundreds of pages of manga each month, *Shojo Beat* will bring you the latest in Japanese fashion, music, art, and culture—plus shopping, how-tos, industry updates, interviews, and much more!

DON'T YOU WANT TO HAVE THIS MUCH FUN?

Only **$34.99** for **12 GIANT Issues!** **51% OFF** the Cover Price!

NANA by AI YAZAWA

Subscribe Now! Fill out the coupon on the other side

Or go to: **www.shojobeat.com**

Or call toll-free **800-541-7876**